## TRUSTS AND PRIVATE WEALTH MANAGEMENT

There has been insufficient literature focusing on the world-changing rise of Asian wealth. Private wealth in Asia is very substantial, with 33 per cent of the global population of high-net-worth individuals based in Asia. Yet, there is a dearth of legal analysis of Asian wealth, particularly by texts written in English. This collection aims to fill that gap, with chapters on legal issues in relation to Asian wealth transmission, investments in international real estate, familial disputes, family offices, and private trust companies. A substantive section of this book also focuses on the changing legal context with chapters exploring trusts and cryptoassets, constructive trust, trustee's discretion and decision-making, changing regulatory environment, and abuse of trust structures. This collection of essays on trusts and wealth management presents a focus on Asian wealth and the changing legal context, and follows the related publication, *Trusts and Modern Wealth Management* (Cambridge University Press, 2018).

Richard C. Nolan is Professor of Law at the University of York and previously Reader in Corporate and Trust Law at the University of Cambridge. His work has been cited by judges in the United Kingdom, Australia, Singapore, New Zealand, and Hong Kong. He has been a consultant to several governmental bodies.

Tang Hang Wu is Professor at the Yong Pung How School of Law, Singapore Management University, researching on equity, trusts, and wealth management. Hang Wu has published widely and advised local and international law firms, high-net-worth individuals, US Department of Justice, and banks and trust companies on trust law.

Man Yip is Associate Professor at the Yong Pung How School of Law, Singapore Management University, researching on equity, trusts, remedies, and private international law. She has published widely in international peer-reviewed journals and her work has been cited in leading treatises and courts.

# Trusts and Private Wealth Management

## DEVELOPMENTS AND DIRECTIONS

Edited by

**RICHARD C. NOLAN**

University of York

**MAN YIP**

Singapore Management University

**TANG HANG WU**

Singapore Management University

CAMBRIDGE
UNIVERSITY PRESS

CAMBRIDGE
UNIVERSITY PRESS

Shaftesbury Road, Cambridge CB2 8EA, United Kingdom

One Liberty Plaza, 20th Floor, New York, NY 10006, USA

477 Williamstown Road, Port Melbourne, VIC 3207, Australia

314–321, 3rd Floor, Plot 3, Splendor Forum, Jasola District Centre, New Delhi – 110025, India

103 Penang Road, #05–06/07, Visioncrest Commercial, Singapore 238467

Cambridge University Press is part of Cambridge University Press & Assessment, a department of the University of Cambridge.

We share the University's mission to contribute to society through the pursuit of education, learning and research at the highest international levels of excellence.

www.cambridge.org
Information on this title: www.cambridge.org/9781009048781

DOI: 10.1017/9781009049399



First published 2023
First paperback edition 2026

*A catalogue record for this publication is available from the British Library*

ISBN 978-1-316-51802-1 Hardback
ISBN 978-1-009-04878-1 Paperback

# Contents

# Contributors

**The Right Hon Lady Arden of Heswall DBE** grew up in Liverpool and read law at Girton College Cambridge and Harvard Law School. Called to the Bar in 1971, she became a Queen's Counsel in 1986 and served as Attorney General of the Duchy of Lancaster between 1991 and 1993. Her judicial career began in 1993 when she was appointed to the High Court of Justice of England and Wales, as the first woman judge assigned to the Chancery Division. Between 1996 and 1999 she served as Chairman of the Law Commission of England and Wales. She was a justice of the Court of Appeal of England and Wales from 2000 to 2018. On 1 October 2018 she became Justice of the Supreme Court of the United Kingdom. She retired on 24 January 2022. Lady Arden has also served as the Member of the Permanent Court of Arbitration in The Hague and as an *ad hoc* UK judge of the European Court of Human Rights.

**Tobias Barkley** is a lecturer at the La Trobe Law School, La Trobe University, Australia. His research interests are the doctrinal foundations and social impact of contemporary trust practice, with a focus on discretionary trusts. Tobias has published a range of articles on issues in trust law, and his work has been presented before the New Zealand Supreme Court.

**Chan Ee Lin** is an internationally recognised trust and wealth planner and family business governance advisor to high net worth families in Asia. Director and SE Asia lead for Family Enterprise Consulting at Deloitte Tax Services, Ee Lin is also a top-rated adjunct professor of executive education and masters programs at Nanyang Technological University and Singapore Management University. She is found in Citywealth's Leaders List and IFC Top 200 Power Women list, holds degrees from Stanford University and Carnegie Mellon University and a doctorate in Jurisprudence from SMU and is an advocate and solicitor of the Supreme Court of Singapore.

**Thomas P. Gallanis** is the Allan D. Vestal Chair in Law and Director of the Global Wealth Management Program at the University of Iowa, a visiting professor at the University of Chicago Law School, and a visiting professor at the KoGuan

Law School of Shanghai Jiao Tong University. His research interests include the laws of property, trusts, succession, and wealth management, particularly in their multinational and cross-border aspects. He was associate reporter (co-author) of the Restatement Third of Trusts and is the executive director of the Uniform Law Commission's Joint Editorial Board for Uniform Trust and Estate Acts.

**Lusina Ho** is the Harold Hsiao-Wo Lee Professor in Trust and Equity at the Faculty of Law, the University of Hong Kong. Her research interests include trusts, unjust enrichment, comparative trusts, and elder law. She has published widely in these areas and has been consulted by the Government of the People's Republic of China and the Government of the Hong Kong SAR on reforms related to trust legislation. Her research led to the setting up of the Special Needs Trust Scheme by the Hong Kong Government.

**James Lee** is Professor of English Law at The Dickson Poon School of Law, King's College London. He is Associate Academic Fellow of the Inner Temple and an academic member of the Chancery Bar Association, the Property Bar Association, and the Property Litigation Association. He works on private law, law reform, and judicial reasoning. With Jamie Glister, he is co-editor of the leading text, *Hanbury & Martin: Modern Equity*, now in its 22nd edition.

**Rebecca Lee** is an Associate Professor at the Faculty of Law, The University of Hong Kong. She teaches and researches in Equity and Trusts, Contracts and Non-profit Law, and has published works in these areas in leading English, Australian, and American law journals. Rebecca has advised the Hong Kong Government and NGOs on trusts/trust-related reforms and initiatives. Currently, she is working on research projects on selected issues in trusts law, charity governance, and special needs support.

**Kelvin F. K. Low** is Professor at the Faculty of Law, National University of Singapore. Kelvin's research interest spans the field of private law but with a particular interest in property. He has published internationally with leading journals, and his works have been cited by courts in Australia, Canada, England and Wales, Hong Kong SAR, Malaysia, New Zealand, and Singapore as well as law commissions and law reform bodies in Australia, England and Wales, Ireland, New Zealand, Scotland, and Singapore.

**Richard C. Nolan** is Professor of Law at the University of York. He has published widely in the areas of company law and trusts, and his work has been cited in the highest UK courts as well as in Australia, Hong Kong, and Singapore. He has been a visiting professor in Australia, Hong Kong, New Zealand, Singapore, and the USA. He has acted on several occasions as a consultant to the Law Commission and governmental bodies in the UK. Professor Nolan is also a barrister and door tenant at Erskine Chambers, Lincoln's Inn, London.

**Vincent Ooi** is Lecturer of Law at the Yong Pung How School of Law, Singapore Management University. His research largely focuses on tax law and private law. Vincent's books include *Singapore Trusts Law* and both tax law volumes of *Halsbury's Laws of Singapore*. He was previously Deputy Head of Tax at a Singapore law firm, Law Supervisor at Peterhouse College, Cambridge, and has held research positions at all three law schools in Singapore. Vincent's work has been cited by leading English and Singapore law texts and by the United Nations Commission on International Trade Law (UNCITRAL).

**Jessica Palmer** is the Pro-Vice-Chancellor of Humanities at the University of Otago. She teaches and researches in contract law, trusts, commercial equity, and restitution. She was a member of the reference group assisting the New Zealand Law Commission in its recent review of the law of trusts and her work has been cited by New Zealand, Australian, and English courts. She has been a judges' clerk and worked in a large commercial law firm.

**David Pollard** is a barrister, practising from Wilberforce Chambers in Lincoln's Inn, London, specialising in pensions, insolvency, and employment law. David previously practised as a solicitor (England and Wales) in London and Singapore and was for 25 years a partner in Freshfields Bruckhaus Deringer LLP. His books include *The Law of Pension Trusts* (Oxford University Press), *Corporate Insolvency: Employment and Pension Rights* (Bloomsbury), and *Pensions Contracts and Trusts: Legal Issues on Decision Making: Applying Braganza* (Bloomsbury). David is a former chair of the Association of Pension Lawyers.

**Tang Hang Wu** is Professor at the Yong Pung How School of Law, Singapore Management University. His research interests include land law, restitution, equity, trusts, wealth management, charity, and non-profit law. Hang Wu has published widely in these areas, and his work has been relied on by all levels of the Singapore courts, Royal Court of Jersey, Court of Appeal in Manitoba, courts in Malaysia, Caribbean Court of Appeal, law reform committees in the Commonwealth, major textbooks, and law journals.

**Edward S. W. Ti,** is an Assistant Professor of Law at the Yong Pung How School of Law, Singapore Management University. Edward's research interests include land law, multi-ownership property rights, urban policy, and property theory. Edward has won prizes for his scholarship and has published in these areas in leading journals.

**Graham Virgo QC (Hon)** is Professor of English Private Law at the Faculty of Law in the University of Cambridge, a fellow of Downing College, Cambridge, and a Bencher of the Honourable Society of Lincoln's Inn. His research interests include equity and trusts, the law of restitution, contract, and criminal law. He has published widely in these areas, particularly *The Principles of the Law of Restitution*

(3rd ed, 2015) and *Principles of Equity and Trusts* (4th ed, 2020). His work has been widely cited in appellate courts in many jurisdictions. He was awarded an Honorary QC in 2017.

**Simone Wong** is Emeritus Reader at Kent Law School where she taught Equity & Trusts and Banking Law. Her research interests include feminist legal studies, equity, trusts, gender, domestic relationships and banking. Her recent publications include (co-authored with R Cain), 'The impact of cuts in Legal Aid funding of private family law cases' (2019) 41(1) *Journal of Social Welfare and Family Law* 3 and 'Tapping into trust assets for redistribution upon divorce in England and Wales', in Richard C. Nolan, H. W. Tang, and K. F. Low (eds), *Trusts and Modern Wealth Management* (Cambridge, Cambridge University Press, 2018).

**Man Yip** is Associate Professor of Law at Yong Pung How School of Law, Singapore Management University. Her research interests include equity and trusts, restitution, remedies, private international law and dispute resolution. Her work has been cited by the Singapore Court of Appeal, the Singapore High Court, the Singapore District Court, and the High Court of England and Wales, as well as leading treatises and journal articles.

# Table of Cases

# Table of Legislation

## UK PRIMARY LEGISLATION

UK STATUTORY INSTRUMENTS



EUROPEAN UNION LEGISLATION



NON-UK PRIMARY LEGISLATION

NON-UK STATUTORY INSTRUMENTS

INTERNATIONAL TREATIES AND CONVENTIONS

# 1

# Introduction

*Richard C. Nolan, Tang Hang Wu, and Man Yip*

This book results from a conference, held in Singapore in August 2019, which we organised to discuss the implications for trust law and wealth management of a topic much discussed in other contexts, but less so in the present context: the enormous and continuing rise of Asian wealth. The world economy has changed and continues to change in focus to a degree not seen since the rise of European maritime powers, beginning in the late fifteenth century. This change is compounded by the accelerating pace of technological change. The law – including trust law and the law of wealth management – must acknowledge and accommodate these developments and their consequences. We hope this volume is a contribution to that process.

Our book begins with an overview on 'Family Trusts Today' by Lady Arden (Chapter 2). This chapter provides an insightful *tour d'horizon* of the problems that are encountered in modern trust law practice. The chapter focuses on four problems that affect modern family trust practice: privacy in family trust litigation, over-dominant settlors and the doctrine of sham trusts, trustees' liability to trust creditors in the event of insolvency, and climate change and the handling of disputes between beneficiaries and trustees. Lady Arden's incisive treatment of the problems highlights the complexity of modern trust practice and provokes us to consider more deeply the fundamental tenets of the trust institution in order to work towards solutions.

On privacy in court proceedings, litigation concerning family trusts is not, by default, heard in private. The court needs to balance between the private interest of protecting beneficiaries' identities (especially the identity of any vulnerable beneficiaries) and the public interests of open justice and transparency. It is interesting to note that some jurisdictions are now offering court-based resolution of disputes in private, but only in the context of 'non-local' disputes, where the public interest in transparency may be less than in a fully domestic context. The Singapore International Commercial Court (which, notwithstanding its name, has jurisdiction to hear trust disputes with an 'international' and 'commercial' character) is one such example. Beyond the litigation context, developments such as trust registration and data protection also enable greater transparency in private trusts but possibly at the cost of a loss of privacy.

As to an over-dominant settlor and the sham trust doctrine, Lady Arden's analysis of the landmark decision of *JSC Mezhdunarodniy Promyshlenniy Bank* v. *Pugachev*[1] raises the profound question as to the proper basis on which to invalidate a trust, even where it satisfies the usual certainty and formality requirements and does not infringe the concept of irreducible core of trustee obligations.

Turning to the trustees' liability to trust creditors in the event of insolvency, the discussion exposes the potential unfairness arising from the unitary nature of the legal personality of the trustee in cases where the trustee has incurred liability on behalf of the trust. Without distinguishing between his or her personal and fiduciary capacities, the trustee's personal assets are put at risk to meet the trust liabilities. The trustee may protect himself or herself through an appropriate contractual limitation clause. Alternatively, the law may consider introducing statutory limitation on trustee liability, such as Article 32 of the Jersey Trusts Law.[2]

Finally, as climate change and sustainability developments have become global concerns, the beneficiaries may disagree as to how trustees, generally guided by the *Cowan* v. *Scargill* principle of maximising financial returns in the absence of explicit direction in the trust deed, should exercise their powers of investment. Unlike the corporate context, where corporate social responsibility is a recognised pillar of corporate governance, it is more difficult to argue that investment in the family trust context should be guided by a sustainability strategy.[3] Lady Arden suggests that on encountering such a disagreement with the beneficiaries, even though there is no obligation on the part of the trustees to consult the beneficiaries, the trustees would be wise to confer with their beneficiaries. There are two clear benefits to a consultative approach to the problem for the trustee. First, where all the trust beneficiaries are of majority age and sound mind, their concurrence in a certain course of action would provide good defence against an allegation of breach of trust raised by them subsequently. Second, such an approach would help to preserve good relations between the beneficiaries and trustees.

Part I of this book considers various legal issues arising from growing Asian wealth. In Chapter 3, Thomas P. Gallanis points out that private wealth in Asia is substantial, representing 33 per cent of the global population of high-net-worth individuals; yet, there is a dearth of legal analysis of Asian wealth, particularly by texts written in English. This part of the collection aims to contribute to the literature by offering chapters on legal issues in relation to Asian wealth transmission, investments in international real estate, familial disputes, family offices and private trust companies. While many issues are considered in this volume, other pressing concerns arising from the growth of Asian wealth have not been aired due to space

1 [2017] EWHC 2426 (Ch).

2 Considered in *Investec Trust (Guernsey) Limited* v. *Glenalla Properties Limited* [2018] UKPC 7.

3 Where pension trusts are concerned, see Susie Daykin, 'Pension Scheme Investment: Is It Always Just about the Money? To What Extent Can or Should Trustees Take Account of Ethical or ESG Factors When Investing?' (2014) 28(4) *Trust Law International* 165.

constraints. This does not mean that these topics are less important. On a macro level, growing Asian wealth raises important issues like inequality, taxation, and philanthropy. Certainly, we are acutely aware that these topics are significant and, indeed, inequality and taxation have been dealt with by Tony Molloy in our previous collection, *Trusts and Modern Wealth Management*, edited by two of the current editors together with Kelvin F. K. Low. Philanthropy is another topic that goes hand in hand with rising wealth. Further, with the growth of wealth, many Asian families seek to increase their philanthropic activities. Thus, philanthropy during the time of COVID-19 was the main theme of our 2021 *Trusts, Wealth and Philanthropy* conference jointly convened by the University of Melbourne, Singapore Management University and the University of York. We hope that this volume will inspire more scholarly work on these and other topics associated with Asian wealth.

In Chapter 3, Thomas P. Gallanis considers the use of US law and legal institutions for wealth transmission by citizens and residents of Japan or China. Five prominent mechanisms found in US law are unpacked, namely wills, revocable and irrevocable trusts, life insurance policies, retirement accounts, and survivorship interests in real property by joint tenancies or transfer-on-death deeds. In exploring these mechanisms, Gallanis expertly tackles the difficult conflict of laws issues in international wealth transmission. He also deals with the implications of US tax in relation to succession. This chapter is invaluable to the wealth advisors of citizens and residents of Japan or China with assets or a significant presence in the United States. Gallanis ends the chapter by identifying five policy questions in relation to Asian wealth in the United States. First, does the United States have the right rules on choice of law given that wealth is mobile and often intangible? Second, should the ability of foreigners to own real estate in the United States be circumscribed? Third, does the United States have the right rules for the treatment of trusts as compared to corporations? Fourth, does the United States have the right rules to determine source and situs of income and capital? Finally, when should the laws and legal institutions facilitate the transmission of private wealth of citizens of another country? No doubt, these penetrating policy questions form an invaluable agenda for research by scholars in the field.

Edward S. W. Ti's chapter (Chapter 4) takes up the second policy question posed by Gallanis albeit from the perspective of Australia, New Zealand, and Canada. The topic of Asian wealth is often tied not just with international trusts but also with investments in foreign real estate. Anecdotally, Asians demonstrate a fondness for real estate investments all over the world. This chapter tackles the topic of the impact of Chinese wealth and their investments in residential property in the West. According to Ti, the recent narrative is that wealthy Chinese people are buying residential property in Western countries such as Australia, New Zealand, and Canada causing the property market to become unaffordable for the local population. Ti helpfully unpacks the Chinese motivations for buying residential property in the West. The reasons include the rise of wealth in China and astronomical housing costs in major cities such as Beijing and Shanghai, making real estate in the West seem like affordable investments. Other soft factors driving these buyers include planning for children who study abroad, possible immigration, diversification of wealth portfolio, and economic and political confidence in those Western countries. According to policymakers, the influx of these foreign buyers has resulted in the local population being outpriced. Hence, governments in those countries had to enact regulatory measures to prevent foreigners from buying real estate. This chapter then embarks on a careful study of the regulatory responses in Australia, New Zealand, and Canada. The regulatory measures include approval by government bodies before purchase and enhanced stamp duties for foreigners buying real estate. In the case of New Zealand, there is an outright ban on foreigners from purchasing residential property.

Ti's thesis appears to be twofold. First, Ti argues that 'if a particular group is specifically highlighted by a country's lawmakers to justify the enactment of a law, there ought to be specific data or evidence to back this up'. Second, the author makes a plea for more temperate remarks in relation to the regulatory responses so as not to stir up anti-Chinese sentiments. Presumably, such anti-Chinese sentiments may have negative repercussions on not just foreigners but also on permanent residents and citizens of those countries who have an Asian background.

In relation to the author's second thesis, the editors are in complete agreement with the need for sensitivity by political leaders. As seen by the recent pandemic, anti-Asian feelings have led to ugly verbal abuse and unprovoked physical attacks on members of the Asian community living in the West, especially women and the elderly. However, Ti's first thesis, that there should be more data before policymakers suggest a particular group is responsible for the rise in the property market, is a more nuanced issue. While the editors agree that it is not a good idea to make intemperate remarks, the point is that there is indeed empirical data from other developed jurisdictions such as Singapore and the United States (as demonstrated by Thomas P. Gallanis's chapter) that Chinese buyers are among the largest group of foreigners buying international real estate. Furthermore, China has also enacted regulatory measures to discourage its citizens from making real estate investments abroad. Indeed, Ti concedes that he is not making the argument that 'Chinese investors are never the cause of housing unaffordability'. It is the present editors' view that regulatory responses to prevent housing prices from becoming unaffordable to its local population are completely justified, though intemperate remarks are unhelpful and potentially dangerous.

Turning to a different topic, Lusina Ho, in Chapter 5, investigates the issue of mental capacity required for wills and lasting powers of attorney in Hong Kong and Singapore. Certainly, this is an important topic given the rapidly greying population of these two jurisdictions – and many other Asian jurisdictions. Specifically, Ho explores the application of mental capacity law derived from England to the cultural contexts of Hong Kong and Singapore. In this chapter, she demonstrates that there are great tensions inherent in efforts to apply English law, which is rooted in notions of individual autonomy, to these Asian jurisdictions. Ho carefully analyses the Hong Kong cases showing that the presumption of testamentary capacity with respect to wills that are duly executed and rational on their face is ambivalent, having only been endorsed in certain first instance decisions. In contrast, Singapore courts embrace the presumption of testamentary capacity but appear to define 'irrationality on the face of the will' differently from their English counterparts. There are hints that a Singapore court may consider a will to be irrational if certain beneficiaries are chosen and other beneficiaries are cut out from inheritance.

In this chapter, Ho also traverses an under-investigated area, that is, mental capacity for executing lasting powers of attorney. While Hong Kong courts have yet to seriously consider undue influence in relation to power of attorney, Singapore courts have had the benefit of several major decisions where the lasting powers of attorney were vitiated on the ground of undue influence. Ho rightly concludes that the key to protecting against both undue influence and testamentary incapacity is to seek good quality legal service in preparing and executing these documents.

The stereotypical Western view of the Asian family is one where the family is a harmonious unit and disputes are rare and frowned upon. However, the next two chapters, Chapter 6 by Rebecca Lee and Chapter 7 jointly written by Yip Man and Tang Hang Wu, demonstrate that this view is misconceived. Asian families, especially wealthy families, like all families do have their fair share of disputes.

In Chapter 6, Rebecca Lee explores inheritance disputes from the Hong Kong perspective. She demonstrates a recurring undercurrent in these cases, namely that Hong Kong law, which is based on English law and like English law shows a firm commitment to testamentary freedom, often clashes with perceived familial obligations arising out of local cultural expectations. These cultural norms include an unspoken expectation that certain family members will inherit some parts of the testator's wealth. When these expectations are frustrated, the family members may be tempted to apply for maintenance from the deceased's estate. Interestingly, Rebecca Lee demonstrates that the Hong Kong statute for maintenance of family members is narrower than its English counterpart, requiring the applicant to have been maintained either wholly or substantially by the testator prior to his or her demise. Hence, in both cases discussed by Rebecca Lee, the applicants failed to obtain any maintenance. She argues that the denial of maintenance in these cases shows that the principle of testamentary freedom remains the dominant legal value found in Hong Kong law despite the perceived importance of familial obligation in Chinese culture.

Outside testamentary disputes, another fertile ground for familial disputes are trust disputes. Wealthy Hong Kong families have for many years settled their wealth on discretionary trusts, both domestically and in offshore jurisdictions, as part of their succession planning. Many of these settlers are domiciled in China and hence subject to Chinese forced heirship rules. Since these trusts effectively oust forced heirship rules, they have become the foci of disputes. Rebecca Lee discusses such a trust dispute in the context of litigation involving HSBC as trustee of the Lo Family Trust. In this case, the matriarch settlor claimed that there was a common understanding between her and the trustee that the trustee was to give overriding weight to her instructions, instead of following the trustee's duty to treat all beneficiaries fairly. Unsurprisingly, Madam Lo's assertion was rejected by the Hong Kong Court *inter alia* on the ground that this would mean that the trust would be a sham. Other reported trust disputes considered by Rebecca Lee include an application to the Royal Court of Jersey for the Court's blessing for transfer of trust assets involving the family of Hong Kong's largest property developer. In conclusion, Rebecca Lee argues that full testamentary freedom appears to be both the prevailing approach and the starting point of Hong Kong succession and trust law.

Continuing with the theme of familial disputes, in Chapter 7, Yip Man and Tang Hang Wu examine the legal contests over the family wealth of high-net-worth families in Singapore. The first part of the chapter demonstrates that for many wealthy Asian families, the members of the family are deeply intertwined with, and often inseparable from, the family wealth and business. The consequent collectivist thinking about family property often gives rise to grave difficulties when deciding the individual ownership of family assets amongst family members on the demise of the family's patriarch or matriarch. The second part of the chapter embarks on a deep dive into five landmark cases in Singapore to extract further insights into family disputes. Several factors emerge as drivers of familial disputes: they include a culture that prefers sons over daughters, a culture of informality in relation to beneficial entitlement of shares in the family company, the unclear ownership status of real estate, and the effect of the declining mental capacity of the family's patriarch or matriarch. The normative implications that emerge from these family wealth disputes are that English property and trusts doctrines, which are received by the courts of Singapore and used by them to unravel these conflicts, are hardly the ideal tools to resolve family disputes caused by a perceived breach of Asian familial and cultural norms. Yip and Tang then proceed to provide a roadmap to careful succession planning to minimise such familial disputes: to bridge the gap between a legal system that still manifests the cultural norms of its English (often nineteenth century) origins and the familial and cultural norms of (twenty-first century) Singapore.

Vincent Ooi and Chan Ee Lin end this part in Chapter 8 by tackling the opaque world of family offices and private trust companies. They also consider the use of Singapore's Variable Capital Company in structuring private wealth. Family offices and private trust companies are commonly used structures by wealthy families all over the world and yet are never mentioned in any of the major trust textbooks. Thus, this chapter contributes to the literature by providing an 'on the ground' survey of how wealthy Asian families are structuring their wealth. Beyond the descriptive account of the structures, Ooi and Chan provide insightful analysis of settlors who attempt to retain control over the trusts they establish and the methods by which the trusts' integrity may be preserved. Ooi and Chan propose certain strategies including setting out clear roles and responsibilities in terms of management of the structures, how decisions are made within the context of the family office or private trust company, and how future disagreements will be handled. This chapter should be read together with the earlier chapters on familial conflict because such disputes are usually framed by these structures. The larger theme that emerges from Ooi's and Chan's piece is that just as companies should have a proper governance structure, wealthy families should also establish proper family governance structures in their trusts, trust companies, and private offices. Indeed, proper family governance structures appear to be one of the most important factors in avoiding family disputes.

The second substantive part of this book is entitled 'The Changing Legal Context'. Legal systems have always been faced with change, but rarely so much change, in so short a time, as today. Both the human and the technological context of trust law is changing rapidly around us. Chapters 9–12 all deal with what might be called the internal development of trust law, whereas Chapters 13–15 address the external regulation of trusts.

Chapter 9, 'Trusts of Cryptoassets', by Kelvin F. K. Low, addresses the changing technological context of trust law. Cryptoassets have very rapidly established themselves in the world economy. Whether that is a good thing, or a bad thing, is for others to decide. But the one thing the law would be very ill-advised to do is simply to try and ignore this genuinely novel phenomenon. The process of common law accommodation, seen so often in other contexts, and particularly in another time of enormous change, the Industrial Revolution of the eighteenth and nineteenth centuries, has once again risen to the challenge. This time, the leading development came in New Zealand, in the *Cryptopia* case,[4] with its recognition of cryptoassets as the subject of property rights and the Singapore Court of Appeal in *Quoine Pte Ltd* v. *B2C2 Ltd*,[5] albeit in the form of *dicta* on the issue of a trust over cryptoassets.

Some cryptoassets are readily assimilable into the existing legal framework as choses in action. In these cases, the new technology of cryptoassets is simply a novel way of recording the existence of, and dealing with, the benefit of obligations – in other words, choses in action. These new means of structuring an existing concept may still raise questions, such as the application of formality rules, but the questions are limited and not particularly difficult in concept.

However, certain other cryptoassets are more fundamentally problematic for the legal order, because they do not constitute a claim on anyone, and so it is hard to view them as choses in action. The very phrase 'chose in action' betrays the problem: a chose in action necessarily involves, as the very words indicate, a claim against someone enforceable (only) by action. But an asset such as a bitcoin is not

4 Ruscoe v. Cryptopia Ltd (in liq) [2020] NZHC 728.
5 [2020] SGCA(I) 2.

a claim against anyone. It is just digital information processed in accordance with the specific programming of a particular computer network. And how often have we been told that information cannot be property? Yet many objections to conceptualising information as the subject matter of property rights do not apply to cryptoassets. Most importantly, the limitless replicability of most information is simply not possible in the context of a bitcoin: the code – the information – constituting a bitcoin is as unique as a particular gold coin bearing a serial number, and that code only has meaning within the specific programming of a particular computer network.

Low makes a very useful contribution to working out some of these problems in the context of trust law. It is an area of enormous importance, where academic investigation and theorisation can be very useful, as witness the work of Fox and Green, cited in the *Cryptopia* case.[6] It is also an area where academics can make a significant contribution through their participation in the many important institutional responses to the rise of cryptoassets by (*inter alia*) the Law Commission of England and Wales (in its Digital Assets Project), the Bank of England (in its Central Bank Digital Currency Taskforce), the Monetary Authority of Singapore (in its Project Ubin), UNIDROIT (in its project on Digital Assets and Private Law) and the Bank for International Settlements' research into, and reaction to, such developments.

James Lee's chapter, Chapter 10, looks at the changing social context of trust law: the ways in which practitioners, acting for settlors, seek to test the boundaries of trust law and develop new structures – or at least seemingly new structures – for the management of wealth. As Lee notes, so far in the United Kingdom, most of the accommodation of these developments – or not – has occurred in judicial decisions, whereas other jurisdictions, particularly New Zealand but also Singapore and many offshore jurisdictions, have recently used statute law to develop their law of trusts.

Lee investigates the doctrine of the 'illusory trust', which was to the fore in the Privy Council decision of *Webb* v. *Webb*.[7] The interrelation of this doctrine and the doctrine of sham trusts could still usefully be clarified in judicial decisions, though conceptually the distinction is clear. Sham trusts involve an apparent or ostensible attempt to create a trust, where, because of proven fraud, the courts are entitled to disregard the language of the trust and use extrinsic evidence to conclude that such language is simply a sham and of no effect, so that the purported trust property is in fact simply held for the benefit of the settlor. Illusory trusts, by contrast, involve an exercise in construction: the very words of the trust instrument, when looked at in the round, and as a whole, lead to the conclusion that there are no trusts for the benefit of people other than the settlor, but simply an outright trust for him or her. In other words, as a matter of construction, the courts reach the conclusion that the settlor has simply remained beneficial owner of the assets. The result of applying each doctrine is the same, but the means of reaching it are distinct.

6 [2020] NZHC 728 at [63]–[65].
7 [2020] UKPC 22.

Lee's chapter also raises two other important themes. First, the extent to which the courts' resolution of ostensibly novel problems can be found in their reaction to developments earlier in time. Second, the question of what might be the best institutional forum for the future development of trust law.

As regards the first of these questions, Lee cites a vitally important point made by Kós P extrajudicially in New Zealand: 'Perhaps in equity more than any other part of our law, one drives ahead safely with one eye on the rear vision mirror'. It is a fascinating realisation that many apparent human changes in the context of trust law are, on closer inspection, nowhere near so novel as the technological changes: human beings change much less fundamentally, and much less rapidly, than technology. For example, trust law has for centuries had to deal with overbearing settlors who wish to retain many powers over the trust assets. One example of this is the law surrounding powers of appointment, from the seventeenth- and eighteenth-century law on general powers to the development of intermediate powers in the 1970s and 1980s. There is much to be learned from the thoughts of our forebears, even if we choose different outcomes today.

As regards the second of these questions, different jurisdictions have found different balances between judicial development and statutory development of trust. Lee points out that the response in the United Kingdom has been largely judicial, though the response elsewhere, for example, in New Zealand and Singapore, has been much more a matter of statute law. It is very hard to say which response is in any sense 'better'. Each response has its merits and demerits. The judicial response is hugely flexible and nuanced, but that may come at the cost of some uncertainty, especially in the early stages of the response. By contrast, the statutory response can provide a sense of clarity – sometimes misplaced, given that statutes have to be interpreted – but that certainty can come at the cost of inflexibility and difficulty in coping with unanticipated situations. The United Kingdom has, historically, shown something of a *via media* through these apparently contrasting approaches: it tends to allow developments to occur initially through the proposals of practitioners in trust instruments, and the disposal of disputes about them by the courts; and then an emerging consensus is often enacted in new trustee legislation.

The contrast between judicial and legislative development of trust law is also apparent in the next two chapters, Chapter 11 by David Pollard and Chapter 12 by Tobias Barkley. Both focus on pension (superannuation) trusts, some of the largest and most economically and socially important trusts in the world today.

Pollard's chapter deals with the developing English law applying public law concepts of good decision-making to private law institutions such as trusts. The judges are the drivers of this process. It is hardly surprising that trusts as big and as important as pension trusts attract more scrutiny, through litigation, than traditional family trusts, and that the judges are more willing to impose stricter (albeit still liberal) standards on decision-making by trustees of such trusts. Crucially, of course, the beneficiaries of such trusts are not volunteers but bought and paid for their rights under the trust. This fact clearly warrants and legitimates greater judicial oversight of pension trustees.

The more difficult question, however, is how far the judges will apply new principles developed in one particular area of trust law – pension trusts – to all trusts, including traditional family settlements where the justification for more intrusive oversight of trustees is less. This question of the scope for application of developing principles raises squarely issues, noted above about judicial development of the law: the possibility of nuance, whereby the judges distinguish between pension trusts and other types of trusts, coupled with uncertainty in the law until such nuance is established – or else is definitively rejected.

Barkley's chapter addresses Australian superannuation law. This provides an interesting counterpoint to the previous chapter, not just because of the difference in jurisdiction, but also because so much regulation of pension trustees in Australia is statutory in origin. And again, the distinction noted above between judicial and statutory development of the law shows itself. Statutory rules are, on their face, clearer, and apply to a clearly defined category of trustees – superannuation trustees. Superannuation trustees are easy to identify, because superannuation trusts require prior administrative approval: the trustees of those trusts that have such prior approval are superannuation trustees, easily identified by reason of that prior approval. (While it is possible that an unapproved superannuation scheme might attract the statutory regulation of its trustees, this situation is not going to be common: in other words, identification of who is a superannuation trustee, as opposed to some other kind of trustee, is, in the vast majority of cases, going to be easy.) So, the scope for application of the new statutory rules is certain, easy to identify, and stable. However, the content of those rules can still leave doubt. And, more interestingly, the possible effect of the new statutory rules by analogy on areas to which they do not directly apply raises difficult and as yet unanswered questions.

Chapter 13, by Simone Wong, moves the discussion into a new area. While this chapter is still concerned with recent changes in the law applicable to trusts – the effect of unexplained wealth orders on trusts in English law – the perspective of her chapter is different. The previous four chapters (Chapters 9–12) were concerned with the development of internal trust law rules, that is, the development (whether by judicial decision or by statute) of the relationship between trustees and beneficiaries, which in turn may have some effect on the extent to which a settlor achieves her or his desired goals. Unexplained wealth orders, an important new weapon in the fight against financial crime, particularly money laundering, concern the external regulation of the holders of wealth, including trustees, by public authorities.

The trust has traditionally been a private institution, in the sense of not being subject to the scrutiny of outsiders, including public authorities, as well as in the sense of being a private law institution. Indeed, historically, one of the great attractions of using a trust structure to manage wealth was its privacy and the absence of public scrutiny, intervention, or supervision. This was seen by settlors and trustees as a considerable advantage of trust structures, as opposed to, say, corporate structures, where some degree of disclosure and publicity has always been part of the legislative scheme establishing corporate law in many (perhaps most) jurisdictions. Unexplained wealth orders radically alter this situation. An unexplained wealth order in the context of a trust will compel a large class of people, including but not limited to the trustees, to provide public authorities with a large amount of information about the origin of specific trust funds or assets.

Wong therefore goes on to investigate the scope of the class of people to whom an unexplained wealth order might apply in the context of trust assets. For obvious reasons, that scope has been very widely defined: if it were not, the fight against financial crime would be made significantly more difficult. Nevertheless, it is reasonable to wonder whether it is appropriate for the law to make such a wide and uncertain class of people subject to coercive state procedures by an unexplained wealth order in the context of a trust relationship, though in the present day and age, such concerns are likely to be dismissed by the state as less important than the fight against financial crime.

The last two chapters (Chapters 14 and 15) in the collection are concerned with direct and indirect challenges to an express trust which has been created or used for self-interested motives. It is well recognised that the express trust accords a great degree of freedom to the settlor in both creation and its structuring. In the wealth management industry, in particular, the modern 'trust' products are settlor-focused and enable the settlor to retain significant control (in the capacity of a trustee, protector, or otherwise) over some aspects of trust administration, even after the trust has been set up and the trustees have taken ownership of the trust assets. Two common questions run through Chapters 14 and 15. First, where should the courts draw the line and push back against too much settlor autonomy? Second, what judicial and legislative techniques may be used to 'look through' the form of trust, or the exercise of rights, to the 'substance' of the matter?

In Chapter 14, Jessica Palmer critically examines the New Zealand courts' indirect challenge to the express trust, through the imposition of a 'reasonable expectations constructive trust' on property already held on an express trust. This specific type of constructive trust arises in circumstances where the third party (e.g. a spouse or de facto partner) has made contributions to the property while it is owned by the trustee such that it could be said that the trustee should reasonably expect to yield an interest in the trust property in favour of the third party. It is an indirect challenge because the express trust is left intact, but the beneficial entitlement is redistributed through the constructive trust. Against the background of an increasing number of discretionary trusts and the concomitant demand for retention of settlor control in New Zealand, this particular type of constructive trust is a judicial technique, in the absence of appropriate statutory intervention, to enable some recourse for creditors, spouses or de factor partners of the settlor. It is a blunt instrument to correct the injustice arising from the reality that a trustee (often the settlor-trustee in the New Zealand trust landscape) has the ability to induce third-party expectations in relation to trust property in exchange for that party's contribution of wealth or value to the trust fund.

As Palmer forcefully points out, however, the New Zealand courts' solution is unprincipled for two main reasons. First, the constructive trust on an express trust analysis not only recognises a new equitable interest in favour of the spouse, partner or, creditor, but also defeats the prior equitable interest of beneficiaries of the express trust, even though the latter have done nothing to justify them losing priority to the later created equitable interest. Second, the constructive trust analysis is a mechanism to reverse unjust enrichment. The more appropriate remedy to award in such cases is arguably a personal award based on unjust enrichment or promissory estoppel, but the success of these actions would depend on the claimant having no notice of the pre-existing express trust. More generally, Palmer's chapter raises the bigger question of how best to respond to the injustice arising from the controlling settlor-trustee's behaviour directly. She concludes with the tantalising suggestion that the answer may lie in a flexible doctrine of illusory trusts, albeit that the existence of the doctrine has yet to be firmly established in the common law world.[8]

In Chapter 15, Graham Virgo argues that a distinct, umbrella doctrine of abuse of trust – targeted at invalidating a settlor's or a trustee's acts based on self-interested purposes – can be identified from the smaller and seemingly disparate doctrines, such as sham trusts, illusory trusts, illegality and fraud on the power. According to Virgo, an abuse of trust is to be distinguished from a breach of trust, the latter of which is concerned with a failure to carry out what the trust requires the trustee to do. An abuse of trust, on the other hand, occurs where 'the purpose of the settlor or trustee in creating the trust or in exercising the power is considered to be inconsistent with the purity of the trust', typically in cases where the settlor or trustee is 'unacceptably motivated by self-interest'.[9] He points out that whilst the common law does not recognise a doctrine of abuse of rights,[10] purposes, and motives are relevant to the exercise of equitable rights.

The value of Virgo's analysis lies primarily in its explanatory power: it helps us identify that a broader principle is at work in trust law which unites a number of invalidating doctrines. But beyond providing a rationalised account of the law, the abuse of rights doctrine also seeks to establish 'illusory trust' as a distinct doctrine. Virgo argues that if the settlor attempts to create what is not a trust by its core requirements based on an objective determination, the attempt is an abuse of trust. It is not enough to simply say no trust is created, a pronouncement that has no moral underpinning. The illusory trust doctrine, on Virgo's analysis, would appear to apply most readily to cases where the settlors or trustees have reserved so much power to themselves (self-interested motivation) that no real trust exists. Given the moral

8 See discussion in Mark Bennett, 'The Illusory Trust Doctrine: Formal or Substantive?' (2020) 51 *VUWLR* 193.

9 See Chapter 15.

10 Cf. Solène Rowan, 'Abuse of Rights in English Contract Law: Hidden in Plain Sight?' (2021) 84(5) *MLR* 1066.

undertone of the doctrine, it should logically follow that illusory trust cases can be distinguished from a scenario where the settlor, through imprudence or ignorance, failed to create a trust due to uncertainty in subject matter or objects. Yet, the illusory trust doctrine can be distinguished from the sham trust doctrine. A sham trust satisfies the core requirements for trust creation on an objective determination, but the trust is invalidated due to the parties' subjective intention to mislead. They never intended to create a real trust. The settlor of an illusory trust intends to create a real trust, but she reserves so much power to herself that no real trust can arise.

Although Virgo does not suggest that the abuse of trust doctrine should supplant the different principles which fall within the purview of this umbrella concept, a reader who has arrived at the conclusion of Chapter 15 will inevitably wonder if the wider doctrine may empower courts to recognise new grounds of invalidity.

It has taken us longer to bring this volume to fruition than we had originally hoped, because of the effects of the worldwide COVID-19 pandemic. We apologise for that to our long-suffering but hugely supportive authors. And we hope this volume is worth the wait.

# 2

# Family Trusts Today

*Lady Arden*

## 1 INTRODUCTION

There is an old Chinese saying about family wealth: 富不过三代 ('Wealth does not pass three generations'). I have taken this saying as the theme for this keynote speech on family trusts. The paradigm trust for my purposes is the family trust set up by a successful business person, who, perhaps starting from humble beginnings, made their fortune and then wanted to keep their wealth in the family for many generations to come.

As the saying indicates, by the time that the business reaches the third generation, the children may be much less interested in the business. There may also be a cultural layer here: it may be that the settlor never really discussed what he wanted because of cultural attitudes which view with disfavour discussions about what is to happen after the most senior family passes on. In some cultures, there is a reluctance to make a letter of wishes or a formal will since it may be thought to be unlucky.

The members of the second generation who enter the business may be perfectly content with the trust arrangements, but, by the third generation, the attitudes and values may have changed. The economic situation may have changed. The family may no longer find it as congenial as it was in the past to continue to be based where the business is located and so on. It is not every third-generation beneficiary who is unhappy with the family trust; there are many family trusts that have survived many generations. However, the saying that 'Wealth does not pass three generations' is valuable because it illustrates how over time disputes may arise within family trusts. If there is a dispute between different branches of the family, then, as a way of dividing the trust assets in the third generation, the assets may, with the consent of all concerned, be put into a number of separate trust companies, marking a shift away from the original trust structure.

There can, of course, be many reasons for wanting to restructure a trust. For instance, the minimisation of tax may be an objective. It may, for that reason, be desired to put the assets forming part of the trust in a jurisdiction with a low tax rate. That may lead to further complications. If, for example, that jurisdiction is not a common law jurisdiction but one which applies, say, Sharia law, it may be found that that system of law does not favour or allow an absolute disposition by a person during his lifetime. The reorganisation of a trust in a different jurisdiction may be referred to as transitioning.

When, however, the third generation takes a different view about the purpose of the trust from the original settlor, there can be tension also between the trustees and the beneficiaries. There may be considerable difficulty for the trustees in deciding how a discretion should be exercised.

I propose to consider four problems affecting family trusts. I believe these to be some of the problems which are uppermost in people's minds in practice today. The four problems are:

(1) Privacy in court proceedings: Issues of privacy may arise when seeking directions from the court, as it may be desirable to keep the details of the trust and the names of the beneficiaries out of the public domain.
(2) The over-dominant settlor and sham trusts: Under this head, I am going to look at the landmark case of *JSC Mezhdunarodniy Promyshlenniy Bank* v. *Pugachev* ('*Pugachev*'),[1] in which professionally drafted discretionary trusts established in New Zealand were set aside by the High Court of Justice of England and Wales. The general issue is what happens when the settlor of a family trust, which he endows with business assets, turns out to be a person who dominates the trust and someone then contends that the trust is not a valid trust.
(3) Insolvency: This may be an issue because the businesses which form part of the assets of the family trust become insolvent in circumstances where there are not enough assets to meet the liabilities incurred by the trustees. So the question arises: can the creditors sue the trustees personally?
(4) Climate change and handling disputes: I will say a little about disputes between beneficiaries and trustees in the particular context of climate change between trustees and beneficiaries.

## 2 PRIVACY IN COURT PROCEEDINGS

Court proceedings can provide important guidance and protection to trustees. The courts in various jurisdictions have provided considerable assistance to trustees to enable them to operate in an efficient fashion. One of the latest of these decisions was the decision in the matter of the *C Trust* by Chief Justice Hargun of Bermuda.[2] The trust in that case made provision for a protector, but the corporate entity that had been acting as a protector for some years had not been properly appointed. The Chief Justice made an order under the inherent jurisdiction of the court to intervene in the administration of the trust to approve certain acts which were in

1 [2017] EWHC 2426 (Ch).
2 [2019] SC (Bda) 44 App.

fact an effective departure from the trust. Chief Justice Hargun relied on *Re New*,[3] *In the matter of the Z settlement*,[4] and *Schmidt* v. *Rosewood Trust Ltd*.[5] Chief Justice Hargun concluded that the court may under its inherent jurisdiction order that the current trustees leave undisturbed the acts or omissions of the previous trustees while there was an issue about the validity of the previous trustees' appointment. In short, the trust could be administered on the same footing as if those acts had been validly done with the authority of the duly constituted trustees. In other cases, the courts have varied the terms of the trust deeds so as to substitute or add a valid provision relating to the perpetuity period.

In connection with court proceedings, however, there is often a desire for anonymity.

### 2.1 *Can There Be Hearings in Private?*

Originally trust proceedings were always heard in private, but this is less so today. In England and Wales, the applicant for a hearing in private has to show that it is necessary to hold the hearing in private. But there are circumstances where applications may have to be heard in private in order to protect beneficiaries, including children who might be kidnapped if it was widely known how wealthy they or their families were. If in these circumstances there is a request for privacy, it may be necessary for the family to disclose their social media history.

Different courts adopt different approaches to the question whether trust disputes should be heard in public. I have been told that in India, for instance, all documents filed in courts can be inspected by the public. *In the matter of G Trusts*,[6] the court held that a directions application should be held in private because it was essentially a matter about internal trust administration in which there was no public interest. This case can be contrasted with that of *MN* v. *OP*,[7] where the Court of Appeal of England and Wales confirmed in a case involving a substantial family trust that there was no presumption that an anonymity order would be made on a variation of trust application.

The Court of Appeal concluded that the judge was entitled to come to the conclusion that a good case for anonymity had not been made. However, it further concluded that there was possible prejudice to minor children so it made orders under section 39(1) of the Children and Young Persons Act 1933 preventing any identification of them in any publication. Information about the assets within the family trust was already in the public domain and the judge had refused anonymity about the adult beneficiaries' interests even though the allocation of their beneficial

3 [1901] 2 Ch 534.
4 [2016] JRC 048.
5 [2003] 2 AC 709.
6 [2017] SC (Bda) 98 Civ.
7 [2019] EWCA Civ 679.

interests had not previously been made public. These cases demonstrate very different approaches. So the practical point here for trustees and those advising them is that trustees need to be sure about the practice of the jurisdiction before making their application for directions or other relief.

Next, there is a question about whether investigative journalists or other members of the public can get copies of the documents filed in court. Here the decision of the Supreme Court of the United Kingdom in *Dring (on behalf of the Asbestos Victims Support Group)* v. *Cape Intermediate Holdings Ltd (Media Lawyers Association intervening)* is of some interest.[8] The Supreme Court held that the principle of open justice extended even to documents which were not part of the records of the court and to documents for whose disclosure there was no rule in the Civil Procedure Rules. The courts had inherent jurisdiction to provide access to any person, and for this purpose, they had to carry out a weighing exercise balancing the open justice principle against other considerations which, depending on the case, would include privacy interests and proportionality. The purpose of the open justice principle was to bring individual judicial officeholders to account and to enable the public to understand what evidence had been before the court and why decisions were made. So a member of the public could apply to see any document placed before the court, including the trial bundle. Subject to questions of, for example, proportionality, a person could apply to inspect documents, which had been produced at a trial he had not attended or which had taken place many months earlier.

People sometimes want information about a trust which is not contained in documents lodged for the purposes of litigation. More and more jurisdictions are deciding that trusts have to be registered and in some cases, this involves revealing the name of the ultimate beneficial owner on a website. Beneficiaries may be able to use the data protection legislation to obtain copies of information about themselves.[9]

## 3 SHAM TRUSTS

This subject has become topical due to the landmark case of *Pugachev*. The settlor was a man said to be Putin's banker, or perhaps his ex-banker. The claimant was a bank from which he was said to have misappropriated substantial funds. He went to New Zealand where a solicitor established discretionary trusts for Mr Pugachev and his family. Mr Pugachev was the first protector. If he came under a 'disability', which was said to have happened because an order had been made against him in England and Wales freezing all his assets, he could not continue to act as protector and his son became protector in his place.

The claimant bank claimed that these trusts should be set aside as illusory trusts or shams, alternatively as transactions to defeat creditors within section 423 of the

8 [2019] UKSC 38.

9 *Dawson-Damer* v. *Taylor Wessing LLP (Information Commissioner intervening)* [2017] EWCA Civ 74.

Insolvency Act 1986. The trial was heard by Birss J, who gave a long and detailed judgment (456 paragraphs). He held that the claimant had established that the trusts were illusory. In short, the judge held that Mr Pugachev had retained beneficial ownership of the assets put into the trust as a matter of the interpretation of the trust deeds. It followed that they were shams.[10] The trusts should not be enforced either on the basis that they were illusory or on the basis that they were a sham.[11] He also held that the section 423 claim succeeded. But it is the first holding with which I am here concerned and which I believe means that it is right to be called the landmark case of recent times. The judge's core holding on illusory trust was:[12]

> The true effect of all the trust deeds in this case, properly construed, is to leave Mr Pugachev in control of the trust assets. Mr Pugachev is the beneficial owner. They amount to a bare trust for Mr Pugachev.

At the start of the passage directing himself on the law on illusory trusts, Birss J cited the following passage from the judgment of the Chief Justice Richard Ground in Bermuda in *Re AQ Revocable Trusts*:[13]

> the concatenation of rights and powers in the settlor, when coupled with the fact that he was the sole trustee at the time of the constitution of the trusts, *rendered this trust illusory during his lifetime* [...] the cumulative effect of the trust documents, when taken with the de facto situation, means that the settlor as trustee could not effectively be called to account in his lifetime. [emphasis original]

Before I venture further, I want to examine the decision of the Chief Justice on which Birss J relied. It is common in the case of lifetime trusts for settlors to reserve powers to themselves, or to appoint themselves as protector of the trust, which gives them power to intervene in the management of the trust. There are also cases where a settlor sets up a trust but appoints himself as trustee, which may lead to him not properly distinguishing between the trust assets and his personal assets.

*AQ Revocable Trusts* is relied on in *Pugachev*, so it is important to be clear about the ratio in that case. The issue which Ground CJ there had to decide was whether the trusts set up by the settlor in his lifetime were valid or whether they were invalid because of the way the trust was operated. If they were invalid, the trust assets fell into testamentary trusts of the settlor and that led to major tax savings by the beneficiaries.

We only have a glimpse into the evidence, but it is apparent that the problem was the settlor's behaviour. The judge found that the over-dominant settlor's conduct showed that he had no intention of abiding by the terms of the trust. At least one of the trustees had no real knowledge of what was happening in relation to the trust assets.

10 [2017] EWHC 2426 (Ch) at [455].
11 ibid at [441]–[442].
12 ibid at [455].
13 ibid at [155], citing *Re AQ Revocable Trusts* [2010] SC (Bda) 40 Civ at [29].

To cap it all, there was a clause in the trust deed that enabled the settlor to give his approval to any transaction and for the trustees to be relieved of their liability if that happened. The trust had been drafted in the United States and was possibly based on an American precedent adapted for use in Bermuda. The Chief Justice found that the settlor had effective sole dominion over the trust assets in this lifetime. Not surprisingly the Chief Justice held that the trusts were ineffective and void.

In reaching his conclusion, the Chief Justice relied on 'the de facto situation', which can only be read as a reference to the evidence he had heard but (perhaps for privacy reasons) was not set out in his judgment. He was influenced by that evidence and by the terms set out in the trust deed, including the one to which I have referred. The judge recalled the beneficiary principle, that is, the principle for a trust to be valid a beneficiary had to be able to enforce the trust. I note in passing that that principle has to work both ways of course. If a beneficiary can enforce the terms of a trust, it can hardly be said to be illusory. In short, in this case, it is clear that the Chief Justice took account of both the evidence and the terms of the trust, thus it may be that we have to read the conclusion of Birss J on illusory trust in that light.

The judge went on to consider whether the *Pugachev* trusts were sham trusts. There was in fact no need for the judge to have recourse to the concept of a sham trust. The judge was able to set the trusts aside simply because the settlor had not respected the fact that when he set up the trust, he transferred control of the assets so transferred to the trustees. A sham, on the other hand, is a transaction into which parties enter with a view to the transaction having a different effect from that that appears to be the effect of the transaction. The test of what is a sham was laid down by Diplock LJ in a case called *Snook* v. *London and West Riding Investments Ltd*. He held[14]:

> [...] it is, I think, necessary to consider what, if any, legal concept is involved in the use of this popular and pejorative word. I apprehend that, if it has any meaning in law, it means acts done or documents executed by the parties to the 'sham' which are intended by them to give to third parties or to the court the appearance of creating between the parties legal rights and obligations different from the actual legal rights and obligations (if any) which the parties intend to create. One thing I think, however, is clear in legal principle, morality and the authorities [...] that for acts or documents to be a 'sham', with whatever legal consequences follow from this, all the parties thereto must have a common intention that the acts or documents are not to create the legal rights and obligations which they give the appearance of creating. No unexpressed intentions of a 'shammer' affect the rights of a party whom he deceived.

There are a number of cases where this has been applied in the context of trusts. For example, in *Midland Bank* v. *Wyatt*,[15] the settlor made a written declaration of trust

[14] [1967] 2 QB 786 at 802.
[15] [1995] 1 FLR 697.

in favour of his wife and children and then put the relevant instrument away in his safe. The court held that the settlor did not intend to benefit his wife and children. He simply wished to bring the trust into existence in case he should need it to avoid paying his creditors. It was held that the trust deed was a sham, but it is to be noted that the only relevant intention was that of the settlor.

As Birss J makes clear, the Court of Appeal of England and Wales (to which I was party) decided in an earlier tax case, *Hitch* v. *Stone (Inspector of Taxes)*,[16] that to find a sham the court had to look at subjective intention. In the same case, I also observed that the court was able to look at the surrounding circumstances and the same, one might imagine, may be true for illusory trusts. It is then open to argument that the judge in *Pugachev* did not go further than look at the trust deeds. But more fundamentally, in *Pugachev*, there was no finding that the irreducible core of the trust, that is, the presence of some minimum obligations enforceable in law, which is fundamental to the concept of a trust (see *Armitage* v. *Nurse*),[17] was not present. If that is so, we must ask whether an illusory trust is an exception to the irreducible core principle so that a trust can be illusory even if the irreducible core is present.

There is authority that this is not so. For instance, in *Citibank NA* v. *MBIA Assurance SA*,[18] Citibank was trustee for the holders of debt notes issued to securitise Eurotunnel debt. Under the notes, MBIA guaranteed repayment of the sums due on their notes. Under the trust deed, MBIA had power, in order to protect its position as guarantor, to give Citibank instructions concerning the exercise of most of its powers as trustee. Those instructions were binding on Citibank and the trust deed specifically provided that Citibank 'need not have regard to the interests of the Noteholders' when following MBIA's instructions. The trust deed also exempted Citibank from all liability to the noteholders when acting on MBIA's instructions. The Court of Appeal of England and Wales, in a decision to which I was party, held that the trust was valid because Citibank continued to have an obligation of good faith and had real discretions to exercise in terms of other powers. Accordingly, the trust created by the notes was valid.

An issue on which opinions differ is the extent, if any, to which the powers of the protector in *Pugachev* went beyond those giving powers of control to protectors and which are commonly met. Other issues arise out of this case, such as whether the law of shams in relation to trusts where the trust as created by a document to which the first trustees are party should require the necessary shamming intent to be shown on the part of trustees as well as the settlor. Where professional trustees are involved, this is likely to be extremely difficult to show. I shall leave those matters there.

[16] [2001] EWCA Civ 63.
[17] [1998] Ch 241 at 253.
[18] [2007] EWCA Civ 11.

## 4 INSOLVENCY

By using a trust, assets are insulated from creditors of the settlor, but this may expose a weakness in the structure – insolvency law of course contains several provisions designed to bring assets back into the pot for the settlor's creditors and one of these is an old statutory provision avoiding transactions designed to defeat creditors. In England and Wales, that is currently section 423 of the Insolvency Act 1986.

There are several issues that have arisen in recent years concerning family trusts. One of them concerns trusts holding businesses in various companies. The trustees may have got into the position of raising substantial loans in their capacity as trustees. It has recently been established by the Privy Council that, unless there is special legislation, the trustees will end up as liable to the creditors, with a right of indemnity against the trust fund. The case in which this was established is *Investec Trust (Guernsey) Ltd* v. *Glenalla Properties Ltd*.[19] The decision establishes the following legal principles:

(1) A trust is not a legal entity with a distinct legal personality separate from the trustee: it is a relationship between the trustee and the beneficiaries in relation to specific property. The trust assets are vested in the trustee, and only the trustee is capable of assuming legal rights and liabilities to third parties on behalf of the trust.
(2) The trustee has the relevant rights and liabilities. The trustee acts as principal and not as agent for the beneficiaries or the other legal entities within the trust. He is not an agent of the trust.
(3) On orthodox trust law principles, the legal personality of a trustee is said to be unitary: there is no distinction between a trustee's personal and fiduciary personality, thus putting at risk not only the trust assets but also the trustee's personal assets.
(4) An unsecured creditor of the trustee has no direct recourse to the trust assets to enforce his debt. He can only sue the trustee. His only way of accessing the trust assets is through subrogation to the trustee's right of indemnity from the trust fund for liabilities reasonably incurred.

All this means that there are limits on the ability of the trust creditor to obtain recourse from the trust assets. If the loan has been improperly incurred, they will have no right of subrogation to the trustee's right of indemnity against the trust assets because the trustee will not be entitled to any such indemnity. A trustee can by contract limit his liability for obligations, which he undertakes as trustee to the trust assets. There are jurisdictions where by statute the liability of the trustee for liabilities incurred on behalf of the trust is limited to the trust assets. In *Investec*, the Privy Council held (by a majority) that the common law would recognise such statutory limits on the liability of a trustee arising under the law pursuant to which the trust was set up.

19 [2018] UKPC 7.

Under English trust law, there is no such statutory provision. No distinction is drawn between the trustee's personal and fiduciary capacities when determining the extent of the trustee's liability for obligations incurred on behalf of the trust. The trustee is (in the absence of some limitation in the contract) liable to the full extent of his personal assets for all liabilities incurred to a third party on behalf of the trust if the trust assets have been exhausted. On that basis, the question of the strength of the covenant of the trust is the same as the question as to the strength of the covenant of the trustee.

## 5 CLIMATE CHANGE AND DISPUTES BETWEEN BENEFICIARIES AND TRUSTEES

One of the issues of the day is undoubtedly climate change. This can affect trustees too. I recall that in 1999 I had a case about contaminated land (*X (claimant)* v. *A, B, and C (defendants)*).[20] There was a landfill site that belonged to the deceased testator who had left his property on trust. The trustees discovered that they had enormous liabilities to deal with the methane gas which was being emitted from this land. There was an issue as to whether the trustees had a lien over the land in respect of their future liabilities to put the property right. I held that there was. There was also a question of whether the trustee had power to invest funds that it held pursuant to its lien. I held that there was a wide power of investment.

There was a further interesting question about consultation with the beneficiaries. Counsel had advised that the trustee had to keep the beneficiaries informed and ascertain their wishes. I held that there was no such obligation, but I repeated what Wilberforce J had said at the end of his judgment in *Re Pauling's Settlement Trust (No.2)*.[21] Here he expressed the hope and understanding that the trustee would give an undertaking that he would confer with the plaintiffs as to the investments held in the trust fund and give consideration to every suggestion made by them with regard to its investment and will not object to any suggestion made on reasonable terms.

I am sure that there will be many such problems in the future and that the wisdom of Wilberforce J will continue to be applicable and provide useful guidance to those who advise trustees of family trusts.

## 6 CONCLUSIONS

The world used to be a smaller place. A landowner would often make a settlement in his lifetime, and he would normally appoint as trustees his closest friends or his solicitor or his accountant. They would have been people he knew and often he would continue to live on the trust estate and he would want to express views on decisions the trustees were about to take or had taken. Now the trust has evolved. It is used in

20 *X (claimant)* v. *A, B and C (defendants)*, Chancery Division, 30 July 1999.
21 [1963] Ch 576.

many cases where families have built up trusts as a result of successfully founding a business. It is a feature of a modern trust that its place of administration may be in one jurisdiction and the beneficiaries in another and this gives rise to legal issues in private international law. Moreover, the settlor may not have a personal relationship with the trustees, and the assets may no longer be physical assets or assets whose management he can monitor. So what has tended to happen is that, as in *Pugachev*, the settlor has become the protector, and there are clauses saying what trustees can or cannot do without his consent. There may be many other clauses not found in trusts of previous generations, such as proper law clauses and 'flee' clauses and all the rest.

I have three concluding thoughts.

First, it is remarkable how trust law has developed. Originally, in England and Wales, trusts were ways of avoiding the law against making a will. You transferred your property to another to the use of the beneficiaries and equity was prepared to enforce those trusts because they were not inconsistent with the law. Another reason in the thirteenth century was that landowners went off to what was called the Holy Land to fight in the Crusades safe in the knowledge that their property would be properly looked after while they were away and if they did not return. Over the centuries, the law of trusts has spread to many countries and been used for a number of purposes, principally for conserving family wealth but also in commercial situations as well.

Second, it is striking how homogenous trust law is. That is why I have been able to cite cases from many different jurisdictions. Many countries recognise trusts. There may, of course, be local differences due to legislation but, by and large, the principles are understood and held in common. There is also a network of practising lawyers who keep in touch with each other and practise in one or more jurisdictions. This is helpful because trusts are often administered in one place when the proper law of the trust is that of another place. There has to be local learning in the place of administration and the judges there have to be familiar with the problems of trust law.

Third, it is apparent to me that practitioners in this field have to be very skilled at keeping all the balls in the air. For example, when all of a sudden a particular place becomes a popular home for substantial trusts (and this may happen in a very short space of time), the practitioners and judiciary in a jurisdiction may need rapidly to build up expertise to deal with the issues to which trusts give rise.

With those thoughts in mind, I welcome this event as providing an excellent opportunity for trust lawyers to get together and compare their views and get up to date. I thank you all for accompanying me on this short *tour d'horizon* of some of the problems that today are commonly met in this field.[22]

[22] The views which I express in this chapter do not preclude me from considering the matter afresh should the matter come before me judicially. The law is stated as at 1 August 2019.

PART I

# The Rise of Asian Wealth

# 3

# Asian Wealth in the United States

## *Some Legal Answers and Policy Questions*

*Thomas P. Gallanis*[*]

## 1 INTRODUCTION

Private wealth in Asia is substantial. In 2019, the Asia-Pacific region had approximately 6.5 million high net worth individuals ('HNWIs')[1] with investable assets of approximately US$22.2 trillion.[2] This represented approximately 33 per cent of the global population of HNWIs and approximately 30 per cent of global HNWI investable wealth.[3] These percentages are larger than the corresponding percentages for any other region. In second place was North America, which had approximately 32.1 per cent of the global HNWI population and approximately 29.3 per cent of global HNWI investable wealth.[4] The largest markets in the Asia-Pacific region are Japan and China, with HNWIs numbering approximately 3.4 million in Japan and approximately 1.3 million in China.[5]

Private wealth often is invested internationally. Such wealth is known as 'outbound' wealth from the perspective of the country of origin and 'inbound' wealth from the perspective of the country of destination. The United States is both a source of outbound wealth[6] and a destination for inbound wealth. Consider one type of inbound investment: residential real estate. During the twelve-month period

* Allan D. Vestal Chair in Law, University of Iowa; Visiting Professor of Law (2017–2027), University of Chicago Law School; Visiting Professor of Law (2019–2022), KoGuan Law School, Shanghai Jiao Tong University. This chapter initially was prepared for a conference held in Singapore in August 2019 on 'Asian Wealth and the Global Context' co-sponsored by the Singapore Academy of Law, the Singapore Management University School of Law and the University of York Law School. It is a pleasure to thank Richard C. Nolan, Tang Hang Wu and Yip Man for the invitation and my students Katlyn Bay and Miles Patton for research assistance.

1 HNWIs have 'investable assets of US$1 million or more, excluding primary residence, collectibles, consumables, and consumer durables'. Capgemini Research Institute, *World Wealth Report 2020*, p. 3.

2 ibid, pp. 6–7.

3 ibid.

4 ibid.

5 ibid, p. 8.

6 For example, the World Bank reports that, in 2019, more than US$71.5 billion was remitted to other countries by US-based migrants. See The World Bank, 'Migration and Remittances Data' (2019) <www.worldbank.org/en/topic/migrationremittancesdiasporaissues/brief/migration-remittances-data> last accessed 26 April 2021.

from April 2019 through March 2020, non-US citizens bought $74 billion of US residential real estate.[7] Of these non-citizen buyers, 39 per cent primarily resided outside the United States.[8] Of the non-citizen, non-resident buyers, the top three countries of origin were China, Canada, and Mexico.[9]

This chapter is about Asian wealth in the United States. Such a broad topic, however, must be narrowed in order to become manageable in one essay.[10] My expertise centers on the role of law and legal institutions in facilitating the donative transfer of private wealth, especially at death. Accordingly, this chapter explores the use of US law and legal institutions to transmit private wealth by individuals who are citizens and residents of Japan or China, the nations in Asia with the greatest number of HNWIs. The wealth transmission examined here occurs in the form of a donative transfer at death, typically within the family and often across generations.

This chapter proceeds in two main parts. The first part focuses on the current law. It examines the use of five prominent mechanisms in US law for the deathtime transmission of private family wealth. These are wills, revocable and irrevocable trusts, life insurance policies, retirement accounts, and survivorship interests in real property by joint tenancies or transfer-on-death deeds. It explores the extent to which these US mechanisms are available to individuals who are citizens and residents of Japan or China. In considering this question, it examines not only US succession and trust law but also US tax law. The second main part turns from law to policy. It raises five policy questions about US wealth transfer law and its use by individuals who are non-citizens and non-residents.

## 2 ASIAN WEALTH IN THE UNITED STATES: SOME LEGAL ANSWERS

This part of the chapter examines the use of five prominent mechanisms in US law for the deathtime transmission of private wealth and the extent to which they are available to individuals who are citizens and residents of Japan or China. The mechanisms are wills, revocable and irrevocable trusts, life insurance policies, retirement accounts, and survivorship interests in real property by joint tenancies or transfer-on-death deeds.

### 2.1 *Wills*

The prototypical mechanism in US law for the transmission of private wealth at death is the will. In the United States, wills and other instruments of succession

7 National Association of Realtors, 2020 Profile of International Activity in U.S. Residential Real Estate (August 2020), pp. 3, 12. This was a decrease of 5 per cent from the prior twelve months. A majority of the properties were in five states: Florida (22 per cent), California (15 per cent), Texas (9 per cent), New York (5 per cent), and New Jersey (4 per cent).

8 ibid.

9 ibid, pp. 3, 13–15.

10 CUP's limit is 10,000 words including footnotes.

are governed by state law, not federal law.[11] The standard formal requirements in US state law for a valid will are writing, signature, and attestation: the will must be in writing, signed by the testator, and attested by credible witnesses.[12] The specific contours of these requirements depend on state law. For example, some US states specify that the testator's signature must be located at the end of the will or that the witnesses must sign in the presence of the testator and the presence of each other.[13] In 2008, the Uniform Law Commission amended the Uniform Probate Code to allow notarisation as a substitute for attestation.[14] In 2019, the Uniform Law Commission approved an Act to authorise electronic wills.[15] The crucial point is that the requirements for a valid will are determined by the law of each US state.

Most US states have enacted statutes recognising as valid a will executed outside that state.[16] For example, section 2-506 of the Uniform Probate Code recognises as valid a will that does not comply with the state's own formalities if the will satisfies the requirements of 'the law at the time of execution of the place where the will was executed, or of the law of the place where at the time of execution or at the time of death the testator is domiciled, has a place of abode, or is a national'.[17] Analogously, the 1961 Hague Convention on the Conflicts of Laws Relating to the Form of Testamentary Dispositions provides that:[18]

A testamentary disposition shall be valid as regards form if its form complies with the internal law:

(a) of the place where the testator made it, or
(b) of a nationality possessed by the testator, either at the time when he made the disposition, or at the time of his death, or
(c) of a place in which the testator had his domicile either at the time when he made the disposition, or at the time of his death, or

[11] An exception must be noted with respect to employee benefits governed by federal statutes. The most important such statute is the Employee Retirement Security Act of 1974, known as ERISA. On ERISA preemption of US state succession law, see Thomas P. Gallanis, 'Will-Substitutes: A US Perspective', in A. Braun and A. Röthel (eds), *Passing Wealth on Death: Will-Substitutes in Comparative Perspective* (Hart Publishing, Oxford, 2016), pp. 26–28 and the sources cited therein.

[12] See Thomas P. Gallanis, *Family Property Law: Cases and Materials on Wills, Trusts, and Estates* (Foundation Press, 8th ed, 2020), pp. 118–119.

[13] For a list of the statutory variations, see Restatement (Third) of Property: Wills and Other Donative Transfers (1999), Statutory Note to §3.1.

[14] See Uniform Probate Code, §2-502(a)(3)(B) and the accompanying Comment. For a discussion of this innovation, see Lawrence W. Waggoner, 'The UPC Authorizes Notarized Wills' (2008) 34 *American College of Trust and Estate Counsel Journal* 83, 83–87.

[15] See the Uniform Electronic Wills Act (2019).

[16] The choice-of-law rules in the US states are summarised in Restatement (Third) of Property: Wills and Other Donative Transfers (1999), Statutory Note to §3.1.

[17] Uniform Probate Code, §2-506. For discussion, see Jeffrey A. Schoenblum, 'Multijurisdictional Estates and Article II of the Uniform Probate Code' (1992) 55 *Albany Law Review* 1291, 1294–1301.

[18] Hague Convention on the Conflicts of Laws Relating to the Form of Testamentary Dispositions, 5 October 1961, in force 5 January 1964, Art. 1.

(d) of the place in which the testator had his habitual residence either at the time when he made the disposition, or at the time of his death, or
(e) so far as immovables are concerned, of the place where they are situated.

Japan is a party to this Convention, but the United States and China are not.[19]

The Washington Convention of 1973 provides a method for making a will that will be recognised as formally valid in all of the countries joining the Convention. In the United States, the Convention is implemented through state legislation originally called the Uniform International Wills Act and now called the Uniform Wills Recognition Act.[20] This Act has been enacted in nineteen US states and the District of Columbia.[21] However, neither Japan nor China is a party to the Washington Convention.[22]

On the death of a decedent who is a citizen and resident of Japan or China, US state law and procedure – including state law on the choice of law – will govern the assets deemed to have situs in that US state.[23] For example, if a person dies who is a citizen and resident of Japan or China and that person owns a vacation home in Chicago, then Illinois law and procedure – including Illinois law on the choice of law – will govern the deathtime transmission of the vacation home. (Note that the United States, Japan, and China are not parties to the 1989 Hague Convention on the Law Applicable to Succession to the Estates of Deceased Persons.)[24] The decedent's foreign will can and possibly should be the governing instrument for purposes of probate in the United States.[25] Experienced lawyers urge caution before having a

[19] See the Convention status table <www.hcch.net/en/instruments/conventions/status-table/?cid=40> last accessed 26 April 2021. Note that the Convention applies in the Special Administrative Region of Hong Kong.

[20] In January 2015, the Uniform International Wills Act was renamed the Uniform Wills Recognition Act.

[21] A list of the enacting US states is available on the website of the Uniform Law Commission <www.uniformlaws.org> last accessed 26 April 2021.

[22] UNIDROIT Convention providing a uniform law on the form of an International Will, Washington, 26 October 1973, in force 9 February 1978: see <www.unidroit.org/status-successions> last accessed 26 April 2021. Here it is stated the Republic of China signed the Convention on 27 October 1973, but that, effective 1 January 1979, the United States recognised the People's Republic of China 'as the sole legal government of China'.

[23] For discussion, see Jeffrey A. Schoenblum, *Multistate and Multinational Estate Planning* (CCH Incorporated, 2014), 3.02, 3.04.

[24] Hague Convention on the Law Applicable to Succession to the Estates of Deceased Persons, 1 August 1989, not yet in force: see <www.hcch.net/en/instruments/conventions/status-table/?cid=62> last accessed 26 April 2021.

[25] See, e.g. Uniform Probate Code, §3-408 ('A final order of a court of another state determining testacy, the validity or construction of a will, made in a proceeding involving notice to and an opportunity for contest by all interested persons must be accepted as determinative by the courts of this state if it includes, or is based upon, a finding that the decedent was domiciled at death in the state where the order was made.') and §3-409 ('A will from a place which does not provide for probate of a will after death, may be proved for probate in this state by a duly authenticated certificate of its legal custodian that the copy introduced is a true copy and that the will has become effective under the law of the other place.'). On the probate of a will written in a language other than English, see Schoenblum, Multistate and Multinational, §15.09.

client execute both a foreign will and a US will. If two wills are used, they must be coordinated carefully in order to ensure that the will executed first is not revoked, wholly or partially, by the will executed second.[26]

## 2.2 *Revocable and Irrevocable Trusts*

The deathtime transmission of private wealth in the United States occurs not only by will but also by a variety of will substitutes.[27] The Restatement (Third) of Property defines a will substitute as 'an arrangement respecting property or contract rights that is established during the donor's life, under which (1) the right to possession or enjoyment of the property or to a contractual payment shifts outside of probate to the donee at the donor's death; and (2) substantial lifetime rights of dominion, control, possession, or enjoyment are retained by the donor'.[28] Whereas a transfer of property by will requires a valid will and the court-supervised procedure known as probate, a will substitute enables the donor's property to pass at death without a will or any court-supervised procedure. The transfer is a 'non-probate' transfer.[29]

One of the leading will substitutes in the United States is the revocable trust. A trust is revocable if the creator of the trust – the settlor – retains the power to revoke it. Under modern US trust law, which is state law rather than federal law, the settlor often is presumed to have retained the power to revoke the trust unless the terms of the trust provide that the trust is irrevocable.[30] Revocable trusts frequently are used as will substitutes, especially in those US states where probate procedure is slow or expensive.[31] Under the terms of a typical revocable trust, the settlor retains the lifetime right to the trust income and in many instances also is a discretionary beneficiary of the trust principal. After the settlor's death, the assets remaining in the trust are distributed to or retained in trust for the surviving beneficiaries. No court-supervised procedure is necessary.

[26] Suzanne L. Shier, '*U.S.-China Planning, Northern Trust Insights on Wealth Planning*' (2016), p. 7 <www.northerntrust.com/documents/commentary/wealthplanning-insights/wealth-planning-insights-on-us-china-planning.pdf> last accessed 26 April 2021.

[27] See Gallanis, 'Will-Substitutes', pp. 9–29.

[28] Restatement (Third) of Property: Wills and Other Donative Transfers (2003), §7.1.

[29] For the seminal scholarly article, see John H. Langbein, 'The Nonprobate Revolution and the Future of the Law of Succession' (1984) 97 *Harvard Law Review* 1108, 1108–1141.

[30] See, e.g. Uniform Trust Code §602. See also Restatement (Third) of Trusts (2003), §63, Comment c ('Where the settlor has failed expressly to provide whether a trust is subject to revocation or amendment, if the settlor has retained no interest in the trust (other than by resulting trust), it is rebuttably presumed that the settlor has no power to revoke or amend the trust. If, however, the settlor has failed expressly to provide whether the trust is revocable or amendable but has retained an interest in the trust (other than by resulting trust), the presumption is that the trust is revocable and amendable by the settlor.').

[31] For a critique of one state's probate courts and procedure, see John H. Langbein, 'The Scandal of Connecticut's Probate Courts' (7 October 2005) (statement to the Connecticut Legislature's Committee on Program Review and Investigations) <https://law.yale.edu/yls-today/news/scandal-connecticuts-probate-courts-statement-prof-john-h-langbein-conn-legislature-committee> last accessed 26 April 2021.

A trust that is irrevocable is not a will substitute in the classic sense, but it is nonetheless a widely used vehicle for family wealth management and transmission. An irrevocable trust can achieve various goals of the settlor. In the modern planning environment, one such goal is the protection of assets from creditors. The spendthrift trust, which insulates some or all of the trust property from creditors of the trust's beneficiaries, is recognised throughout the United States, albeit with some variation from state to state.[32] In addition, nearly twenty US states authorise an asset protection trust,[33] which shields trust property not only from creditors of the beneficiaries but also from creditors of the settlor.[34] Some US-based trust companies actively market US asset protection trusts to clients in Asia.[35]

The validity of a trust with multijurisdictional contacts is determined under US law by the relevant rules on choice of law. (Note that the United States is not a party to the Hague Convention on the Law Applicable to Trusts and on their Recognition; neither is Japan nor China.)[36] The relevant provision in the US Uniform Trust Code is section 403, which provides that an inter vivos trust 'is validly created if its creation complies with the law of the jurisdiction in which the instrument was executed, or the law of the jurisdiction in which, at the time of creation: (1) the settlor was domiciled, had a place of abode, or was a national; (2) the trustee was domiciled or had a place of business; or (3) any trust property is located'.[37]

The law governing a trust after its creation also is determined by the relevant rules on choice of law. Section 107 of the Uniform Trust Code provides that the 'meaning and effect of the terms of a trust are determined by: (1) the law of the jurisdiction designated in the terms unless the designation of that jurisdiction's law is contrary to a strong public policy of the jurisdiction having the most significant relationship to the matter at issue; or (2) in the absence of a controlling designation in the terms of the trust, the law of the jurisdiction having the most significant relationship to the matter at issue'.[38] This provision, like the Hague Convention, allows the trust's settlor to designate the

[32] See Gallanis, *Family Property Law*, pp. 588–611.

[33] *E.g.* Alaska, Connecticut, Delaware, Hawaii, Indiana, Michigan, Mississippi, Missouri, Nevada, New Hampshire, Ohio, Oklahoma, Rhode Island, South Dakota, Tennessee, Utah, Virginia, West Virginia, and Wyoming.

[34] For discussion, see 'Henry Christensen III/McDermott, Will & Emery', *International Estate Planning* (Matthew Bender, 2nd edn. 2020), ch. 10. See also Melissa Meyer and Jack Millhouse, 'Evaluating Foreign and Domestic Asset Protection Trusts', Bloomberg Law News, 9 December 2020.

[35] See Roddy Balfour, 'U.S. trusts for Asian clients – a growing market', Equiom Group (10 December 2020) <www.equiomgroup.com/news/us-trusts-asian-clients-growing-market> last accessed 26 April 2021.

[36] See the Convention status table <www.hcch.net/en/instruments/conventions/status-table/?cid=59> last accessed 26 April 2021. Note that the Convention applies in the Special Administrative Region of Hong Kong.

[37] Uniform Trust Code, §403.

[38] Uniform Trust Code, §107. For variations in the enactment of this provision by US states, see Thomas P. Gallanis, 'The Use and Abuse of Governing-Law Clauses in Trusts: What Should the New Restatement Say?' (2018) 103 *Iowa Law Review* 1711, 1726–1727.

governing law, within limits. The provision also provides a rule – the 'most significant relationship' rule – for trusts having no effective designation of governing law. The application of the 'most significant relationship' rule is explained in the Uniform Trust Code's Official Comment: 'Usually, the law of the trust's principal place of administration will govern administrative matters and the law of the place having the most significant relationship to the trust's creation will govern the dispositive provisions'.[39] The Uniform Trust Code gives the settlor great latitude in designating the trust's principal place of administration. Section 108(a) provides that the 'terms of a trust designating the principal place of administration are valid and controlling if: (1) a trustee's principal place of business is located in or the trustee is a resident of the designated jurisdiction; or (2) all or part of the administration occurs in the designated jurisdiction'.[40]

Under these choice-of-law rules, an individual who is a citizen and resident of Japan or China may establish a revocable or irrevocable trust under the law of a US state and may designate the law of that state to govern the trust. That designation generally will be respected by the US courts if certain conditions are met. One way to meet the conditions is to select a trustee in that state and provide that the state shall be the trust's principal place of administration.

### 2.3 *Life Insurance*[41]

A life insurance policy is a contract between an insurance carrier and the owner of the policy. It also is a will substitute. If the insured person – who may, but need not, be the owner – dies while the policy is in force, a death benefit is paid from the carrier to the named beneficiaries who survive the insured. No court-supervised procedure is necessary.

The availability of US life insurance for an individual who is neither a citizen nor a resident of the United States varies by the country of residence, in two respects. First, the country of residence must permit the purchase. Some countries, such as Japan, prohibit their residents from purchasing US life insurance.[42] China, on the other hand, permits it. Second, the country must be on the life insurer's list of approved countries. Each insurer assigns to an approved country a letter rating – for example, 'A', 'B', 'C', or 'D' – to indicate the level of risk and life expectancy. Some US insurers classify China as a 'B' country;[43] some others distinguish the major cities in China (classified as 'B') from other

39 Comment to Uniform Trust Code, §107.

40 Uniform Trust Code, §108(a).

41 On the types of life insurance policies and the tax treatment of life insurance, see Bruce A. Tannahill and Melisa Seyhun, 'Life Insurance: What Attorneys and Trustees Should Know' (November/December 2020) *Probate & Property* 38, 38–52.

42 See Zhaneta Gechev, 'Life Insurance for Foreign Nationals' (24 February 2021) <https://onestoplifeinsurance.com/life-insurance-for-foreign-nationals/> last accessed 28 April 2021.

43 See Insurance & Estates Blog, '*Life Insurance for Non U.S. Residents & Foreign Nationals*' (20 May 2018) <www.insuranceandestates.com/life-insurance-for-non-u-s-residents-and-foreign-nationals/> last accessed 28 April 2021.

regions of China (classified as 'C').[44] The letter rating affects, among other things, the terms of the policy and the amount of coverage that will be available for purchase.

If a prospective purchaser is a resident of an approved country, two additional requirements are imposed by US life insurers. These requirements are nexus and need. Nexus means a connection; each US life insurer requires a prospective purchaser to have a sufficient connection to the United States. What counts as a sufficient connection varies from one insurer to another.[45] For example, an insurer may require the prospective purchaser to spend a certain number of days per year in the United States, and/or to have one or more family members residing in the United States, and/or to have certain US assets, such as US real estate or a US business. In addition to nexus, a prospective purchaser of US life insurance must show a need for the coverage. Wealth preservation and income protection are examples of typically accepted needs.[46]

A final point to mention is that all steps in the life insurance transaction must occur in the United States – including the application, the underwriting (including any medical examination), and the delivery of and payment for the policy. This means that a US bank account typically is required.[47]

### 2.4 *Retirement Accounts*

An individual retirement account ('IRA') arises from a contract between an individual and a provider. The individual contributes funds, which then are invested according to the menu of options offered by the provider. Once the individual retires, the individual controls the timing and amount of distributions from the account, subject to federal rules on minimum required distributions that govern once the individual reaches age 72.[48] Funds remaining in the IRA at the individual's death are distributed to the surviving beneficiaries as designated by the individual or, if no designation was made, to the beneficiaries as defined by the IRA's governing documents. No court-supervised procedure is necessary.

In order to contribute in any given year to an IRA, an individual (or the individual's spouse, if a joint income tax return is filed) must have US taxable compensation that year.[49] Taxable compensation means compensation earned from working – for example, wages, salaries, commissions, or self-employment income. It does not include

44 See X and Y Advisors, '*About Buying Life Insurance as Non-U.S. Citizens*' (13 March 2018) <www.xandyadvisors.com/blog/about-buying-life-insurance-as-non-us-citizens> last accessed 28 April 2021.

45 For discussion, see Insurance & Estates, 'Life Insurance for Non U.S. Residents & Foreign Nationals'.

46 See Insurance & Estates, 'Life Insurance for Non U.S. Residents & Foreign Nationals'.

47 See ibid.

48 See Gallanis, 'Will Substitutes: A US Perspective', p. 14. The former triggering age of 70½ was raised to 72 by the Setting Every Community Up for Retirement Enhancement (SECURE) Act of 2019, Pub. L. No. 116-94, enacted as Div. O. of Further Consolidated Appropriations Act 2020. For discussion, see Richard L. Kaplan, 'Estate Planning for Retirement Benefits after the SECURE Act' (2020) 46 *American College of Trust and Estate Counsel Law Journal* 79, 79–84.

49 See Internal Revenue Service, Publication 590-A: Contributions to Individual Retirement Arrangements (IRAs) (2020), pp. 5–6, 39.

other forms of income, such as interest or dividend income, or earnings or profits from real estate.

If an individual is a citizen and resident of Japan or China, it is very unlikely that the individual will satisfy the taxable compensation requirement. This means that, ordinarily, a citizen and resident of Japan or China cannot open and contribute to an IRA.

### 2.5 *Survivorship Interests in Real Property by Joint Tenancies or Transfer-on-Death Deeds*

Joint tenancy of real property is a form of co-ownership; each joint tenant owns a present undivided interest in the real property. Joint tenancy also is a will substitute.[50] The interest of each joint tenant includes a right of survivorship. At the death of one joint tenant, the ownership shifts immediately to the surviving joint tenant(s). For example, suppose that *A*, *B*, and *C* own real property as joint tenants and that they die in alphabetical order. Upon *A*'s death, the property automatically belongs to *B* and *C*. Upon *B*'s later death, the entire property automatically belongs to *C*. No court-supervised procedure is necessary.

For an owner of real property who wants the survivorship feature of joint tenancy but not the co-ownership, there is an alternative: a transfer-on-death deed.[51] More than half the states in the United States have enacted statutes authorising transfer-on-death deeds of interests in real property.[52] Pursuant to these statutes, a person who owns an interest in real property may execute and record a transfer-on-death deed designating one or more beneficiaries. While the property owner is alive, the deed is revocable and the beneficiaries have no interest in the property. If the deed remains in force at the owner's death, the property then passes directly to the beneficiaries as specified in the deed. No court-supervised procedure is needed.

An individual who is a citizen and resident of Japan or China can acquire real property in the United States and can hold the property in joint tenancy or execute and record a transfer-on-death deed. Unlike China, which restricts the ability of foreigners to acquire land-use rights in real property,[53] the United States has no comparable restrictions on land ownership as a general matter. Some US states impose certain restrictions on the ownership of land, especially agricultural land, by a non-resident alien, but many US states do not.[54] Indeed, the statistics quoted earlier in the chapter about the purchases

50 See Gallanis, *Family Property Law*, p. 353.

51 See, e.g. the Uniform Real Property Transfer on Death Act (2009).

52 See Gallanis, *Family Property Law*, p. 354.

53 Typically, a foreigner must live and work in China for a year in order to be allowed to acquire land-use rights in Chinese residential real property. See <www.mohurd.gov.cn/wjfb/201102/t20110218_202615.html> last accessed 28 April 2021.

54 Some US states have specific restrictions. For example, the State of Iowa requires a non-resident alien who has acquired agricultural land by descent or devise to be divested of all interest in the land within two years. See Iowa Code, §9I.5. For another example, the law of the State of Kentucky provides that land acquired by a non-resident alien may escheat to the state after eight years if the alien has not become a citizen of the United States. See Kentucky Revised Statutes, §381.300. For

of US residential real estate by individuals overseas[55] show that many individuals who are citizens and residents of China own interests in US real property.[56]

## 2.6 *US Federal Taxation*

The United States imposes two forms of federal tax[57] relevant to inbound wealth from Japan or China: income tax and transfer tax. With respect to the federal income tax, an individual who is neither a citizen nor a resident of the United States is called a 'nonresident alien'.[58] Residence in this context is based largely on whether the individual has a US green card or been present in the United States for a certain number of days in the current year and the preceding two years.[59] A nonresident alien is subject to federal income taxation only on income 'effectively connected with the conduct of a [US] trade or business'[60] and on income 'derived from sources within the [US]'.[61] Sometimes the sourcing rules are what one would predict, but sometimes they are not.[62] For example, dividends paid by a US corporation to a nonresident alien are considered US-source,[63] but gains from the sale of investments in US securities, such as stocks, are sourced to the residence of the seller, meaning that such gains accruing to a nonresident alien are exempt from federal income taxation.[64] Similarly, income from the sale of real property located in the United States is US-source income and therefore is subject to federal income taxation,[65] but income from the sale of tangible personal property located in the United States is sourced, as a general matter, to the residence of the seller, meaning that such income accruing to a nonresident alien generally is exempt from federal income taxation.[66]

a state-by-state analysis, see Gary A. Goodman and Elizabeth A. Gable, 'Restrictions on Foreign Investment in Real Property', in J. Eugene Marans et al (eds), *Manual of Foreign Investment in the U.S.* (Thomson/West, 3rd ed, 2013), ch. 19, appendix 19-1.

55 See notes 7–9 and the accompanying text.

56 Note, however, that the Foreign Investment in Real Property Tax Act of 1980 ('FIRPTA') imposes tax withholding on nonresident aliens or foreign corporations disposing of US interests in real property. See <www.irs.gov/individuals/international-taxpayers/firpta-withholding> last accessed 7 October 2021.

57 Taxes imposed by US states or localities are beyond the scope of this chapter.

58 See, e.g. 26 USC, §2(d).

59 See 26 USC, §7701(b). For discussion, see Thomas S. Bissell, *U.S. Income Taxation of Nonresident Alien Individuals* (Bloomberg Tax Management Portfolio 6400-1st), Part III.

60 26 USC, §872(a)(2).

61 ibid, §872(a)(1). Income that is effectively connected with a US trade or business is taxed at normal graduated rates. See 26 USC, §871(b). US-source income that is not effectively connected with a trade or business is generally taxed at a flat 30 per cent rate. See 26 USC, §871(a). However, there are exceptions. For example, a nonresident alien may elect to treat income from real property as income effectively connected with a trade or business. See 26 USC, §871(d).

62 For a detailed analysis, see Ansgar A. Simon, *Source of Income Rules* (Bloomberg Tax Management Portfolio 6620-1st).

63 See 26 USC, §861(a)(2).

64 See ibid, §865(a)(2); IRS PLR 9847016 (1998).

65 See ibid, §897(a)(1)(A).

66 See ibid, §865(a)(2). This assumes that the tangible personal property is not depreciable and is not inventory property, see ibid, §865(b), (c)

So far, we have been speaking about the income taxation of an individual, but it is possible that the income is incurred instead by a trust or a corporation. Here, the tax rules are too detailed to summarise in this chapter, other than to make three general observations. First, federal income tax law distinguishes between a domestic trust and a foreign trust.[67] A domestic trust is treated as a US person and is subject to federal income taxation on its worldwide income, whereas a foreign trust is treated as a non-resident alien individual and is subject to federal income taxation only on US-source income and on income effectively connected with the conduct of a US trade or business.[68] Second, there are comparable rules for determining the US taxable income of a foreign corporation.[69] Third, the 2017 US legislation known as the Tax Cuts and Jobs Act[70] reduced the corporate income tax rate and retained certain income tax deductions for corporations while limiting those deductions for individuals and trusts; one effect of the Act may be that non-resident aliens will prefer to hold US assets, such as US real estate, through a corporation.[71]

One final point must be made about the federal income tax as it relates to a non-resident alien who is a resident of Japan or China. The US has signed tax treaties with Japan[72] and China[73] designed to avoid the double taxation of income. As amended in 2013, the treaty with Japan provides in pertinent part:[74]

67 See ibid, §7701(a)(30)(E) (defining certain trusts as equivalent to a 'United States person'); ibid, §7701(a)(31)(B) (defining a foreign trust as 'any trust other than a trust described in').

68 See ibid, §641(b); Treas. Reg. §1.641(b)-1. For discussion, see Thomas S. Bissell, Tax Planning for Portfolio Investment into the United States by Foreign Individuals (Bloomberg Tax Management Portfolio 6420-1st), Part V.A.2.

69 See, e.g. 26 USC §881 (imposing a tax on US-source income not effectively connected with the conduct of a US trade or business), §882 (imposing a tax on income effectively connected with the conduct of a US trade or business). For discussion, see Bissell, Tax Planning for Portfolio Investment, Part III.E.

70 Tax Cuts and Jobs Act of 2017, Pub. L. No. 115-97.

71 See Amy Heller and Eric Fischer, 'Impact of US Tax Reform on Cross-Border Estate Planning' (2019) 25 *Trusts & Trustees* 153, 153–154.

72 The Convention between the Government of the United States of America and the Government of Japan for the avoidance of double taxation and the prevention of fiscal evasion with respect to taxes on income and capital gains, Washington, 6 November 2003, in force 30 March 2004: see <www.treasury.gov/resource-center/tax-policy/treaties/Documents/japantreaty.pdf> last accessed 28 April 2021. For the U.S. Treasury Department's Technical Explanation of the treaty see <www.irs.gov/pub/irs-trty/japante04.pdf> accessed 28 April 2021. The treaty was amended in 2013. For the amending protocol see <www.treasury.gov/resource-center/tax-policy/treaties/Documents/Treaty-Protocol-Japan-1-24-2013.pdf> last accessed 28 April 2021. For the US Treasury Department's Technical Explanation of the amending protocol see <www.treasury.gov/resource-center/tax-policy/treaties/Documents/2013-Technical-Explanation-Between-US-Japan.pdf> last accessed 28 April 2021.

73 The Convention between the Government of the United States of America and the Government of the People's Republic of China for the avoidance of double taxation and the prevention of tax evasion with respect to taxes on income, Beijing, 30 April 1984, in force 1 January 1987: see <www.irs.gov/pub/irs-trty/china.pdf> last accessed 28 April 2021. For the US Treasury Department's Technical Explanation of the treaty see <www.irs.gov/pub/irs-trty/chintech.pdf> last accessed 28 April 2021.

74 Art. 23(1).

> Subject to the provisions of the laws of Japan regarding the allowance as a credit against the Japanese tax of tax payable in any country other than Japan, where a resident of Japan derives income from the United States which may be taxed in the United States in accordance with the provisions of this Convention, the amount of the United States tax payable in respect of that income shall be allowed as a credit against the Japanese tax imposed on that resident. The amount of credit, however, shall not exceed the amount of the Japanese tax which is appropriate to that income. For the purposes of the preceding provisions of this subparagraph, income beneficially owned by a resident of Japan which may be taxed in the United States in accordance with the Convention shall be deemed to arise from sources in the United States.

Similarly, the treaty with China provides in pertinent part:[75]

> Where a resident of China derives income from the United States, the amount of the United States income tax payable in respect of that income in accordance with the provisions of this Agreement shall be allowed as a credit against the Chinese tax imposed on that resident. The amount of credit, however, shall not exceed the amount of the Chinese tax computed with respect to that income in accordance with the taxation laws and regulations of China.

We now turn from income taxation to transfer taxation. There are three transfer taxes imposed at the federal level in the United States: an estate tax, a gift tax, and a generation-skipping transfer ('GST") tax. This chapter focuses on the deathtime transfer of wealth, so the relevant transfer taxes are the federal estate and GST taxes.[76]

The statutes and regulations governing the federal estate tax do not use the term 'nonresident alien'; instead, they use the term 'nonresident not a citizen of the United States' ('NRNC').[77] The federal estate tax determines residence based on domicile. As stated in the applicable Treasury regulation, a nonresident decedent 'is a decedent who, at the time of his death, had his domicile outside the United States'.[78] The regulation offers a description of what 'domicile' means: 'A person acquires a domicile in a place by living there, for even a brief period of time, with no definite present intention of later removing therefrom. Residence without the requisite intention to remain indefinitely will not suffice to constitute domicile, nor will intention to change domicile effect such a change unless accompanied by actual removal'.[79] In the words of the US Supreme Court, 'domicile is established by physical presence in a place in connection with a certain state of mind concerning one's intent to remain there'.[80] For purposes of this

75 Art. 22(1).

76 For a discussion of the application of the federal gift tax to non-citizens, see Michael A. Heimos, *Non-Citizens – Estate, Gift, and Generation-Skipping Taxation* (Bloomberg Tax Management Portfolio 837-4th).

77 See, e.g. 26 USC, §2101(a).

78 Treas. Reg., §20.0-1(b)(2).

79 ibid, §20.0-1(b)(1).

80 *Mississippi Band of Choctaw Indians* v. *Holyfield*, 490 US 30 at 48 (1989).

chapter, assume that we are discussing a non-citizen who is also a non-domiciliary, hence an individual qualifying as an NRNC under the federal estate tax.

With respect to an individual who is an NRNC, the federal estate tax applies only to property 'which at the time of [...] [the individual's] death is situated in the United States'.[81] The rules for determining the situs of property often are what one would predict. For example, real property located within the United States is situated in the United States.[82] Similarly, tangible personal property located within the United States generally is situated within the United States,[83] though there is a statutory exception for works of art in the United States on loan for exhibition.[84] Shares of stock are deemed to be situated in the United States if the shares were issued by a US corporation;[85] the location of the stock certificates is irrelevant.[86] But not all of the situs rules are as one might predict. For example, the proceeds of a US life insurance policy on the life of a decedent NRNC are deemed to be situated outside the United States.[87] Note that this rule applies only to life insurance on the decedent, not to life insurance purchased by the decedent on someone else, such as the decedent's spouse.[88] Another unusual situs rule concerns bank deposits. Sums on deposit with a US bank or an offshore branch of a US bank are deemed to be situated outside the United States as long as the deposit is not connected with a US trade or business.[89] One of the most interesting situs rules governs beneficial interests in a trust. The US Internal Revenue Service has taken the position that, with respect to a beneficial interest in trust held by an NRNC, the 'situs of an equitable interest in a conventional private trust is determined by reference to the underlying assets'.[90]

Once one identifies the property situated in the United States, the federal estate tax applies to the NRNC's 'gross estate' – property situated in the United States which the NRNC owned, had an interest in at death, or had sufficient rights or powers over at death such that the property is included within the gross estate. The rules for determining inclusion in the gross estate of an NRNC generally are the same as for determining inclusion in the gross estate of a US citizen or resident.[91] For example, property in a decedent's revocable trust is treated as if it were owned outright by the decedent.[92] Similarly, property over which the decedent held a general

81 26 USC, §2106(a).
82 See Treas. Reg., §20.2104-1(a)(1).
83 See ibid, §20.2104-1(a)(2).
84 See 26 USC, §2105(c).
85 See ibid, §2104(a).
86 See Treas. Reg., §20.2104-1(a)(5).
87 See 26 USC, §2105(a).
88 See Treas. Reg., §20.2105-1(g).
89 See 26 USC, §§2105(b)(1), 2015(b)(2); Treas. Reg., §20.2105-1.
90 See Rev. Rul. 55-163, 1955-1 C.B. 674. Note, however, that the trust at issue in that Revenue Ruling was a revocable trust.
91 See 26 USC, §2103. For discussion, see Heimos, *Non-Citizens*, Part VI.B.
92 See ibid, §2038(a)(1).

power of appointment is treated as if it were owned outright by the decedent.[93] These rules apply equally to the NRNC as to the US citizen or resident. US-situs property falling into these categories is included in the gross estate of an NRNC just as it would be included in the gross estate of a US citizen or resident.[94] However, not all of the inclusion rules are the same. Consider property owned in joint tenancy by the decedent and the decedent's spouse. If the decedent is a US citizen or resident, 50 per cent of the value of the joint-tenancy property is included in the decedent's gross estate.[95] However, if the decedent is an NRNC, the amount included is 50 per cent only if the surviving spouse is a US citizen; otherwise, the amount included is 100 per cent of the value of the joint-tenancy property, except to the extent that the surviving spouse provided consideration for the property's acquisition.[96]

Even greater differences arise with respect to credits and deductions. A US citizen or resident is entitled to a credit that, in 2021, shelters US$11.7 million from federal transfer taxation.[97] Put bluntly: Only very wealthy US citizens or residents pay federal transfer tax. In contrast, the federal estate tax credit for an NRNC shelters only US$60,000.[98] Another stark difference pertains to the marital deduction, which is a deduction for property passing outright or in certain restricted forms to the decedent's surviving spouse. A US citizen or resident is entitled to an unlimited marital deduction;[99] even the wealthiest decedent will owe no federal estate tax if the decedent's property passes outright or in certain restricted forms to the surviving spouse. In contrast, an NRNC is entitled to a marital deduction only if the surviving spouse is a US citizen or if the property passes to a qualified domestic trust.[100]

There is no tax treaty between the United States and China pertaining to transfer taxes. The reason is that China does not impose transfer taxes, so there is no risk of double taxation. Instead, the risk is of substantial taxation by the United States. Japan imposes an inheritance tax on the recipient of property from a decedent,[101] and there is a US–Japan tax treaty, signed in 1954, covering the US federal estate and gift taxes. Article V, paragraph 1, of that treaty provides in pertinent part:

> Where either contracting State imposes the tax by reason of the nationality thereof or the domicile therein of a decedent or a donor or a beneficiary of a decedent's estate or of a gift, such State shall allow against its tax (computed without application of this Article) a credit for the tax imposed by the other contracting State

93 See ibid, §2041(a)(2).

94 See ibid, §2103.

95 See ibid, §2040(b)(1).

96 See ibid, §§2040(a), 2056(d)(1)(B); Treas. Reg. §20.2056A-8(a).

97 See ibid, §2010; Rev. Proc. 2018-57, §3.41.

98 See ibid, §2102. The credit is $13,000, which shelters $60,000 of property from tax.

99 See ibid, §2056(a), (b).

100 See ibid, §2056(d).

101 If the decedent was a citizen and resident of Japan, the transfer is taxable under Japan's inheritance tax on a worldwide basis. See Christensen/McDermott, Will & Emery, *International Estate Planning*, 19.11[1].

> with respect to property situated at the time of the transfer in such other State and included for the taxes of both States (but the amount of the credit shall not exceed that portion of the tax imposed by the crediting State which is attributable to such property).[102]

To reduce or avoid US federal estate taxation of inbound wealth, experienced lawyers often recommend the use of a foreign corporation.[103] Recall that shares of stock are deemed to be situated in the United States only if they are issued by a US corporation.[104] This means that shares issued by a foreign corporation are not situated in the United States, hence are not subject to federal estate taxation. This technique does not work, however, if the foreign corporation is a sham.[105] As one practitioner explains:[106]

> [I]n evaluating the bona fides of a foreign holding company, all the formal actions of the NRNC decedent, the family, and the company vis-à-vis the alleged corporate property will be scrutinized. [...] Accordingly, all investment accounts and other assets must be maintained in the company's name, and all transactions, of any sort, must be logged in the company's books appropriately, and made pursuant to the company's governing rules as well as the applicable laws of the company's domicile. The formalities of dealings between the company and the subject NRNC need to also be given close attention. The NRNC must have neither possession nor the rights to possession of the company's assets, and all of the indicia of ownership must be in the company. The NRNC must have no rights, present or future, to the return of the assets. [...] A rule of thumb would be to assume that the IRS will be looking at each transaction, which should, therefore, be effectuated and documented accordingly.

Note that a foreign corporation is needed only where the underlying assets otherwise would be included in the decedent's gross estate. Assets such as certain deposits in a US bank or life insurance proceeds on the life of the NRNC decedent are not treated as situated in the United States[107] and are not included in the gross estate.[108]

The federal GST tax is a tax on gratuitous transfers that skip a generation.[109] The US Congress designed the GST tax to ensure that a tax is paid when property skips one or more generations or when it passes through one or more generations in a form that would allow it to escape estate or gift taxation in the skipped generation(s). Three examples will illustrate.

[102] For the text of the treaty see <https://taxtopics.net/Japan.html> last accessed 28 April 2021.
[103] For discussion, see Heimos, *Non-Citizens*, Part VIII.B.
[104] See 26 USC, §2104(a).
[105] See *Fillman* v. *United States*, 355 F.2d 632 (Ct. Cl. 1966) (concluding that the foreign corporation was a sham). For a discussion of *Fillman*, see Heimos, *Non-Citizens*, Part VIII.B.
[106] ibid.
[107] See 26 USC, §2105(a), (b); Treas. Reg. §20-2105-1.
[108] See ibid, §2103.
[109] See Gallanis, *Family Property Law*, pp. 1088–1091.

(1) G's will transfers property to G's grandchild, X. At G's death, the property is subject to estate taxation and to GST taxation. In the terminology of the GST tax, the transfer is a 'direct skip';[110] the transfer has skipped one or more generations.
(2) G's will creates a trust directing the trustee to pay income annually to G's child, A, for A's lifetime and at A's death to distribute the trust principal to A's then-living descendants. The trust property will be subject to estate taxation at G's death.[111] At A's death, there is no estate taxation because A's interest ends at A's death, but the trust will incur GST tax. In the terminology of the GST tax, a 'taxable termination'[112] has occurred because there has been a termination of an interest in trust – A's lifetime interest – and after the termination all of the remaining interests in the trust are held by persons two or more generations below G. In the parlance of the GST tax, such persons are called 'skip persons'.[113]
(3) G's will creates a trust of $100 million authorising the trustee to distribute income and/or principal to G's descendants. The following year, the trustee distributes $100,000 to G's child, A, and $100,000 to G's grandchild, X. X is liable for GST tax.[114] In the terminology of the GST tax, the distribution to X is a 'taxable distribution'[115] – a distribution, other than a direct skip or a taxable termination, from a trust to a person two or more generations below G (a 'skip person').

The GST tax on transfers made by an individual who is an NRNC is governed by a US Treasury regulation.[116] In the parlance of that regulation, the individual is a non-resident alien transferor ('NRA transferor').[117] The regulation provides that the GST tax applies to a direct skip from an NRA transferor to a skip person only to the extent that the transfer is subject to the federal estate or gift tax;[118] the GST tax applies to a taxable termination or a taxable distribution only to the extent that the initial transfer into the trust by the NRA transferor was subject to the federal estate or gift tax.[119] Thus, for transfers occurring at death, the rules discussed above governing situs and inclusion in the gross estate for purposes of the federal estate tax apply also to the federal GST tax.

Recall that a US citizen or resident has a high transfer tax exemption amount: US$11.7 million in 2021.[120] The GST exemption amount for an NRA transferor is only US$1 million.[121]

[110] See 26 USC, §2612(c)(1).
[111] See ibid, §2033.
[112] See ibid, §2612(a)(1).
[113] See ibid, §2613(a).
[114] See ibid, §2603(a)(1).
[115] See ibid, §2612(b).
[116] Treas. Reg., §26.2633-2.
[117] ibid, §26.2633-2(a).
[118] See ibid, §26.2633-2(b)(1).
[119] See ibid, §26.2633-2(b)(2).
[120] See 26 USC, §§2010, 2631; Rev. Proc. 2018-57, §3.41.
[121] See Treas. Reg. §26.2633-2(a).

## 3 ASIAN WEALTH IN THE UNITED STATES: SOME POLICY QUESTIONS

The prior discussion focused on the law. This part of the chapter highlights five questions of policy.

Question 1: Choice of law. Does the United States have the right rules on choice of law? Wealth is mobile and often intangible. Roscoe Pound phrased it best: 'Wealth, in a commercial age, is made up largely of promises'.[122] Today's trusts and other property arrangements often are multijurisdictional. How much weight should US law give to a designation of one jurisdiction's governing law, either in the terms of a trust or in another instrument?[123] When there is no effective designation of the governing law, how should US law determine which jurisdiction's law governs? How workable or desirable is the current approach, which seeks to identify the jurisdiction with the most significant relationship to the matter at issue? Consider a multinational trust. If the settlor is domiciled in country *A*, the trustee is domiciled in country *B*, the trust director is domiciled in country *C*, the beneficiaries are domiciled in countries *D* and *E*, and the assets are situated in multiple countries, which jurisdiction has the most significant relationship? Alternatively, is there a better approach to choice of law that can provide clearer and superior rules?

Question 2: The ability to own real property. Does the United States have the right rules on foreign ownership of real property? Unlike China,[124] most US states freely allow the acquisition of interests in real property without regard to citizenship, domicile, or residence.[125] Is this the best approach? Real property remains a significant source of a nation's wealth even in a commercial age. Should there be restrictions on foreign ownership of land – for example, on the type of land or on the duration of ownership?

Question 3: The treatment of trusts compared to corporations. Does the United States have the right rules for the treatment of trusts compared to corporations? Current US federal tax law respects the corporation as a legal entity, for example, by providing that shares in a foreign corporation are deemed to be situated outside the United States.[126] This opens the door to the use of a foreign corporation to shield assets from federal taxation. In contrast, US federal estate tax law provides that, for the purpose of determining the tax liability of an NRNC, the situs of an asset held in trust is determined according to the asset's situs.[127] In form, the tax distinction is consistent with current private-law doctrine: the

[122] Roscoe Pound, *An Introduction to the Philosophy of Law* (Yale University Press, 1922), p. 236.

[123] For discussion, see Gallanis, 'Use and Abuse of Governing-Law Clauses', pp. 1719–1723.

[124] See <www.mohurd.gov.cn/wjfb/201102/t20110218_202615.html> last accessed 28 April 2021.

[125] See Goodman and Gable, 'Restrictions on Foreign Investment in Real Property', appendix 19-1.

[126] See 26 USC, §2104(a).

[127] See Rev. Rul. 55-163.

corporation is a legal entity whereas the trust is not.[128] But in substance, US trust law is moving in the direction of treating the trust as an entity,[129] and in some respects, US federal income tax law is already there, for example, by requiring a trust to have its own tax identification number and its own income tax return.[130]

Question 4: The federal tax rules determining source and situs. Does the United States have the right rules for determining US source and situs for purposes of federal taxation? Some of the distinctions drawn by the current law seem odd. For example, why is the stock of a foreign corporation deemed to be located outside the United States for purposes of the federal estate and GST taxes even if the corporation has US assets and is conducting a trade or business within the United States?[131] Why are the proceeds held by a US life insurer deemed to be situated outside the United States if the policy is owned by and on the life of an NRNC?[132] Some of these rules have the odor of interest-group lobbying.[133]

Question 5: Use of a nation's wealth transfer system. When should the laws and legal institutions of a country facilitate the transmission of the private wealth of citizens and residents of another country? Do the rationales for facilitating wealth transmission for one's own citizens and residents apply also to citizens and residents of other nations? US law strongly embraces the principle of donative freedom. In the words of the Restatement (Third) of Property: 'The organising principle of the American law of donative transfers is freedom of disposition'.[134] The machinery of US law aims to implement this principle. When should the principle of donative freedom and its associated legal machinery extend beyond US citizens and residents?

Of the five policy questions, the fifth is the most fascinating, the most over-arching, and the most undertheorised. The scope of this chapter hardly permits a full answer, but having raised the question, the chapter can offer the following framework by way of a preliminary response.

The starting point is to recognise that nations act in their own interest. This is the most realistic[135] and pragmatic approach to any matter involving the behaviour

[128] See Restatement (Third) of Trusts (2003), §2 (defining a trust as 'a fiduciary relationship with respect to property').

[129] See the discussion in Restatement (Third) of Trusts (2012), §105, Reporter's Notes (describing the modern trend allowing lawsuits against the trustee in a representative capacity).

[130] See, e.g. Internal Revenue Service, Instructions for Form 1041 (2019), pp. 5, 13, 18. Here I am speaking of a trust that is not a 'grantor trust' – a term referring to a trust that is not treated as a separate taxable entity for income tax purposes. For the rules governing grantor trusts, see 26 USC, §§671–679.

[131] See Treas. Reg. §20.2105-1(f).

[132] See 26 USC, §2105(a).

[133] See Heimos, *Non-Citizens*, Part IV.C.3 (describing the situs rule for life insurance proceeds as a 'concession to domestic life insurers').

[134] Restatement (Third) of Property: Wills and Other Donative Transfers (2003), §10.1, Comment a.

[135] For an overview of the realist school(s) of international relations, see William C. Wolforth, 'Realism', in Christian Reus-Smit and Duncan Snidal (eds), *Oxford Handbook of International Relations* (Oxford University Press, 2008).

of nations. Even when a nation appears to act altruistically or in support of a supra-national principle – for example, to foster global peace or to protect the planet's environment – the nation is acting in accordance with its own interests as it defines them.

From this realistic recognition of national interest, we can derive the following principle: A nation should open its laws and legal institutions to facilitate the transmission of the private wealth of citizens and residents of other nations where doing so is in the interest of the host nation. 'Interest' means more than economic interest; it means interest in the fullest sense and as each nation defines for itself.

Another way to express this principle is: A nation should open its laws and legal institutions to facilitate the transmission of the private wealth of citizens and residents of other nations where the benefits to the host nation ($b_{hn}$) exceed the costs to the host nation ($c_{hn}$). 'Benefits' and 'costs' are not limited to the economic. Where $b_{hn} > c_{hn}$ the nation is furthering its interests. Where $b_{hn} < c_{hn}$ the nation is harming its interests.

## 4 CONCLUSIONS

The United States has a longstanding commitment to the principle of freedom of disposition. It also has laws and legal institutions – as well as law firms, trust companies, and financial institutions – with expertise to offer in the management and transmission of private wealth.[136] Therefore, the United States has interests both economic and non-economic in facilitating the freedom of disposition beyond its borders, even if some of the specifics of US law discussed in this chapter might be improved. In general, $b_{hn} > c_{hn}$ for the United States.

Private wealth in Japan, China, and Asia generally is growing substantially. The United States is, and should be, positioned to assist individuals and families in Asia with wealth management and transmission.

[136] In a similar vein, I explored the contribution that can be made by Anglo-American fiduciary law to civilian legal systems in Thomas P. Gallanis, 'The Contribution of Fiduciary Law', in Lionel Smith (ed), *The Worlds of the Trust* (Cambridge University Press, 2013), pp. 397–405.

# 4

# Regulation of Residential Property in the West

## *The Impact of Chinese Money*

*Edward S. W. Ti*

### 1 INTRODUCTION

The narrative pertaining to Chinese real estate investors in some Western jurisdictions reads like this: Noveau riche Chinese buyers are attracted to a westernised education for their children, an agreeable and law-abiding civic society all whilst living in a clean and pleasant environment. The flood of Chinese wealth has impacted residential housing markets resulting in locals being outpriced. To combat unaffordability, governments have had no choice but to impose regulatory measures preventing foreign (mainly Chinese) capital from overrunning the market. Is this story cogent?

The place-specific nature of real estate means that its economic value is ultimately dependent on policy processes.[1] Lord Wilson defines policy as the 'actions, objectives and pronouncements of governments [. . .] and the steps they take to implement them'.[2] Guided by this articulation, this chapter discusses the policies meant to address the 'emerging global trend of foreign liquidity in local property markets'.[3] In particular, this chapter explores the propriety and logic of some of the articulated housing policies which have led to legislative amendments made by governments in Australia, New Zealand, and Canada, purportedly in response to the fact that Chinese nationals[4] have been driving up prices in residential markets.

[1] David Adams, Craig Watkins and Michael White (eds), 'Examining Public Policy and Property Markets' in *Planning, Public Policy & Property Markets* (Blackwell Publishing 2005), p. 239.

[2] Richard Wilson, *'Policy Analysis as Policy Advice' in Michael Moran*, Martin Rein and Robert Goodin (eds), *The Oxford Handbook of Public Policy* (Oxford University Press 2008), p. 154.

[3] Ashok Bardhan and Cynthia Kroll, 'Globalization and the Real Estate Industry: Issues, Implications, Opportunities' (Sloan Industry Studies Annual Conference, Cambridge, MA, 26 April 2007) <www.web.mit.edu/sis07/www/kroll.pdf> accessed 14 October 2019.

[4] Chinese nationals include not just mainland Chinese but also those from Greater China (especially Hong Kong SAR). Other Asian buyers residing outside China, as well as the Chinese diaspora in Asia (e.g. Singapore, Malaysia and other parts of Southeast Asia) also invest in the West but are not included as 'Chinese buyers' for the purpose of this chapter as references by governments to 'Chinese buyers' typically refer to the former.

This chapter finds that some of the policy reactions by the surveyed jurisdictions appear to have resulted not because Chinese investors have been proven to affecting affordability. Instead, the adopted policies are to appease the feelings of local residents who believe that Chinese investors are the root of the problem. This is a significant enquiry traversing both property rights and ethnocentrism. Singling out or blaming a particular nationality, one that is so closely linked to ethnicity, for something as sensitive as housing is controversial. History teaches us that majoritarian belief that a certain 'group' is to be blamed for a social ill is a dangerous, slippery slope. Many of the jurisdictions analysed in this chapter have significant ethnic Chinese communities. While the political statements mentioned by the lawmakers roundly clarify that Chinese *nationals* cause high prices, it would be surprising if ethnic Chinese communities would be wholly unaffected if strong anti-Chinese national sentiment took root. Rogers and Dufty-Jones observe that in Australia, the singling out of buyers of Chinese heritage can lead to cultural profiling of people of Asian appearance who buy property. They note the societal occurrence of labelling Australian-Chinese citizens as Chinese foreign investors as a conceptual problem which 'feeds parochial discourses in the public debate'.[5] In Vancouver, Ley and Murphy's scholarship demonstrates that in the early 2000s, the cultural profiling and misrepresentation of local Chinese communities in Vancouver's mainstream media reinforced negative stereotypes of these migrant groups in Canada.[6] A few clarifications about the scope of this chapter are in order.

First, my analysis whether the presence of Chinese buyers becoming a legitimate political issue is justified or merely a convenient excuse for 'political hysteria'[7] is qualitative and where data is referred to, I explicitly rely on the quantitative analysis done by others. Second, this chapter is not looking at the effects of Chinese buyers in non-Western jurisdictions. Foreign buyers, including Chinese investors, are buying property around the globe, including in many non-Western jurisdictions. Indeed, Hong Kong,[8] Malaysia,[9] Singapore,[10] Thailand,[11] and the Philippines[12] all

5 Dallas Rogers and Rae Dufty-Jones (eds), '21st-Century Australian Housing: New Frontiers in the Asia Pacific' in *Housing in Twenty-First Century Australia: People, Practices and Policies* (Routledge 2016), pp. 221–236.

6 David Ley and Peter Murphy, 'Immigration in Gateway Cities: Sydney and Vancouver in Comparative Perspective' (2001) 55(3) *Progress in Planning* 119, 165.

7 Norman Miller, Michael Sklarz, and Nocholas Ordway, 'Japanese Purchases, Exchange Rates and Speculation in Residential Real Estate Markets' (1988) 3(3) *Journal of Real Estate Research* 39, 48.

8 Hong Kong imposes a 15 per cent surcharge on home purchases by non-nationals.

9 Most Malaysian States require foreigners wishing to invest in residential real estate to be limited to those above RM$1M.

10 Non-nationals are limited to owning apartments and are subject to additional stamp duty of between 5 per cent (permanent residents) and 20 per cent (foreigners).

11 Non-Thais limited to purchasing condominiums that have at least 51 per cent Thai ownership.

12 Foreigners cannot own the land but can own a house – essentially requiring them to enter into a long lease for the underlying land.

have laws meant to limit foreign home buyers and 'anti-Chinese' sentiment in these jurisdictions may be even more intense than those in the West. Third, this chapter limits itself to the effect Chinese buyers are said to have on direct investments in residential property, which typically engenders stronger sentiments than commercial property. Fourth and finally, the focus is not on general macroprudential measures which aim to reduce speculation in property per se, but which are not specifically aimed at reducing demand from foreign buyers. While reducing demand from foreign buyers has the concurrent effect of reducing demand in the market in general, I focus on the changes to the law that have taken place, which were expressly intended to respond to foreign, and in particular, Chinese buyers.

Using the legislative reactions to Chinese money in six Western jurisdictions: Australia (Victoria, New South Wales ('NSW'), and Queensland), New Zealand, and Canada (Ontario and British Columbia), this comparative exercise seeks to identify the policy rationale behind the law and analyse its propriety.

## 2 CHINESE MOTIVATIONS FOR BUYING IN THE WEST

There are many reasons why Chinese nationals are motivated to buy residential property in the West. Endogenous reasons include an increase in disposable savings coupled with the lack of appealing investment opportunities at home. The continuing rise in Chinese wealth eclipses the similar trajectory enjoyed by the Japanese in the 1980s. Meanwhile, housing prices in China have also risen significantly, with *average* housing costs in Beijing and Shanghai ranging from US$350 to US$460 per square foot.[13] Relatively speaking therefore, buying in the 'West' may not be as expensive.

Exogenous reasons may include the desire to send children to study abroad, future preparations for possible immigration, exposure to safe-haven currencies, and belief in the inherent strength of Western economies, as well as diversification benefits.[14] One commentator has also suggested that Canada's agreeable environment may have been a pull factor. According to the Chairman of the Asia Pacific Foundation of Canada, John Bruk, 'members of China's middle class, who have lot of money to spare and who are living in overcrowded and polluted cities, are looking for a more pleasant environment for themselves or their children'.[15] In the context of Australia, its low-risk business environment, educational opportunities, lifestyle, and

[13] Peter Wang, 'The 10 Chinese Cities with Most Expensive Home Prices' (China Whisper, 2019) <www.chinawhisper.com/the-10-china-cities-with-most-expensive-home-prices> accessed 14 October 2019.

[14] Clemon Sirmans and Elaine Worzala, 'International Direct Real Estate Investment: A Review of the Literature' (2003) 40 (5–6) *Urban Studies* 1081, 114.

[15] John Bruk, 'Canada's Housing Crisis: The Time for Study Has Passed' (The Globe and Mail, 8 July 2016) <www.theglobeandmail.com/report-on-business/rob-commentary/canadas-housing-crisis-the-time-for-study-has-passed/article30801183/> accessed 14 October 2019.

large ethnic Chinese population have been said to make the country an attractive destination for buyers from China.

Foreign buyers will not assimilate as well as locals. Their money is made outside the country and is brought in to compete with locals for residential housing within a particular locale. Depending on the reason of the purchase, the foreign buyers may keep their properties largely empty, adding to the frustration of local residents. These are some of the postulations that may be justified in some cases but pure politics in others. For instance, Miller, Sklarz, and Ordway note that Japanese buyers were singled out as the main cause of the rapid housing price appreciation in parts of Hawaii in the 1980s. Their analysis however rejects any causation, concluding instead that price increases were more a symptom of Hawaii's long-evolving housing shortfall: rapidly growing populations and severely restrictive land use controls were driving up average home prices long before the Japanese took an interest in Hawaii.[16] Conversely, a recent paper analysing the Vancouver residential market indicates a statistically strong correlation between foreign ownership and unaffordability.[17]

## 3 WHAT HAVE HOST COUNTRIES DONE?

The jurisdictions discussed below have all enacted laws guided by their articulated policy beliefs that the free market has failed and some degree of control of the local residential market is needed. Affordability is typically the policy goal cited but how this is achieved may not necessarily coincide with the *response* that voters may want implemented. As governments come in and out of power, differing mindsets or agendas might permeate, with sentiments amorphous and disparate. Yet the enactment of legislation is supposed to be a technical expression of this sentiment. What follows is a breakdown by jurisdiction of the measures and legislation implemented in response to Chinese buyers, and some comparative observations before concluding.

### 3.1 *Australia*

Foreign ownership of residential property in Australia has sometimes been described as an emotionally charged issue with locals pointing the fingers at foreign buyers when property prices increase in Australia's capital cities. Indeed 'foreigners-make-housing-expensive' was a central economic tenet of the Abbott government. This

16 Miller, Sklarz and Ordway, 'Japanese Purchases, Exchange Rates and Speculation in Residential Real Estate Markets'.

17 Josh Gordon, Vancouver's Housing Affordability Crisis: Causes, Consequences and Solutions (Centre for Public Policy Research, Simon Fraser University) (2 May 2016) <www.sfu.ca/mpp/centre_for_public_policy_research/cppr.html> accessed 14 October 2019.

has been described as a political gambit designed to play to the assumed xenophobic instincts of the electorate.[18] Unfortunately, some of this 'assumed xenophobia', particularly against the Chinese, appears true. In 2014, well-known Australian businessman and politician Clive Palmer said in the context of an iron ore dispute in Western Australia, *'I don't mind standing up against the Chinese bastards and stopping them from (taking over)'*.[19] Recently, Jason Clare of the Labour Party noted the inherent tension between the importance of foreign investment and the lack of its popularity, particularly in respect of Chinese investment. Addressing the House in August 2018, the five-time Federal Member of Parliament (MP) observed that Australia is a country built on foreign investment. He noted that even though China is only the overall ninth biggest foreign investor, increase in community concern was disproportionately higher compared to other inbound nations (such as the United States). Seventy-two per cent of Australians polled in the Lowy Institute Poll 2017 agreed that 'the government was allowing too much investment from China'.[20] It remains to be seen whether his exhortation will be followed:

> We've got to talk up the benefits of foreign investment, but we also can't ignore community concerns, because if we do they fester, they get worse and it makes it harder to do the things that we think are so important to create the country we want to build.[21]

As discussed below, a good majority of foreign investors in Australia are Chinese nationals. However, there is doubt about whether concerns pertaining to affordability are proportional to the actual effect Chinese investors have had on residential property in Australia. Guest and Rohde[22] find that increases in foreign investment have accounted for 20–30 per cent of the housing price increases between 2004 and 2014 in Melbourne and Sydney. In contrast, a paper by the Australian Treasury[23] has expressed the view that the recent price growth experienced in Australia is largely not attributable to foreign demand. The Treasury paper notes the research by Guest

[18] Chris Berg, 'You Can't Blame Foreigners for High House Prices' (ABC News, 17 February 2015) <www.abc.net.au/news/2015-02-17/berg-you-cant-blame-foreigners-for-high-house-prices/6125500> accessed 14 October 2019.

[19] Phillip Coorey and Joanna Heath, 'Chinese Bastards' Want to Take Over Australia: Palmer, (Australian Financial Review, 19 August 2014) <www.afr.com/news/politics/national/chinese-bastards-want-to-take-over-australia-palmer-20140819-j8vpx> accessed 14 October 2019.

[20] Jason Clare MP, *Ministerial Statements – Investment Statement 2018* (Hansard, House of Representatives, 20 August 2018) <www.aph.gov.au/Parliamentary_Business/Hansard/Hansard_Display?bid=chamber/hansardr/66d5616d-41f7-432b-b370-a62012124e44/&sid=0194> accessed 14 October 2019.

[21] ibid.

[22] Ross Guest and Nicholas Rohde, 'The Contribution of Foreign Real Estate Investment to Housing Price Growth in Australian Capital Cities' (2017) 53(3) *ABACUS* 304.

[23] Chris Wokker and John Swieringa, 'Foreign Investment and Residential Property Price Growth' (Treasury Working Chapter, December 2016) <www.rse.anu.edu.au/media/1845323/Swieringa-Chapter-2017.pdf> accessed 14 October 2019.

and Rohde but disagrees with its findings. The Treasury expresses the view that its research had the benefit of far more granular data (monthly Foreign Investment Review Board ('FIRB') approvals at the postcode level), while Guest and Rodhe's chapter was limited to annual, State-level data. The Treasury noted that foreign investors account for an increasing share of demand for residential property, with approximately 70 per cent of FIRB approvals made by Chinese national applicants. However, it concluded that there is only a small positive relationship of less than 1 per cent between foreign investment approvals and residential property price growth. Additionally, the Treasury's research found that foreign demand has been successful in achieving the national policy of increasing *supply* of housing – more developers were incentivised to construct new dwellings to satisfy the increasing demand from foreigners, who are limited to buying new properties.

Chung has noted that there is very little research on the impact of buyers with Chinese backgrounds on the Australian property market, and most of the negative commentary on the Chinese was 'based on media and real estate agent speculation'.[24] Her research indicates that there is inconclusive evidence whether Chinese investment has resulted in higher home prices. In respect of Australia's Business Innovation and Investment visa program (which starts at A$1.5M worth of investment and goes up to A$15M), Chung states that 90 per cent of applicants from that program in 2014–2015 were Chinese. She proffers the view that the rapid prominence of the Chinese in Australia may have attracted envy by some Australians who in response have made Chinese scapegoats for high housing prices.

### 3.1.1 Australia's Foreign Investment Review Board

From a legal perspective, the regulation of foreign[25] investment into Australian residential property is administered by the FIRB, a non-statutory body established in 1976 to advise the Federal Treasurer and the Government on foreign investment matters. Technically, the FIRB has only advisory functions and cannot make binding decisions on foreign investment for the government. Under Part 3 of the *Foreign Acquisitions and Takeovers Act 1975* ('the Act'),[26] the Treasurer is responsible for making decisions on foreign investment policy and investment proposals. In practice though, FIRB officers are empowered to make decisions 'consistent with the foreign investor framework',[27] with the FIRB being described as a 'de facto part of

[24] Mona Chung, 'New Research Questions Impact of Chinese Buyers on Australian House Prices' (Deakin University media release, 18 September 2017) <www.deakin.edu.au/about-deakin/media-releases/articles/new-research-questions-impact-of-chinese-buyers-on-australian-house-prices> accessed 14 October 2019.

[25] A 'foreign person' refers to all individuals 'not ordinarily resident' in Australia (Foreign Acquisitions and Takeovers Act 1975 (No. 92, 1975), s. 4).

[26] Foreign Acquisitions and Takeovers Act 1975 (No. 92, 1975).

[27] Foreign Investment Review Board, *Annual Report 2017–2018* (February 2019), p. 3.

the Treasury'.[28] Policy advisers in the Central Bank believe that an increase in the level of demand for new housing will lead to an increase in housing supply.[29] In furtherance of this policy, foreign investors are prohibited from purchasing 'established dwellings'[30] under section 95(4) of the Act, unless able to get an exemption certificate under section 37. In practice, virtually all foreign investors are limited to purchasing newly built or off-plan dwellings. There is data suggesting that first home buyers generally purchase established rather than new dwellings.[31] This may suggest that limiting foreign buyers to new dwellings is complementary.

Even in respect of new dwellings, section 3 of the Act states that the Treasurer, in relation to a foreigner intending to acquire real estate, is entitled to:

(1) Decide that the Commonwealth has no objection;
(2) Impose conditions on the purchase;
(3) Prohibit the purchase; or
(4) Require the action to be undone (e.g. requiring the disposal of an interest that has been acquired).

In practice, the vast majority of applications for new dwellings are approved (with the condition of the application fee paid); the approach at the federal (FIRB) level is to charge an application fee which entitles the foreign investor to make the investment sought. Every purchase by a foreigner requires FIRB approval with application fees proportional to the price of the property purchased.[32]

While Chinese nationals are currently significant segment of inbound foreign investors to Australia,[33] 'China was an isolated communist state'[34] when FIRB was established in 1976. The meteoric growth experienced by China starting from the 1990s was also a crucial factor in Australia's own prosperity, especially through demand for minerals and other resources. The Federal government's White Paper *Australia in the Asian Century*[35] notes that the Australian economy and society

[28] Chris Paris, 'The Super-Rich and Transnational Housing Markets: Asians Buying Australian Housing' in Ray Forrest, Sin Yee Koh and Bart Wissink (eds), *Cities and the Super-Rich: Real Estate, Elite Practices and Urban Political Economies* (Palgrave Macmillan 2017), pp. 63, 71.

[29] Maurice Gauder, Claire Houssard and David Orsmond, *Foreign Investment in Residential Real Estate*, Reserve Bank Bulletin (June 2014), p. 15.

[30] Defined as simply 'not new dwellings' under s. 4 of the Foreign Acquisitions and Takeover Act 1975 (No. 92, 1975).

[31] Maurice Gauder, Claire Houssard and David Orsmond, *Foreign Investment in Residential Real Estate*, Reserve Bank Bulletin (June 2014), p. 16.

[32] This is set out in Part 2 of the Foreign Acquisitions and Takeovers Fees Imposition Act 2015 (No. 152, 2015).

[33] China is now the second largest foreign investor source country in Australia, behind the United States. However, while only 17 per cent of US investment in Australia is in real estate, 54 per cent of inbound Chinese capital is placed in property: Foreign Investment Review Board, *Annual Report 2017–2018* (February 2019), p. 1.

[34] Paris, The Super-Rich and Transnational Housing Markets, p. 71.

[35] Australian Commonwealth Government (2012) 6.

have progressively become more integrated into the Asia-Pacific region. The White Paper also notes that by 2025, Asia-Pacific will account for half of the world's output. The inherent policy tensions in respect of dealing with Chinese money has led to the FIRB taking a fairly robust attitude towards foreign investment. For instance, Kelly O'Dwyer MP lamented that since 2006, there has not been a single prosecution against foreign investors who failed to comply with FIRB notifications.[36] The Reserve Bank has stated that 'foreign investment has been a longstanding feature of Australia's housing market'.[37]

It should be noted that the FIRB fees only give the foreign investor the right to purchase housing in Australia and foreign investors are subject to taxation at the State level as well. All six States[38] in Australia now impose additional acquisition taxes for foreign investors. Of these, three States, and in particular their major cities – Victoria (Melbourne), NSW (Sydney), and Queensland (Brisbane) attract more than 90 per cent of the Chinese money coming into Australia.[39] This chapter thus focuses on these three States. Tevfik and Liu note that according to government statistics in 2015–2016, 25 per cent of new dwellings in NSW are acquired by foreigners, of which 80 per cent are Chinese nationals. In Victoria, 16 per cent of new dwellings are acquired by foreigners.[40] These statistics are compelling but must be looked at in the context of the entire property market. For instance, in their submission to Australia's Parliament,[41] a non-profit organisation representing Australia's property developers ('NPO') said that based on FIRB and data from the Australian Bureau of Statistics, Chinese contribution to the total foreign investment in residential real estate from 2010 to 2013 was approximately A$5 billion per annum, in a market worth A$250 billion. The NPO expressed the view that 'while

36 Kelly O'Dwyer MP, *Matters of Public Importance – Prime Minister* (Hansard, House of Representatives, 4 December 2014) <www.aph.gov.au/Parliamentary_Business/Hansard/Hansard_Display?bid=chamber/hansardr/200bef5f-bafa-4738-b150-7dbac05c37e0/&sid=0147> accessed 14 October 2019.

37 Maurice Gauder, Claire Houssard and David Orsmond, *Foreign Investment in Residential Real Estate*, Reserve Bank Bulletin (June 2014), p. 18.

38 Victoria: 8 per cent pursuant to the *Duties Act 2000* (w.e.f. 1 July 2019); New South Wales: 8 per cent pursuant to the *Duties Act 1997* (w.e.f. 1 July 2017); Western Australia: 7 per cent pursuant to the *Duties Act 2008* (w.e.f. 1 January 2019); South Australia: 7 per cent pursuant to the *Stamp Duties Act 1923* (w.e.f. 1 January 2018); Queensland: 7 per cent pursuant to the *Duties Act 2001* (w.e.f. 1 October 2016); and Tasmania: 3 per cent pursuant to the *Duties Act 2001* (w.e.f. 1 July 2018). Only the territories (Northern Territory and Australian Capital Territory) do not.

39 Colin Tincknell, *Duties Amendment (Additional Duty for Foreign Persons) Bill 2018* (Second Reading), Parliamentary Debates (WA) Hansard (20 September 2018) <www.parliament.wa.gov.au/Hansard/hansard.nsf/0/48B47D6FA0BDEA2B482583130017613C/$file/C40%20S1%2020180920%20All.pdf> accessed 14 October 2019.

40 Hasan Tevfik and Peter Liu, *Australian Investment Strategy: Shanghai? Shenzhen? Sydney!* (Credit Suisse Research Note, March 2017) <www.businessinsider.com.au/foreign-investment-in-australian-housing-2017-3> accessed 14 October 2019.

41 At the request of the House of Representatives (Standing Committee on Economics), in contribution to Parliament's *Report on Foreign Investment in Residential Real Estate* (November 2014).

2% of the market is a worthy contribution to new housing, it is not considered to be at a level to warrant the community concerns and intense media scrutiny of late'. The NPO also indicated that with American and Canadian investment in Australia at levels very close to the Chinese, the focus on Chinese investment was similarly not warranted. As foreigners are legally limited to purchasing only new dwellings, a high proportion of Chinese buying such properties may not necessarily have a large impact on the larger housing market, which comprises both new dwellings and resale homes.

What follows is a discussion on the three States most affected by Chinese buyers – Victoria, NSW, and Queensland. Outside these States, the impact of Chinese investors is certainly more muted. Hansard parliamentary debates involving the enactment of the relevant additional tax for foreigners in South Australia,[42] Tasmania, and Western Australia do not single out Chinese investors as a cause for housing affordability in their respective States.

### 3.1.2 Victoria

As of July 2019, Victoria has increased its additional foreign buyer's stamp duty for residential property to 8 per cent.[43] With its base stamp duty rate of 5.5 per cent,[44] foreigners pay a 13.5 per cent transaction tax at the State level. As mentioned above, 16 per cent of new dwellings are acquired by foreigners. While there is no specific data on what proportion of this is fuelled by Chinese buyers, there is certainly evidence that curbing Chinese investors coming into the state remains a political issue. During the legislative assembly debates on the amendment of the *Duties Act*, Judith Graley MP (Labour) said, 'if you go out and talk to people in the community you will hear the average Australian saying that it is a good thing to tax Chinese investors on property. That is a good thing. People support that'.[45] There was no other justification offered in support of the proposed amendment of the Act. Absentee land tax has also increased from 1.5 to 2 per cent in Victoria.[46]

42 Notably, in South Australia, there were parliamentary comments on the impact of Chinese investment, albeit in relation to farm property: '*Well, you know, it's sort of a bit like this: the Chinese have got more guns than we've got, and they've got bigger guns than we've got, and if we are going to kick their arse'—excuse the language—'they're going to kick ours 10 times harder.' That is a very concerning statement for a senator to make, given that this was an evening where he was addressing food producers. For him to say that we are fast becoming a foreign-owned country is very disturbing.*' (18 July 2012) <http://hansardpublic.parliament.sa.gov.au/Pages/HansardResult.aspx#/docid/HANSARD-10-11952> accessed 14 October 2019 (Ann Bressington MLC quoting Senator Barnaby Joyce).

43 Duties Act 2000, s. 28A.

44 ibid, s.28, for properties more than A$960,000.

45 Judith Graley, *State Taxation Acts Amendment Bill*, Parliamentary Debates (Vic) Hansard (22 May 2018), p. 1484 <www.parliament.vic.gov.au/images/stories/daily-hansard/Assembly_2018/Assembly_Daily_Extract_Tuesday_22_May_2018_from_Book_6.pdf> accessed 14 October 2019.

46 Land Tax Act 2005, Part 3.

### 3.1.3 New South Wales

Like Victoria, NSW imposes an 8 per cent additional 'surcharge purchaser's duty' for residential property acquired by foreigners.[47] Also similar to Victoria, NSW imposes a base transfer tax of 5.5 per cent[48] meaning that foreigners pay 13.5 per cent transaction tax to the NSW government. Further, with effect from 31 December 2017, the State also enhanced its 'surcharge land tax' for foreign-owned residential property to 2 per cent per annum.[49] This is markedly different from Victoria's absentee land tax[50] (which applies to unused properties regardless of who owns them).

As mentioned above, the data in respect of Chinese buyers in the State appears compelling; approximately 20 per cent of new dwellings were purchased by Chinese nationals who comprise 80 per cent of all foreign buyers.[51] However, this statistic may not evidence a cause of housing unaffordability as Chinese buyers *cannot* directly affect the secondary market. It is also incongruous that an NSW legislator should refer to statistics in the country to support legislative change for addressing the problem of housing affordability *within the State*. In his speech to NSW's Upper House, Lou Amato MP said:

> [...] in recent times the Australian housing market has seen exponential price increases far exceeding the potential of most Australians to service [...] Unlike our sometimes novel discussions on the cause, New Zealand has identified the main culprit without engaging in a pseudointellectual debate on the issue. The problem it seems is that foreign buyers are pushing up house prices and restricting New Zealanders' access to the market. Presently one in four properties sold in our country is being purchased by foreign buyers who consistently outbid Australians. It is obvious there is a correlation with spiralling property prices and foreign investors bidding up prices way beyond market value.[52]

As a State legislator, Amato should have confined himself to evidence and data of the State; the parliamentarian's dramatic conclusion of an 'obvious' correlation between 'spiralling property prices and foreign investors bidding up prices way beyond market value' is also not persuasive, perhaps betraying politicisation of the housing issue. The statistic that Amato cited also grossly misrepresents. In fact, one in four *new* properties was purchased by foreign buyers, with most property transactions occurring in the secondary market.

47 Duties Act 1997, s. 104U

48 ibid, s. 32, (for properties above A$1,013,000).

49 Land Tax Act 1956, s. 5A(2).

50 Land Tax Act 2005, Part 3

51 Tevfik and Liu, 'Australian Investment Strategy: Shanghai? Shenzhen? Sydney!'.

52 Lou Amato, *Housing Affordability*, Legislative Council Hansard (21 November 2017) <www.parliament.nsw.gov.au/Hansard/Pages/HansardResult.aspx#/docid/HANSARD-1820781676-75074> accessed 14 October 2019.

There is at least one paper that concerns itself with public sentiment regarding the unpopularity of Chinese investors in NSW. Rogers, Wong, and Nelson[53] surveyed 899 Sydney residents, looking at their perceptions of foreign and Chinese investment. They found high levels of public concern and discontent about foreign investment amongst Sydneysiders, with Chinese investors being a key target of this discontent. In the context of high housing prices in Sydney, there were widely held concerns about housing affordability. According to the researchers, survey respondents had a sophisticated understanding of what influences house prices, but overemphasised the role of foreign investment. They found a general lack of support for policy that encourages foreign investment, and a lack of confidence in how the government is regulating foreign investment. The paper found that half of the participants reported that they would not welcome Chinese foreign investment in their suburb.

### 3.1.4 Queensland

On top of its marginal transfer duty rate of 5.75 per cent,[54] Queensland has imposed an 'additional foreigner acquirer duty' of 7 per cent under section 244 of the *Duties Act 2001*. This means that the State imposes a total transfer tax of 12.75 per cent on foreigners.

It is interesting to note that during the parliamentary debates regarding the imposition of the additional tax for foreign buyers, Queensland's Premier, Annastacia Palaszczuk, said that one of the purposes of the tax was to increase funding of the homeowner's grant (from A$15,000 to A$20,000).[55] Queensland's Treasurer Curtis Pitt similarly said that the tax would be to 'make foreigners pay for the infrastructure and services they will use'.[56] A further justification for the additional tax was simply that NSW and Victoria had imposed similar taxes.[57] The position of the Queensland government is thus to treat the additional foreigner acquirer duty as a wealth tax, which allows the State to redistribute to first time homeowners who need help.

Laudably, there has been no indication by any Queensland legislator that the purpose of the additional tax was to curtail foreign or Chinese investment so as to

53 Dallas Rogers, Alexandra Wong and Jacqueline Nelson, 'Public Perceptions of Foreign and Chinese Real Estate Investment: Intercultural Relations in Global Sydney' (2017) 48(4) *Australian Geographer* 437–455.

54 Duties Act 2001, sch 3 (for properties above A$1M).

55 Annastacia Palaszczuk, *Questions Without Notice* (Hansard, Queensland Parliamentary Debates) 3204 (31 August 2016) <www.parliament.qld.gov.au/documents/hansard/2016/2016_08_31_WEEKLY.pdf> accessed 14 October 2019.

56 Curtis Pitt, *Questions Without Notice* (Hansard, Queensland Parliamentary Debates) 3205 (31 August 2016) <www.parliament.qld.gov.au/documents/hansard/2016/2016_08_31_WEEKLY.pdf> accessed 14 October 2019.

57 Annastacia Palaszczuk, *Questions Without Notice* (Hansard, Queensland Parliamentary Debates) 3845 (13 October 2016) <www.parliament.qld.gov.au/documents/hansard/2016/2016_10_13_WEEKLY.pdf> accessed 14 October 2019.

increase affordability. This is despite a recent newspaper report[58] indicating that Chinese property investment has risen in tandem with a record number of students of Chinese nationality enrolling in universities in Queensland. The report notes that data from Queensland's Foreign Ownership of Land Register show that Chinese investors spent about A$1.5b on Queensland properties in 2016–2017, up from $872 million two years earlier and that nearly all the money was spent on properties in the Brisbane and Gold Coast area.

### 3.2 *New Zealand*

New Zealand has one of the most austere legislative responses to foreign buyers of residential property in the Western world. On 15 August 2018, the labour-led coalition government passed the *Overseas Investment Amendment Bill* which bans virtually all foreign investors from purchasing residential property. Under the revised provisions, which came into force on 22 October 2018, Schedule 1 to the Overseas Investment Act 2005[59] defines residential property as 'sensitive land'. Under clause 4 to Schedule 2 of the Act, only 'qualifying individuals' are permitted to acquire such properties, barring extraordinary ministerial approval. These include NZ nationals and permanent residents, as well as due to free trade agreements, citizens and permanent residents of Australia and Singapore.[60] Residential tenancies of up to five years are exempted from the prohibition against foreign acquisition.[61] Foreigners are also permitted to purchase up to 60 per cent of new strata units which must be sold off-plan by developers constructing at least twenty new dwellings; foreigners are not permitted to buy already built units.[62] Similar to the position in Australia, this exception appears to increase the number of new dwellings in the market. Enforcement under the Act is robust, and includes allowing the government to issue a 'notice requiring a disposal of property' to a non-qualifying person who has acquired sensitive land.[63]

An appreciation of the politicking behind this amendment provides the context behind the rule change. A major campaign issue for all political parties in NZ's 2017 General Elections was reported severe housing unaffordability in several major cities. While both the Labour Party (46) and New Zealand First (9) won less seats than New Zealand National (56), the former two parties succeeded in forming government in New Zealand's 120-seat house through a coalition agreement with the

58 Kristian Silva and Kirrin McKechnie, 'Chinese Property Investment Soars in Qld as Record Number of Uni Students Enrol' (ABC News, 25 June 2018) <www.abc.net.au/news/2018-06-25/chinese-property-investment-soars-in-south-east-queensland/9905558> accessed 14 October 2019.

59 Overseas Investment Act 2005 (No. 82 of 2005).

60 Overseas Investment Act 2005, sch 2, cl 4 read with the Overseas Investment Regulations 2005 (SR 2005/220), reg. 30.

61 ibid, sch 3, cl 3.

62 ibid, sch 3, cl 4 read with the Overseas Investment Regulations 2005 (SR 2005/220), reg. 32.

63 ibid, s. 41F.

Green Party (8). Both Labour and New Zealand First had run a tried-and-tested recipe: blame foreigners for house price rises; both parties made election promises to restrict investment by foreigners.

Labour Minister for Trade and A-G David Parker who introduced the Bill to the House said during the first reading, 'We think that it is the birthright of New Zealanders to own our homes'.[64] Parker relied on vague generalities in his endeavour to justify the new policy:

> We know that more and more of the world's wealth is accumulating in the hands of a very small minority—less than 1 percent. We know from the Panama Chapters and from Piketty's book Capital in the Twenty-First Century that many of these people pay low or no tax on their income overseas. In the face of that reality, the Government has the right and the duty to protect their local citizens from overseas accumulators of wealth impacting on the New Zealand housing market. Therefore, this bill brings residential land within the category of 'sensitive land' in the Overseas Investment Act.

Gerry Brownlee MP (National Party ('National')) countered that the data regarding foreign buyers did not justify the legislation. He pointed out that statistics from Q3,2017 show that only 3 per cent of properties were owned by foreigners, the vast majority of which are Australians (which the Act exempts).[65] Even within Auckland, data from that quarter shows that 9.8 per cent of transfers were made to foreigners.[66] Most recent data from Q4,2018 shows that only 2.3 per cent of home transfers were made to non-residents or citizens.[67] It is also alarming that Michael Woodhouse MP (National) noted that New Zealand First Party had expressed negativity towards 'Chinese-sounding surnames'[68] in expressing their desire to slash migration and prevent foreigners from buying houses. Stories of wealthy Chinese 'outbidding New Zealanders on suburban homes in Auckland' may also smack of representative bias.[69] Mercifully, Forestry Minister Shane Jones (NZ First) was candid enough to admit that the policy change was political rather than data-driven:

[64] David Parker, *Overseas Investment Amendment Bill (First Reading)*, Hansard, 19 December 2017 <www.parliament.nz/en/pb/hansard-debates/rhr/combined/HansDeb_20171219_20171219_16> accessed 14 October 2019.

[65] Gerry Brownlee, *Overseas Investment Amendment Bill (First Reading)*, Hansard, 19 December 2017 <www.parliament.nz/en/pb/hansard-debates/rhr/combined/HansDeb_20171219_20171219_16> accessed 14 October 2019.

[66] Stats NZ, *One in 19 Inner City Auckland Home Transfers Go to Overseas People* (30 October 2018) <www.stats.govt.nz/news/one-in-10-inner-city-auckland-home-transfers-go-to-overseas-people> accessed 14 October 2019.

[67] Stats NZ, *Overseas Home Buyers' Share Relatively Unchanged in December Quarter* (8 February 2019) <www.stats.govt.nz/news/overseas-home-buyers-share-relatively-unchanged-in-december-quarter> accessed 14 October 2019.

[68] Michael Woodhouse, *Overseas Investment Amendment Bill (First Reading)*, Hansard, 19 December 2017 <www.parliament.nz/en/pb/hansard-debates/rhr/combined/HansDeb_20171219_20171219_16> accessed 14 October 2019.

[69] Nick Perry, 'New Zealand bans most foreigners from buying homes' (AP, 15 August 2018) <www.apnews.com/cb80e520c0e045da9e129302256dca97> accessed 14 October 2019.

> But this bill will pass, and I just want to remind the House: where do we get our mandate to make such a fundamental change towards property ownership in New Zealand and the numbers of non-Kiwis holding such a privilege? We fought an election on this particular issue.[70]

Even apart from the opposition, there were several quarters who found the legislative amendments ill-conceived. In December 2017, New Zealand's own Treasury released a Regulatory Impact Assessment ('RIA')[71] on the intended Bill to Cabinet. The RIA observed several problems, including:

(1) 'the nature of the [intended] benefits is unclear as it is difficult to assess the extent and nature of the behavioural responses that will result from the policy';
(2) 'there is lack of empirical data on current levels of overseas investment in the housing market';
(3) 'some of the design choices may be sub-optimal or have unintended consequences'.

In April 2018, the International Monetary Fund ('IMF') expressed reservations about New Zealand's general ban on foreign ownership. The IMF noted that 'a ban of residential real estate purchases by non-residents is unlikely to have a significant impact on housing affordability' and further, that 'foreign buyers seem to have played a minor role in New Zealand's residential real estate markets recently'.[72] The IMF's Mission Chief for Australia and New Zealand, Thomas Helbling, said that putting capital flow controls were only appropriate when they were 'very large, disruptive inflows of money'. Helbling also opined that 'when you look at the statistic for New Zealand as a whole, and even Auckland as a whole, the role of foreign buyers is much less prominent'.[73]

## 3.3 *Canada*

There are no legislative measures at the federal level restricting or controlling foreign investment in residential property. The chapter's discussion on Canada focuses on the two provinces which have introduced measures to tax foreign buyers with

70 Shane Jones, *Overseas Investment Amendment Bill (First Reading)*, Hansard, 19 December 2017 <www.parliament.nz/en/pb/hansard-debates/rhr/combined/HansDeb_20171219_20171219_16> accessed 14 October 2019.

71 The Treasury, 'Regulatory Impact Assessment: Screening Overseas Investment in Sensitive Residential Land' (11 December 2017) <https://treasury.govt.nz/sites/default/files/2018-01/ria-tsy-srl-dec17.pdf> accessed 14 October 2019.

72 IMF, *New Zealand: Staff Concluding Statement of the 2018 Article IV Mission* (17 April 2018) <www.imf.org/en/News/Articles/2018/04/16/ms041618-new-zealand-staff-concluding-statement-of-the-2018-article-iv-mission> accessed 14 October 2019.

73 Rob Stock, 'IMF Not Keen on Proposed Foreign Buyer Ban for Houses' (Stuff, 6 July 2018) <www.stuff.co.nz/business/money/105284813/imf-not-keen-on-proposed-foreign-buyer-ban-for-houses> accessed 14 October 2019.

additional acquisition tax; Ontario and British Columbia. David McKay, the Chief Executive of the Royal Bank of Canada, has commented that foreign inflows are distorting Canada's already constrained housing market and that such investments are unproductive capital.[74] While perhaps less glaring than in Australia and New Zealand, public sentiment suggests that a good majority of these foreign buyers originate from China and Greater China. As discussed below, a less common narrative that should be noted is that Canada encouraged such investments in the first place and could be a victim of its own success. Educating Canadians on this could perhaps go some way to soothe some of the anti-Sino sentiments which may have arisen in the first place.

### 3.3.1 Ontario

On 21 April 2017, the Ontario government introduced several measures, including rent control rules, to rein in the housing market. The measures appeared most focused on the capital, Toronto, with the provincial government is also considering implementing a vacancy tax for empty homes.

Most notable of the implemented measures was the imposition of a 15 per cent transfer tax on foreign buyers, pursuant to section 2.1 of the *Land Transfer Tax Act*.[75] As the marginal transfer tax in Ontario is 2.5 per cent,[76] the total tax exposure for foreigners is 17.5 per cent. Dubbed the 'non-resident speculation tax', the tax applies to non-Canadian citizens and non-residents (including non-Canadian companies and taxable trusts) who purchase residential property in the Greater Golden Horseshoe ('GGH') region[77] in Southern Ontario.

Section 1(1)(a) of the *Land Transfer Tax Act* limits the application of the tax to residential land that contains up to six 'single family residences'. The Act defines single family residences 'as a unit or proposed unit under the *Condominium Act 1998* or a structure or part of a structure that is designed for occupation as the residence of a family'. The provision thus looks at how many single family residences are contained on the residential land lot in question, imposing the tax on foreigners buying single dwelling (stand-alone) property as well as condominium units that contain up

[74] Doug Alexander, 'RBC chief Issues Warning to Foreign Investors in Canadian Real Estate' (Bloomberg, 6 March 2018) <www.theglobeandmail.com/report-on-business/rbc-chief-issues-warning-to-foreign-investors-in-canadian-real-estate/article38218144/> accessed 14 October 2019.

[75] Land Transfer Tax Act R.S.O. 1990, c. L.6. Notably, due to coronavirus emergency legislation, a discretionary waiver of this tax is possible where the foreign buyer occupies the residence as his or her principal residence within 60 days of purchase, and where the purchase was made between 17 January 2020 and 24 July 2020: <www.fin.gov.on.ca/en/bulletins/nrst/#covid> accessed 30 October 2020.

[76] Land Transfer Tax Act R.S.O. 1990, c L.6, s. 2(1), for properties above C$2M.

[77] The GGH region centres itself around Toronto. With a population close to eight million people, the GGH region accounts for approximately 20 per cent of the population of Canada and close to 60 per cent of the population of Ontario.

to six apartments. The non-resident speculation tax does not apply to the purchase of a condominium unit in a building containing seven or more dwellings.

Explaining the stated purpose behind the tax from the government's perspective, Ontario's Minister of Finance Charles Sousa said that the non-resident speculation tax 'is about discouraging those who are capitalising on the speculation on homes, driving up prices, creating vacant homes and crowding out families looking to buy'.[78] Member of Provincial Parliament (MPP) Yvan Baker MPP similarly said that the policy aims to 'discourage those who have never even set foot in Ontario but who are impacting a tight property market, creating vacant homes and contributing to a speculative market'. Affordability was a key policy behind the legislative change. Baker also stated that the people of Ontario should be able to enter the property market without having to make undue sacrifices or taking on a huge amount of risk.[79] At least at first glance, these policy motivations appear reasonable, particularly because at the time the legislation was introduced, Toronto had experienced a 33 per cent year-on-year increase in residential prices.[80] Closer inspection however suggests that there may be a disconnect between the alleged problem (foreign speculators) and the legislative changes.

The first point is that there are several cogent allegations critical of the policy-making process in respect of the non-resident speculation tax made by opposition MPPs during the legislative assembly debates. Tellingly, these allegations have all remained unrebutted,[81] even though the Speaker of the House granted airtime to Minister Charles Sousa, the main target of the criticism by his peers. During the Bill's technical briefing, Victor Fedeli MPP reported that senior civil servants from the Ministry of Finance said there was no hard data on why the GGH area was established as the relevant boundary affected by the tax, instead explaining that it 'was a political decision', and further that the Ministry decided to follow 'the British Columbia model as we heard they did it in the greater Vancouver area'.[82] When probed further on the legislative justifications, Fedeli said that the senior

78 Charles Sousa, *Orders of the Day – Time Allocation* (Hansard, Legislative Assembly of Ontario, Session 41:2) 31 May 2017 <http://hansardindex.ontla.on.ca/hansardeissue/41-2/l088.htm> accessed 14 October 2019.

79 Yvan Baker, *Budget Measures Act (Housing Price Stability and Ontario Seniors' Public Transit Tax Credit)* (Hansard, Legislative Assembly of Ontario, Session 41:2) 30 May 2017 <http://hansardindex.ontla.on.ca/hansardeissue/41-2/l087.html> accessed 14 October 2019.

80 ibid.

81 Similar allegations critical of Finance Minister Charles Sousa have also been reported in Toronto's *The Star*, the newspaper with the largest circulation in Toronto. See Martin Cohn, *How Charles Sousa woke up from his housing hibernation: Cohn* (The Star, 21 April 2017) <www.thestar.com/news/queenspark/2017/04/21/how-charles-sousa-woke-up-from-his-housing-hibernation-cohn.html> accessed 14 October 2019.

82 Victor Fedeli, *Budget Measures Act (Housing Price Stability and Ontario Seniors' Public Transit Tax Credit)* (Hansard, Legislative Assembly of Ontario, Session 41:2) 30 May 2017 <http://hansardindex.ontla.on.ca/hansardeissue/41-2/l087.htm> accessed 14 October 2019.

civil servants shared that the reason was simply that 'the government felt it had to do something'. Describing the legislation as an 'ill-planned project', Fedeli also noted the absence of a nexus between alleged policy problem and policy goal given that there was 'no credible data on foreign buyers in the housing market'.[83] At an earlier legislative assembly debate, Peter Tabuns MPP similarly observed that the enactment of the non-resident speculation tax by the Liberal government was trying to score 'cheap political points by talking about foreign speculators'.[84] He noted that if preventing speculation was the policy goal, why were there no rules set in place to prevent speculation by locals. As Toronto's *The Star* noted sarcastically, 'Foreign speculators be damned and banned. Domestic speculators, mind you, can carry on as before'.[85]

The second point is that it is somewhat unclear why the non-resident speculation tax is limited to residential land containing up to six single family residences. In the entirety of Hansard proceedings concerning the Bill, this point was only mentioned once,[86] but none of the parliamentarians cite any reasons why the anti-speculation tax is limited to the purchase of units in a building that contains six dwellings or less. As there are no laws preventing a foreign investor from purchasing all the units in say a seven-unit condominium (without any speculation tax involved), one justification could be to encourage developers to build apartment buildings with more than six dwellings – this serves the twin purpose of increasing the supply of housing units while also making such projects more attractive to foreign investors. Under section 82.1 of Ontario's *Condominium Act 1998*,[87] a wholly owned or vastly majority-owned foreign condominium building can be collectively redeveloped or sold by an 80 per cent (as opposed to unanimous) majority consent.[88] In a comparative paper including Canada and Australia, I had previously made suggestions how the collective sale process of strata buildings could be improved.[89] If increase in number of residential dwellings is a policy goal, then one further amendment to the Ontario Act could be to introduce a requirement to increase the number of dwellings following a collective sale. Currently, there is no requirement for this in all jurisdictions that allow a strata sale by majority, despite the fact that many of these jurisdictions have a housing supply issue.

83 ibid.

84 Peter Tabuns, *Housing Policy* (Hansard, Legislative Assembly of Ontario, Session 41:2) 3 May 2017 <http://hansardindex.ontla.on.ca/hansardeissue/41-2/l076.htm> accessed 14 October 2019.

85 Cohn, 'How Charles Sousa woke up from his housing hibernation'.

86 Yvan Baker, *Budget Measures Act (Housing Price Stability and Ontario Seniors' Public Transit Tax Credit)* (Hansard, Legislative Assembly of Ontario, Session 41:2) 30 May 2017 <http://hansardindex.ontla.on.ca/hansardeissue/41-2/l087.htm> accessed 14 October 2019.

87 *Condominium Act 1998* S.O. 1998, c. 19.

88 This particular section allowing for a collective sale by 80 per cent majority is legislated for but not in force yet, pending proclamation by the Lieutenant Governor.

89 Edward S. W. Ti, 'Collective Best Interests in Strata Collective Sales' (2019) 93(12) *Australian Law Journal* 1025–1040.

One of the key criticisms about the way Ontario has dealt with the foreign buyers, tax is the paucity of data; this is reflected in the way the legislators endeavoured to explain the tax in the provincial parliament. While it is known that Toronto is very popular with Chinese buyers, it is not possible to conclude what relationship if any, this has had on the enactment of the non-resident speculation tax. Troublingly, the Canadian Broadcasting Corporation recently reported that the Ontario government has stopped publishing statistics on foreign buyers, tax on residential property, with the Finance Minister unable to explain why this is the case.[90]

### 3.3.2 British Columbia

Vancouver has been described as one of the least affordable places to live in the developed world resulting in many ordinary residents, particularly young workers, being forced to live far away from the metropolitan area. Gordon notes that debt levels of first time buyers have surged while at the same time communities are weakened by empty or underused dwellings owned by non-nationals.[91] Gordon's chapter presents a comprehensive and persuasive report which argues that Chinese investment is the primary reason for housing unaffordability in Vancouver. In reaching this conclusion, he accounts and excludes other possible reasons as the primary cause – low interest rates, desirability and strength of the Vancouver economy, zoning and geographical limitations, and insufficient social housing.[92] Elsewhere, Rose has also excluded the constrained supply of housing units hypothesis as the cause of unaffordability; his research similarly indicates that foreign speculators are driving prices up.[93] While these findings are persuasive, it is interesting to note that Canada may have been a victim of its own success; Chinese investors were initially encouraged to invest in Canadian cities.

Mike de Jong, then Finance Minister of British Columbia, shared in July 2016 that more than 90 per cent of foreign buyers are Chinese or Greater Chinese nationals.[94] Similarly, the evidence presented by Ley also indicates that almost all of Vancouver's foreign investors are from Greater China,[95] and that this stemmed from a series of 'business immigration programs' starting as early as

[90] Mike Crawley, 'Ontario's Foreign Buyers Tax Figures Are Now a Mystery – and the Finance Minister Says He Doesn't Know Why' (CBC News, 13 May 2019) <www.cbc.ca/news/canada/toronto/doug-ford-ontario-foreign-buyers-tax-real-estate-statistic-1.5131759> accessed 14 October 2019.

[91] Gordon, 'Vancouver's Housing Affordability Crisis: Causes, Consequences and Solutions'.

[92] ibid.

[93] John Rose, 'The Housing Supply Myth' (Working Chapter, 24 November 2017) <www.kpu.ca/sites/default/files/The%20Housing%20Supply%20Myth%20Report%20John%20Rose.pdf> accessed 14 October 2019.

[94] Bruk, 'Canada's housing crisis: The time for study has passed'.

[95] David Ley, 'Global China and the Making of Vancouver's Residential Property Market' (2017) 17(1) *International Journal of Housing Policy* 15–34.

1978 established by the Canadian government to encourage investment in the country. Canada's 'investor stream'[96] initiated in 1986 by the Mulroney government appears to have been at least partially opportunistic. The anticipated return of Hong Kong to China in 1997 created uncertainties among many of the wealthy in Hong Kong and the investment scheme allowing for migration captured a sizeable segment of this group. These investor schemes no doubt snowballed over the years, and it would be surprising if the presence of the early Chinese investors did not encourage further Chinese settlement and investment in Canada. Indeed since 2002, more than 60,000 millionaire migrants and their family members have settled in Vancouver.[97]

Notwithstanding that the Canadian governments' own policies probably precipitated housing unaffordability in its cities, regulatory measures to curb these effects have been introduced. In February 2018, the government of British Columbia issued a White Paper listing a 30-point plan for housing affordability.[98] In August 2016, the government had earlier imposed an additional tax of 15 per cent on residential property transfers to foreign nationals.[99] Effective 21 February 2018, the White Paper led to this tax being increased to 20 per cent for certain core central areas in Vancouver.[100] With a basic marginal transfer tax of 2 per cent,[101] this means that foreigners buying residential property in British Columbia will have total transfer tax liability of 17 or 22 per cent. Another legislative reaction to curb foreign investment was the introduction of a vacancy tax[102] via the Vancouver Charter read with the *Vacancy Tax (Empty Homes Tax) Bylaw 11674*.[103] The rule requires Vancouver city

96 Under this scheme, foreigners were granted residency in exchange for giving the Canadian government a 5-year interest free loan of C$400,000, as well as having a net worth above C$800,000.

97 Ian Young, 'Foreign Home Buyers in Vancouver Hit with HK-style 15pc Tax, but Millionaire Migrants Will Be Exempt' (SCMP, 26 July 2016) <www.scmp.com/print/news/world/united-states-canada/article/1994773/foreign-home-buyers-vancouver-hit-hk-style-15pc-tax> accessed 14 October 2019.

98 BC Government, *Homes for BC, A 30-Point Plan for Housing Affordability in British Columbia* (February 2018) <www.bcbudget.gov.bc.ca/2018/homesbc/2018_homes_for_bc.pdf> accessed 14 October 2019.

99 *Property Transfer Tax Act* [RSBC 1996] (Cap 378), s. 2.01 adopts the definition of 'foreign national' as stated in the *Immigration and Refugee Protection Act* SC 2001, c. 27, s. 2(1) which states that 'foreign national means a person who is not a Canadian citizen or a permanent resident, and includes a stateless person'. This 15 per cent additional tax was imposed for transfers within the Metro Vancouver Regional District comprising most of the city.

100 Property Transfer Tax Act [RSBC 1996] (Cap 378) ('the Act'), s. 2.02. Pursuant to s. 3 of the Act, transfer taxes to Canadian nationals or permanent residents are no more than 3 per cent of the property's value (1 per cent of the first C$200,000, 2 per cent for the next C$1.8M and 3 per cent for amounts in excess of C$2M).

101 ibid, s. 3.01.

102 Vancouver Charter [SBC 1953] (Cap 55), Part XXX. Under rule 2.3, Bylaw, a property is deemed vacant if it is left unoccupied for six months during the vacancy reference period.

103 Vacancy Tax (Empty Homes Tax) Bylaw 11674 <https://bylaws.vancouver.ca/11674c.PDF> accessed 14 October 2019.

homeowners to file an annual declaration on the occupancy status of their residential home – owners who fail to file or declare a home empty pay a vacancy tax of 1 per cent[104] of the property's assessed taxable value.

Have these legislative reactions been successful in achieving their stated policy aim of achieving housing affordability? A preliminary assessment would suggest at least some success in this respect. In July 2017, a year after the 15 per cent additional property transfer tax was imposed, the Real Estate Board of Greater Vancouver reported that price growth declined while volume of sales dropped across all segments of the housing market.[105]

In Vancouver, the additional transfer tax applied to transfers to 'foreign nationals' excludes permanent residents of Canada, regardless of nationality. The policy could thus be criticised for focusing on whether a buyer was foreign or non-resident instead of whether the money came from overseas, thus downplaying the impact of foreign capital. There are perhaps two ways this policy be tweaked. First, as Gordon has suggested, the emphasis should be on limiting the impact of foreign capital brought into Canada by permanent residents, that is, the additional transfer tax should also apply to such buyers. This could limit the possibility of foreign buyers using permanent residents as the registered owners to hold the property on trust for them. A second possibility would be to adopt a more restrictive definition of a 'local', being limited to Canadian citizens only.

## 4 REGULATION AND PROPERTY RIGHTS

Globalisation has led to foreign liquidity playing an increasingly important role in shaping property markets.[106] In all cities, housing scarcity can be a sensitive policy issue when local residents feel outpriced. The tension between attracting capital on one hand and affordability on the other is one that all major cities grapple with. The effects of legislation meant to curb foreign investment and thereby increase affordability are, like all policy tools, not always easy to measure, and a robust, long-term quantitative analysis is needed at a city-level to examine the cost-benefits of a policy. While politicians are quick to claim credit when changes in law or policy coincide with lower prices and hence 'affordability', unintended ancillary effects must also be considered to avoid only superficial analysis. Apart from Vancouver, the rest of the jurisdictions surveyed in this chapter do not show a robust, data-driven relationship to justify the policy of enacting additional acquisition tax for

104 Rule 2.4, Bylaw. Failure to pay the 1 per cent vacancy tax attracts a 5 per cent penalty: Rule 2.7, Bylaw.

105 A year following the introduction of the 15 per cent additional property transfer tax, Vancouver's composite benchmark of house prices still rose 8.7 per cent but volume declined by 8.2 per cent year-on-year.

106 Liao Wen-Chi et al., 'Foreign Liquidity to Real Estate Market: Ripple Effect and Housing Price Dynamics' (2015) 52(1) *Urban Studies* 138, 154.

foreigners. The emotive and sometimes dramatic language used by lawmakers suggests that in general, politics has trumped good policymaking.

Of course, politicians may not necessarily routinely make sound policy and legislative changes based on hard data. Where property is concerned however, perhaps one should expect, if not hope, for very cogent reasons when rights are affected. It should be recognised that any change in policy affecting the transfer of property amounts to a certain extent, imposition of property itself. From an economic perspective, property is often seen as bundle of rights,[107] though all governments impose regulations limiting what can be done to or on land.[108] As property tax rates increase for instance, regulation shades into appropriation at a certain point. Sometimes governments realise this and have to make reversals of policy. In 2004, Sri Lanka imposed a 100 per cent tax on foreigners buying property in the country, citing fears of foreigners buying up prime beachfront hotels and bungalows. In 2011, in order to 'promote foreign investment and tourism', the tax was scrapped.[109] The imposition of punitive transfer taxes distorts the free market. Property prices are determined by the interaction of supply and demand in the market, with the price mechanism operating to return supply and demand to a state of equilibrium.[110] Ball, Lizieri, and MacGregor find that, for equilibrium to be feasible, 'buyers and sellers must be able to use the full available information when making their decisions and operate according to the arguments of their demand and supply schedules'.[111] Rapaczynski notes the biggest threat to private property rights is often the State itself.[112] Similar concerns have been expressed by Dan Morrison, President of the Real Estate Board of Greater Vancouver, who denounced the abruptness of the foreign transfer tax:

> Implementing a new real estate tax with just eight days' notice and no consultation with the professionals who serve home buyers and sellers every day needlessly injects uncertainty into the market. Government has had a long time to take action on the affordability issue, yet they decide to bring this new tax in over a long weekend, with no notice, and no time to prepare. It would have been prudent to seek consultation from the people most knowledgeable about the impact.

[107] Harold Demsetz, 'Towards a Theory of Property Rights' (1967) 57(2) *American Economic Review* 347–359.

[108] Edward S. W. Ti, 'Compensating Regulation of Land: UK and Singapore Compared' (2019) 11(2) *Journal of Property, Planning and Environmental Law* 135–150.

[109] Bandula Sirimanna, '100% Land Sale Tax for Foreigners to Be Scrapped' (Business Times, 18 September 2011) <www.sundaytimes.lk/110918/BusinessTimes/bt01.html> accessed 14 October 2019.

[110] David Adams, Neil Dunse and Michael White, 'Conceptualising State-Market Relations in Land and Property: The Mainstream Contribution of Neo-Classical and Welfare Economics' in David Adams, Craig Watkins and Michael White (eds), *Planning, Public Policy & Property Markets* (Blackwell Publishing 2005), p. 19.

[111] Michael Ball, Colin Lizieri and Bryan MacGregor, *The Economics of Commercial Property Markets* (Routledge 1998), p. 63.

[112] Andrzej Rapaczynski, 'The Roles of the State and the Market in Establishing Property Rights' (1996) 10(2) *Journal of Economic Perspectives* 87, 92.

## 5 CONCLUSION

From one perspective, the policy responses by the jurisdictions surveyed do not appear unreasonable. China is the largest international property investor in the world, having grown twenty-five fold between 2010 and 2017 alone. Former NSW premier Bob Carr expressed the view at a leadership summit that Sydney and Australia as whole should 'get used to investment from China and India because the economic centre of gravity is shifting to Asia'.[113] This chapter does not argue that Chinese investors are never the cause of housing unaffordability. The point made is that if a particular group is specifically highlighted by a country's lawmakers to justify the enactment of a law, there ought to be specific data or evidence to back this up.

In four out of six of the surveyed jurisdictions (Victoria, NSW, New Zealand, and Toronto), comments by parliamentarians suggest that it is the mere *belief* that Chinese investors affect housing affordability that precipitated legislative change, despite no or even opposing data shown. Unhelpful, sensational headlines such as '*Country is at risk of becoming the 24th province of China*'[114] are seen in major newspapers, often times with limited analysis on whether the underlying causal relationship is shown.

Housing policy is deeply complex, and this chapter does not suggest that jurisdictions should not have the liberty to impose enhanced taxation on foreigners. Indeed, it is conceded that foreign buyers may leave their investment homes empty; unused homes certainly do not benefit a city's flourishing. A vacancy tax that applies uniformly to all owners but has a greater effect on foreign buyers appears to be more palatable than one that specifically targets foreigners. Respectfully, I would suggest that regulations targeting foreigners should be backed by data. Local residents concerned about Chinese buyers should not be advised to 'simply get over it'[115] – advice which assumes that Chinese buyers have in the first place, been the cause of housing unaffordability. As an Australian MP wisely observed, allowing anti-foreigner sentiment to fester has the potential to disintegrate social fabric.[116] Hansard from

113 Benedict Brook, 'Get Over It: Bob Carr's Advice to Prospective Homeowners Concerned about Chinese Buyers' (news.com.au, 5 July 2019) <www.news.com.au/finance/economy/get-over-it-bob-carrs-advice-to-prospective-homeowners-concerned-about-chinese-buyers/news-story/b9f053eb0bd99e20412a2b628133bb87> accessed 14 October 2019.

114 Alexis Carey, 'Fears One Million Aussie Homes Could Soon Be Owned by Foreign Buyers' (news.com.au, 16 February 2019) <www.news.com.au/finance/real-estate/buying/fears-one-million-aussie-homes-could-soon-be-owned-by-foreign-buyers/news-story/c50a4112bab4f3ed8fae27277f313f54> accessed 14 October 2019.

115 Brook, Get over it: Bob Carr's advice.

116 Jason Clare MP, *Ministerial Statements – Investment Statement* 2018 (Hansard, House of Representatives, 20 August 2018) <www.aph.gov.au/Parliamentary_Business/Hansard/Hansard_Display?bid=chamber/hansardr/66d5616d-41f7-432b-b370-a62012124e44/&sid=0194> accessed 14 October 2019.

Queensland records that the only purpose of the additional transfer tax on foreigners is to fund help-to-buy housing policies.[117] This is far healthier than politicians who permit, or worse, encourage unhealthy beliefs relating to Chinese buyers not positively borne out by the data.

117 Annastacia Palaszczuk, *Questions Without Notice* (Hansard, Queensland Parliamentary Debates) 3204 (31 August 2016) <www.parliament.qld.gov.au/documents/hansard/2016/2016_08_31_WEEKLY.pdf> accessed 14 October 2019.

# 5

# An Asian Approach to Mental Capacity for Wills and Lasting Powers

*Lusina Ho*[*]

## 1 INTRODUCTION

The populations in Hong Kong and Singapore are ageing rapidly; the cities' oldest baby boomers turned 75 in 2021.[1] Combined with increasingly complex family structures and considerable wealth accumulation over the last few decades of unprecedented economic growth, contests over wills and lasting powers of attorney ('LPAs')[2] are likely to become more common than ever in these two cities.

Currently, capacity tests with respect to wills and LPAs in these jurisdictions are based on the approach in England and Wales, where judges place increasing emphasis on the need to respect individual autonomy in capacity assessment.[3] It has been well established, following the stipulation in the Mental Capacity Act 2005 ('MCA'), that unwise decisions or decisions that conflict with conventional values are insufficient alone to establish the incapacity of the decision-maker.[4] However, there has been surprisingly little discussion of balancing autonomy with family protection in Hong Kong and Singapore courts. These two Asian jurisdictions present interesting case studies of how English legal rules, grounded in liberalism, have

[*] I am grateful to Mandy Choi, Jason Fee and Carl Tong for their research assistance. The research undertaken for this project was funded by the Research Grants Council of Hong Kong (Project Number 17614318).

[1] In 2018, people aged 65 or above accounted for 18 per cent of the Hong Kong population, compared with 8 per cent in 1988: K. Wong and M. Yeung, 'Population Trend of Hong Kong', Office of the Government Economist – Economic Letter 2019/02, 28 January 2019, p. 2. In 2019, people aged 65 or above accounted for 14 per cent of Singapore's population, compared with 6 per cent in 1990: Singapore Department of Statistics, *Key Indicators on the Elderly, Annual* (2020) <www.tablebuilder.singstat.gov.sg/publicfacing/createDataTable.action?refId=14914> accessed 30 April 2021.

[2] Currently, Hong Kong uses the term 'enduring powers of attorney', but it has introduced 'continuing powers of attorney'. Singapore uses the term 'lasting power of attorney'. For ease of reference, this chapter will use 'lasting powers of attorney' to refer to the durable powers in both jurisdictions.

[3] The United Kingdom and China (on behalf of Hong Kong) are signatories of the UN Convention on the Rights of People with Disability, 2006, 2515 UNTS 3. Article 12 of the Convention prohibits denying legal capacity based on a person's disability in decision-making. Singapore is not a signatory of the Convention.

[4] Mental Capacity Act 2005, s. 1(4).

been interpreted by judges in societies with values centred upon kinship ties and the family as a unit of care.[5] The succession context throws this issue into sharp relief, because succession law is closely linked to the cultural context in which it operates.

This chapter addresses the tension associated with applying English capacity law in the predominantly Chinese cultural contexts of Hong Kong and Singapore. Some judges in these Asian jurisdictions interpret even the most basic elements of the law to take into account the value of family protection. Some judges are committed to respecting the autonomous preferences of individuals in much the same way as their English counterparts. The tension in the courts' approach mirrors that in Hong Kong and Singaporean societies, where a predominantly Chinese culture is constantly evolving in response to western values. This chapter considers this tension with respect to wills and LPAs, arguing that respect for autonomy requires outcome-based considerations to be relevant only to demonstrate the coherence of the decision-making process.

The discussion proceeds as follows. Part 2 describes capacity tests in England and the approach adopted by English judges to reflect the value of autonomy. Using the English approach as a baseline, Part 3 compares the interpretation of these tests in Hong Kong and Singapore. With respect to wills, this comparison focuses on two core components in capacity assessment: (1) the allocation of the burden of proof and (2) the relevance of outcome (as reflected by the rationality of the will) in the evaluation of testamentary capacity. Part 4 turns attention to LPAs, which raise the additional concern of self-impoverishment, and examines the protective approach taken towards donors of LPAs in Singapore. Part 5 concludes by observing the practical constraints in placing responsibility on lawyers to examine the capacity of testators and donors of LPAs.

## 2 CAPACITY TESTS FOR WILLS AND LASTING POWERS: THE ENGLISH APPROACH

A natural starting point in examining the English approach to testing capacity for wills and LPAs is provided by *Banks* v. *Goodfellow*, which laid down the capacity test for wills, and in the MCA, which established the general test for capacity that is applicable to lasting powers.[6]

5 For discussion of the relevance of Confucian values in related contexts in Singapore law, see M. Chen-Wishart, 'Legal Transplant and Undue Influence: Lost in Translation or a Working misunderstanding?' (2013) 62 *International Comparative Law Quarterly* 1 (undue influence). Also see K. Low, 'Victoria Meets Confucius in Singapore' in Y. K. Liew and M. Harding (eds), *Asia-Pacific Trusts Law: Theory and Practice* (Hart Publishing, 2021), pp. 97–120; Chapter 7 (Yip and Tang); M. Yip, 'Comparing Family Property Disputes in English and Singapore Law: "Context Is Everything"' (2021) 41 *Legal Studies* <https://doi.org/10.1017/lst.2021.10> accessed 17 May 2021; T. E. Chan, 'Advance Care Planning: A Communitarian Approach' (2019) 26(4) *Journal of Law and Medicine* 896 (advance directives).

6 *Banks* v. *Goodfellow* (1870) LR 5 QB 549; Mental Capacity Act 2005. The MCA test is a general test which also applies to other context such as healthcare decision-making.

The burden of proof in relation to testamentary capacity was clarified by Briggs J (now Lord Briggs) in *Re Key (Deceased)*.[7] While the propounder of a will bears the burden of establishing testamentary capacity, if the will is duly executed and appears rational on its face, then the court presumes capacity.[8] The challenging party may adduce evidence to raise a real doubt as to capacity, and if a real doubt is raised, the evidential burden shifts to the propounder of the will to establish capacity.[9]

The capacity test defined in *Banks* v. *Goodfellow* comprises four limbs as follows:[10]

It is essential [...]

(1) that a deceased shall understand the nature of the act and its effects;[11]
(2) [that the deceased] shall understand the extent of the property of which he is disposing;
(3) [that the deceased] shall be able to comprehend and appreciate the claims to which he ought to give effect; and
(4) with a view to the latter object, that no disorder of the mind shall poison his affections, pervert his sense of right, or prevent the exercise of natural faculties – that no insane delusion shall influence his will in disposing of his property and bring about a disposal of it which, if the mind had been sound, would not have been made.

The MCA stipulates as its first key principle that a person is presumed to have capacity unless the contrary is established.[12] Although the MCA capacity test comprises two parts, a functional test and a diagnostic test, it does not differ significantly from the four-limbed test in *Banks*. The functional test states that a person lacks capacity if at the time of making the decision in question, he is unable to (a) understand, (b) retain, (c) use or weigh information relevant to that decision or (d) communicate it to others.[13] Relevant information includes not only the purpose and effect of the decision but also the reasonably foreseeable consequences of deciding one way or another or of making

[7] *Re Key (Deceased)* [2010] EWHC 408 (Ch), [2010] 1 WLR 2020, adopted most recently in *Clitheroe* v. *Bond* [2021] EWHC 1102 at [31].

[8] ibid at [97].

[9] *Symes* v. *Green* (1859) 1 Sw & Tr 401; *Sutton* v. *Sadler* (1857) 3 CBNS 87 at 98; *Cowderoy* v. *Cranfield* [2011] EWHC 1616 (Ch), [2011] WTLR 1699 at [133].

[10] *Banks* (1870) LR 5 QB 549 at 565. The test has been applied widely in the common law world. See, e.g. *Bailey* v. *Bailey* [1924] HCA 21 at 57 (Australia); *Drivas* v. *Jakopovic* [2019] NSWCA 218 (Australia); *Loosley* v. *Powell* [2018] NZCA 3(New Zealand); *Dujardin* v. *Dujardin* [2018] ONCA 597 at 423 DLR (4th) 731 (Canada).

[11] The phrase ‘shall understand’ refers to the capacity to understand: *Harwood* v. *Baker* (1840) 3 Moo PC 282 at 290; *Hoff* v. *Atherton* [2004] EWCA Civ 1554 at [34] (Peter Gibson LJ); applied in *Re Simon (Deceased)* [2014] EWCA Civ 280 at [40] (Lewison LJ).

[12] MCA, s. 1(2).

[13] MCA, s. 3(1). The functional test should be considered before the diagnostic test: *PC* v. *City of York Council* [2013] EWHC Civ 478, [2014] Fam 10 at [58]–[60]; *Kings College Hospital NHS Foundation Trust* v. *C* [2015] EWCOP 80, [2016] COPLR 50 at [33], [71], [93].

no decision at all.[14] The diagnostic test stipulates that the inability to make the decision is caused by a permanent or temporary impairment of the mind or brain.[15]

The *Banks* and MCA tests reflect the value of autonomy, both in principle and practically. In terms of principle, these tests require the ability to conduct a thought process from the assessment of evidence to the possible outcomes of decisions and the ability to weigh the consequences of alternative courses of action. The tests thus focus exclusively on the functional aspect of the decision-making process, and may be satisfied irrespective of the outcome of that process. Both tests emphasise that a decision is not to be treated as having been made without capacity merely because it is unwise or improvident.[16] If these principles are strictly adhered to, the outcome of a decision or rationality of a will is only relevant as *evidence* to demonstrate a lack of basic coherence in the decision-making process. An example of this would be to show that a decision-maker did not desire the consequences of a course of action but still chose to perform it over a course of action that would have produced the outcome he or she desired.

At a practical level, many examples exist in the healthcare context wherein the MCA test is satisfied despite the outcome being undesirable. For example, a socialite who rejected life-saving treatment for kidney failure because she chose not to become dependent or impoverished was held to have capacity to make such a choice,[17] as was a patient with paranoid schizophrenia who refused to have her gangrenous leg amputated.[18]

The MCA test of capacity is applicable to LPAs. In *re Collis*, Senior Judge Lush held that to have capacity, a donor must be able to understand the effect of the lasting power, which gives a person (in this case, an attorney) complete authority over the donor's property, as if they were the owner.[19] Furthermore, the donor must be aware of the foreseeable consequences of not executing an LPA.[20] As LPAs must be created with independent certification of capacity, there are very few legal disputes involving capacity requirements for an LPA.[21] Rather, the MCA provides

14 MCA s. 3(4); *B* v. *A Local Authority* [2019] EWCA Civ 913, [2020] Fam 105 at [9]–[10].

15 MCA, s. 2(1).

16 MCA, s. 1, third and fourth principles; MCA Code of Practice, [2.10]–[2.11]. A similar view has been expressed in relation to wills ('a testator is permitted to be capricious and improvident'): *Bird* v. *Luckie* (1850) 8 Hare 301 at 306. See also *Clitheroe* [2021] EWHC 1102 at [73], in which Falk J observed that an irrational will 'may be relevant to the enquiry of the testator's soundness of mind. It is not itself a reason to treat a will as invalid'.

17 Kings College Hospital NHS Foundation Trust [2016] COPLR 50.

18 *Heart of England NHS Foundation Trust* v. *JB* [2014] EWHC 342 (COP). See also *In Re SB (A Patient: Capacity to Consent to Termination)* [2013] EWHC 1417 (COP), [2013] 3 FCR 384 at [44]; *In Re C* (Adult: Refusal of Medical Treatment) [1994] 1 WLR 290, [1994] 1 All ER 819; *Re B (Adult: Refusal of Medical Treatment)* [2002] EWHC 429 (Fam), [2002] 2 All ER 449.

19 *In the Matter of Collis*, 27 October 2010, discussed in D. Lush and C. Bielanski, *Cretney and Lush on Lasting and Enduring Powers of Attorney*, 8th edn (LexisNexis, 2017), [3.41].

20 MCA, s. 3(4).

21 MCA, sch 1, para. 2(e)(i), discussed in Lush and Bielanski, Cretney and Lush, [6.2]–[6.6].

a remedial mechanism whereby the court may revoke LPAs obtained by fraud or undue influence, as well as those where donees contravene their authority.[22] Such an intervention may only take place if the donor lacks the capacity to revoke the LPA concerned, a standard that reflects the importance of donor autonomy.[23]

Turning to the context of testamentary capacity, judges have shown commitment to the value of autonomy by downplaying requirements that may interfere with the functional approach to capacity. One example is the requirement that a will be rational on its face before the court will presume capacity.[24] If judges interpret this requirement by reference to the will's conformity with conventional values, testamentary freedom will be curtailed.

Earlier authorities' discussion of the requirement of rationality is highly confusing due to imprecise judicial language. Often, judges attached the label of rationality to wills that appeared to them 'proper and natural', without clarifying the criteria used to reach this conclusion.[25] For example, in *Banks* v. *Goodfellow*, Cockburn CJ contrasted a rational will with one that was inofficious, 'in which natural affection and the ties of near relationship have been disregarded'.[26] With these references, Cockburn CJ provided precedence to support determining as irrational wills that disinherit children or spouses in contravention of social mores.

Fortunately, in the last few decades, English judges have exercised constraint in imposing their own values or traditional values and have instead required a high degree of irrationality to deny the presumption of capacity. They have strived to interpret 'irrationality on the face of the will' as referring to extreme cases where the will manifests such inconsistency with long-held beliefs of the deceased as to indicate the absence of a sound and disposing mind.[27] Mummery LJ in *Re Burgess's Estate* aptly described the terms of such a will as 'irrational and inexplicable'.[28] In line with this approach, it has been held that it is not irrational on the face of the

22 MCA, s. 22(3).

23 MCA, s. 22(4). See *SAD, ACD* v. *SED* [2017] EWCOP 3, [2017] WTLR 1439.

24 *Symes* (1859) 1 Sw & Tr 401; *Sutton* (1857) 3 CBNS 87 at 98.

25 *Cartwright* v. *Cartwright* (1793) 1 Phill Ecc 90 at 91, (1793) 161 ER 923 at 924: 'I think it clearly appears the will is as proper and natural as [the testatrix] could have made, and it is likewise as conformable to her affections at the time'.

26 *Banks* (1870) LR 5 QB 549 at 570 (Cockburn CJ); J. Brook, '*Banks* v. *Goodfellow* (1870): Defining Testamentary Capacity', in B. Sloan (ed), *Landmark Cases in Succession Law* (Hart Publishing, 2019), pp. 60–61.

27 J. Brook, 'The Neighbour, the Carer and the Old Friend – The Complex World of Testamentary Capacity' in H. Conway and R. Hickey (eds), *Modern Studies in Property Law*, vol 9 (Hart Publishing, 2017), pp. 123–124. For cynical views, see K. Schulman et al, '*Banks* v. *Goodfellow* (1870): Time to Update the Test for Testamentary Capacity' (2017) 95 *Canadian Bar Review* 251, 257–258.

28 *In Re Burgess's Estate* [2013] EWCA Civ 94, [2013] WTLR 453 at [57] (Mummery LJ); cited in *Re the Estate of Beryl Parsonage (deceased)* [2019] EWHC 2362 (Ch), [2019] 9 WLUK 75 at [27]; *Todd* v. *Parson* [2019] EWHC 3366 (Ch), [2020] WTLR 305 at [138]. See also J. R. Martyn and N. Caddick, *Williams, Mortimer and Sunnucks on Executors, Administrators and Probate*, 21st edn (Sweet & Maxwell, 2018), 10–26: describing an irrational will as one that is 'incoherent, irrational or strange'.

will to benefit only two of five children,[29] to make a gift of £600 to two daughters but leave the rest of a substantial estate to a son,[30] or to leave a harp to a son and leave the rest of the estate to a daughter and a grandchild by the son.[31] In contrast, a will that left the entire estate to two employees to the exclusion of the deceased's daughters was deemed 'very surprising' and a bequest that 'no reasonable deceased would do'.[32]

Given this high threshold for irrationality, the requirement of rationality on the face of the will is easily satisfied and seldom warrants detailed discussion in judicial decisions.[33] Where the issue has been discussed, the judgments reflect conscious deference to testamentary autonomy. For example, judges who have held that a will was rational on its face have typically said that it was 'not irrational',[34] not concerning themselves with identifying a good reason for the disposition, but merely stating that there is an understandable reason for it.

In *Schrader* v. *Schrader*, Mann J further reduced the circumstances in which courts may substitute the moral values of the deceased through the requirement of rationality.[35] His Lordship held that the requirement simply meant that a will was grammatical, made legal sense, and contained no inconsistency in its terms.[36] He distinguished rationality of the will *on its face*, which is determined by considering the terms of the will alone, from rationality *in its context*, which may be evidenced by the deceased's failure to provide a reason for disinheriting a potential heir.[37] If adopted, Mann J's narrow interpretation of 'rationality on its face', significantly reduces the hurdles to obtaining a presumption of testamentary capacity.

Even if the presumption of capacity is triggered, this is but a starting point that alleviates the need for the propounder of a will to adduce evidence of capacity in the application for probate. If the contestant of the will disputes testamentary capacity and raises an issue with the court, the court will assess the totality of the evidence to determine whether testamentary capacity still exists. In doing so, the court may take into account the rationality of the will (in its context).[38]

To prevent consideration of rationality from becoming a tool to displace the autonomous preferences of the deceased, the courts do not treat rationality as a

29 *Ledger* v. *Wootton* [2007] EWHC 2599 (Ch), [2008] WTLR 235.

30 *Re the Estate of Maudlin Bascoe (deceased)* [2019] EWHC 3344 (Ch), [2020] WTLR 67.

31 *Re Hayward (deceased)* [2016] EWHC 3199 (Ch), [2017] 4 WLR 32.

32 *Sharp* v. *Adams* [2006] EWCA Civ 449 at [64].

33 In most cases where the issue is mentioned, the discussion takes up no more than one paragraph, often just one sentence, in the whole judgment: *Goss-Custard* v. *Templeman* [2018] EWHC 2476 (Ch), [2018] WTLR 893 at [113], [117]; *Re the Estate of Maudlin Bascoe (deceased)* [2019] EWHC 3344 (Ch) at [97]; *Re Hayward* [2016] EWHC 3199 (Ch) at [127]; *Ledger* [2007] EWHC 2599 (Ch) at [6]; *Markou* v. *Goodwin* [2013] EWHC 4570 (Ch), [2014] WTLR 605 at [26], [45].

34 *Goss-Custard* [2018] WTLR 893 at [117]; *Markou* [2014] WTLR 605 at [45]; *Ledger* [2008] WTLR 235 at [6].

35 *Schrader* v. *Schrader* [2013] EWHC 466.

36 ibid at [76].

37 *Schrader* [2013] EWHC 466 at [77].

38 ibid at [78].

requirement over and above the capacity test, but instead as evidence pertaining to the third limb of the *Banks* test, namely the ability to appreciate the claims of potential heirs.[39] For example, an understandable reason for disinheriting potential heirs may be presented to demonstrate that the deceased was aware of their claims and thus was not lacking capacity.[40]

This brief survey shows not only that the *Banks* and MCA tests are grounded on the value of autonomy but also that English judges would resolve the ambiguity in these tests in line with this value. The judges' commitment to a functional, as opposed to outcome-based, assessment of capacity demonstrates respect for an individual's autonomy to make decisions that judges may disagree with.

## 3 AN ASIAN APPROACH TO TESTAMENTARY CAPACITY

Due to their common lineage as former British colonies, Hong Kong and Singapore apply testamentary capacity law first developed in Victorian England. This part considers how Hong Kong and Singapore courts accommodate Chinese values within the English rules with respect to (1) the triggering of the presumption of testamentary capacity and (2) the relevance of the outcome or rationality of the will in assessing capacity.

### 3.1 *Triggering the Presumption of Capacity: Rationality on the Face of the Will*

Although capacity disputes seldom hinge on the presumption of testamentary capacity, affirmation of such a presumption nonetheless reflects a significant commitment to the value of autonomy. The approach in Hong Kong adheres less to this principle than that in England and Singapore, where there is clear affirmation of such a presumption, even if the presumption is not automatic and arises only if the will is duly executed and rational on its face.[41]

The position of Hong Kong courts is more ambivalent: the presumption of testamentary capacity has only been endorsed in certain first instance decisions, all of which were decided by deputy judges.[42] The majority of decisions on testamentary

39 *Edkins* v. *Hopkins & Ors* [2016] EWHC 2542 (Ch), [2017] WTLR 39 at [49].

40 ibid.

41 For Singapore, see *George Abraham Vadakathu* v. *Jacob George* [2009] SGHC 79, [2009] 3 SLR(R) 631 at [33]; *Chee Mu Lin Muriel* v. *Chee Ka Lin Caroline* [2010] SGCA 27, [2010] 4 SLR 373 at [40]; *Ng Bee Keong* v. *Ng Choon Huay* [2013] SGHC 107 at [50]; *Soong Ah Kiow* v. *Yvonne Markham* [2014] SGDC 319 at [23]; *Lian Kok Hong* v. *Lian Bee Leng* [2015] SGHC 205 at [40], [42], [54]–[72], overruled on other grounds in [2016] SGCA 24, [2016] 3 SLR 405 (CA); *ULV* v. *ULW* [2019] SGHCF 2, [2019] 3 SLR 1270 at [26]; *UWF* v. *UWH* [2020] SGHCF 22 at [217].

42 *Chan Tin Lam* v. *Chan Lai Chun* [2000] HKCFI 130, [2000] HKCU 785; *Lau Chi Ying* v. *Lau Wai Keung* [2011] HKCFI 1927, [2012] HKCU 27 at [127] (DHCJ Au-Yeung); *In Re the Estate of Kwok Sze* [2014] HKCFI 961, [2014] HKCU 1287; *In Re the Estate of Wong Yin Sheung* [2014] HKCFI 1172, [2014] 4 HKLRD 685. The issue of testamentary freedom is also raised in the related context of statutory family provisions, for which see Chapter 6 (Lee).

capacity in Hong Kong recite the general principle laid down by Ribeiro PJ in *Nina Kung* v. *Wong Din Shin*, which makes no mention of the presumption of capacity.[43] In this case, Ribeiro PJ held that the persuasive burden is on the party propounding a will to prove that the will was duly executed and the decedent was of *testamentary* capacity.[44] As testamentary capacity was not disputed in the *Nina Kung* case, it was not necessary for the court to indicate whether and when it would presume testamentary capacity. However, the judge's silence on the point should not be interpreted as a rejection of the availability of the presumption.

A better approach, found in first instance decisions by deputy judges mentioned above, is to recognise the presumption of testamentary capacity with respect to wills that are duly executed and rational on their face.[45] This principle and its moral justification in the value of autonomy were clearly articulated by Deputy High Court Judge Yee in *In Re the Estate of Kwok Sze*,[46] who remarked that 'the starting point [in assessing capacity] should be the freedom of testamentary dispositions'.[47] The judge's decision was affirmed by the Court of Appeal.[48]

### 3.2 *Rationality as Reasonableness versus Rationality as Lack of Unreasonableness*

Singapore courts embrace the presumption of testamentary capacity mentioned above; however, it is unclear if they define 'irrationality on the face of the will' by the same standard as English courts. Singaporean judges have not yet adopted Mann J's approach in *Schrader* v. *Schrader* (checking only that the will was grammatical, made legal sense and contained no inconsistency in its terms).[49] In earlier landmark decisions,[50] Singapore courts might have drawn on their own moral values more than English judges do. However, Singapore's courts have shown an increasing tendency to align with the English approach and respect the autonomic choices of the deceased.

Singapore courts do not interpret rationality narrowly as Mann J did. For example, in the landmark case of *Chee Mu Lin Muriel* v. *Chee Ka Lin Caroline*, Chan CJ observed that '[a]n indication of testamentary capacity would be the rationality of the will having regard to its terms *and the identities of the beneficiaries*'.[51] Other

43 *Nina Kung* v. *Wong Din Shin* [2005] HKCFA 54, (2005) 8 HKCFAR 387.

44 ibid at [173], citing *Barry* v. *Butlin* (1838) 2 Moo PC 480, 12 ER 1089 at [176]. Applied in *In Re the Estate of Au Kong Tim* [2018] HKCA 210, [2018] 2 HKLRD 864 (CA) at [45]; *In Re Chiu Yau Chuen* [2012] HKCFI 82, [2012] HKCU 220 (CFI) at [48]–[49]; [2013] HKCA 293, [2013] HKCU 1395 (CA).

45 See cases referred to at footnote 42.

46 *In Re the Estate of Kwok Sze* [2014] HKCFI 961 at [39], [176].

47 ibid at [35].

48 See generally *In Re the Estate of Kwok Sze* [2015] HKCA 157.

49 *Schrader* [2013] EWHC 466.

50 *George Abraham* [2009] SGHC 79; *Chee* [2010] SGCA 27.

51 *Chee* [2010] SGCA 27, [2020] 4 SLR 373 at [40] (emphasis added).

courts in Singapore also tend to examine the deceased's reasons for choosing certain beneficiaries and cutting out potential claimants from inheritance, whereas Mann J would consider these matters as falling within rationality in the context of the will.[52]

Singapore's approach provides an interesting contrast to the explicit endorsement of *Schrader* v. *Schrader* by the Hong Kong Court of First Instance in the case *In Re Kwok Sze*. Here, DHCJ Yee endorsed counsel's submission, based on *In Re Key (Deceased)*, that:[53]

> rationality required of by the presumption is internal in nature. So long as there is no internal inconsistency within the will, the rebuttable presumption of testamentary competency is triggered.

That being said, other decisions in Hong Kong have paid little attention to this point or the possibility of applying a presumption of testamentary capacity.

As a general principle, the legal requirement of rationality is a matter of degree. The higher the threshold for rationality required, the smaller the scope of the presumption of testamentary capacity. The modern English approach requires a high degree of irrationality to disprove capacity, namely a will that is so strange or inexplicable that no reasonable person would have made it. Because higher courts in Hong Kong have not explicitly recognised the presumption of testamentary capacity, there is limited discussion in Hong Kong jurisprudence about the requisite threshold for rationality on the face of the will. In a notable exception, *In Re Kwok Sze*, DHCJ Yee made observations that closely reflect the English approach:[54]

> A deceased may disinherit either wholly or partially, his children, and leave his property to strangers to gratify his spite, or to charities to gratify his pride, and the court must give effect to his testamentary dispositions however much the course he has pursued is condemnable, so long as he has the requisite testamentary capacity. In short, the court is not required to carry out an objective assessment of the fairness and/or reasonableness of his testamentary dispositions.

In contrast to the Hong Kong approach, landmark cases in Singapore have yet to explicitly embrace the English approach in full. The traditional understanding of rationality stated in *Banks* v. *Goodfellow* was reiterated in the landmark cases of *George Abraham* v. *Jacob George* and *Chee Mu Lin Muriel* v. *Chee Ka Lin Caroline*, both of which were decided by Chan CJ.[55] In *George Abraham*, George George ('GG') executed a will to leave his entire estate to his nephew and nieces, omitting his younger brother, who challenged the will. As GG had been suffering from

[52] Ng [2013] SGHC 107 at [109]–[119]; *Lian* [2015] SGHC 205 at [54]–[68]; *UWF* [2020] SGHCF 22 at [217]–[218]. Cf *Schrader* [2013] EWHC 466.

[53] *In Re Kwok Sze* [2014] HKCFI 961 at [176].

[54] ibid at [45]. See also Martyn and Caddick, *Williams, Mortimer and Sunnucks on Executors, Administrators and Probate*, 10-03.

[55] *George Abraham* [2009] SGHC 79.

schizophrenia since he was 18 years old (he made his will at approximately 60 years of age), the High Court relied heavily on *Banks* v. *Goodfellow*, in which the deceased had been suffering from delusions for many years. After citing passages from *Banks*,[56] the court observed:[57]

> The rationality of a will has a significant bearing on the deceased's rationality, and is a sound indication of testamentary capacity. In *Banks* [...], **the courts took into account the 'inofficiousness' of the will as indicating a lack of testamentary capacity**. In my view, just as an inofficious will is some evidence of an irrational deceased, a rational will is some evidence of a rational deceased.

The court proceeded to hold that the will was not inofficious, but 'rational and something that was naturally expected', noting that as a brother, 'GG was under no familial or moral duty to give anything to the [younger brother]' and that he had detested the younger brother but been fond of his nephews and nieces.[58]

The court's reasoning in *George Abraham* is illustrative of both the importance and the ambiguity of rationality. The court not only attached significant evidential weight to the rationality of the will but also considered the rational content of the will as directly reflecting the rationality of the deceased. Relying heavily on earlier English authorities such as *Banks*, the court replicated the ambiguous language used in those cases. For example, it did not clarify whether rationality was determined by GG's natural affection or binding familial duties, citing both in holding that GG's will was rational.

It was against the background of this case that *Ng Bee Keong* v. *Ng Choon Huay* clarified that rationality refers to the deceased's natural affection rather than his moral duties, a significant milestone in Singapore law defining rationality.[59] After quoting *George Abraham*, Ang J added:[60]

> Whether the deceased disregarded natural affection and claims of near relationship is a question of fact rather than of biological ties.

The judge held that a will that solely benefited the executor's nephew, to the exclusion of the deceased's wife and siblings, was rational. In assessing rationality, Ang J considered the deceased's emotional rather than biological ties with the potential claimants and held that given the deceased's close relationship with the nephew, his estrangement from his wife soon after the marriage and his annoyance with his sister and her family for repeated requests for financial help, 'it is unlikely that the deceased felt any moral obligation to make provision for his relatives except the [nephew]'.[61]

[56] ibid at [61].
[57] ibid at [67] (emphasis in the original); see also [32](d).
[58] ibid at [67].
[59] Ng [2013] SGHC 107.
[60] ibid at [50].
[61] Ng [2013] SGHC 107 at [50].

A further step in enhancing the value of autonomy in the courts was made in *Lian Kok Hong* v. *Lian Bee Leng*, where Prakash J adopted counsel's submission that an enquiry about rationality should focus on whether the terms of the will are 'so odd or inexplicable that it should cast doubt on the testamentary capacity of the deceased'.[62] Such an interpretation aligns with English law at the doctrinal level.

In *Lian Kok Hong* v. *Lian Bee Leng*, the only son of the deceased sought to propound a secret handwritten will made by the deceased a few months before he passed away. The will provided for the sale of the family house after the testator's and his wife's passing and donation of the proceeds to various charities in China. The house was a substantial part of his S$7 million estate. The son's application was opposed by his sister and niece, with whom his mother sided. Prakash J rebutted all of the sister's arguments that the will was irrational on its face, noting that although the deceased had not previously donated large sums to Chinese charities, it was not irrational for him to do so in a will when he was free from any concern about his own needs.[63] That the will failed to provide for the deceased's wife was also deemed not irrational, as the will implicitly allowed her to stay in the family house during her lifetime.[64] The judge's separate finding that the deceased lacked both knowledge and approval of the will was overturned by the Court of Appeal, and thus the will was ultimately held to be valid.[65] As the will made no provision about the residuary estate, the deceased's wife and daughter were able to inherit the residuary estate through intestacy rules.

The approach in *Lian Kok Hong* v. *Lian Bee Leng* was reinforced in the recent decision of *UWF* v. *UWH*, in which Judicial Commissioner Tan of the Singapore High Court (Family Division) emphasised that 'the court must be mindful not to displace [the deceased's] subjective preferences, especially when the Will is rational on its face'.[66] The court thus held as rational a will that made a pecuniary gift to the son with whom the deceased mother was not on good terms, with the rest of the estate divided to give each of her other three sons equal shares and her daughter half of the amount that the sons received, due to the mother's traditional Chinese belief that daughters should inherit less.[67]

These three recent decisions, *Ng Bee Keong* v. *Ng Choon Huay*, *Lian Kok Hong* v. *Lian Bee Leng*, and *UWF* v. *UWH*, affirmed the validity of wills that are rational, just as the court did in *George Abraham*. However, the rhetoric used by the judges in these three decisions represent a significant milestone in the development of the notion of rationality on the face of the will in Singaporean jurisprudence. They

62 *Lian* [2015] SGHC 205 at [54].
63 ibid at [57]–[58].
64 ibid at [65]. The judge found that the deceased lacked knowledge and approval of the will, but this finding was overturned by the Court of Appeal and thus the will was held valid.
65 *Lian* [2016] 3 SLR 405 (CA) at [71]–[78].
66 *UWF* [2020] SGHCF 22.
67 ibid at [218].

have steered the law away from the potentially interventionist approach in *George Abraham* and *Chee* v. *Chee*, by emphasising that the court is concerned with the *fact* of the deceased's emotional attachment and his or her own perception of moral duties, and recognising that a will is considered irrational only when it is so odd as to suggest a lack of testamentary capacity.

### 3.3 *Irrationality as Evidence of Incapacity*

When the contestant of a will adduces evidence to show incapacity, the court's task is to assess the totality of the evidence to determine whether there was testamentary capacity. English law recognises the irrationality of the will as a part of the totality of the evidence. However, rationality is not an additional condition to the *Banks* capacity test. Nor is it sufficient, when trying to establish that a will is not rational, to show that it is not fair or unreasonable. Only the extreme case of irrationality will amount to evidence that the deceased's decision-making power was affected by delusional beliefs or an inability to appreciate and weigh the claims of his or her natural heirs. The following subsections analyse the divergent approaches in Hong Kong and Singapore in relation to the evidential role of the rationality of the will as evidence of capacity.

#### 3.3.1 Hong Kong

At first sight, Hong Kong law on testamentary capacity appears to be the same as English law, as courts in Hong Kong have expressly adopted the *Banks* test.[68] However, whilst the majority of Hong Kong decisions follow the English approach closely, a recent decision interpreted the basic elements of this test in a markedly different manner.

The majority approach, emphasising the importance of autonomy, is exemplified in a number of decisions. In *In Re Chiu Yau Chuen*, a taxi mogul with sixteen children drafted a will that expressly disinherited nine of them (born to his ex-wife) and made no provisions for the others, naming his mistress as the sole beneficiary.[69] The will was a departure from his previous will, which had left the estate to all of his children born at the time of the will. Some of the disinherited children relied on the irrationality of the last will as 'the principal factor' to dispute the deceased's testamentary capacity.[70] This argument was rejected by Poon J at first instance, who observed that the terms of the last will were explicable both by the deceased's estrangement from

68 *In Re Au Kong Tim* [2017] HKCFI 1182, [2017] 4 HKLRD 284 (CFI), affirmed by the CA: [2018] 2 HKLRD 864 (CA); *In Re Chiu Yau Chuen* [2012] HKCFI 82; *In Re Lam Chok Wai* [2020] HKCFI 3047, [2020] HKCU 4328.

69 *Re Chiu Yau Chuen* [2012] HKCFI 82; for a similar approach, see *Re Wong Yin Sheung* [2014] HKCFI 1172 at [206].

70 *Re Chiu Yau Chuen* [2012] HKCFI 82 at [71].

his family due to some unhappy incidents and by the deceased's personal tendency to act in an unfair or disproportionate manner.[71] The court laid down the principles applied in the ruling: first, irrationality is only one of many factors used to assess testamentary capacity.[72] Second, if the irrationality is due to an unsound mind, such a mind usually exhibits signs and symptoms of cognitive impairment. Thus, in the absence of such symptoms, irrationality can only support an inference of incapacity in exceptional circumstances.[73] Poon J's decision was affirmed on appeal.[74]

Poon J's observations were endorsed in *In Re Kwok Sze*,[75] in which the lower and upper courts both rejected counsel's 'simplistic' assertion that it had been irrational and out of character for the deceased, a traditional Chinese man, to leave the whole of his estate to grandchildren who did not carry his surname. At first instance, DHCJ Yee held that the deceased had his own reasons to do so, as he was closest to the grandson who had returned from the United Kingdom to take care of him.[76]

Another decision arguably exhibiting the same approach, although articulated less explicitly, is the Hong Kong Court of Appeal's decision in *In Re Au Kong Tim*.[77] The dispute involved a will written by the deceased in 2008 whilst in hospital. The testator was so frail that when he signed the document, his elder son, a beneficiary of the will, had to 'support' his hand. The solicitors who prepared the will had been hired by the son and had never met the deceased prior to the day the will was executed. The will gave the estate to his two sons in equal shares (omitting his daughter) and replaced an earlier will that had omitted the sons and given the estate to the deceased's grandchildren (two from the elder son and four from the younger son), including his granddaughters, in equal shares.

At first instance, Chow J applied *Banks* v. *Goodfellow*. However, instead of applying the three limbs[78] of the *Banks* capacity test, he assessed the totality of the evidence and placed great weight on the testimonies of the solicitor and trainee solicitor that there was capacity. He also singled out rationality of the will as 'an important factor or indicator of testamentary capacity'.[79] It is not clear whether this was intended to give additional evidential weight to the rationality of the will, thus departing from *In Re Chiu Yau Chuen*. The judge held that it was rational for the 2008 will to leave

71 ibid at [181], [217].

72 ibid at [80].

73 ibid at [81], citing *Boughton* v. *Knight* (1873) LR 3 P & D 64 at 69.

74 *Re Chiu Yau Chuen* [2013] HKCU 1395 (CA).

75 *In Re Kwok Sze* [2014] HKCFI 961 affirmed in [2015] HKCA 157 at [74].

76 ibid at [187], [190], endorsed by the Court of Appeal, ibid at [74].

77 *Re Au Kong Tim* [2017] HKCFI 1182; [2018] 2 HKLRD 864 (CA); [2018] HKCFA 61, [2018] HKCU 4382 (CFA) (leave to appeal against the CA decision refused).

78 Hong Kong courts have treated *Banks* v. *Goodfellow* as comprising three limbs, and appeared to treat the fourth limb, regarding potential 'disorder of the mind', as part of the evidence to establish any or all of the first three limbs.

79 *In Re Au Kong Tim* [2017] HKCFI 1182 at [47]. See also *In Re Lau Heung* [2018] HKCFI 121, [2018] HKCU 297 at [68](4) (Chow J).

his daughter out of the will, as this was consistent with the deceased's long-held preference for male descendants.[80] Chow J's decision was overturned by the Court of Appeal for not having specifically examined each of the three limbs of the *Banks* test, thus leaving gaps in the evidence as to whether the second and third limbs, regarding appreciation of the estate and comprehension of claims, were satisfied.[81] The Court of Appeal did not provide any specific comment on the evidential role of rationality, let alone the degree of irrationality required to demonstrate lack of capacity.

In contrast, the Court of First Instance, in deciding *In Re Lam Chok Wai*, was quick to assume that the deceased had acted irrationally in failing to provide for the legal and moral claims of his divorced wife and children.[82] In this case, the owner of a successful electrical appliance retail chain, Tai Lin, had made three wills. The first will was made in favour of his wife and two sons born to her. The other two wills left his entire estate to Madam Tam, with whom he had had an affair that led to the end of his marriage. The estranged family challenged the deceased's capacity to make the last two wills.

The dispute centred on the second will, which was executed at a solicitors' office a few months after the deceased had suffered a second stroke, close to his 54th birthday. After evaluating the evidence of the solicitor and medical experts, Chan J held that the deceased did not have capacity to make this will. The court applied the *Banks* test but interpreted the basic elements of the *Banks* test in a dramatically different way from that suggested by Cockburn CJ in *Banks* v. *Goodfellow*. For example, Cockburn CJ intended the first limb of the test to mean that the deceased understands both 'the nature of the business he is engaged' in and that is he or she is expressing his or her wishes for gifts to be made on his or her death.[83] Chan J, however, interpreted the same criterion to mean that the deceased understood that the will would 'deprive the plaintiffs of their *moral* entitlement under the [previous] will' and deprive the '*moral* claims' of all of his children.[84] The same observations were reiterated in relation to the third limb, whereby the judge emphasised:[85]

> Comprehending and appreciating the legal and moral claims of these claimant would *render it necessary* for these claimants to be specifically catered for.

The court held that the will was 'irrational having regard to the various legal and moral claims to which the deceased ought to give effect' given that the deceased was a responsible person who ensured his children were properly educated.[86]

[80] *In Re Au Kong Tim* [2017] HKCFI 1182 at [73].
[81] *In Re Au Kong Tim* [2018] 2 HKLRD 864 (CA).
[82] *Re Lam Chok Wai* [2020] HKCFI 3047.
[83] *Banks* (1870) LR 5 QB 549 at 565–567; B. Sloan, *Borkowski's Law of Succession*, 3rd edn (Oxford University Press, 2002), pp. 71–72.
[84] *Re Lam Chok Wai* [2020] HKCFI 3047 at [132].
[85] ibid at [139] (emphasis added).
[86] ibid at [141].

The decision likely produced a fair result, as it transpired that Madam Tam had not looked after the deceased after the second will was made. The deceased had been left to live the last few years of his life alone in Shenzhen, at times in a factory dormitory. Furthermore, Madam Tam's brother had kept the deceased's travel documents and prevented his estranged family from gaining access to him. The deceased had died of sepsis, with multiple bed sores, in a home for older people, indicating a serious lack of care. That being said, the court's reasoning as to the role and meaning of rationality is remarkable for three reasons. First, as explained above, Chan J's interpretation of the first limb of the *Banks* test was much more stringent than that intended by Cockburn CJ himself. Second, under English law, the third limb of the *Banks* test, regarding the deceased's ability to appreciate the moral claims of others, does not state that such claims must be catered to. Yet Chan J opined that appreciating the claims would 'render it necessary' for the deceased to cater to them. Third, whilst it would be rational for the deceased, who was responsible and cared about his children's education, to provide for them in a will, it would also be rational for him to disinherit his estranged wife and her grown children, who were in their early 20s. Given his close relationship with Madam Tam at the time the will was executed, it is equally plausible that he wished to provide for her and, through her, their young children. Ultimately, it was not for the court to determine whether the will was rational in the sense of being fair and reasonable, and rationality has never been a condition of validity. Instead, the court should have asked whether the will was so irrational that it provided cogent evidence of the deceased's incapacity. One only hopes that *Re Lam Chok Wai* is an outlier and the decision is confined to the unique facts of that case.

### 3.3.2 Singapore

Whilst the court in *George Abraham* appeared to attach considerable weight to the rationality of the will, recent decisions in Singapore tend to focus on medical or other factual evidence about the functional abilities of the deceased. This approach aligns better with the functional test of capacity.

In *George Abraham*, the Singapore Court of Appeal emphasised that assessment of capacity is a judicial function and that the court must decide the issues of fact after taking into account medical and factual evidence.[87] The court singled out the rationality of the will as a piece of evidence in this overall assessment. On the facts, the court observed that it need not accept the medical expert's opinion that

[87] *George Abraham* [2009] SGHC 22 at [66]. See also *Chee* [2010] SGCA 27 at [40]. For a similar approach in relation to the MCA test, see *Re BKR* [2015] SGCA 26, [2015] 4 SLR 81 at [134]–[135], where the court observed that whilst experts are better placed to answer the diagnostic question of whether an individual suffers from a mental impairment, it is the court's role to answer the functional question.

the deceased lacked capacity, as this opinion was not supported by the objective evidence of the testator's being in remission from schizophrenia. It held that the lower court had been overly deferential to the expert, and 'should have given more weight to the non-medical evidence. One such piece of evidence is the rationality of the Will itself'.[88] The court overturned the lower court's decision on the basis that it had ignored this 'rather commonsensical view'.[89]

Recent cases addressing capacity in Singapore have typically reached conclusions based on the totality of the evidence, in particular, medical and other factual evidence about the deceased's functional abilities, rather than outcome-based considerations such as the rationality of the will.[90] That being said, the courts' rulings on capacity typically correlate with their views on the rationality of the will. For example, in *Ng Bee Keong* v. *Ng Choon Huay*, the deceased was determined to make a will that disinherited his estranged wife and a sibling, and he did so in the hospital shortly before he died.[91] Even though the deceased's lawyer failed to ask specific questions to ascertain his ability to appreciate the claims of his natural heirs (the third limb of the *Banks* test), the court inferred from his furious reaction to his estranged wife's intended visit that he had an understanding of the people who would have natural claims to his estate.[92]

In *Lian Kok Hong* v. *Lian Bee Leng*, the deceased made great efforts to draft a will without his wife's knowledge, with the aim to donate his estate to charities in China.[93] He wrote many drafts and sought his son's assistance to execute his will. After holding that the will was rational on its face and therefore that capacity was presumed, Prakash J examined contrary medical evidence of the deceased's low oxygen saturation and held that his ailments did not amount to any mental impairment that would rebut the presumption.[94]

Finally, in the most recent decision of *UWF* v. *UWH*, the testator had suffered bipolar disorder for some 20 years when she executed the contested will, which provided uneven gifts to her children.[95] The court closely examined the medical evidence and determined that her illness had been in remission when she had written the will and that she had not held any irrational beliefs regarding the son who received the smallest gift. The court held, based on the facts, that the will was rational in light of her relationships with the respective beneficiaries.[96]

88 *George Abraham* [2009] SGHC 22 at [66].

89 ibid at [69].

90 *Ng* [2013] SGHC 107 at [100]–[119]; *Lian* [2015] SGHC 107 (HC) at [53], [73]–[85]; *UWF* [2020] SGHCF 22 at [146]–[210], [216]–[219].

91 *Ng* [2013] SGHC 107 at [27]–[33].

92 ibid at [132]–[133], [136].

93 *Lian* [2015] SGHC 205 (HC) at [84]; [2016] 3 SLR 405 (CA) at [28], [35].

94 *Lian* [2015] SGHC 205 (HC) at [72]–[85].

95 *UWF* [2020] SGHCF 22 at [1]–[3], [62]–[70].

96 ibid at [154]–[210], [216]–[218].

Clearly, the courts in Hong Kong and Singapore are increasingly conscious of the need to apply each of the limbs of the *Banks* test; they assess the functional abilities of the deceased with respect to these limbs. However, Singapore's *UWF* v. *UWH* and Hong Kong's *In Re Lam Chok Wai*, both decided in the same month, display a sharp contrast in approach. *In Re Lam Chok Wai* weighed the deceased's moral duties towards his expected heirs heavily and treated his failure to provide for them in his will, despite being a responsible man, as irrational and demonstrating failure to satisfy the *Banks* test. The Hong Kong court did not appear to analyse expert opinions very closely, addressing them in only four of the judgment's 183 paragraphs and concluding that there was no testamentary capacity.[97] By contrast, *UWF* v. *UWH* involves the Singapore court's detailed examination of expert evidence as to whether the deceased with schizophrenia was in remission or influenced by overvalued beliefs, maintaining a clear respect for the subjective preferences of the deceased. It is hoped that the Hong Kong Court of Appeal will have the opportunity to review the approach adopted in *In Re Lam Chok Wai* and clarify the role and meaning of the will's rationality in capacity assessment.

## 4 CAPACITY FOR EXECUTING LPAS

Although LPAs and wills differ significantly in legal effect, they are often executed together in estate and incapacity planning, and they involve similar risks. However, as an instrument that takes effect during the lifetime of the donor, the LPA is subject to the additional risk that an errant attorney will divert the donor's assets when the donor most needs them.[98]

As compared to England, Hong Kong and Singapore adopt a more cautious and protective approach to LPA execution, requiring certain formalities. Hong Kong requires certification of the donor's capacity or the appearance of such capacity by a medical practitioner or solicitor, respectively.[99] Singapore requires certification of capacity by a qualified psychiatrist, medical practitioner, or solicitor.[100] By contrast, England does not require the person certifying capacity to be a professional; the donor may choose a layperson who has known him or her for more than two years as of the signing of the LPA.[101]

97 *Re Lam Chok Wai* [2020] HKCFI 3047 at [146]–[149].

98 See *Re Ko Siu Yung* [2018] HKCFI 1797, [2018] HKCU 2582 at [3], where an attorney holding enduring power transferred over HK$1.2 million from her mother's bank account to her own within months of the appointment.

99 Enduring Powers of Attorney Ordinance (Cap 501), s. 5(2)(a)(i)–(ii).

100 Mental Capacity Act (Cap 177A, 2010), §43(1)-(3) (Sing.). See also Form 1, OFF. OF THE PUB. GUARDIAN, LASTING POWER OF ATTORNEY (LPA): FORM 1 (2020) 6, 12 <www.msf.gov.sg/opg/AnalyticsReports/ LPA_Form_1_2020.pdf> accessed 30 April 2020.

101 MCA, sch 1, para. 2(e)(i), discussed in Lush and Bielanski, Cretney and Lush, [6.2]–[6.6]; The Lasting Powers of Attorney, Enduring Powers of Attorney and Public Guardian Regulations 2007 (SI 2007 No. 1253), reg. 8(1).

Following a widely reported case of abuse of an LPA,[102] the Singapore Mental Capacity Act 2010 was amended in 2016 to give the court power to revoke an LPA 'in respect of all or such of the matters to which the lasting power of attorney relates as the court thinks fit'.[103] This power can be used pre-emptively, before a finding of fraud or dishonesty in a criminal proceeding, and differs significantly from both English and Hong Kong legislation.[104]

Courts in Singapore also adopt a more protective approach in addressing concerns of undue influence than those in Hong Kong. Hong Kong courts have paid very little attention to the role of undue influence in invalidating LPAs, whether the undue influence is used as a way to establish incapacity or as a separate ground of invalidity. In *In Re Chui Kwok Ying*, Burrell J of the Hong Kong Court of First Instance recognised that influence was 'relevant to' the issue of mental capacity but did not explain how it was relevant.[105] In *In Re A: Mental Health*, Lok J quickly rejected a claim of undue influence based primarily on the donor mother's isolation from the younger sister by the donee, the other's reposition of trust and confidence on the donee, and the execution of an enduring power of attorney and a deed of gift over her entire estate (of some HK$22 billion) in favour of the donee.[106]

By contrast, a more proactive approach has been taken by the Singapore courts. In the case of *BKR*, the Singapore Court of Appeal explained that the presence of undue influence is relevant to establish incapacity under the Singapore Mental Capacity Act 2010, which was modelled closely after the English MCA, by providing material *evidence* of mental impairment or by helping establish *causation* between the impairment and incapacity.[107] As to its evidential role, undue influence may demonstrate decision-makers' inability to understand information relevant to the decision, such as the presence of conflicting interests, as the result of ignorance about such influence having been applied to them. Similarly, decision-makers' susceptibility to undue influence and consequent inability to use and weigh information may provide evidence of their mental impairment.[108] Alternatively, whilst a

102 *TDA* v. *TCZ* [2016] SGHC 63, [2016] 3 SLR 329; *Public Prosecutor* v. *Yang Yin* [2015] SGHC 3, [2015] 2 SLR 78; *Chung Khin Chun K* v. *Yang Yin* [2015] SGHC 215, [2015] 5 SLR 467.

103 Mental Capacity Act (Cap 177A, 2010), § 17(5A) (Sing.).

104 H. W. Tang, 'Financial Planning Mechanisms Available to Persons with Special Needs in Singapore', in L. Ho and R. Lee (eds), *Special Needs Financial Planning: A Comparative Perspective* (Cambridge: Cambridge University Press, 2019), p. 218.

105 *Re Chui Kwok Ying* [2016] HKCFI 237, [2016] HKCU 379 at [33], [59]–[60].

106 *In Re A: Mental Health* [2018] HKCFI 467, [2018] 2 HKLRD 1105 at [118], [128]–[129]. The decision involved an application for the appointment of a committee of estate, where undue influence was pleaded as a separate ground to incapacity.

107 *BKR* [2015] SGCA 26, discussed in H. W. Tang, 'Equity and Trusts' (2015) 16 *Singapore Academy of Law Annual Review* 450, 452; A. Peng and K. W. Tan, 'The Deputy Regime under Singapore's Mental Capacity Act: An Introduction' (2020) 32 *Singapore Academy Law Journal* 167, [35]–[37].

108 *BKR* [2015] SGCA 26 at [125].

person with mental impairment may make a decision with assistance, undue influence render him or her unable to benefit from such assistance.[109] In this way, undue influence, combined with cognitive impairment, is a potential cause of incapacity.

The court held that BKR was subject to undue influence from her younger daughter. References were made to this daughter's isolation of BKR from her siblings and BKR's revocation of instructions to the bank that were favourable to the daughter when unaccompanied by the daughter.[110] The court held that the undue influence hindered BKR, who exhibited mental impairment, from obtaining facilitative assistance.[111]

The *BKR* principle was applied in *BUV* v. *BUU*.[112] In this case, a mother executed an LPA that appointed her elder son as sole attorney over her entire estate with no restriction on cash gifts. Abdullah J invoked the equitable doctrine of presumed undue influence and held that because the mother placed her trust and confidence in the son and the LPA called for explanation (such as by giving him 'benefits and control over [...] her property and affairs'),[113] a presumption of undue influence arose. The son failed to rebut the presumption by claiming that he was his mother's favourite child. The undue influence operated together with the mother's mental impairment such that she could not benefit from others' assistance in making decisions.[114] Abdullah J proceeded to revoke the LPA on the ground that it had been procured by undue pressure under section 17(3)(a)(ii) of the Singapore Mental Capacity Act. As Chan rightly noted, the court's decision implies that 'undue pressure' in the statute may comprise presumed undue influence.[115]

*BUV* v. *BUU* has potentially far-reaching consequences, as the overwhelming majority of LPA donors appoint as attorney someone in whom they repose trust and confidence, typically a family member, and may be unconcerned with granting wide powers that allow donees to benefit themselves. If LPAs with such powers are held to call for explanation, the presumption of undue influence would apply to a majority of them. A wide scope of the doctrine of undue influence with respect to LPAs may put family attorneys/carers in the unenviable position of having to rebut the presumption and may reduce family members' willingness to provide support for the elderly.[116] In this light, there is much to be said for applying the presumption

109 ibid at [126].

110 ibid at [197], [202].

111 ibid at [207].

112 *BUV* v. *BUU* [2019] SGHCF 15. See also *Goh Karen* v. *Goh Kelvin* [2020] SGHC 195 with respect to powers of attorney.

113 *BUV* [2019] SGHCF at [90].

114 ibid at [90]–[92].

115 G. Chan, 'Assessing Mental Capacity' (2020) 32 *Singapore Academy Law Journal* 287, [33].

116 For similar arguments, see B. Chen, 'Family Fiduciaries in the Protective Jurisdiction' (2020) 44(1) *Melbourne University Law Review* 55; B. Chen, 'Elder Financial Abuse: Fiduciary Law and Economics' (2020) 34 *Notre Dame Journal of Law, Ethics, and Public Policy* 307.

only to LPAs that contain unusual terms that make little legal sense, such as that the power is irrevocable without written approval from the donee.[117]

## 5 CONCLUSION

While these jurisdictions determine the proper balance between autonomy and protection against both undue influence and testamentary incapacity, testators and LPA donors may best avoid their wills and LPAs ending up in the court system by securing quality legal service in preparing and executing these legal documents. An important theme of court decisions with respect to wills and LPAs is the importance of high-quality legal services in preparing and executing these legal instruments. The Singapore Court of Appeal in *Chee* v. *Chee* so observed:[118]

> The judicial process is not the best mechanism to determine the testamentary capacity of a testator, and solicitors who draw up wills bear a special responsibility to the testator and the legitimate beneficiaries not to have their handiwork picked over by psychiatrists acting on imperfect information in a court of law.

Echoing these comments is the call made by Cheung JA in *In Re Au Kong Tim* for law schools and the professional body at large to properly train solicitors in the preparation and execution of wills.[119]

Whilst no one doubts the good sense of these remarks, the reality of will-making by solicitors cannot be ignored. The solicitor in *In Re Au Kong Tim* charged only HK$2,000,[120] roughly the market rate in 2008, to prepare the will in question and execute it at the testator's elderly home. At such a rate of pay, solicitors are unlikely to find it commercially attractive to invest time and resources to improve their will-making services. State-funded financial support, whether by way of fee subsidy or training non-lawyers in will-making, is necessary to increase the availability of affordable, high-quality will-making service. In this connection, it is worthy to note that the OCBC Bank in Singapore has launched an Online Will Generator to facilitate will-making by the general public.[121] There is also an increasing number of will-writing companies in Singapore that provide affordable will-writing services. Ultimately, it is crucial for testators with complex family dynamics to appreciate the benefits of investing in a duly executed will in avoiding many of the issues that give rise to expensive court cases. Until there is sufficient demand in society for high-quality will-writing services, there is unlikely to be a significant rise in the supply of such services.

117 See *Goh Karen* [2020] SGHC 195. The power of attorney for the sale of the donor's property also provides for the entire proceeds to be transferred to the son of the donee, and only states that the donee 'request' the son to hold the proceeds upon trust, but not that the son should accede to the request.

118 *Chee* [2010] SGCA 27 at [62].

119 *Re Au Kong Tim* [2018] HKCA at [4]; see also Kwan JA at [75]–[76].

120 ibid at [37].

121 See <www.ocbc.com/personal-banking/lifegoals/willgenerator/#/> accessed 17 May 2021.

# 6

# Testamentary Freedom and Inheritance Disputes in Hong Kong

*Rebecca Lee*[*]

## 1 INTRODUCTION

'[A]n Englishman still remains at liberty at his death to dispose of his own property in whatever way he pleases'.[1] This statement summarises the principle of testamentary freedom in English succession law, which confers extensive rights on a testator to dispose of his estate in whatever manner he chooses.[2] In the recent case of *Ilott* v. *The Blue Cross*,[3] the UK Supreme Court restated the principle's centrality as the organising principle of English succession law. The principle of testamentary freedom, which in effect amounts to dead hand control, is commonly justified on two overlapping grounds. First, from a wider perspective, a fundamental principle of private law is that legal norms are organised to enhance personal autonomy. Thus, as an incident of property, an individual should have the freedom to dispose of his property both during and after his lifetime.[4] Second, turning to the perspective of the individual testator, he possesses better and more complete information and knowledge than the legislature or courts about the best distribution of his property to family members or other donees. As Cockburn CJ stated in *Banks* v. *Goodfellow*:[5]

* Faculty of Law, The University of Hong Kong. Research for this chapter was funded by the RGC General Research Fund 2018–2019 (project number: 17607418).

1 *Re Coventry* [1979] 2 WLR 853 at 864–865 (Oliver J); approved by Buckley LJ on appeal: [1980] Ch 461 at 495.

2 The freedom of testation also underlies US succession law. See, for example, Restatement (Third) of Property: Wills and Other Donative Transfers (2003), § 10.1; *Fischer* v. *Heckerman*, 772 SW2d 642 at 645 (Clayton J): 'the right of a testator to make a will according to his own wishes is jealously guarded by the courts, regardless of a court's view of the justice of the chosen disposition'.

3 *Ilott* v. *The Blue Cross* [2017] UKSC 17, [2018] AC 545.

4 See Alec Samuels, 'Inheritance (Provision for Family and Dependants) Act 1975' (1976) 39(2) *Modern Law Review* 183: 'freedom of testation is an incident of property. It allows for flexible dispositions to suit the situation in the individual family, whose members may be rich or poor, deserving or undeserving or whatever'.

5 *Banks* v. *Goodfellow* (1879) LR 5 QB 549 at 564 (Cockburn CJ).

> [Al]though in some instances, caprice, or passion, or the power of new ties, or artful contrivance, or sinister influence, may lead to the neglect of claims that ought to be attended to, yet the instincts, affections, and common sentiments of mankind may be safely trusted to secure, on the whole, a better disposition of the property of the dead, and one more accurately adjusted to the requirements of the particular case, than could be obtained through a distribution prescribed by the stereotypes and inflexible rules of general law.

Accordingly, effectuating a testator's wishes maximises his satisfaction. It also promotes capital accumulation and strengthens family ties.[6]

As a former British colony,[7] Hong Kong also enshrines the principle of testamentary freedom in law. This chapter considers the principle's application in inheritance disputes, namely will and trust disputes, in Hong Kong. Part II first examines recent will disputes in which the principle of testamentary freedom was applied to explore how the balance between personal autonomy and familial obligation is struck and identifies the differences between the English and Hong Kong approaches in upholding the principle in will disputes. The preference for testamentary freedom also informs the law of private express trusts. Accordingly, Part III of the chapter then draws upon the emergent use of the trust (including the offshore trust) and family trust litigation involving some of Hong Kong's wealthiest families to highlight the use of the trust as a tool to safeguard testamentary freedom and maximise control. It will also delineate the limits of freedom of testation in trusts, as gleaned from the disapproving remarks of the English judiciary and offshore judiciaries when dealing with aggressive tax avoidance cases where mistakes in trust planning have occurred. In so doing, the chapter reflects on how Asian trusts are established and administered in a globalised world.

## 2 TESTAMENTARY FREEDOM AND WILL DISPUTES

### 2.1 *Centrality of the Principle of Testamentary Freedom in Will Disputes in Hong Kong*

Death is still very much a taboo subject in Asian cultures. However, although no one likes to talk about death, there is increasing awareness that the only proper way to plan for one's succession and avoid legal complications is to ensure that proper estate planning tools are in place. A will is the most affordable estate planning tool for those with modest wealth, whilst trusts provide wealthier individuals who own

[6] Daniel B. Kelly, 'Restricting Testamentary Freedom: Ex Ante versus Ex Post Justifications' (2013) 82 *Fordham Law Review* 1135, 1137.

[7] Hong Kong's legal rules are primarily transplanted from the English law that prevailed in the colonial period. Since the resumption of Chinese sovereignty over the territory in 1997, article 8 of the Basic Law, Hong Kong's mini constitution, preserves the application of common law and rules of equity in Hong Kong.

property and/or have more sophisticated considerations with more flexible options, including tailor-made property-holding arrangements. In recent years, globalisation has increased mobility, with increasing numbers of people living and owning property outside their countries of origin. There is thus greater awareness of disparities in dispositive freedom and a growing desire to make property arrangements that maximise testamentary freedom while minimising liability to estate duty. The topic of testamentary freedom has thus enjoyed renewed interest in recent years.

The principle of testamentary freedom has long been enshrined in Anglo-Hong Kong law. Indeed, the principle has been upheld by the highest court in Hong Kong, which noted – in a lengthy and dramatic series of family legal battles involving Nina Wang[8] – that its role in construing a will is to effectuate the testator's intent. Nina Wang was before her death in 2007 reputed to be one of the wealthiest women in Asia. The final episode in the legal saga, *SJ* v. *Joseph Lo Kin Ching*,[9] focused on Nina's 2002 homemade will, which comprised just four clauses written in Chinese passing on her entire estate, valued at an estimated HK$83 billion (US$10.6 billion), to the Chinachem Charitable Foundation ('the Foundation'). Clause 1 contained a gift of all of her properties to the Foundation, whereas clause 2 provided the following:

> After I pass away, I wish to entrust 'Chinachem Charitable Foundation Limited' to the supervision of a managing organisation jointly formed by the Secretary General of the United Nations; the Premier of the PRC Government as well as the Chief Executive of the Hong Kong Special Administrative Region. Under its supervision, the Foundation must continue all its current projects and set up a Chinese prize similar to that of the Nobel Prize.

The case thus concerned the construction of Nina's will. It is clear that the principle of testamentary freedom was upheld by Hong Kong's highest court. The Court of Final Appeal ('the CFA') reaffirmed its role in construing a will as effectuating the testator's intent. The Foundation argued that it should receive Wang's entire estate as an absolute gift to be used for various charitable purposes as they arose. The Secretary for Justice, however, contended that a charitable trust had been established, and hence that the Foundation, as trustee, was bound to give effect to the

8 Nina Wang, together with her late husband Teddy Wang, ran the Chinachem Group. The initial dispute began with a fight between Nina and her father-in-law over Teddy's estate, which was alleged to have been left to Nina by way of a will: *Nina Kung* v. *Wong Din Shin* [2005] HKCFA 54, (2005) 8 HKCFAR 387, where the Hong Kong Court of Final Appeal held that the handwritten will Teddy Wang created in 1990, which named his wife Nina as the sole beneficiary of his estate, was his last valid will, and thus awarded his estate to Nina. When Nina died in 2007, an alleged secret lover claimed to hold a valid will to her entire estate, which launched a new set of legal battles: *Chinachem Charitable Foundation Ltd* v. *Chan Chun Chuen* [2010] HKCFI 88, where it was held that Nina's alleged secret lover had presented a forged will, with the one held by the Foundation declared to be genuine. Leave to appeal to the CFA was denied: *Chinachem Charitable Foundation Ltd* v. *Chan Chun Chuen* [2011] 14 HKCFAR 798 at [106].

9 *SJ* v. *Joseph Lo Kin Ching* [2015] 8 HKCFAR 169.

directions specified in the will. Lord Walker NPJ (sitting as non-permanent judge on the CFA), in delivering the CFA's unanimous judgment, dismissed the Foundation's argument, holding 'that the Foundation [should] hold N[ina]'s estate as a trustee' and be obliged to give effect to her will and use the estate for the specific purpose stated therein so far as possible.[10]

In arriving at this conclusion, the CFA adopted a holistic approach and looked at all relevant circumstances pertaining to the testatrix when she made the will to ascertain her true intention.[11] As a general rule,[12] a bequest to a charitable company is construed as an absolute gift unless there are circumstances showing that a trust was intended.[13] Such circumstances prevailed in the case before the CFA. The Foundation's argument for a gift proceeded on the basis that the precatory word 'wish' in clause 2 reflected Nina's aspiration alone, and hence that the will's directions concerning the creation of a managing organisation and the establishment of the Chinese prize constituted only non-binding guidance. The CFA rejected that argument, holding that it was perfectly understandable that Nina had used the word 'wish' because, however strong her desire to entrust the Foundation to the distinguished persons named, it was entirely up to them whether they decided to participate. In fact, her use of 'wish' demonstrated her clear intention not to simply give the Foundation and its directors free rein after her death.[14] Accordingly, Nina Wang's will imposed conditions on her gift to the Foundation, and the Foundation could not simply do as it wished with her estate,[15] as it did not hold that estate as absolute owner, but merely on trust. The CFA's strong preference for privileging and facilitating the testatrix's intent could not be clearer. Although some of the conditions on her gift such as the establishment of a Nobel-like Chinese prize and the formation of a managing organisation with members of unquestionable integrity, experience, and judgment were unworkable as drafted, they were nonetheless considered valid conditions;[16] with any uncertainties to be rectified 'and clarified by the [Anglo-Hong Kong] law's benevolent treatment of charitable trusts.'[17]

### 2.2 *Testamentary Freedom versus Familial Duty*

Even in one of the oldest expressions of the principle of testamentary freedom, the principle was not divorced from the importance of familial obligation. Thus in *Banks* v. *Goodfellow*, Cockburn CJ stated the following:[18]

[10] *SJ* v. *Lo* [2015] 8 HKCFAR 169 at [13].
[11] Based on the so-called arm-chair principle laid down in *Boyes* v. *Cook* (1880) 14 Ch D 53 at 56.
[12] *Re Vernon's Will Trusts* [1972] 1 Ch 300 at 303E-G (Buckley J).
[13] *SJ* v. *Lo* [2015] 8 HKCFAR 169 at [40].
[14] ibid at [62]–[64].
[15] ibid at [52].
[16] ibid at [77].
[17] ibid at [52].
[18] *Banks* (1870) 5 LR QB 549 at 563 (Cockburn CJ).

> Yet it is clear that, though the law leaves to the owner of property absolute freedom in this ultimate disposal of that of which he is enabled to dispose, a moral responsibility of no ordinary importance attaches to the exercise of the right thus given.

Accordingly, the principle of testamentary freedom, which seemingly grants unrestricted rights to the disposal of one's own property, is qualified by legislation and the courts in circumstances in which some level of responsibility to provide for his family is imposed on the testator or where there are unforeseen contingencies not provided for by the testator. These qualifications and restrictions are examined below. As will be seen, in determining the extent to which the freedom to testate should be qualified or restricted, there is tension between individualism, which allows for flexible dispositions to suit the needs of the individual testator, and his moral, familial obligation to provide for his immediate family members. It must be noted that decisions in this area are highly fact-specific, and, given that the courts have wide discretionary powers, different courts may reach different decisions on the same facts depending on their views about the operation of the principle of testamentary freedom vis-à-vis the testator's moral obligation to provide for his family out of his estate.

In both England and Hong Kong,[19] a disinherited family member can apply, pursuant to family provision statutes, specifically the Inheritance (Provision for Family and Dependants) Act 1975 ('IPFDA') and the Inheritance (Provision for Family and Dependents) Ordinance ('IPFDO'), respectively, for court-based discretionary relief to obtain a share of the testator's estate only where the deceased's will or the default intestacy rules fail to make suitable provision. To file such an application, the disinherited family member must bear a certain relationship to the testator, in most cases being his or her spouse (or former spouse or unmarried cohabitant) or child. The application is then followed by the familiar two-stage approach to family provision claims under the IPFDA/IPFDO. In the first stage, the court considers whether, from an objective perspective, the will and/or intestacy rules make 'reasonable financial provision' for the applicant's maintenance (and thus focuses on considering the applicant's future needs on the date of the hearing). The inquiry is concerned with whether the deceased failed to make reasonable financial provision; thus the test is not whether it would have been reasonable for the applicant to receive more from the estate, but whether it was unreasonable for the applicant not to have done so. The second stage of the inquiry then addresses whether the court should exercise its judicial discretion if reasonable financial provision has not been made. Here, the court will intervene only if the testator's decision was unreasonable

[19] See, generally, Richard Hedlund, 'The end to testamentary freedom' *Legal Studies* (forthcoming) for a discussion of the introduction of the family provision rule in England. See Brian Sloan, 'The "Social Contract", Care and Inheritance in Hong Kong' (2020) 50 *Hong Kong Law Journal* 139, 149–154 for a comparative discussion of the family provision rules in England and Hong Kong.

in light of his moral duties because, given the testamentary freedom principle, the court will not normally want to review a testator's discretion and replace it with rules akin to forced heirship. Hence, discretionary relief is to be granted only on a case-by-case basis subject to judges' discretion.

### 2.3 Ilott *v.* The Blue Cross *and Its Implications*

In *Ilott* v. *The Blue Cross*,[20] the UK Supreme Court for the first time considered a claim for discretionary relief under the IPFDA. More specifically, it considered whether an estranged and disinherited but financially strained adult child should be entitled to such relief at the expense of the principal beneficiaries of a testator's will. The testatrix in the case, Mrs Jackson, had been a widow with one daughter, now Mrs Ilott. At the time of Mrs Jackson's death in 2004, mother and daughter had been estranged for twenty-six years, ever since the latter had eloped with her boyfriend at the age of seventeen. At the time of her mother's death, Mrs Ilott was married with five children. Her family had limited financial means and was entitled to various social benefits. Although there had been three attempts at reconciliation prior to Mrs Jackson's death, all had foundered, and Mrs Ilott had lived her entire married life completely isolated from her mother. Mrs Jackson decided to make no provision for her daughter in her will, instead leaving the majority of her estate to three charities (Blue Cross etc.). The daughter subsequently contested the will under the IPFDA on the ground that it failed to make reasonable financial provision for her maintenance.

The district judge found that the testatrix had unreasonably excluded her daughter from receiving any financial provision despite her straitened financial circumstances and awarded the daughter £50,000 (about 10 per cent of the estate). The daughter appealed on the basis that the award was inadequate, claiming that she should get more than 10 per cent. Arden LJ, delivering the leading judgment of the Court of Appeal, reversed the district judge's decision on the ground that he had committed two errors. First, the district judge had not properly considered the effect of the long period of estrangement and the daughter's independent life, and in particular what the award would have been without these factors. Second, the district judge had not properly considered the effect of the award on the daughter's current entitlement to means-tested state benefits.[21] After weighing up these factors, the Court of Appeal increased the award to £143,000 to enable the daughter to purchase the house in which she was living and afforded her an option to receive a further £20,000 to meet her financial needs without affecting her state benefit entitlement.

20 *Ilott* [2018] AC 545.

21 *Ilott* v. *Mitson* [2015] EWCA Civ 797, [2016] 1 All ER 932 at [35]–[36].

The three charities appealed. The Supreme Court held unanimously that the district judge had made neither alleged error.[22] Consequently, the Court of Appeal's decision was reversed and the district judge's award was restored. What is significant for our purposes is that the Supreme Court reaffirmed the principle of testamentary freedom by noting that the Court of Appeal's observation that the charities had no expectation of benefit[23] should be treated with caution. Apart from the fact that charitable operations are heavily dependent on testamentary bequests, the Supreme Court emphasised that the testatrix had chosen the specified charities as her beneficiaries. Therefore, they did not have to justify their claim to the estate on the same basis of need as the testatrix's daughter.[24] The Supreme Court decision thus sends an important message about testamentary freedom to all potential protagonists. It reassures testators that their wishes have an important role to play in family provision claims in that the court *must* take those wishes into account in deciding whether to exercise its powers to grant discretionary relief under the IPFDA. Further, the testators' wishes should not be overridden lightly (even though they may not always be respected in full, as the final decision in *Ilott* shows). The decision also reassures chosen beneficiaries that they are not required to justify their claim to an estate on the basis of need. Disinherited family members, in contrast, may now find it more difficult to obtain discretionary relief from the court under English law, and, even if they succeed, the relief obtained may be modest (as it was in the case of the daughter in *Ilott*).

Despite *Ilott's* affirmation of the centrality of the principle of testamentary freedom, two points are worthy of note with regard to claims for financial provision by disinherited children. First, insofar as claims by adult children are concerned, English courts may continue to override a will (as *Ilott* shows) and restrict testamentary freedom. *Nahajec* v. *Fowle*[25] was the first case to apply *Ilott*. Just as in *Ilott*, an estranged daughter succeeded in claiming, under section 2 of the IPFDA, a share of her late father's estate despite his clear wish to disinherit her. The father had left the whole of his estate, the net value of which was £265,710, to his long-time friend and executor, Mr Fowle. The daughter was one of the deceased's three children. The daughter said that she had had no relationship with her father because he had cut himself off from the family and that his subsequent attempt to rekindle the relationship had not succeeded because he disapproved of her boyfriend. The daughter lived by herself, worked as a retail assistant, and wished to become a veterinary nurse, having previously worked in a veterinary surgery. She had debts of £6,600.

[22] *Ilott* [2018] AC 545 at [32]–[41]. First, the IPFDA does not require the court to make a hypothetical assessment of reasonable financial provision. In the case in question, the district judge had been entitled to give weight to the estrangement, the testatrix's clear wish to benefit the named charities and the daughter's lack of expectation of any benefit. Second, the district judge had indeed addressed the impact of his award on the daughter's state benefits.

[23] *Ilott* [2016] 1 All ER 932 at [51].

[24] *Ilott* [2018] AC 545 at [46] (Lord Hughes).

[25] *Nahajec* v. *Fowle* [2017] EW Misc 11 (CC).

The judge applied the two-stage test laid down in *Ilott* and noted, in particular, that a single assessment of reasonable financial provision must be made in light of all of the factors in section 3 of the IPFDA.[26] The test was not whether it was unreasonable to make provision for the defendant but, objectively, whether the deceased had failed to make reasonable provision for the applicant.[27] On the facts, the Court agreed that reasonable financial provision had not been made. It recognised that the daughter needed money for her studies and to pay off her debts and did not live an extravagant life, and also approved of her aspiration to become a veterinary nurse. Although the Court also recognised that Mr Fowle had financial difficulties, possibly because he had neglected his work to look after the deceased, those difficulties did not render it reasonable for the father to leave nothing in his will to his daughter. After balancing these factors, the Court awarded the daughter £30,000 in maintenance.[28]

Second, and in contrast, the English courts' approach to claims brought under the IPFDA by minor children has not changed, as illustrated by the recent case of *Ubbi* v. *Ubbi*.[29] In that case, whilst the court concerned explicitly recognised the importance of testamentary freedom in family provision claims[30] in applying the *Ilott* guidelines, it obviously accorded considerable weight to the fact that the claim was brought by the deceased's minor children as a vital part of the factual matrix. The deceased, Malkiat Ubbi, had been a pharmacist who had built up a pharmacy business together with his wife, with whom he had two children. Malkiat's subsequent affair with his mistress led to the birth of two additional children, whom he failed to provide for in his will. It was no surprise that the Court held that reasonable financial provision had not been made by Malkiat's will and, accordingly, was ready to provide for the maintenance of the mistress's minor children, including housing, education, and childcare costs.

### 2.4 *The Hong Kong Approach*

In Hong Kong, there is a strong culture of concern with familial duty.[31] However, notwithstanding the impact of Chinese culture and traditions, the principle of testamentary freedom has generally been honoured. Two notable recent family inheritance cases which hinge on the principle's application are examined here

26 ibid at [29]–[68], [85].

27 ibid at [20].

28 *Nahajec* [2017] EW Misc 11 (CC) at [103]. Note also that one of her half-brothers had previously made a claim under the IPFDA that had been settled by a payment of £22,000 while the other had not made a claim.

29 *Ubbi* v. *Ubbi* [2018] EWHC 1396 (Ch).

30 ibid at [14].

31 See, e.g. N. W. S. Chow and T. Y. S. Lum, *Trends in Family Attitudes and Values in Hong Kong: Final Report to Central Policy Unit, Hong Kong SAR Government* (The University of Hong Kong, 2008), pp. 1–37; Sammy Chiu and Victor Wong, 'East Asian Welfare Regimes in Transition', in Alan Walker and Chack-kie Wong (eds), *East Asian Welfare Regimes in Transition: From Confucianism to Globalisation* (Bristol University Press, 2005), p. 88.

to illustrate how the balance between personal autonomy and familial obligation is struck under Hong Kong law. They show that personal autonomy is a strong guiding principle that the courts have endeavoured to uphold despite enjoying the judicial discretion to rescue disinherited family members under the IPFDO. The more restrictive language of the Hong Kong statute distinguishes the Hong Kong approach from its English counterpart insofar as claims by adult children are concerned.

Just as in England, the Hong Kong judiciary has repeatedly affirmed the principle of testamentary freedom.[32] Testamentary freedom has always been central to wills because they serve as a useful approximation of a testator's preferences. However, statutory recognition of the need to make reasonable financial provision for adult children out of a deceased's estate is much narrower in Hong Kong than in England. In England, the first hurdle to overcome in making an application is the relationship requirement, that is, the disinherited member must have had a certain relationship with the testator. Most commonly this is the testator's spouse (or former spouse or unmarried cohabitant) or child, as set out in section 1 of the IPFDA. The starting point in Hong Kong is strikingly different. Whilst the Hong Kong statute is largely the same as its English counterpart, it imposes a specific requirement of maintenance if an adult child is making an application for financial provision: 'an adult child of the deceased who immediately before the death of the deceased *was being maintained*, either wholly or substantially, by the deceased'.[33] That position is materially narrower than in English law, where there is no such restriction.[34] Thus, for example, it was not necessary for the adult daughter in *Ilott* to prove that she had been maintained by her mother in order to bring a claim for discretionary relief (even though the Supreme Court emphasised the importance of limiting awards to 'maintenance'). This may explain why even though the UK Supreme Court rejected the interventionist approach of the Court of Appeal – an approach that might pose a challenge to testamentary freedom – it still affirmed an award to an adult child, who was not only able-bodied and financially independent, but also long estranged from her mother. That award was also contrary to her mother's express wish that she be disinherited.

In contrast, it would be impossible for the adult daughter in *Ilott* to succeed in a Hong Kong court. The narrower statutory recognition in Hong Kong of the need to make reasonable financial provision for adult children may explain why the Hong

[32] See, e.g. *Lau Kin Wing Ken* v. *Deng Yujiao* [2019] HKCA 769 at [69]; *Li Wai Chu* v. *Li Wai Ling* (unrep, HCAP 6/2012, Court of First Instance, 20 June 2017) at [136] and *Tang Tim Chue* v. *Tang Ka Hung Robert* (unrep, Court of First Instance, 7 June 2012) at [15].

[33] Inheritance (Provision for Family and Dependants) Ordinance (Cap 481), s. 3(1)(vi) (emphasis added).

[34] However, as is the case in England, the level of financial provision granted by the courts in Hong Kong is limited to what is reasonable in all circumstances for the applicant to receive for his or her maintenance.

Kong courts are more reluctant than the English courts to grant such applications. *Tang Tim Chue* v. *Tang Ka Hung Robert* is a recent case in point.[35] The applicant, an adult child, applied under section 3(1)(vi) of the IPFDO for financial provision from the estate of his late father, whose will specified no such provision. Indeed, the deceased father had stipulated that the applicant was to be excluded from both his funeral and obituary.[36] The trial judge ruled that the applicant had failed to prove that he had been maintained either wholly or substantially by his father immediately before the father's death. On appeal, the Court of Appeal held that it would not interfere with the trial judge's findings of fact unless they were plainly wrong. The Court noted, in particular, that there was evidence that the father had believed that the applicant had instigated his former wife's divorce proceedings. It was thus unlikely that he would have been generous to the applicant, particularly as the applicant's mother had already obtained a sizeable lump sum. This evidence of the father's hostile attitude towards the applicant was completely contrary to the applicant's suggestion that his father had been providing him financial maintenance.[37]

This deferential approach is equally applicable to family provision claims made by parents, as illustrated by a family inheritance case involving a local celebrity. Madam Tam was the mother of the late Anita Mui, a well-known pop singer. In 2003, a month before her death, Anita executed a will leaving her entire estate to a discretionary trust for which HSBC acted as the trustee. Litigation ensued because Madam Tam was dissatisfied with what she received under the trust, namely monthly maintenance of HK$70,000 (US$8,965). In previous proceedings, she had unsuccessfully challenged the validity of both the will and the trust on various grounds, including a lack of testamentary capacity.[38]

In one of the latest installments of the protracted litigation, *Tam Mei Kam* v. *HSBC International Trustees*,[39] Madam Tam appealed against the trial judge's decision to refuse her application for a lump sum order under section 4(1)(b) of the IPFDO out of Anita's net estate. Instead, the judge had made a provision under that section for periodic payments for Madam Tam's medical expenses. In determining whether Madam Tam was entitled to a lump sum under section 4(1)(b), the Hong Kong Court of Appeal affirmed that 'reasonable financial provision' is defined as 'such financial provision as it would be reasonable in all the circumstances of the case for the applicants to receive for [their] maintenance'. Statutory power is thus an evaluative judgment based on objective considerations rather than the subjective view of the applicant. In making reasonable financial provision for an applicant, the court is empowered to consider a range of orders under section 4(1) with regard to matters in section 5. With respect to

35 *Tang Tim Chue* v. *Tang Ka Hung Robert* [2018] HKCA 514, [2018] 4 HKLRD 277.
36 ibid at [21].
37 *Tang Tim Chue* [2018] HKCA 514 at [40].
38 *Tam Mei Kam* v. *HSBC International Trust Ltd* [2011] 14 HKCFAR 512 at 525, 529.
39 *Tam Mei Kam* v. *HSBC International Trustees* CACV 18/2016, Court of Appeal, 10 February 2017.

Madam Tam, because she was Anita's parent, the court had to take into account both the applicant's age and the monetary contribution she had received prior to the death of the deceased pursuant to section 5(3).[40] Furthermore, it was also correct for the trial judge to consider whether there were sufficient funds in the estate for the requested payment to be made. Taking these issues into account, the Court of Appeal held that there was no legal basis for Madam Tam to contend that a lump sum was insufficient. In reaching that conclusion, the Court – applying *Re Coventry* – noted that the purpose of the IPFDO is to ensure 'reasonable maintenance', not to 'provide legacies' for an applicant to 'divert [...] assets where [they] would be most useful and appreciated'.[41]

To conclude, the principle of testamentary freedom prevails in Hong Kong succession law. The legislature has tempered the principle in favour of protecting the family of testators, and thus family provision claims can be made against a testator's estate as a moral measure to protect his dependants. Nonetheless, at least insofar as adult children are concerned, the statutory language provides some justification for a more favourable attitude towards testators against claims made by adult children.[42] More significantly, freedom of testation also has a significant role to play in resolving inheritance disputes in Hong Kong even prior to *Ilott*.[43] Despite the time-honoured tradition and perceived importance of familial obligation in Chinese culture, the Hong Kong courts do not lightly distribute a testator's assets to family members whom they view as having a superior moral claim to the testator's assets to protect them from disinheritance or to ensure that the testator's familial duty is met. This judicial reluctance to grant discretionary relief reflects the principle of autonomy of will in succession law, and in turn, enhances testators' testamentary freedom, giving them greater autonomy in succession planning.

## 3 TESTAMENTARY FREEDOM AND DISCRETIONARY TRUSTS

The preference for testamentary freedom also informs the law of private express trusts. Hong Kong law, following English common law, embodies the law of trusts. The asset protection function of trusts is beyond dispute. For example, an

40 Section 5(3) reads: '[...]where an application for an order under section 4 is made by virtue of section 3(1)(iv), the court shall, in addition to the matters specifically mentioned in paragraphs (a) to (f) of that subsection, have regard to the age of the applicant and the contribution (if any) in money or money's worth made by the deceased towards the needs of the applicant immediately before the death of the deceased'.

41 *Re Coventry* [1979] 2 WLR 853 at 864; cited by the Court of Appeal in *Tam Mei Kam* CACV 18/2016 at [44].

42 Apart from awarding statutory discretionary relief, the courts may also make use of other tools to restrict testamentary freedom, such as insistence on strict compliance with will formalities and the doctrine of undue influence: see, e.g. Melanie B. Leslie, 'The Myth of Testamentary Freedom' (1996) 38 *Arizona Law Review* 235, 243–258.

43 Note that thus far, only the English Court of Appeal but not the UK Supreme Court decision in *Illot* has been considered by Hong Kong courts.

offshore trust can be set up to protect the settlor's assets against divorce claims.[44] However, a trust is not only an asset protection device; it also safeguards testamentary freedom. The following discussion addresses two main issues. First, why is the trust an attractive device for safeguarding testamentary freedom – and control – in the Asian wealth management context? It will be shown that trusts safeguard testamentary freedom by ousting any applicable forced heirship rules, maximising settlor control and preserving confidentiality. Second, does the principle of testamentary freedom have any limits in the trust context? To answer this, the cautionary remarks of both the English judiciary and offshore judiciaries will be examined.

### 3.1 *Ousting Applicable Forced Heirship Rules*

Trusts are immune from discrimination challenges in the selection of beneficiaries, and the trust legislation in many jurisdictions provides for protection against foreign forced heirship rules. In common law jurisdictions, children have no right to their parents' property. Intestacy rules do not override a testator's wishes, properly expressed, in most situations. Imposing restrictions on testamentary freedom by way of forced heirship rules, in contrast, is generally a feature of civil law jurisdictions. Forced heirship rules operate to constrain a person's testamentary freedom to dispose of his property according to his wishes, instead of vesting rights in surviving spouses and children (forced heirs) to fixed shares of the testator's estate. The result is that the bulk of a testator's property must pass upon his death to his forced heirs immediately and unconditionally, in fixed shares per stirpes, regardless of the testator's wishes or his descendants' needs and also usually irrespective of whether his assets are located in or outside his country of residence. China has a limited forced heirship regime under which dependants of the deceased are entitled to succession to the extent that they otherwise cannot support themselves. Article 1141 of the Civil Code of the People's Republic of China (2020) provides as follows:[45]

> Reservation of a necessary portion of an estate shall be made in a will for a successor who neither can work nor has a source of income.

44 Note, however, that efforts to place assets in offshore trusts beyond the reach of family courts in divorce litigation have not always proved successful, as illustrated by the English Court of Appeal decision in *Charman* v. *Charman (No 4)* [2007] EWCA (Civ) 503, which was subsequently applied by the Hong Kong CFA in *Kan Lai Kwan* v. *Poon Lok To Otto* [2014] 17 HKCFAR 414.

45 See also Art. 1130 of the Civil Code for a similar provision in relation to intestate succession. Other notable features of Chinese inheritance law include: disinheriting successors if they have committed serious acts of misconduct towards the deceased (Art. 1125) and rewarding those who have cared for the deceased (Art. 1130 & Art. 1131). For a critique of the potential conflicts between Chinese inheritance and trust laws, see Frances H. Foster, 'The Dark Side of Trusts: Challenges to Chinese Inheritance Law' (2003) 2 *Washington University Global Studies Law Review* 151.

Given the differences between testamentary freedom and forced heirship, it is not surprising that many desire greater freedom of disposition. The offshore trust offers a way to overcome the restrictions of forced heirship rules in certain civil law jurisdictions. It plays a crucial part in bringing greater dispositive freedom to civilian systems. To make the trust an attractive estate planning tool, some offshore trust jurisdictions have expressly guaranteed that their trusts are not vulnerable to foreign disruption. For example, the Cayman and Jersey trust laws provide as follows:

> [N]o trust is void, voidable, liable to be set aside or defective [...] by reason that 'the trust or disposition avoids or defeats rights, claims or interests conferred by foreign law upon any person by reason of a personal relationship to the settlor or by way of heirship rights [...]'.[46]
>
> [T]he law of Jersey prevails even if [...] 'the trust or disposition avoids or defeats rights, claims, or interests conferred by any foreign law upon any person by reason of a personal relationship or by way of heirship rights [...]'.[47]

Consequently, not only does the trust (the offshore trust in particular) continue to serve as a vital element of dispositive freedom in Hong Kong's common law system, enabling people to make arrangements for the management, use, and enjoyment of their property, but it has also become an increasingly popular instrument in civil law jurisdictions such as mainland China. In recent decades, with wealth accumulating at an astonishing rate in mainland China, Hong Kong has become a trust service hub for mainland Chinese entrepreneurs. These Chinese billionaires, who may be subject to (limited) forced heirship laws and hefty inheritance taxes in mainland China, are motivated to set up trusts to achieve tax mitigation, asset protection and, not least, testamentary freedom. For example, it was reported in January 2019 that four Chinese tycoons whose companies are listed on the Hong Kong stock market had transferred more than US$17 billion in assets to offshore family trusts in late 2018.[48] They probably did so in anticipation of the tightening up of local tax laws and to protect themselves against the risk of forced heirship.

### 3.2 *Maximising Control and Freedom of Testamentary Disposition*

Inherent in the desire to attain testamentary freedom is the desire to retain control. At the same time, given settlors' general unfamiliarity with trusts, they naturally want to seek extra protection against the risk of using an alien trust structure. This is particularly likely to be so if they are amongst the first generation of wealthy entrepreneurs in Hong Kong, who may not understand the mechanics of a trust

46 Cayman Islands: The Trusts Law (1998 Revision), s. 91(b).
47 Trusts (Jersey) Law 1984, Art. 9(2)(b).
48 Venus Feng and Blake Schmidt, 'Four Chinese Tycoons Just Transferred $17 Billion to Trusts' (Bloomberg, 16 January 2019) <www.bloomberg.com/news/articles/2019-01-15/four-chinese-tycoons-just-transferred-17-billion-to-trusts> last accessed 17 June 2022.

and may not want to relinquish control over the trust assets. Amongst the most prevalent, and innovative, features of the trust in enabling the settlor to maximise his control over the trust property are the use of letters of wishes, protectors, and the presence of reserved powers by settlors. An outline of these features is in order before we turn to a local case involving an intense battle for control over a trust between the settlor and trustees.

First, modern family trusts are usually settled as discretionary rather than fixed trusts, which has led to a surge in the use of letters of wishes drawn up by the settlors.[49] In these letters, settlors express non-binding requests to trustees concerning how the latter's wide dispositive discretion is to be exercised within the parameters intended by the settlors.[50]

Second, a settlor may also ensure that the trust is administered in accordance with his wishes through the appointment of a third party, who is usually a close friend or family member of the settlor, to act as the protector of the trust to monitor trustees in the administration of the trust.[51] The office of protector is now well-established and allows settlors some degree of influence over a trustee's exercise of discretion.

Third, settlors who do not wish to lose control over their assets may reserve significant and substantive decision-making powers for themselves under modern trust instruments (offshore trust instruments in particular). This situation is in stark contrast to the traditional English trust, wherein the settlor retains no control over the trust assets after the trust's creation. It is customary for Anglo-Hong Kong settlors to reserve the power to direct trustees to make investments; to add or remove beneficiaries; to appoint income or capital to beneficiaries; to appoint or remove trustees; to revoke the trust;[52] and to veto the trustee's administrative or dispositive decisions. Further, entrepreneur-settlors may now transfer their companies into a trust, and so naturally want to retain management of the corporate assets rather than leaving such management to the trustee, who has less knowledge of the company's affairs than the settlor and may lack the expertise to supervise its conduct. Accordingly, the trust deed may contain 'anti-*Bartlett*' clauses to exclude the trustee's duty of care[53]

[49] Alternatively, the trust may be accompanied by an internal memorandum of the settlor's wishes drawn up by the trustees. See, e.g. *Tam Mei Kam* v. *HSBC International Trustee Ltd* [2011] 14 HKCFAR 512.

[50] See *Hartigan Nominees Pty Ltd* v. *Rydge* (1992) 29 NSWLR 405 at 408; *Breakspear* v. *Ackland* [2009] Ch 32 at [5]; *In re* Rabaiotti 1989 Settlement [2000] JLR 173 at 173–174.

[51] Donovan W. M. Waters, 'The Protector: New Wine in Old Bottles?', in A. J. Oakley (ed), *Trends in Contemporary Trust Law* (Oxford: Oxford University Press, 1996); Matthew Conaglen and Elizabeth Weaver, 'Protectors as Fiduciaries: Theory and Practice' (2012) 18(1) *Trusts & Trustees* 17, 19–20.

[52] In relation to the power to revoke a trust, see, generally, *Fonu* v. *Merrill Lynch Bank & Trust Co* [2011] UKPC 17, which held that an unfettered power to revoke can be treated as a type of property that can be claimed by the settlor's receivers for the benefit of his creditors.

[53] The trustee's duty of care was laid down in *Bartlett* v. *Barclays Trust Co Ltd* [1980] 2 WLR 430, which has now been codified by statute: English Trustees Act 2000, s. 1; Hong Kong Trustee Ordinance, s. 3A.

in the management of the company's affairs unless he has actual knowledge of dishonesty on the part of the company's directors or officers.[54]

Recent family trust litigation highlights the intense battle for control over a trust that sometimes occurs between a settlor and trustees. *Tao Soh Ngun (also known as Lo To Lee Kwan)* v. *HSBC International Trustee Ltd*[55] also constitutes one of the most recent family inheritance dispute to reach the Hong Kong courts. Madam Lo was the widow of the tycoon Lo Ying-shek. She and her late husband had co-founded the Hong Kong property giant Great Eagle Holdings ('GE'). In 1984, the couple set up two discretionary trusts for the purpose of long-term succession planning and to minimise the estate duty payable, although Mr Lo would retain effective control over the trust assets during his lifetime. The two trusts were subsequently merged into the Lo Family Trust ('the Trust'). The Trust has a wide class of beneficiaries and confers wide powers on its trustee, HSBC International Trustee. A subsequent family feud split the couple's nine children into two rival camps, one siding with Madam Lo and the other with the third son, KS. Madam Lo requested that HSBC stock up on shares in GE to prevent KS from gaining a controlling shareholding in the company. HSBC refused and sought to remove itself as trustee.

Madam Lo claimed that there was a common understanding between herself and the trustee that the trust had been established solely for the purpose of minimising her husband's estate duty. By reason of that common understanding, she claimed, HSBC should give heavy weight to her instructions, with those instructions overriding HSBC's duty to treat all beneficiaries equally. However, HSBC had departed from their common understanding and was refusing to follow her requests (set out in ten letters) regarding the administration of the trust, namely the purchase of additional GE shares.

When the case went to trial in 2018, Madam Lo, aged 98, was called to testify before the court. Chan J rejected her arguments on, inter alia, the following two grounds. First, with regard to the common understanding she supposedly shared with HSBC, the court held that the trust would be a sham if the trustee were obliged to comply with whatever Madam Lo asked it to do. There can be no fetter on the discretionary powers of the trustees of discretionary trusts, and, accordingly, the contention that significant weight should be accorded to Madam Lo's requests was legally unsustainable.[56] In any event, Madam Lo could not establish the existence of such an understanding, as the trust deed was conclusive.

Second, the dual purpose of the Trust was succession planning and the avoidance of estate duty. It was never its purpose to preserve a 'controlling shareholding' in GE.

54 The effectiveness of anti-*Bartlett* clauses was recently affirmed by the Hong Kong Court of Final Appeal in *Zhang Hong Li* v. *DBS Bank (Hong Kong) Ltd* [2019] HKCFA. See, further, Rebecca Lee and Man Yip, 'Exclusion of Duty and the Irreducible Core Content of Trusteeship: A Re-assessment' (2020) 14 *Journal of Equity* 131.

55 *Tao Soh Ngun (also known as Lo To Lee Kwan)* v. *HSBC International Trustee Ltd* [2019] HKCFI 1268.

56 *Tao Soh Ngun* [2019] HKCFI 1268 at [42]–[43].

With regard to Madam Lo's request to purchase additional shares in GE, HSBC had a general duty of prudence in investment, which includes the possibility of diversification.[57] On the facts, HSBC was legally entitled to be concerned about the concentration risk of purchasing additional GE shares, and it could, and genuinely did, take into account that risk in refusing to do so. There had been no gross negligence or wilful default on HSBC's part in refusing Madam Lo's request. The weight accorded to a given consideration is a matter for the trustee, which is not obliged to give reasons for its decisions. Thus, HSBC need not 'attend or respond promptly' to Madam Lo's requests, consider them 'as the primary or material consideration' or provide 'good, legitimate and/or sufficient reason' for any refusal to implement them.[58] Despite the trustee's victory, the case provides an apt illustration of some settlors' attempts to retain aggressive control over 'their' assets even after the establishment of the trust.

### 3.3 *Preserving Confidentiality in Testamentary Disposition*

Confidentiality is one of the principal advantages that a trust enjoys over other property-holding arrangements. As a general rule, trustees must keep the affairs of the trust confidential. The existence of a trust, as well as the names of its settlor and beneficiaries, does not appear in the public record. Needless to say, the fact that well-known families and celebrities can deal with their financial affairs privately without being subject to public scrutiny is a major appeal of the trust.[59] Confidentiality can also serve as an important shield against political risks such as nationalisation and the expropriation of assets, particularly when the trust is located offshore.

The operation of confidentiality in trust arrangements is well-illustrated by *HSBC Trustee (CI) Limited* v. *Siu Hing Kwong*,[60] which also illustrates the desire for settlor control. In that case, the settlor achieved such control by establishing a complex structure involving a series of corporate vehicles and offshore trusts, with the trusts holding shares in the companies established. The Kwok family is one of the wealthiest families in Hong Kong, having founded the Sun Hung Kai Properties empire, Hong Kong's largest property developer by market capitalisation. Madam Kwong, the mother of Walter, Thomas, and Raymond Kwok, established four discretionary offshore trusts that owned holding companies that held shares in a series of underlying companies, which in turn owned substantial properties in Hong Kong. In 2007, relations between Walter and his brothers deteriorated. In 2014, the settlor, that is, Madam Kwong, and all three sons entered into Heads of Agreement that divided the assets held by the four

57 ibid at [380].
58 ibid at [407].
59 Furthermore, settlors sometimes do not want their beneficiaries to have full access to trust information because they do not want their descendants to have knowledge of the large trust established on their behalf owing to the risk of a forced heirship attack. As a result, some offshore trusts stipulate that a beneficiary's right to trust accounts and information is not absolute.
60 *HSBC Trustee (CI) Limited* v. *Siu Hing Kwong* [2017] JRC 214A.

trusts amongst trusts established for the three branches of the family (those headed by Walter, Thomas, and Raymond) in a fair and tax-efficient manner. Top-up payments were also arranged to equalise the amounts segregated into each branch. The Heads of Agreement were intended to avert the need for litigation. The trustees would transfer 15 per cent of the other assets to trusts for Walter and his family. All of these arrangements were made privately, keeping the family's affairs out of the public spotlight. However, Walter objected to the 15 per cent calculation, and HSBC thus applied for the Jersey Court's blessing for the aforementioned asset segregation decision.

The Court's blessing was duly granted. It held that it was perfectly reasonable for the trustees to proceed on the basis that the settlor's request represented her genuine wishes and that she had not been unduly influenced by Thomas or Raymond. The trustees' decision had been made in good faith, and they had acted reasonably in terms of disclosure and the ascertainment of the family assets in segregating the trusts despite Walter's objection. The trustees had considered the matter very carefully and taken detailed legal advice from lawyers in both Hong Kong and Jersey and from senior English counsel. They had also appointed independent financial advisers and consulted widely, and the minutes covered all pertinent issues thoroughly.

As previously noted, confidentiality is one of the trust's principal advantages over other property-holding arrangements. A trust can be used in conjunction with an underlying company to convert onshore assets (e.g. substantial properties in Hong Kong) into offshore assets and to interpose an additional layer of confidentiality in the chain of ownership. Had Walter not objected to the proposed segregation of assets, the Kwok family's distribution of assets and succession planning arrangements would never have entered the public domain.[61]

## 3.4 *Testamentary Freedom and Mistakes in Trust Planning*

In some cases, a settlor may make transfers to a trust based on a mistaken belief, induced by his trustees or professional advisors, as to the tax implications of doing so. Since *Pitt* v. *Holt*,[62] it is settled in English law that the courts have equitable jurisdiction to set aside a disposition on the ground of a mistake, with the gravity of the mistake to be assessed in terms of the unconscionability or injustice of leaving the mistake

[61] It is worthy of note that the Jersey Court considered the issue of the publication of its judgment in a subsequent decision: *HSBC Trustee (CI) Limited* v. *Siu Hing Kwong* [2018] JRC051A. In general, a judgment will be issued in anonymous form if the hearing takes place in private. In the present case, however, anonymisation of the parties concerned would have been ineffective, as the essential features of the case were already in the public domain. Hence, the Court had to choose between not publishing the judgment at all or publishing it without anonymisation. It came down firmly in favour of publication because the information was already in the public domain and the right of privacy cannot outweigh the interests of public justice.

[62] *Pitt* v. *Holt* [2013] UKSC 26, [2013] 2 AC 108. Thus far, these equitable principles have not been applied by the Hong Kong courts.

uncorrected. Significantly for present purposes, an interesting issue arises as to how the freedom of testation interacts with the court's overall assessment of unconscionability in granting relief for mistakes in trust planning. In *Pitt* v. *Holt*, Lord Walker remarked that the court may withhold rescission 'in some cases of artificial tax avoidance'.[63]

Although his Lordship's dictum is controversial, and its existence as a principle of current law has subsequently come under doubt,[64] it remains a powerful and influential remark, being made by the highest English court and signifying judicial disfavour of aggressive trust planning on the public policy ground that artificial tax avoidance is a social evil that smacks of a want of good citizenship.[65] Offshore courts appear to be moving in the same direction. Whilst offshore courts have traditionally been relatively tolerant of tax avoidance schemes,[66] the tide appears to have turned, with the artificial nature of tax mitigation schemes now potentially featuring in offshore courts' overall assessment of unconscionability. Two Jersey cases decided in 2019 serve to illustrate this point. In both cases, the Jersey Royal Court made repeated cautionary remarks against 'aggressive tax avoidance schemes', noting their relevance in the exercise of the court's discretion. In *In the matter of the J Settlement*, the Jersey Royal Court affirmed (in *obiter*) that allegations of 'aggressive tax avoidance schemes' are potentially a matter that goes to the exercise of the Court's discretion.[67] In *IFM Corporate Trustees Limited* v. *Helliwell*, a case concerning the rescission of a mistake on the ground of rectification, the Jersey Royal Court remarked that it was 'open to argument' that judicial discretion ought not to be exercised if 'the scheme in question is lawful but appears to be so contrived and artificial that it leaves the Court with distaste if, in effect, it is required to endorse it'. The relevant paragraph in the case deserves to be quoted in full:[68]

> Historically, the courts have always applied the principles of law rather than what are perhaps inchoate and uncertain ethical considerations in this area. What seems to us perhaps to be open to argument is whether, in an area which involves the exercise of a judicial discretion in cases where the court's assistance is being sought for a mistake that has been made, there is room for the argument that the discretion ought not to be exercised if, on the facts of a particular case, the scheme in question is lawful but appears to be so contrived and artificial that it leaves the Court with distaste if, in effect, it is required to endorse it.

63 ibid at [135].

64 See, e.g. *Van der Merwe* v. *Goldman* [2016] EWHC 926 (Ch) at [9].

65 *Pitt* [2013] 2 AC 108 at [135].

66 See, e.g. Jersey: *Re the Strathmullan Trust* [2014] JRC 056, 17 ITELR 819 at [25]; Guernsey: *Nourse* v. *Heritage Corporate Trustees Ltd* [2015] 18 ITELR 502 at [16]; Cayman Islands: A. Smellie CJ, 'Dealing with Mistakes of Trustees or Settlors: The Outlook from the Offshore Bench' (2014) 20 *Trusts & Trustees* 1101, 1109.

67 *In the matter of the J Settlement* [2019] JRC 111 at [38].

68 *IFM Corporate Trustees Limited* v. *Helliwell* [2015] JRC 160 at [13]; cited in *Representation of Pinnacle Trustees re: the D and E Trusts* [2019] JRC 246 at [25].

To conclude, whilst testamentary freedom is safeguarded by the use of the trust device, care must be taken in succession planning that involves measures that could potentially be challenged as constituting an 'aggressive tax avoidance scheme'. As such measures will be closely scrutinised by the court when deciding whether to exercise its discretion to grant relief for mistakes in trust planning.

## 4 CONCLUSION

Freedom of testation has long been exalted in Anglo-Hong Kong law. It prevails over intestate distribution schemes. As a result, if a deceased person executed a valid will that expresses his genuine wishes, that will prevent the court from rearranging his estate plan unless the court exercises its statutory power to make discretionary provisions to rescue disinherited family members. Full testamentary freedom is both the prevailing approach and the starting point in Hong Kong succession law. However, the legislature has tempered the principle in favour of protecting family members of the deceased in certain circumstances via various family provision rules. This chapter has examined recent will disputes in which the principle of testamentary freedom was applied to examine how the balance between personal autonomy and familial obligation is struck. The cases under examination demonstrate that personal autonomy is a strong guiding principle that the courts have endeavoured to uphold despite their judicial discretion to rescue disinherited family members under the relevant statute. The system preserves testators' freedom to decide, and that freedom is also valued and respected by courts in Hong Kong. Not only has Hong Kong inherited the common law principle of freedom of testation, but it has also cultivated a robust commitment to it.

A person may still be able to get around the rules on family provision in various ways. For example, he can make inter vivos gifts that will diminish his estate upon his death, and he can also set up a testamentary trust for specified beneficiaries. Such gifts or trust property will not be available to satisfy a family provision claim. Turning to the use of the trust to promote testamentary freedom and family responsibility by granting settlors maximum flexibility to provide for their loved ones, the emergence of offshore, private-client trusts has extended the boundaries of the trust from commercial use to private client asset protection and estate planning. Two points have emerged from the discussion above. First, as recent trust litigation in Hong Kong shows, managing Asian wealth requires sensitivity to the peculiar characteristics of Asian entrepreneurs who desire their trust to safeguard testamentary freedom and maximise the possible amount of control that comes with such freedom. Second, however, as remarks by both the English and offshore judiciaries in the context of mistakes in trust planning demonstrate, aggressive trust planning and tax avoidance schemes are likely to be viewed by the courts with great circumspection.

# 7

# Crazy Rich Families in Singapore

## *Property, Trust and Business Disputes, and the Incompatibility of English Principles*

*Man Yip*[*] *and Tang Hang Wu*[**]

### 1 INTRODUCTION

The 2018 Hollywood movie 'Crazy Rich Asians', directed by Jon M Chu, caused a lot of buzz. It told the story of a fictional Young family who became ultra-rich through investment in real estate. The plot was rich in money-fueled politics of the Young family and complete with a steely and fearsome matriarch played by Michelle Yeoh. In these respects, the movie is not too far from reality. But being a romantic comedy, it had a happy ending. The stories of real-life crazy rich Asian families, on the other hand, are no fairy tales. Unlike the movie where the male lead was the only son and sole heir to the wealth of his branch of the family, many rich Asian families have a number of heirs to the family business and wealth, each vying to be the patriarch/matriarch's favourite. The non-fictional stories often have tragic endings where family relations break down and family businesses are broken up.

This chapter examines the legal contests over family wealth in rich families in Singapore. These disputes tell a cautionary tale that has two core messages. First, it warns against heads of household in over-estimating his or her enduring control over both family and family business affairs and blurring the line between the two at will. Second, it reveals the potential inadequacies of current legal principles, many of which have Western origins, in dealing with the Asian family wealth disputes. This chapter proposes that the best way to avoid tragic endings is to prevent litigation from arising through careful succession planning carried out on the basis of open and transparent communications with each other to avoid unhappiness and misunderstanding.

The discussion comprises three main parts. The first part, by way of background, paints the hallmark features of the complex family dynamics of wealthy Asian

* Associate Professor, Yong Pung How School of Law, Singapore Management University.
** Professor, Yong Pung How School of Law, Singapore Management University.

families. The discussion shows that where wealthy Asian families are concerned, the concept of 'family' is intertwined with the 'family business,' which is the source of the family's influence, wealth, and social standing. The second part provides an in-depth analysis of a selection of representative family wealth disputes in Singapore, with particular focus on how the background family dynamics, which evolve over the years, have brewed a perfect litigation storm in the foreground. The third part offers two reflections: first, taking an *ex post* perspective, what the cases reveal about the mismatch between hard-nosed legal principles and nuanced Asian familial and cultural norms; and secondly, taking an *ex ante* perspective, what families should do, before conflicts arise, to preserve family relations and the family business in the long term.

## 2 THE DYNAMICS OF ASIAN FAMILY BUSINESS AND FAMILY

### 2.1 *The Complexities of the Rich Asian Family*

'Family' is a complex concept, whether in the Asian or Western culture. The rich Asian family is particularly complex in two related ways. First, the wealth of the family typically originates from a successful business enterprise created and managed by the founder family member who is the patriarch or matriarch of the family. The founder would generally wish to keep the business within the family for multiple generations. For this reason, the family is inextricably intertwined with the family business, as family members control and/or influence the affairs of the company. And many family businesses are major business empires. According to a study on Asian family firms, drawing on the annual reports with the financial year ending October 2010 to September 2011, 60.8 per cent of the SGX-listed firms comprise family firms.[1] Family firms have a dominant presence in industries such as construction hotel and restaurants, properties, and manufacturing.[2] Putting aside the founder's sentimental attachment to the enterprise he or she built (often from scratch), this approach also gives the family business the advantage of having longer planning horizons.[3] However, the transfer of ownership to the next generation is likely to lead

1 M. Dieleman, J. Shim, and M. Ibrahim, 'Asian Family Firms: Success sand Succession – A Study of SGX-listed Family Firms' (DBS Bank Ltd & Centre for Governance, Institutions and Organisations, May 2013), p. 8, <https://bschool.nus.edu.sg/cgs/wp-content/uploads/sites/7/2018/10/Success-and-Succession-2013.pdf> last accessed 21 September 2021. This percentage is arrived at based on the application of a broad definition of 'family firm', commonly used in academic research, to refer to firms 'where (co-)founders or heir family members are present among the 20 largest shareholders or as board members'.

2 Dieleman, Shim, and Ibrahim, 'Asian Family Firms: Success sand Succession', p. 11.

3 This assumes that the family remains united and unity is generally present when the dominant control is consolidated in the hands of the patriarch/matriarch.

to fragmentation of ownership and control[4] as there are usually more family members in the next generation than the previous one. Moreover, the increase in the number of shareholders will increase and intensify internal conflicts which will lead to the segmentation and even splintering of the family and the business which supports it.[5]

The second complexity concerning Asian families is the tendency to blur the line between family and business,[6] as well as between the self and the collective. There may be a number of explanations for this behaviour. In some family firms, owing to the consolidated control in the hands of the patriarch/matriarch, capital and assets are easily transferrable across the family group of businesses because they are treated as belonging to a common budget, controlled by the patriarch/matriarch for the common good of the family.[7] The patriarch/matriarch's mindset is, therefore, that the business assets represent family fortunes. His or her actions are also rarely questioned at the corporate level.[8] Moreover, the communitarian culture of prioritising the family and common good above the individual, or more accurately, the expectation of the family members to exhibit such communitarian values by the patriarch/matriarch may partly explain this behaviour in the family. The communitarian value, in the context of Chinese family businesses in Singapore, is often attributed to Confucianism which requires prioritising one's obligation to the family above one's obligations to oneself.[9] Given that '[m]aintaining the continuity of the family is the most important responsibility,' family members 'are obliged to be loyal to the father and to safeguard his business'.[10] A more cynical explanation is that such behaviour manifests from the patriarch/matriarch's unrelenting desire to retain control at home and in the business and his or her intention for no one heir to truly own any of the family wealth or business assets while he or she is still alive.[11]

4 S. Wong, 'The Chinese Family Firm: A Model' XXXVI *The British Journal of Sociology* 58.

5 See, for example, the Eu Yan Sang third-generation family conflict which 'made the conglomerate a mere shadow of its former self by the 1980s'. 'Eu Yan Sang breaks third-generation curse' (15 May 2015), <https://business.inquirer.net/191881/eu-yan-sang-breaks-third-generation-curse> last accessed 21 September 2021.

6 For example, in *Geok Hong Co Pte Ltd* v. *Koh Ai Gek* [2019] 1 SLR 908, the patriarch of the family allowed one of his sons and his family to stay rent free in a property registered in the name of the company for 40 years.

7 Wong, 'The Chinese Family Firm', 64. See also L. H. Tan, 'Family-Owned Firms in Singapore: Legal Strategies for Constraining Self-Dealing in Concentrated Ownership Structures' (2011) 23 *Singapore Academy of Law Journal* 890, 895.

8 See, for example, *Chan Tong Fan* v. *Chiam Heng Luan Realty Pte Ltd (Chiam Toon Tau and anor, non-parties)* [2013] SGHC 192.

9 L. S. Tsui-Auch, 'The Professionally Managed Family-Ruled Enterprise: Ethnic Chinese Business in Singapore' (2004) 41 *Journal of Management Studies* 693, 695–696.

10 ibid.

11 See Tan, 'Family-Owned Firms in Singapore', 890, 893–894.

## 2.2 *The Features of the Generalised Life Cycle of a Rich Asian Family and Its Business*

According to common wisdom, family wealth does not last beyond three generations. This wisdom is shared across cultures and countries,[12] and is backed by data. According to an American consultancy, the Family Business Institute, 'only 30% of family businesses survive into the second generation and 12% into the third,' and 'merely 3% make it into the fourth and beyond'.[13] The downfall of the family business is frequently considered from the angle of corporate governance and in the Asian context, some have attributed the eventual disintegration to the family's general resistance against professional management of the family business.[14] Indeed, according to the 'Asian Business Families Research Survey 2013,' 77 per cent of the founder generation 'have a distinct preference for a family member to continue managing the family business,' but 65 per cent of the second generation in such family businesses indicated that 'they are open to the possibility of either a family member or a non-family member' to succeed the management of the family business.[15]

This chapter is not disagreeing that retaining management within the family in successive generations may have an impact on the fortune and destiny of both the family business and the family. It seeks to offer complementary perspectives based on cultural values and social norms to draw attention to the underlying conflicts and tension which pre-exist in the family even before the first succession. These undercurrents help to explain why the successive generations are unable to keep the family and the business together. The discussion will highlight the features of the generalised life cycle of a rich Asian family and its business. The life cycle is modelled based on the paradigmatic traditional Asian family where the patriarch (or the matriarch) has built a successful business from scratch on his or her own or with other partners and he or she is succeeded by several children in the second generation.[16]

12 The American version of this saying is 'from shirtsleeves to shirtsleeves in three generations'; in Italian, it is 'from stables to stars to stables'.

13 'To have and to hold' The Economist (Special Report: Family Companies) (18 April 2015) <www.economist.com/sites/default/files/20150418_family.pdf> last accessed 21 September 2021.

14 See, for example, L. K. Hing et al, 'Robert Kuok: Family, Dialect, and State in the Making of Malaysian Magnate' (2013) 53 *Australian Economic History Review* 268, 271; Tan, 'Family-Owned Firms in Singapore', 890, 894. Cf. Dieleman, Shim, and Ibrahim, 'Asian Family Firms', pp. 29–30; The picture of change in management in listed family firms in Singapore is more nuanced.

15 Deloitte and Singapore Management University, Business Families Institute, 'Asian Business Families Succession: Going the Distance with the Next Generation' (2013), pp. 8–9 <www2.deloitte.com/content/dam/Deloitte/sg/Documents/finance/sg-fas-bfi-smu-deloitte-report.pdf> last accessed 21 September 2021.

16 The analysis draws inspiration from the insightful discussion in Wong, 'The Chinese Family Firm'.

When the patriarch/matriarch is still in his or her prime and in full control of the business empire and his or her children are young and unmarried, the family, at least on the surface, is more or less a picture of harmony. This is the first phase of the family. The children are extremely respectful and deferential towards their father and mother. Even so, undercurrents might start to build up at this stage at home because the patriarch and matriarch may have a 'favourite child'. In Asian families, this would usually be the son – it could be the firstborn son with whom the patriarch reposes great expectations or the youngest son with whom the patriarch shares a special bond. The preferential treatment of boys over girls can be chalked up to the tradition of sons carrying the family name whereas the daughters are married off to take on their husbands' surnames and become part of their family.[17] The patriarch is thus less willing to involve daughters in key management roles in the business[18] or to give them substantial shareholding.[19] Parental favouritism is known to have 'detrimental and long-lasting effects on children' which can carry into their adulthood.[20] Parental favouritism in a wealthy Asian family is, therefore, all the more likely to breed deep resentment in the less favoured children towards the favoured child given how much is at stake, thereby accounting for their brittle relations when they reach adulthood. In fact, even the competition between brothers when they are growing up can be intense. As Wong (a sociologist) explains, the eldest brother is usually best placed to succeed the patriarch as the chief executive because 'he has the earliest opportunity to work in the firm and establish himself there'.[21] The younger brothers' strategy is to create 'distinct spheres of influence': they would either acquire a different skillset to complement the strengths of the eldest brother so that they can become his trusted deputies, or they would ask to head up new ventures.[22] The emergence of 'distinct spheres of influence' of the family would in due course account for the decentralisation of decision-making and splintering of the family business.

As the siblings are progressively inducted into the management of the family business, the family enters the second phase. The sibling, usually the eldest brother, who is being given the greatest responsibility and groomed to take over the mantle in due course, neither enjoys the absolute control that the reigning patriarch has nor does he command the respect and deference of his siblings. This in part has to do with the 'inconsistent preparation of the brothers for their adult roles' – the eldest brother

17 'Do you have a "favourite" child?' *Today* (16 December 2017) <www.todayonline.com/singapore/do-you-have-favourite-child> last accessed 21 September 2021.

18 The selective grooming of sons as the successors of the business can be seen in *Thio Syn Kym Wendy* v. *Thio Syn Pyn* [2018] 2 SLR 788.

19 See *Ong Bee Dee (executor of the estate of Ong Tuan Seng, deceased)* v. *Ong Bee Chew* [2017] 3 SLR 579.

20 'Do you have a "favourite" child?' *Today* (16 December 2017) <www.todayonline.com/singapore/do-you-have-favourite-child> last accessed 21 September 2021.

21 Wong, 'The Chinese Family Firm', pp. 58, 66

22 ibid

yields to the younger brothers when they were children but as adults, the latter is expected to yield to the former's authority.[23] As the siblings set up their own families and have their own children, the relations are likely to grow more brittle. There will be more heirs in the second succession (the third generation) and each sibling's family (the second generation) may be given a different share of the family wealth based on the number of children it has, fomenting further discontent between the different family members.[24] In fact, it has been argued that the 'most fragile family bonds are to be found among first cousins'.[25]

As the patriarch and matriarch age, their control and power in the business as well as at home may wane due to declining energy and health, as their children continue to strengthen their positions in the business. This is the third phase of the family. The once straightforwardly deferential relationship between the children and the patriarch or matriarch (as the case may be) may also change due to differing expectations on when the second generation will fully take over the business. According to the 'Asian Business Families Research Survey 2013', in respect of the founder generation respondents who prefer to have the management of the family business succeeded by a family member, 62 per cent indicated that they would only hand over the reins to the next generation when they are in their 70s. This is in sharp contrast to the expectations of the second generation who prefers that the incumbent generation cedes control earlier, in their 50s and 60s.[26] Such differences in views could lead to a power tussle between the waning patriarch and matriarch and their intended successors.[27] Moreover, in these later years of the patriarch's or matriarch's life, his or her affection towards each of his or her children may oscillate, depending on which child is the primary caregiver, whether the children remain respectful or have defied their arrangements for them, etc. The power dynamics between the patriarch or matriarch and their children (and perhaps even their

23 M. Wolf, 'Child Training and the Chinese Family, in M. Freedman, *Family and Kinship in Chinese Society* (Stanford University Press, 1970), p. 61.

24 See *Thio Syn Kym Wendy* v. *Thio Syn Pyn* [2017] SGHC 169 at [12]. Following the birth of twin sons by one of his sons (who were the first grandsons to bear the family surname), the patriarch proposed bonus shares be issued to his grandsons and further, the amendment of constitutions of various family-run companies to allow 'only his descendants bearing the Thio surname to hold shares in these companies'. The patriarch's other children were not in favour of it.

25 Wong, 'The Chinese Family Firm,' pp. 58, 68.

26 'Asian Business Families Succession,' p. 9.

27 In *Thio Keng Poon* v. *Thio Syn Pyn* [2010] 3 SLR 143 at [7], the Court of Appeal noted that the patriarch of the family, Mr Thio 'became dissatisfied because his previously unchecked powers of control over the business were progressively being reined in by his family members'. Mr Thio thought that as the founder of the family-run business and the patriarch of the family, 'he was entitled to retain the various offices in the Thio Group on a permanent basis until such time as he chose to retire, or until he passes away, whichever first occurs'. Mr Thio was later removed as the chairman, managing director and director of two of the Thio group companies following an audit engaged by one of the companies.

grandchildren) are likely to undergo change, as the patriarch or matriarch becomes increasingly frail and less lucid over time.

When the patriarch or matriarch passes on, which brings the family to the fourth phase, undercurrent tension and cracks in family relations could erupt into major disagreements as the heirs fight over the family assets, as well as management and ownership of the family business. The family bickering and conflicts could ripen into courtroom drama[28] such as inheritance disputes; shareholder disputes (e.g. minority oppression) and corporate mismanagement disputes (e.g. breach of director's duties); property contests over family or family business assets; and challenges to the patriarch's capacity in respect of his decisions.

## 3 LITIGATION BETWEEN FAMILY MEMBERS: INSIGHTS AND REFLECTIONS

In Part III, to supplement our discussion in Part II, we scrutinise five landmark cases in Singapore from which we can extract further insights into the complex family dynamics inherent in the wealthy families in Singapore. More importantly, important reflections emerge from these decisions.

### 3.1 *Selective Grooming of Sons to Be Successors: The Thio Family Fallout and Corporate Divorce*

In *Thio Syn Kym Wendy* v. *Thio Syn Pyn*,[29] the Court of Appeal considered six appeals that arose out of a series of suits between the members of the Thio family. A detailed account of the family history was set out in the judgment by the High Court,[30] which reveals that the family feud had been a long time coming. The Thio family fallout, in a nutshell, is a tale of parental favouritism and power tussle amongst the family members.

Mr Thio was described as a 'traditional autocratic patriarch' of the Thio family[31] whose fortune could be traced to a successful joint venture that Mr Thio had entered into in 1963 with the Australian Dairy Produce Board to manufacture and market sweetened condensed milk in Singapore and Malaysia (the 'MDI'). The joint venture company now manufactures and distributes a wide range of products under two well-known brands in the region, Vitagen and Marigold. Subsidiary companies were incorporated in due course to form the Thio group of companies (the 'Thio Group'). Over the years, Mr Thio progressively distributed the family wealth to his sons by allotting shares in the family-run companies to them with the intention that they be groomed to take over the

[28] See generally 'Family Feuds over Fortunes and Business Empires: 7 Cases That Have Grabbed Headlines' *Straits Times* (2018), <www.straitstimes.com/singapore/from-the-straits-times-archives-family-feuds-over-fortunes-and-business-empires> last accessed on 21 September 2021.

[29] *Thio Syn Kym Wendy* [2018] 2 SLR 788.

[30] *Thio Syn Kym Wendy* [2017] SGHC 169.

[31] ibid at [10].

business. He initially had no intention to provide for his three daughters (Vicki, Serene, and Wendy) and only did so, upon his wife's insistence that they be given some form of financial provision. He gave them bonus shares in companies in the Thio Group but he retained full power in respect of the shares through blank transfer forms and powers of attorney executed in his favour. He also generally acted as their proxy at shareholder meetings. Given his clearly preferential treatment of the sons, the Court of Appeal noted that there was no relationship of trust and confidence between the plaintiffs (which comprised two daughters (Wendy and Serene) and a son named Michael who was not in the key management role) and Mr Thio.[32]

Even so, Mr Thio's relations with his sons eventually deteriorated due to disagreements. Two of his sons (Patrick and Ernest), who ultimately gained majority control of MDI, objected to his proposal to give shares to his grandsons and to only allow grandsons to own shares in the Thio group companies. The other children were also not in favour of such arrangements. This disagreement was ultimately resolved through the execution of a deed of settlement between the family members which led to the appointment of the daughters and Mr Thio's other son, Michael as directors of each of the Thio Group. The conflict between Mr Thio and Patrick and Ernest grew as the latter continued to disagree with his instructions to them. Moreover, Mr Thio's affair with another woman had left them deeply upset with the hurt that was caused to their mother whom they regarded as a devoted and dutiful wife.

By 2007, Mr Thio had not been actively involved in the management of the Thio Group for a decade. Following an audit of his travel expenses which he sought to claim from the companies, the Board of Directors of MDI, which included his children, met and resolved to remove him from his positions in the company. Perhaps, this outcome was unsurprising, in view of the bitter relations between Mr Thio and his children. Later, Mr Thio was also removed from his offices in other companies in the Thio Group. To cut the long story short, this provoked Mr Thio to sue his wife and children and various Thio Group companies for minority oppression. The breakdown of family relations quickly extended to the second generation following the litigation with the patriarch. Subsequent events taking place at the corporate level of the Thio Group led Wendy, Serene, and Michael to claim against Ernest, Patrick, and their mother (who allegedly supported the brothers) for minority oppression. Three main categories of complaints were put forward, including conducting corporate affairs in a vindictive manner to punish the plaintiffs for their refusal to sell their shares at an undervalue, such as removing the two sisters as directors of two companies, reduction of Michael's salary in Malaysian companies and removing Michael and Serene's car benefits in MDI.

The Court of Appeal, affirming the High Court's ruling, found that oppression relief in the form of a buyout order was appropriate in the case of a traditional family

32 *Thio Syn Kym Wendy* [2018] 2 SLR 788 at [6].

company run by an automatic patriarch which did not fall into the category of a quasi-partnership. The Court of Appeal, however, extended the buyout order to the plaintiffs' shares in both MDI and the holding company. This decision has been applauded for its 'pragmatic approach in recognising the need for the oppression remedy to extend beyond quasi-partnerships – particularly to autocratic patriarch companies', which are a common feature of the Singapore business landscape and most at risk of majority shareholder abuse given the immense power wielded by the patriarch over the companies.[33] Importantly, the Court of Appeal recognised, by way of obiter, that a case might be made for creating a new framework to assess minority oppression in the context of traditional family-run companies:[34]

> We observe, parenthetically, that this might be perceived by some as a widening conception of what constitutes minority oppression for traditional family companies where the family patriarch wields extreme amounts of control over the company and selectively grooms his successors. Such companies would not usually constitute quasi-partnerships because of a lack of *mutual trust* and confidence, but even if the parties do not expressly set out their legitimate expectations, there may still be unwritten expectations that the family shareholders in management cannot expend corporate resources for personal reasons to punish other family members and that any benefits previously agreed upon between the family members should not be arbitrarily reduced or removed. We leave open the question of whether these expectations establish a new intermediate ***legal*** standard of conduct applicable to traditional family companies *or* merely constitute ***factual*** *instances* that do not carry normative or legal significance as such…

Three important reflections can be derived from this decision. First, the patriarch of a family should rethink engaging in preferential treatment of his children which would inevitably sow rancour and mistrust in the family, reducing the prospects of the children collaborating in the running of the family company. Second, the patriarch should not overestimate his authority and power both at home and in the company. The entire family should be professionally advised and properly educated on the succession of ownership and management of the family-run business early on. Finally, as a matter of law, *Thio Syn Kym Wendy* suggests s. 216 of the Companies Act[35] on minority oppression, which was derived from s. 210 of the UK Companies Act 1948 and s. 186 of the Australian Companies Act, could be adapted to meet the unique challenges arising from traditional family companies. Indeed, it has been forcefully argued that the creation of a new legal standard or 'code of conduct' for autocratic patriarch companies would be a sensible move to respond to commercial realities of Singapore, in view that traditional family companies lie 'at the core of Singapore's economy'.[36]

33 C. H. Tan and S. Tang, 'Company Law' (2018) 19 *Singapore Annual Review* 227, para. 9.18.
34 *Thio Syn Kym Wendy* [2018] 2 SLR 788 at [28] (emphasis as original).
35 Companies Act (Cap 50, Rev Ed 2006).
36 Tan and Tang, 'Company Law,' para. 9.23.

### 3.2 *Blurring the Line between Family Assets and Family Business Assets: The Tan Siblings' Contest over the Beneficial Ownership of Shares*

The second case is *Tan Yok Koon* v. *Tan Choo Suan* which was described by the Court of Appeal as a 'very unfortunate' story of a 'total breakdown in familial ties' between siblings, a state of affairs which would have made their father, the deceased patriarch 'profoundly disappointed' or even 'heartbroken'.[37] The dispute concerned, amongst other issues, the beneficial ownership of shares in the family company.

Mr Tan, the patriarch, set up the family company in 1916, which shares were held by the Tans and Bajumis (the family of Mr Tan's business partner) from 1968 to 2004. Mr Tan brought his children in as shareholders of the Company in 1968, issuing forty shares to each child. Mr Tan expected his children, especially his sons, to enter the family business. His children, except for his eldest daughter (T1), did get involved in the business for most of their adult lives.[38] By the mid-1970s, Mr Tan ceased being actively involved in the Company, and in late 1974, he and his wife moved permanently to Hong Kong. The day-to-day management of the Company was left to his four children, T2, T3, T4, and T5, although he was updated and consulted on major decisions concerning the Company. Mr Tan then fully divested his shares in the Company to his three sons, T2, T3, and T5. He also bought shares from the Bajumis to be transferred to his sons. Thus, in 1985, the Tans owned 50 per cent of the shares and the Bajumis owned the other 50 per cent. Amongst the Tans, the percentage of shareholding at the time was as follows: N (2.22%), T1 (4.44%), T2 (13.70%), T3 (13.70%), T4 (4.44%), and T5 (11.48%).

Relations between the Bajumis and the Tans subsequently deteriorated which culminated in the Tans' acquisition of Bajumis' 50 per cent shareholding in 2004. The acquisition was funded by a loan for which the Tan family members were intended to be responsible. The acquired shares were transferred to Mrs Tan. Between 1986 and 2008, T2, T3, T4, and T5, deferring to Mr Tan's wishes, had transferred their shares in the Company to T1 for no consideration in anticipation of the establishment of a family trust. The trust was, however, never set up. In 2008, thus, T1 and Mrs Tan held 47.78 per cent and 52.22 per cent shareholding in the Company, respectively.

Relevantly, following the Tans' acquisition of Bajumis' shareholding in 2004, T1, who was not involved in the family business before, began to 'exert greater control over [the Company] and greater influence over her parents'.[39] When Mr Tan passed away in late 2008, the siblings' relations rapidly deteriorated. First, T1 refused to return the shares that her siblings had earlier transferred to her. T1 claimed that

37 [2017] 1 SLR 654 at [1].

38 See *Tan Yok Koon* [2017] 1 SLR 654 at [15].

39 *Tan Yok Koon* [2017] 1 SLR 654 at [36]–[37]. For example, in 2007, T1 proposed to Mr Tan that T5 should resign as the Company's managing director. She was then appointed as the managing director by the Company's board of directors.

the siblings previously held the company shares as Mr Tan's nominees and after the transfers, T1 held the shares on trust for Mr Tan's estate. T1 also removed T2, T4, and T5 from their offices in the Company and then barred them from entering the Company's premises. T2–T5 commenced proceedings against T1 and Mrs Tan, seeking inter alia a declaration that they were beneficially entitled to the shares in the company in the percentages as in 1985.

The resolution of the dispute centred heavily on the transferor's intention. First, in respect of Mr Tan's transfer of the Company shares to his children, whether he intended the transfers as gifts. Assuming the transfers were gifts from Mr Tan to his children, in respect of T2–T5's transfer of the Company shares to T1, whether T2–T5 intended to relinquish their beneficial interest in Mr Tan's favour. The case presented unique challenges to finding the answers to the two questions. There was 'a dearth of clear and objective evidence' due in part to the 'more informal manner in which the family business was run'.[40] Mr Tan was also noted by the Court of Appeal to be 'an autocratic patriarch who demanded and generally received utmost respect' from his children and he drew 'no distinction between the assets of this family members and those of his companies'. Further, Mr Tan had never expressly indicated in his letters that the Company belonged to his children pursuant to the various share transfers. The Court of Appeal attributed this to Mr Tan's ambivalence about handing over the reins to his sons. It was observed that:[41]

> Mr Tan…on one hand desiring to retain control (or at least influence) in the affairs of [the Company] as its founder and as the patriarch of the family, and, on the other hand, recognising ultimately that he was past the retirement age of the era, that he had been away for health reasons, and that he had to cede control to the next generation if [the Company] was to be the lasting legacy that he surely wanted it to be.

Finally, Mr Tan executed two statutory declarations in 2008 which stated that he had retained beneficial ownership in the company shares. Mr Tan's post-transfer conduct was held to be admissible.[42]

Notwithstanding these difficulties, the Court of Appeal ultimately concluded that Mr Tan did gift the shares to his children out of his love because he considered them to be the successors of the business and had wished to incentivise them to work hard at the family business.[43] As to the second question on the intention of T2–T5 in respect of their transfer of shares to T1, the Court held that they did not intend to relinquish the beneficial interest. The court cautioned against inferring the children's rights to the Company shares based simply on their general deference

40 See *Tan Yok Koon* [2017] 1 SLR 654 at [2].
41 ibid, [87].
42 The Court of appeal relaxed the rule in *Shephard* v. *Cartwright* [1955] AC 431. See *Tan Yok Koon* [2017] 1 SLR 654 at [106]–[110].
43 *Tan Yok Koon* [2017] 1 SLR 654 at [84].

to Mr Tan's authority and that Mr Tan conventionally regarded business assets as family assets.[44] The court also ascribed no weight to Mr Tan's post-transfer conduct in executing the statutory declarations because they 'were too far removed in time' from the transfers which took place between 1968 and 1985 and executed at a time when he was under T1's influence and in poor health.[45] In this connection, the court took the view that the statutory declarations reflected Mr Tan's disappointment with T2–T5 in 2008 and not his intention at the time of the transfers. The court accepted T1's evidence that Mr Tan was disappointed with his sons as they were 'no longer as welcoming and deferential and that they hardly visited him in Hong Kong'.[46] It is interesting to note that the Court of Appeal had resolved the question concerning Mr Tan's intention based on evidence, instead of resorting to the use of presumptions of resulting trust and advancement. As See points out, 'this development may be attributable to the judicial realisation that presumptions, while providing an intuitive solution in simple familial arrangements, are inadequate in dealing with more complex ones'.[47] Perhaps, the court realised that these presumptions, being derived from English equity, are less applicable to deducing the probabilistic intentions of an autocratic Asian patriarch. When one considers Mr Tan's pattern of behaviour as the patriarch of the family and the founder of the business empire, one gets a sense that the patriarch might never had a clear intention as to whether his children became the owner of the Company shares. He might have operated under the stubborn belief that all company assets were family assets held collectively by the family and to be distributed according to the wishes of the head of the household. Perhaps, to an Asian patriarch, the question is not one of ownership but one of authority and control. His 2008 statutory declarations might have reflected his grave disappointment with his sons but concurrently, they might have reflected his deep-seated belief that he continued to control the family assets. If this was, indeed, the mindset of Mr Tan, would it be realistic to speak of intention at discrete points of time?

### 3.3 *Real Estate and the Family Business: The Swee Kee Chicken Rice Dispute and Deference to Legal Documentation*

Another feature in family businesses in Singapore is the prominence of real estate in the family's asset portfolio. In many cases, the dispute between the family members revolves around the beneficial ownership of real estate. *Moh Tai Siang* v. *Moh Tai Tong and another*[48] is an illustration of such a dispute. The Moh family was in the

44 ibid, [86] and [93].
45 ibid, [117].
46 *Tan Yok Koon* [2017] 1 SLR 654 at [117].
47 A. See, 'Transferor's Intention, Trustees' Undertaking and the Scope of Fiduciary Liability' (2018) 32 *Trust Law International* 50 at 52.
48 [2018] SGHC 280.

food business with the patriarch being one of the pioneers of the famed, Swee Kee Chicken Rice & Restaurant, reputedly an establishment which introduced chicken rice in Singapore. Since they had a prosperous business, the family was able to make several property investments. This case involves a dispute between the Moh siblings over a property located at Branksome Road which was worth S$ 16 million. The property was purchased by the patriarch in 1957 and used as the family home. In 1974, the patriarch conveyed the property in the following manner:

(a) One-quarter share to Tai Sing, the first son;
(b) Three-quarter share to himself, the matriarch, and Tai Sing to hold on trust for Freddy (the second son), Tai Siang (the third son), and Royston (the fourth son).

At the time of the 1974 conveyance, the three younger siblings had not reached the age of majority. In April 1985, when all the siblings were adults, the matriarch and Tai Sing executed an indenture of conveyance transferring the trust property to Freddy, Tai Siang, and Royston in equal shares. Therefore, all the Moh siblings had one-quarter share of the property. On the same day of the indenture of conveyance, Tai Siang transferred his one-quarter share to Tai Sing, Freddy, and Royston for a consideration of $ 200,000. Many years later, Tai Siang, who was the plaintiff, sued his brothers over this transfer. Tai Siang disputed receiving the $ 200,000 and claimed he was told by the matriarch that his brothers would hold Tai Siang's share in the property on trust for him. His brothers, who were the defendants, claimed that the indenture of conveyance evidenced an outright sale of Tai Siang's interest to them.

In pursuing his claim, Tai Siang's characterisation of the family dynamics presents a fascinating, albeit contested, window into the Singaporean business family. Tai Siang described the Moh family as closely knit traditional Hainanese clan who lived under the thumb of the matriarch and Tai Sing, the eldest son, after the patriarch's demise. According to Tai Siang's account, the family had a long-held practice of transferring assets among family members to protect these assets from creditors. This was the rationale of the 1974 trust where the patriarch was seeking to circumvent claims from a bank by transferring the property into his wife's and son's names. Since Tai Siang was facing financial problems, the matriarch and Tai Sing instructed Tai Siang to transfer his interest in the property to his brothers. In contrast, the other siblings said that the conveyance was a sale from Tai Siang to his siblings.

The judge, Aedit Abdullah J, dismissed Tai Siang's claim. Given the passage of time and the fact that the patriarch, matriarch, and eldest son had passed away, Abdullah J said it was difficult to place significant weight on the existence or non-existence of family practices. In this regard, the learned judge said:

> There is also the further task of persuading the court of the inferences to be drawn from family customs and practices, as well as the relevance of and weight to be placed on those inferences to the immediate issue at hand. The strength that can

> be attributed to evidence of custom or practice as part of a chain of inferences about the facts in issue is likely, in most cases, to be weak: alternative explanations come readily to mind… What matters more is the direct evidence of the intention of the testator or person disposing of the property at the time of the legacy or gift. If there exists a document, evidence of custom or practices have to be particularly cogent to overcome the documentary evidence; even on the standard of a balance of probabilities.

Abdullah J found that since the indenture was a document which properly signed, sealed, delivered, and witnessed by a solicitor, cogent evidence would be needed for the court to disregard the clear contents of the documents. On the facts, the learned judge found that cogent evidence was not presented in the present dispute to rebut what was recorded in the indenture.

Besides illustrating the prominence of real estate in the Singapore business family, *Moh Tai Siang* v. *Moh Tai Tong and another* emphasises that in legal disputes among family members, the court gives primacy to the effect of signed legal documents instead of assertions of oral arrangements between family members. This is especially if these contested arrangements happened a long time ago and the main witnesses have passed away.[49] Thus, for any claims based on informal family arrangements to succeed, cogent evidence is required to persuade the court to disregard the formal position as shown in the legal documents.[50]

### 3.4 *Business Legacy Planning Going Awry: The Ong Family*

'The frustrated intentions of a dead man are at the heart of this case,' declared Valerie Thean JC (as she then was) who heard the dispute in *Ong Bee Dee (executor of the estate of Ong Tuan Seng, deceased)* v. *Ong Bee Chew and others*.[51] While succession planning is paramount in preventing family disputes, this case was a situation where the patriarch, Ong Tuan Seng, had his business legacy planning going awry leading his children and grandchildren to a legal dispute.

The patriarch had six sons and four daughters. While the patriarch only spoke the Hokkien dialect and had a basic grasp of Mandarin, he was an extremely successful entrepreneur with a forklift, textile, and property business. The family business

49 For example, in *Geok Hong Co Pte Ltd* v. *Koh Ai Gek* [2019] 1 SLR 908 counsel for the defendants argued successfully in resisting the claim that the claimant had to prove 'what one dead man said to another dead man 40 years ago'. The claim failed because the Court of Appeal did not believe that the relevant representations were indeed made.

50 Cf. *Chia Kok Weng* v. *Chia Kwok Yeo* [2017] 2 SLR 964 where the Court of Appeal found that there was undisputed evidence of a 'family compact' to transfer the property amongst family members when the family was facing financial difficulties. The legal documentations used in such transfers were via sale and purchase transactions. However, the court found that these were not true sale and purchase and the claim for resulting trust was allowed.

51 [2017] 3 SLR 579.

was structured along the lines of several companies which included Chen Hock Heng Machinery Pte Ltd ('CHHMPL'), Ong Tuan Seng Development (Pte) Ltd ('OTSDPL'), and Ong Tuan Seng Pte Ltd ('OTSPL'). OTSDPL functioned as the Ong's family holding company in which all the Ong siblings held shares in the company. Like many family businesses in Singapore, the crown jewel of their assets comprised real estate. At the heart of the dispute is the ownership of two hotels situated at 757 Geylang Road and 12 Lorong 12 Geylang. Initially, these two hotels were owned by CHHMPL and the patriarch wanted to restructure the ownership of the hotel prior to his death.

The patriarch's overarching intention was for his family to retain the hotels for at least 30 years. Several complicated steps were taken in connection with this purported plan. The hotel at 757 Geylang was transferred from CHHMPL to OTSDPL. OTSDPL had an initial paid-up capital of $4 with shares owned by the patriarch and his sons, Bee Dee (the plaintiff), Bee Chip, and Bee Song. The four shareholders were also directors of OTSDPL. After a series of share transfers, the shares of CHHMPL were held by the patriarch, Bee Leng (one of the sons and 1st Defendant), Chong Ho (Bee Leng's son), Bee Beng (one of the sons), and Yongxiang (Bee Beng's sons). At all material times, Bee Leng and his wife, Guat Leng (the 2nd Defendant) helped the patriarch manage CHHMPL. It is interesting that the daughters of this family and their children were not given shares in these companies. Instead, the patriarch gave each of his daughters $ 450,000. In late 2011, the patriarch transferred 320,000 shares in CHHMPL to Bee Leng and his son Zhi Jie (the 3rd Defendant) making his branch of the family the majority shareholders. A further issue of 340,000 new CHHMPL shares was given to Bee Leng and Zhi Jie in early 2012. This resulted in Bee Leng's family owning 51 per cent of the CHHMPL. The patriarch also transferred 26,000 OTSDPL shares to Bee Leng and made him a director of the company.

An aborted shareholders' agreement was the catalyst for the dispute to burst into open. The lawyers drafted a shareholder agreement that gave Bee Leng extensive powers over CHHMPL which included being the managing director, the right to nominate his younger son to be a director and all management decisions to be affirmed by him. Another clause in the draft shareholder agreement provided that CHHMPL will not sell its real estate for a period of 30 years. When the draft shareholder agreement was presented to the family at the lawyer's office in March 2012, an uproar ensued, and the family members started quarrelling in front of the lawyers. Members of the family refused to sign the agreement and stormed off. Subsequently, the patriarch, through his newly appointed lawyers, wrote to Bee Leng demanding that he reverse the various share transfers in CHHMPL and OTSPDL that were transferred to Bee Leng and his sons. In May 2021, the patriarch wrote to Bee Leng asking him to reverse the increase in shareholding in CHHMPL and return the shares in OTSDPL alleging *inter alia* misrepresentation, conspiracy, breach of fiduciary duty, and *non-est factum*. Ultimately, this claim failed because

Thean JC found that the Bee Leng and his wife were not fiduciaries of the patriarch and that *non-est factum* was not applicable to the facts of the case.

Several interesting observations emerge from this case. First, this decision illustrates that in some traditional Chinese business families, the daughters are excluded from the succession of the family business. In the Ong family, the patriarch only included the male lineage of the family in the companies although he did ensure that his daughters would be provided for by giving each daughter close to half a million dollars. Second, this case also highlights a common dynamic that exists within a traditional family where the patriarch maintained dominance over the family members and family business. The exchange between the patriarch and the lawyer who advised on the aborted shareholder agreement is particularly telling. Ms Yui, who drafted the agreement, queried the patriarch whether the other shareholders would sign the document considering that the patriarch was only a minority shareholder. The patriarch confidently replied in the Hokkien dialect, '*wo si lao pa*' ('I am the old father') and that the children would comply. Unfortunately, for the elderly patriarch, he must have overestimated his influence over the family. In the end, the children did not comply with his wishes which resulted in this dispute. Finally, this case is an example of a patriarch having a romanticised view of keeping certain real estate in the family for a stated period. This is often a source of dispute for the family. In this instance, the overarching aim of keeping the hotels in the family for 30 years resulted in one branch of the Ong family maintaining a majority shareholding and dominance in management in the family company, which is a consequence which the patriarch may not have foreseen or wanted.

## 3.5 *Mental Capacity as Locus of Family Disputes: The Case of the Waning Matriarch*

Another fertile source of disputes for wealthy families is when the mental capacity of the patriarch or matriarch wanes. *Re BKR*[52] is an illustration of such a dispute where an application is made pursuant to the Mental Capacity Act (2010)[53] for a declaration that the matriarch is unable to make decisions because of an impairment of or disturbance in the function of her mind. Consequently, the application sought for deputies to be appointed to make on her behalf all decisions in relation to her property and affairs. The respondent, Madam BKR, has three children, her eldest daughter, NG, her son CK and the first respondent. Madam BKR inherited a vast fortune from her father approaching $200 million. Unfortunately, there was considerable friction and animosity between Madam BKR's offsprings and they split into two camps with NG and CK aligned with each other against the first respondent. Madam BKR began to suffer from memory deficits from 2005 and this was noticed

52 [2015] 4 SLR 81.
53 (Cap 177A, 2010 Rev Ed).

by her bankers, JP Morgan. Madam BKR would forget her own instructions to JP Morgan. As a result, JP Morgan ceased to accept her oral instructions unless CK also reviewed and confirmed those instructions.

The dispute revolved around the settlement of a trust in 2010 with DBS. Prior to the DBS trust, Madam BKR had two other trusts with JP Morgan and UBS. The JP Morgan trust provided for herself whereas the UBS trust provided for the education of her eight grandchildren. In relation to the DBS trust, the terms of the trust stated that it would provide for Madam BKR during her lifetime and that it would make donations to charitable organisations after her death. The first respondent was appointed as the protector of the trust. Upon Madam BKR's death, the trust provided that S$10 million would be injected into a bank account of a company and that company would become the sole property of the protector. Excluded persons were named in the trust, that is, those people who were entirely excluded from any benefits of the trust. NG and CK were named as excluded persons, and the trustee or protector was also an excluded person for the duration of their occupation of the said positions. Madam BKR purportedly wrote to UBS to transfer all the assets in the UBS trust to DBS. UBS arranged a face-to-face meeting with her and the meeting included Madam BKR's sister, the first appellant. After the meeting on 23 November 2010, Madam BKR revoked her instructions to UBS to transfer the assets to DBS and authorised UBS to disclose her account information to her two sisters, CK and Madam BKR's personal assistant. However, on 29 November 2010, Madam BKR faxed fresh instructions to transfer all her assets in UBS to DBS within a week. CK also discovered that Madam BKR had recently purchased a bungalow in the name of the first respondent's husband (the second respondent). Subsequently, JP Morgan had a meeting with Madam BKR in Hong Kong, in the presence of her lawyer, Mr L and two bankers from DBS. At the meeting, Mr L spoke on her behalf and instructed that all the assets in the JP Morgan trust be transferred to the DBS trust. A similar meeting took place with UBS and instructions were given to transfer the funds to DBS. In 2011, Madam BKR's sisters commenced proceedings under the Mental Capacity Act 2010.

Ultimately, Sundaresh Menon CJ who delivered the judgment in *Re BKR* found that Madam BKR did not have mental capacity. While a closer examination of the law of mental capacity is beyond the scope of this chapter, the learned Chief Justice seemed troubled by Madam BKR's purpose in setting up the DBS trust. When asked about the DBS trust, Madam BKR said she created the trust to hide money from people, and from her son, CK. Madam BKR said this trust was for her survival and she 'felt so relieved' that CK was shocked at being unable to find her money. She kept on saying the reason for transferring money into the DBS trust is 'so that nobody knows' and 'nobody can find'. Menon CJ found that this belief was problematic because it arose suddenly in her mind without any apparent cause and there was no perceptible factual basis for the belief. Hence, the learned Chief Justice found that the basis for setting up the trust was motivated by a paranoid belief which was caused in part by her mental impairment.

Besides illustrating family feuds which is a result of the second generation not getting along, *Re BKR* demonstrates that mental capacity battles may become the locus for family disputes. With people living longer and the advance in medical science, it is likely that family patriarchs and matriarchs may enjoy greater longevity; however, there will usually be a twilight period when the mental capacity of patriarchs and matriarchs begin to wane. This is the period when the warring camps in the family may begin to contest the mental capacity of the patriarchs or matriarchs. If the patriarchs or matriarchs are declared to be mentally incapable, it is likely that one or more of the children will be appointed to be the deputy with the corresponding right to make decisions in relation to property and affairs. Since deputies control the property and affairs of the patient, one can immediately see the high stakes involved in these mental capacity fights. Hence, *Re BKR* is a cautionary tale of the importance of careful succession planning which includes situations where mental capacity is lost.

## 4 NORMATIVE IMPLICATIONS OF FAMILY WEALTH DISPUTES: INCOMPATIBILITY OF ENGLISH PROPERTY AND TRUST DOCTRINES WITH ASIAN FAMILIAL AND CULTURAL NORMS

The preceding sections demonstrate that the court is far from the ideal forum to resolve family wealth disputes. A recurring difficulty in this area is the sheer incompatibility of English property and trust doctrines with Asian familial and cultural norms in the context of family wealth disputes. In this area, the doctrines that are often pleaded are the resulting and common intention constructive trusts.[54] For both these doctrines, the key element is the proof of intention of the parties. However, the unspoken norm in many Asian families, at least where the patriarch and matriarch are controlling the family, is that there is a family-oriented collectivism.[55] In many cases, the assertion is that the property and wealth are regarded as owned by the family as a collective whole. Yet, such an unspoken norm is difficult to prove in a court of law, especially when the patriarch and matriarch have passed away.

Even if a common intention that the assets are held for the family may be proven, a potential difficulty is showing the necessary detriment and reliance. In many of these cases, the family members might have conducted their social and professional lives in accordance with the wishes of their parents. But it remains controversial whether such conduct may be regarded as sufficient reliance and detriment to establish a common intention constructive trust over alleged family assets. Furthermore, the case law shows that there is a high degree of a culture of informality between family members in relation to their business and real estate interests. Often, the

54 See M. Yip, 'Comparing Family Property Disputes in English and Singapore Law: "Context Is Everything"' (2021) 41 *Legal Studies* 474.

55 See Wong, 'The Chinese Family Firm', p. 58.

ownership of business and real estate may be transferred from one offspring to another offspring in deference to the wishes of the patriarch and matriarch.[56] The difficulty with applying property and trust doctrines to a situation where the familial relationship breaks down shows that the court of law is hardly the ideal forum to resolve such disputes. Hence, it is crucial that careful succession planning must be carried out to prevent disputes. It is to this topic that we now turn to in the next section.

## 5 CAREFUL SUCCESSION PLANNING TO MINIMISE DISPUTES

In this section, we consider the practical steps that families may take to minimise family wealth disputes. The most obvious solution is for the family to embark on careful succession planning with open and transparent communications with each other to avoid unhappiness and misunderstanding. Although such a process is paramount to avoid disputes, there are several usual impediments to this sensible course of action. For some families, there is a cultural distaste especially among the older generation to think about one's mortality. Hence, there is the tendency to put off the process of formal succession planning until it is too late. In other families, the relationship between family members is so dysfunctional that succession planning is difficult to be carried out. Decades of enmity and ill-feeling among members have fossilised the dynamics of the family so much so that open conversations about succession planning are all but impossible. Further, in some of these families, the patriarch or matriarch might not have a communicative relationship with their family members and instead rely on unspoken cultural expectations like filial piety and family norms to govern the relationship between family members.[57] Yet, these expectations and norms are fragile and may lead to disputes when members of the younger generation do not display conduct expected by the patriarch or matriarch.[58] As seen by the case law above, the usual catalyst for legal disputes is when these norms and expectations are not met.

Thus, it is important that the succession planning process be carried out to avoid disputes. Several basic steps should be taken. First, the matriarch and patriarch must execute a will setting out clearly the entitlement of the family members. In drafting the will, the lawyer should take great care that this is done properly to avoid the will be challenged.[59] Also, if there is long-simmering tension between family members, the will should contemplate bequests to family members which allow them to have a 'clean break' from each other. Unrealistic expectations and complicated

[56] As seen in the cases of *Tan Yok Koon* [2017] 1 SLR 654; *Ong Bee Dee (executor of the estate of Ong Tuan Seng, deceased)* 3 SLR 579; *Moh Tai Siang* [2018] SGHC 280.

[57] See, for example, *Ong Bee Dee (executor of the estate of Ong Tuan Seng, deceased)* [2017] 3 SLR 579.

[58] As demonstrated by *Tan Yok Koon* [2017] 1 SLR 654.

[59] See *Low Ah Cheow and others v. Ng Hock Guan* [2009] 3 SLR(R) 1079 at [72]–[74].

family entanglements are best avoided. Bequests of business and real estate interests that force family members to work and live together is a recipe for future disputes. Particularly, succession planning which envisages that certain real estate be kept in the family business for a period of time is generally not a good idea.[60] Disputes are often precipitated by family members who feel hard done by and left out of the family inheritance and, hence, proper thought should be given to each family member's entitlement. The execution of the will should be done with the benefit of a skillful and experienced legal advisor ensuring that the bequests in the will are regarded as fair to the family members. As far as possible, the legal advisor should also advise the patriarch and matriarch from entrenching impractical dynastic considerations in their will. Second, apart from executing a will, the patriarch or matriarch should sort out the precise beneficial entitlement of joint properties, bank accounts, gifts to family members, properties held on trust for family members. Often, disputes arise because family members allege that there is some resulting or common intention constructive trust over certain assets. Such claims may be easily avoided by putting in relevant clauses in the will or recording the intention of the relevant parties clearly by way of a sworn statement. For good measure, the recorded intention of the relevant parties should be circulated to all family members so that everyone will know where they stand.

Finally, careful planning for the loss of mental capacity of the patriarch and matriarch ought to be carried out. As demonstrated by the case law above, one of the major pressure points for disputes is when the patriarch or matriarch loses mental capacity. A carefully considered lasting power of attorney should be executed with the patriarch and matriarch recognising that the donee of the lasting power of attorney will wield vast power over his or her estate. Joint donees may be considered although this may prove to be cumbersome and result in a deadlock if there is a disagreement between donees. Such disagreements may become a trigger point for disputes. Also, thought should be given to limiting the powers of the donee. In some cases, it may be prudent to limit the powers of the donee to buy and sell business and real estate interests, vary pre-existing trust structures, and set up new trust structures. Otherwise, if the succession planning process had already been documented in the will, this can be easily disrupted by a donee going rogue. For ultra-high net worth families, suitable trust structures or foundations may be considered.[61] In some families, they may consider setting up private trust companies, enact a family constitution, and sign relevant shareholder agreements. Properly executed and with open and transparent communication between family members, these mechanisms may avoid disputes between family members.

60 See, for example, *Ong Bee Dee (executor of the estate of Ong Tuan Seng, deceased)* [2017] 3 SLR 579.

61 See H. W. Tang, 'From Waqf, Ancestor Worship to the Rise of the Global Trust: A History of the Use of the Trust as a Vehicle for Wealth Transfer in Singapore' (2018) 103(5) *Iowa Law Review* 2263.

## 6 CONCLUSION

This chapter has examined the legal contests over family wealth in rich families in Singapore. It seeks to shine a spotlight on family cultures, norms, and behaviour in rich Asian families that are likely to foment long-term resentment and irreconcilable conflicts in the family, contributing to a 'time bomb' for the family business if not handled with care.[62] Nobody wins when the matter is in the courtroom. No judge can fully grasp the complexity of emotions at the family layer. Nor can the legal principles assist the court in accurately divining the parties' intentions given the general informality of family dealings. The central message is this: neither the family wealth nor the family may last beyond three generations unless the patriarch or matriarch proactively undertakes succession planning with the aid of professional advisors and through open and transparent communications with the family members and recording the family agreements and arrangements in formal documents. This is no easy task, as this chapter has explained. Importantly, the patriarch or matriarch must start by altering the traditional mindset of avoiding discussing his or her demise and expecting full deference from his or her children by reason of filial piety and family loyalty. These are necessary first steps towards preserving the family and its fortune.

[62] 'Lesson from Stanley Ho's Family Feud: How to Spot a Time Bomb' Forbes (21 March 2011), <www.forbes.com/sites/russellflannery/2011/03/21/lesson-from-stanley-hos-family-feud-how-to-spot-a-time-bomb/?sh=790bb8c410c2> last accessed 25 August 2021.

# 8

# Family Offices, Private Trust Companies, and Trust Integrity Issues

## *Problems and Solutions*

*Vincent Ooi*[*] *and Chan Ee Lin*[**]

## 1 INTRODUCTION

In recent years, the rapid increase of ultra-high-net-worth ('UHNW') individuals in Asia has placed the actions and choices of this class of financial elites and their affairs in the spotlight. In this chapter, we consider structures such as Family Offices and Private Trust Companies ('PTCs') that are commonly used by the Asian ultra-wealthy, focusing on the composition of their management boards. We also consider the use of the new Variable Capital Company ('VCC'). UHNW families typically own family businesses, the original source of their wealth that eventually gets managed by their Family Offices and/or PTCs. Altogether these family businesses, Family Offices, and PTCs, are known as family enterprises. Several family governance issues commonly arise in practice, such as control and management, duties owed by the managers, succession planning, and how to resolve possible conflicts between beneficiaries. These issues must be borne in mind when evaluating which structures to adopt so that the families are able to sustainably maintain them effectively over time. In addition, where settlors attempt to retain considerable control over the trusts (for example, through 'double hatting'), trust integrity issues may arise, which increases the risk of trusts being treated as sham or illusory trusts. In this chapter, we propose several solutions to resolve the trust integrity issues highlighted, including focusing on the importance of establishing effective family governance, proper administration processes, succession planning strategies, and employing professionals with good trust experience to assist in managing the trusts. The discussion centres around developments in Singapore, though the insights and analysis from this article remain applicable across most common law jurisdictions.

[*] Lecturer, Yong Pung How School of Law, Singapore Management University.

[**] Non-practicing Advocate and Solicitor of the Supreme Court of Singapore; Adjunct Faculty, Lee Kong Chian School of Business, Singapore Management University.

## 2 THE CONCEPT OF A FAMILY TRUST

### 2.1 *General Definition of Family Offices*

Family Offices are commonly understood to refer to a broad category of entities that conduct the day-to-day administration and management of the assets and investments of UHNW individuals or families for the purposes of wealth creation, preservation, and enhancement for future generations.[1] While Family Offices are typically independent legal entities, they are generally not statutorily defined.[2] That being said, there are two main types of Family Offices: (1) Single Family Offices ('SFOs') that manage the assets of a single family and (2) Multi-Family Offices, ('MFOs') that manage the wealth of multiple unrelated families. While an SFO is owned by the family it serves, MFO owners also include institutionally backed entities, for example, subsidiaries of banks or financial institutions.[3] Some SFOs perform so successfully that they evolve into family-owned MFOs, and may form another family business for the original SFO-owning family. SFOs and family-owned MFOs often involve family members serving as board directors and/or employees working alongside non-family professionals.

Another feature of SFOs is their inherent variability of internal organisation and functional structure since they are highly customised to serve the needs of one particular family. Some families operate their Family Offices alongside their family businesses, while others may have sold their family businesses and only retain a SFO to manage their enlarged personal assets. Some families have established PTCs and private wealth arrangements such as trusts, private foundations, and/or charitable foundations which in turn may or may not be managed by the SFO. Nonetheless, most Family Offices generally function as a central administrative facility to identify and cost-effectively procure the necessary services needed by the family/families and provide a forum for each generation to articulate its goals and needs.[4]

### 2.2 *General Functions of Family Offices*

While Western Family Offices tend to offer a broad range of services including insurance and risk management, budgeting, life planning, charitable giving or tax compliance services,[5] Family Offices in Asia typically focus primarily on basic wealth management services such as: (1) investment management services (including

1 R. Wilson, *The Family Office Book: Investing Capital for the Ultra-Affluent* (John Wiley, 2012), p. 4.
2 B. Hauser, 'The Family Office: Insights into Their Development in the US, a Proposed Prototype, and Advice for Adaptation in Other Countries' (2001) 4(2) *Journal of Wealth Management* 15.
3 ibid.
4 R. Pease, 'Family Offices and Fiduciaries: Friend or Foe?' (2002) *Private Client Business* 184.
5 Wilson, *The Family Office Book*, p. 18.

recommending and selecting fund managers, managing the family's cash and liquidity requirements,[6] and drafting the family's Investment Policy Statement ('IPS'));[7] (2) tax planning; (3) overseeing directly owned businesses (including managing good corporate governance, monitoring and reporting on business performance and strategic direction);[8] (4) business and financial advisory;[9] (5) family philanthropic strategies (including forming and maintaining family foundations and advising and facilitating effective charitable donations);[10] (6) oversight of estate and wealth transfer strategies (including facilitating wealth transfer between generations and managing family trusts);[11] and (7) concierge services.[12]

## 3 THE CONCEPT OF A PTC

### 3.1 *General Definition of PTCs*

PTCs are entities which are trustees of the assets of a wealthy individual (or of related individuals) that have been transferred into trust.[13] In Singapore, the PTC gains its power to act as trustee from its trust instrument, the Trustees Act[14] and common law. Generally, a PTC can only provide trust and fiduciary services to a limited class of family members and, in some cases, charities and family employees.[15]

In Singapore, PTCs are defined as a corporation 'the purpose of which is solely to provide trust business services in respect of a specific trust or of specific trusts' and where the settlors and beneficiaries of the trusts, which it provides services to, must be connected persons, and which does not provide trust business services to the public.[16]

PTCs are exempted from the requirement in the Trust Companies Act to hold a trust business licence, but must engage a licensed trust company to carry out trust

6 ibid.

7 The IPS defines the family's investment objectives and parameters, benchmark performance standards, as well as roles and responsibilities for staff, asset managers, custodians and advisers. See S. Campbell and D. Bailin, 'Investment Management Best Practices for Family Offices', <https://www.privatebank.citibank.com/newcpb-media/media/documents/Investment-Management-Best-Practices-for-Family-Offices.pdf> last accessed 15 June 2022.

8 R. Joynt and I. Slack, 'What Is a Family Office and Why Do High Net Worth Individuals Want One?' (2014) *Private Client Business* 242, 243.

9 Ernest & Young, 'EY Family Office Guide', 10, <https://assets.ey.com/content/dam/ey-sites/ey-com/en_gl/topics/family-business/ey-the-asian-family-office.pdf> last accessed 15 June 2022.

10 Wilson, *The Family Office Book*, p. 18.

11 ibid.

12 K. Rosplock, *The Complete Family Office Handbook* (John Wiley, 2014), p. 47.

13 I. Ivsan, 'Emerging Challenges in Asset Protection Planning' (2016) 24 *University of Miami Business Law Review* 135, 141.

14 Trustees Act 1967 (2020 Rev Ed).

15 A. Ytterberg and J. Weller, 'Managing Family Wealth through a Private Trust Company' (2010) 36 *American College of Trust and Estate Counsel Law Journal* 623, 624.

16 Trust Companies (Exemption) Regulations (R1, 2006 Rev Ed), r. 2.

administration services for the purposes of conducting checks to prevent money laundering or the financing of terrorism.[17] Thus, even though PTCs are exempt persons, they are indirectly subject to the regulatory oversight of MAS.[18]

The board of directors of the PTC typically comprises the settlor's family members and/or trusted advisors[19] although the board may solely consist of trusted advisors where it is impractical or undesirable for family members to be in direct control of the PTC. The PTC's Investment Committee, which is responsible for the investment management of the trust assets, also typically comprises family members[20] since control of the family wealth is usually a key reason for creating a PTC.[21] The PTC may also have other committees such as distribution, philanthropic, business advisory, and director appointment committees.[22]

### 3.2 *General Functions of PTCs*

PTCs are generally formed only to serve as trustees of the assets of one family and are not usually profit-seeking. In Singapore, they are not required to have any material operations, assets, or income but may not provide trust services to the public at large. Their popularity is due to the fact that, unlike a traditional trust arrangement whereby an external trust company is typically appointed as trustee to manage trust assets, a PTC structure allows the settlor to retain control over managing the trust assets by sitting on the board of directors of the PTC[23] while not directly owning the wealth for tax and other purposes.[24] Other reasons why UHNW families use PTCs include:

(1) Remedying Absence of Suitable Corporate Trustees: PTCs serve to remedy the family's difficulty in finding good corporate trustees which give appropriate weight to the family's decisions, their wish for less involvement of the trustees in the management of their family business, and to address the issue of undiversified trust assets since their family wealth is typically highly concentrated.[25]

(2) Limitation of Liability: A PTC functions as an independent legal entity that will itself be liable if there is any breach of fiduciary duties, rather than the

17 ibid, r. 4.

18 Trust Companies Act 2005 (2020 Rev Ed).

19 3E Accounting, 'Private Trust Setup in Singapore', <www.3ecpa.com.sg/services/trust-services/private-trust-setup> last accessed 15 June 2022.

20 Ytterberg and Weller, 'Managing Family Wealth through a Private Trust Company', 625.

21 ibid.

22 J. McLeod, 'Private Trust Companies', <www.ttn-taxation.net/pdfs/Speeches_NewYork_2014/NY14-JohnMcLeod.pdf> last accessed 15 June 2022.

23 A. L. Jek and D. Tan, 'The Growth of the Private Wealth Management Industry in Singapore and Hong Kong', 6(1) *Capital Markets Law Journal* 104, 107–108.

24 Ytterberg and Weller, 'Managing Family Wealth through a Private Trust Company', 639.

25 L. Wintriss, 'Working with a Family Office' (2000) 26 *American College of Trust and Estate Counsel Notes* 194, 195.

individuals who may serve as trustees. This provides individual family members with greater protection from litigation and limits exposure of the trust assets.[26] However, in some instances, the corporate veil of the PTC may be pierced and the separate legal personality of the PTC will be disregarded when there is an abuse of the corporate vehicle. This may occur when the PTC is the *alter ego* of its controller.[27]

(3) Control over Administration: The ability to make rapid decisions, particularly where the trust holds shares in operating companies of the family group, is of great importance to the entrepreneur-settlor. A trustee which is a subsidiary of a major bank or corporate service provider may not be able to make important decisions affecting a billion-dollar empire without first consulting its head office or legal department for clearance. Meanwhile, independent trustees may be unavailable or difficult to contact on short notice for the purposes of making snap decisions. In contrast, the entrepreneur-settlor may be able to have directors on the board of the PTC who are highly familiar with his business affairs and able to make quick decisions.[28]

(4) Cost: PTCs may be fairly expensive for smaller trusts with assets of less than USD 50 million, but for larger trust assets, the overall cost may be significantly less than the fees typically charged by a trust company owned by a major bank or financial institution.[29]

(5) Ease of Change of Personnel: Changing a trustee is invariably time-consuming: deeds need to be drawn up, indemnities negotiated and final accounts prepared. By contrast, the removal and appointment of new directors of a PTC is a swift and usually painless procedure.[30]

(6) Ease of Change of Service Provider: Typically, the PTC will contractually delegate the tasks of record-keeping, accounting, and other administrative services and often investment advice and management and certainly custody of the investment assets to suitable service providers. These arrangements can be re-negotiated or terminated without major difficulty by the PTC board of directors, often more easily than with a major independent trust company.[31]

## 4 COMMON OWNERSHIP STRUCTURES AND ARRANGEMENTS

Family Offices and PTCs co-exist together as wealth management strategies for UHNW families but are not substitutes for each other given that PTCs serve primarily

26 ibid.

27 C. H. Tan, SC, 'Some Current Issues in Singapore Corporate Law' (2019) 31 *Singapore Academy Law Journal* 1008, [4].

28 Pease, 'Family Offices and Fiduciaries', 189.

29 ibid.

30 ibid, 190.

31 ibid.

as private trustees to the family, while Family Offices serve as private fund managers (and often much more). Nevertheless, the two are often confused in general parlance. While PTCs have been noted to be a natural and logical extension of the services provided by and through Family Offices,[32] families have been known to refer to their PTC as their SFO, since they regard the PTC as functioning as the family's all-encompassing wealth management and administrative body. Regardless, PTCs and Family Offices typically function as separate entities for different purposes and their appropriateness depends entirely on the needs and objectives of the family concerned.

### 4.1 *Ownership Structures of Family Offices*

In Singapore, Family Offices are typically structured as companies limited by shares, where family and non-family professionals may serve as members.[33] The governing rules of ownership and control rights are typically determined by a shareholders' agreement which does not have to be made publicly available and provides members with a high degree of freedom in determining the division of ownership and control among the members.[34] Alternatively, Family Offices may also be structured as partnerships.[35] In the absence of shares, both ownership and control are jointly exercised through the partnership interest. Three types of partnerships exist in Singapore: general partnerships, limited partnerships, and limited liability partnerships.

### 4.2 *Ownership Structures of PTCs*

The settlor and/or family members can hold the PTC shares either directly or indirectly. As in the case of Family Offices, direct ownership may give rise to unfavourable tax consequences and even compromise the degree of confidentiality provided by the PTC serving as private trustee. Furthermore, animosities may develop among family members who are shareholders against those who are not. Since the main purpose of the PTC is to act as a control and wealth preservation structure rather than a wealth creation structure, some families prefer a professional trustee to be a member of the PTC.

A non-charitable 'purpose trust' may be used for the sole purpose of owning the shares of the PTC, to orphan the PTC. It is usual for a person or entity separate from the trustee, typically a trusted family advisor, to fulfill the role of enforcer. Included among the powers of the enforcer could be the power to remove the trustee of

[32] ibid, 184.

[33] Ernest & Young, 'EY Family Office Guide', 58.

[34] Financial Action Task Force, *Concealment of Beneficial Ownership* (Egmont Group, 2018), p. 22, <https://www.fatf-gafi.org/media/fatf/documents/reports/FATF-Egmont-Concealment-beneficial-ownership.pdf> last accessed 15 June 2022.

[35] Ernst & Young, 'EY Family Office Guide', 58.

the purpose trust and appoint an alternative.[36] It is currently not possible to create non-charitable purpose trusts in Singapore, although the idea has been mooted by the Singapore Academy of Law's Law Reform Committee.[37]

A less common alternative is the company limited by guarantee ('CLG'), where members of the company do not own shares. Their interest in the company does not amount to property, and the rights which they enjoy as members may lapse on specified events, for example, death, and there is nothing to fall into the deceased member's estate.[38] A CLG may be developed to very closely simulate a discretionary trust without actually creating a trust. However, a PTC limited by guarantee may have to do annual financial reporting as required by some jurisdictions. This includes Singapore, where the filing of annual returns mandated under Section 197 of the Companies Act extends to CLGs.[39] Such reporting will be made public, which would reveal the management and finances of the PTC. For clients who highly value privacy and confidentiality, such a structure may not be ideal.[40]

Another structure that is growing in popularity is the new VCC, which became available as a structuring option on 14 January 2020. A VCC can potentially be used in place of a PTC and offers several advantages such as flexibility in paying out dividends, privacy, and ring-fencing of the various sub-funds,[41] although it can only be used for collective investment schemes. A number of VCCs have been established in the past year by MFOs for families who are attracted to the fact that different branches of the family may have different asset allocations and investment strategies within the VCC structure while remaining confident that risk contagion from other family branch portfolios will not spill into theirs. Nonetheless, SFOs have not been able to avail themselves of VCCs due to regulations that require VCCs to be managed by firms with a capital markets services licence for fund management, by exempt financial institutions, or by registered fund management companies.[42]

36 McLeod, 'Private Trust Companies'.

37 Singapore Academy of Law, *Report on the Enactment of Non-Charitable Purpose Trusts*, <www.sal.org.sg/sites/default/files/SAL-LawReform-Pdf/2021-05/Report%20on%20the%20Enactment%20of%20Non-Charitable%20Purpose%20Trusts.pdf> last accessed 15 June 2022. Specific to the context of family businesses, the Committee noted that a non-charitable purpose trust could be used to run and prolong family business without fear of asset fragmentation among members of the family. Assets may also be partitioned and devoted to short-term ventures that dilute risk away from the established family business. See pp. 36–38.

38 Pease, 'Family Offices and Fiduciaries', 190–191.

39 Companies Act 1967 (2020 Rev Ed).

40 A. Ip, 'Trust Focus Week: Private Trust Companies' (*Hugill & IP Solicitors*, March 2019), <www.hugillandip.com/2019/03/trust-focus-week-private-trust-companies> last accessed 15 June 2022.

41 For more on the features and advantages of the VCC structure, see V. Ooi, 'A New Structuring Option for Funds: The Singapore Variable Capital Company' (2021) 42(5) *Company Lawyer* 177.

42 G. Cua, 'Plan to Tweak VCC Framework to Draw More Single Family Offices', <www.businesstimes.com.sg/banking-finance/plan-to-tweak-vcc-framework-to-draw-more-single-family-offices> last accessed 15 June 2022.

Unlike MFOs, many SFOs do not have the relevant licences since they do not manage third-party monies and thus, prior to the introduction of the VCC, had no need to obtain such licences. However, the Monetary Authority of Singapore ('MAS') is currently considering measures to further boost adoption by widening the scope of permissible fund managers. If this happens, the VCC may become an even more attractive structuring option, though it is noted that Family Offices are still unlikely to be allowed to manage third-party monies without a licence.[43]

Apart from the legal structuring above, some commonly seen arrangements used by UHNW families involving FOs and PTCs include the following: (1) Family Office Managing Family Wealth and Family Business, (2) Family Office Managing Non-Business Family Wealth only, (3) PTC as Trustee of Family Business held under Trust, and (4) PTC as Trustee of Family Business and Family Office held under Trust. These are just some examples of arrangements used by UHNW families and serve to illustrate the extreme variability of the use of Family Offices and PTCs in their highly customised wealth preservation strategies. Each will be dealt in turn.

### 4.2.1 Family Office Managing Family Wealth and Family Business

A family whose wealth is primarily tied up with the family business may have a Family Office which assists the family in overseeing the family business, as well as the family's pooled wealth. If the family has a professionally managed trust, the Family Office usually oversees it on behalf of the family.

### 4.2.2 Family Office Managing Non-business Family Wealth Only

After a major liquidity event such as the sale of the family business, a family may establish a Family Office to manage the substantial sale proceeds and other family assets such as real estate holdings, yachts, private jets, art collections, etc. For tax and other reasons, some of these assets may be held in professionally managed trusts or civil law foundations, which the Family Office may oversee on behalf of the beneficiary family members. Family Offices may also manage funds specially set up to house family wealth to benefit from the various tax incentive schemes available in Singapore.[44]

### 4.2.3 PTC as Trustee of Family Business Held under Trust

Families whose portfolios feature heavily concentrated or illiquid family assets (such as privately held family businesses) are the most common users of PTCs, for

43 ibid.

44 For example, the Onshore Fund Tax Exemption Scheme (s. 13O) and the Enhanced Tier Fund Tax Exemption Scheme (s. 13U). See V. Ooi, 'Tax Considerations for Funds Structuring in Asia' (2020) 38(1) *Journal of Taxation of Investments* 49, 52–53.

the reasons outlined earlier. Such families need to fully understand what they are signing up for and have the proper training and resources required for adequate day-to-day management of the PTC.[45]

### 4.2.4 PTC as Trustee of Family Business and Family Office Held under Trust

PTCs may also be used to concurrently manage both the family business and an existing SFO for cost efficiency. If a family owns a family business and a SFO that are held under a professionally managed single trust or several separate trusts, the family may decide to consolidate them all under one PTC umbrella, to wrestle control back from professional trustees, reduce fees and better co-ordinate asset management. In such an instance, the PTC would function less as an administrative centre (since the Family Office already provides such services) but purely to manage the family's trusts.[46]

## 5 GENERAL ISSUES RELATING TO FAMILY OFFICES AND PTCs

### 5.1 *Unhappiness with Performance*

Families face increasingly complex decision-making, particularly when more generations, different cousins, or branches of the family work together, bringing disparate views on the objectives of the business or the management of the family's wealth. This may lead to perceived unfairness in decision-making or rifts created due to feelings that opinions were neither aired nor duly considered.[47] Common frustrations relating to Family Office or PTC management commonly stem from the following:[48]

(1) Heirs/Successors: Succession is a process fraught with tension, further heightened by familial ties oft burdened with years of emotional baggage. Where succession is unclear or not well managed, disputes can arise between rival next-generation successors wrestling for control or influence over the Family Offices and/or PTCs and adding complexity to their management. When the

45 C. Weeg, 'The Private Trust Company: A DIY for the Über Wealthy' (2017) 52(1) *Real Property, Trust and Estate Law Journal* 121, 130.

46 ibid, 126.

47 E. Trovato, 'Family Offices Find New Role Smoothing Succession Planning', *Professional Wealth Management*, 3, <www.pwmnet.com/Wealth-Management/Business-Models/Family-offices-find-new-role-smoothing-succession-planning?ref=%2FWealth-Management%2FBusiness-Models%2FFamily-offices-find-new-role-smoothing-succession-planning> last accessed 15 June 2022.

48 Moore Stephens and The Aster Club, 'Succession Planning for Business Families and Family Offices', <https://channelislands.moorestephens.com/MediaLibsAndFiles/media/channelislands.moorestephens.com/Documents/Succession-planning-report.pdf> last accessed 15 June 2022 ('The Stephens Report'), 6.

disputes are left unresolved, they can badly damage the family enterprise as well as irreparably fracture family harmony.

(2) Even when a successor has been designated, the heir may experience frustration when the family head fails to provide empowerment or sufficient latitude to make impactful decisions.[49] Fearing mistakes or doubting the next generation's ability is particularly damaging since the earlier generation must give their intended successors opportunities to gain real experience, provide objective feedback, and a chance to learn from their mistakes.[50]

(3) Culture Clash: Asian enterprise-owning families often face a culture clash between a Western-educated next generation and a more traditional 'Asian' set of founders, who may not have benefitted from the abundance of higher education and coaching opportunities now available to the younger generation.[51] This culture clash, along with the inevitable inter-generational age clash, can exacerbate frustrations of younger members who resent that decisions are made without any real input from them[52] despite their extensive qualifications.

(4) Extended Family Members: As the family grows into the second and third generation of wealth ownership, decision-making becomes spread across various branches of the family. As extended family members seek to exercise their ownership rights and exert greater influence over management issues,[53] informal decision-making and communication that was exercised in the first generation of wealth creators[54] becomes less and less feasible. Family dynamics is exacerbated by family members spread across geographies, with widely different upbringings bringing increasingly disparate and opposing interests.[55] Both non-family professionals and family members employed in the FOs and/or PTCs may be frustrated by constant squabbles and frequent changes in decisions and investment strategies, resulting in a talent retention challenge.

### 5.2 *PTCs: Reduced Ability of Beneficiaries to Sue*

A PTC may be challenged by a beneficiary claiming that the PTC was established to retain control of the trust assets and that it was never the settlor's intention for the PTC to fulfill its fiduciary duties. To avert this, the board and trustees should ensure that the decisions made by the PTC are in accordance with its fiduciary duties, in

[49] ibid.
[50] ibid, 3.
[51] The Stephens Report, 6.
[52] Rosplock, *The Complete Family Office Handbook*, p. 271.
[53] The Stephens Report, 6.
[54] Rosplock, *The Complete Family Office Handbook*, p. 270.
[55] Squire Patton Boggs, 'Family Office Insights 2018 Collection', 23, <www.squirepattonboggs.com/~/media/files/insights/publications/2019/01/family-office-insights-2018-collection/33058corporatefamily20office20insights2020182020collectionbrochure.pdf> last accessed 15 June 2022.

particular, the duties of acting in good faith and the no-profit rule, and that all other aspects of the PTC are respected, that is, all filings are made on time, the structure is correctly administered, the PTC has sufficient trust experience within its board of directors, etc.[56] Settlors could also include a no-contest clause in the trust that severs a beneficiary's interest if he or she unsuccessfully challenges the trust.[57]

While the issue of forced heirship may not arise in jurisdictions such as Singapore and Guernsey, forced heirship is a common consideration, for example, in some Middle Eastern countries where Islamic Shariah Law prevails. The forced inheritance provisions uphold the right of family members who cannot be disinherited by the lawful owner of the asset, and the assets have to be apportioned among his living successors as provided by the forced heirship law. It is commonly said that Singapore trust law contains anti-forced heirship provisions and foreigners who set up local trusts are exempted from these forced heirship limitations, allowing a testator to freely distribute assets to chosen persons.[58] The Trustees Act provides for an anti-forced heirship rule, stating that no rule relating to inheritance or succession shall affect the validity of a trust or the transfer of property to be held on trust.[59]

## 5.3 *PTCs: Conflicts of Interest and Misuse of Powers*

PTCs also run into problems inherent to their structure as both trust and company due to the significant representation and strong influence that the client's family members can exert in the management of the company. While the issues vary with the exact structure and composition of the PTC, the issues faced can be broadly classified into two categories: Trustee's Independent Decision Making (Or Lack Thereof) and Directors' Misconduct (Breach of Duty/Abuse of Powers).

### 5.3.1 Trustee's Independent Decision Making (or Lack Thereof)

As a trust, the PTC is usually established by the family head for the management and preservation of the family wealth. The family head thus often functions as both the settlor who appoints the trustees for the PTC and as a director for the PTC as a corporation. Furthermore, other family members are often appointed as directors on the board of the PTC or trustees of the various managed trusts.

Therein lies a conundrum due to the structuring of the PTC's ownership and management around the family and its assets, which in many cases results in the family head or other family members becoming the beneficiaries of the trust as well.

56 McLeod, 'Private Trust Companies'.
57 Justia, 'Trust Contests', <www.justia.com/estate-planning/trusts/trust-contests/> last accessed 15 June 2022.
58 Hawksford, 'Singapore Trust Advantages', <www.guidemesingapore.com/business-guides/taxation-and-accounting/tax-and-wealth-planning/singapore-trust-advantages> last accessed 15 June 2022.
59 Trustees Act 1967 (2020 Rev Ed), s. 90(2).

Family governance may break down here as the decisions made by the board will often affect the interests of the board members as beneficiaries.

This leads to an issue of 'double hatting,' where the director or settlor and the beneficiary may be one and the same person, and thus have vested interests that may influence the ability of the board of directors and/or the board of trustees from making their own independent and well-informed decisions solely for the benefit of the PTC and its beneficiaries. Where the settlor and the trustee are at odds with each other in the management of the family assets under trust, further complications may arise from the replacement of trustees and allegations of breach of trust duties.

Under such circumstances, the trustee could apply to the court for relief due to his honest and reasonable conduct.[60] This refers to the prudent businessman standard as established under the standard of care for trustees.[61] However, it is important to note that the *relief remains purely discretionary*.[62] This means that even if the trustee can prove that it was acting honestly and reasonably, no relief may be granted.[63] Furthermore, it is argued that the nature of the PTC's assets and holdings makes such legal action impractical, as most PTCs are unlikely to have anything to meet the claim except their minimal paid-up share capital.[64]

### 5.3.2 Directors' Misconduct (Breach of Duty/Abuse of Powers)

In cases where the duties imposed on the trustees or directors are breached, or where the powers of the trustees or directors are misused, the issue of enforcement from the position of the beneficiary/shareholder in holding the directors/trustees accountable for their actions is a thorny one. Where the board of the PTC is affected by family divisions or where there are additional conflicts of interest, it may be unable or unwilling to take proceedings against the specific director for his misconduct. Aggrieved beneficiaries under such circumstances will be unable to sue the director directly because the director, as a third party, generally owes no duty of care to the beneficiary.[65] The beneficiary has two choices under such circumstances. He

[60] Trustees Act 1967 (2020 Rev Ed), s. 60.

[61] For the *locus classicus*, see *Speight* v. *Gaunt* (1883) LR 9 App Cas 1 applied by the Singapore Court of Appeal in *Ng Eng Ghee* v. *Mamata Kapildev Dave* [2009] 3 SLR(R) 109 (CA). Also see *Santander UK Plc* v. *RA Legal Solicitors* [2014] EWCA Civ 183.

[62] *Rajabali Jumabhoy* v. *Ameerali R Jumabhoy* [1998] 2 SLR(R) 434 (CA) at [102].

[63] ibid.

[64] E. Weaver, 'Private Trust Companies: A Future for Derivative Claims?' (2011) 17(3) *Trusts & Trustees* 177.

[65] Weaver, 'Private Trust Companies', 178. Directors are generally held accountable through a variety of shareholder protection measures available in Singapore. However, beneficiaries do not tend to hold legal title to shares, making it difficult for them to avail themselves of these protection measures directly (see V. Ooi and C. H. Tan, 'Singapore Company Law and the Economy: Reciprocal Influence over 50 Years' (2019) 27(1) *Asia Pacific Law Review* 14, 32–35.

could bring an administrative claim against the trustee to compel it to sue the third party or he may be able to bring a claim in the name of and on behalf of the trustee directly against the third party.[66]

The ability of a beneficiary to bring such a derivative claim was recently affirmed in the English Supreme Court in *Roberts* v. *Gill*. The court held, however, that such a claim could only arise under special circumstances,[67] but declined to define the nature of the 'special circumstances' that would qualify[68] (due to the case being decided on a procedural point: the inability of the claimant to amend to join the trustee as a party because of a limitation defence).[69] However, there remains a serious question about the merits of suing the third-party director, given the costs and risks of monetary and reputational loss[70] tied to disputes regarding the management of family businesses and assets, which may complicate and hinder the mere initiation of a derivative action.

Another possible avenue would be for the beneficiary to bring a claim against the directors of a PTC directly as a beneficiary. This would be categorised under a 'dog-leg claim' on the basis that a corporate trustee owes a duty to its beneficiaries to avoid causing loss to the trust funds, and that this trustee could only have acted through its directors. A director of a corporate trustee owes duties to the company including a duty to exercise reasonable skill care and diligence and to act in the best interests of the company. Hence, in performing their duties to the company in so far they affect the trust, the directors are performing the company's duty to the trust. Where a director acts in relation to the trust, the benefit of what he does and his duties and obligations in so acting form part of the trust's assets. This can be argued to be analogous to cases where the benefit of a contract between the trustee and a third-party agent acting for the trust becomes trust property.[71] A beneficiary should be able to bring a derivative action against a third party to enforce a claim which is trust property. Following this reasoning, the beneficiary should be entitled to bring a derivative claim against a director if the corporate trustee is unable or unwilling to sue.

However, this has been rejected in the decision of *Gregson* v. *HAE Trustees Ltd*, where the High Court of England and Wales held[72] that allowing the dog-leg claim would circumvent the clear principle that directors of trust companies owe no duty of care to the beneficiaries of the trust. It further stated that there was no legal basis or mechanism whereby the director's duty to the company became trust property. The court further rejected[73] the analogy with advisers to the trust company on the

66 E. Weaver, 'Private Trust Companies', 178.
67 *Roberts* v. *Gill* [2011] 1 AC 240 at [22], [78], and [103].
68 ibid at [75]–[76].
69 ibid at [70]–[72].
70 E. Weaver, 'Private Trust Companies', 178.
71 ibid, 180.
72 *Gregson* v. *HAE Trustees Ltd* [2009] 1 All ER (Comm) 457 at [46].
73 ibid at [54].

basis that advisers were engaged by the trustee in the course of administration of the trusts but directors were appointed by the organs of the company (either the board or the shareholders in general meeting) not appointed by the trustee. It thus appears that, barring future developments, this category of claims will not at present be available to beneficiaries seeking legal remedy against director misconduct within the PTC.

## 6 TRUST INTEGRITY ISSUES

For PTCs owned by a non-charitable purpose trust, the settlor may have divested himself of legal ownership of the trust assets. The settlor may be a beneficiary and, in certain circumstances, he may also act as a co-trustee by sitting on the Board of Directors of the PTC. The settlor may also retain a degree of control over the trust by reserving the exercise of certain powers to himself (or a third person), such as the power to approve distributions, the power to appoint and remove trustees, and the power to revoke the trust. However, it is essential to the validity of a trust that the settlor actually dispossesses himself of the trust assets.[74]

### 6.1 *Sham Trusts*

A sham trust arises where the parties intend to give third parties or the court the appearance of creating between the parties legal rights and obligations different from the actual legal rights and obligations (if any) which the parties intend to create.[75] If the trustee allows the settlor to run the company as if the settlor still owned it, the trust may be challenged as a sham.[76] However, it is not determinative that a trust is a sham if the settlor retains complete control of a trust. For example, it might be a bare trust.[77]

To establish a sham, there is a need for a common intention of the parties to mislead.[78] This intention is determined at the outset of creation of the trust.[79] The court will have to determine whether the documents were intended to create legal relationships and whether the parties did actually act according to the apparent purpose and tenor of the documents.[80] The court is not restricted to the usual rules

74 Ogier, 'Offshore Trusts' (26 February 2018), <www.ogier.com/publications/offshore-trusts> last accessed 15 June 2022.

75 *Chng Bee Kheng* v. *Chng Eng Chye* [2013] 2 SLR 715.

76 Yip Man, 'Trust Owned Companies: Understanding the Trustee's Duties' (2017) 31(4) *Trust Law International* 185, 195.

77 Russell AM QC & Toby Graham, 'Sham Trusts and *Pugachev*, the International Academy of Estate and Trust Law' (2018) 24(1) *Trusts & Trustees* 1.

78 Alvin See, 'Revisiting Sham Trusts: Common Intention, Estoppel and Illegality' (2018) *The Conveyancer and Property Lawyer* 31–44.

79 *Shalson* v. *Russo* [2005] Ch 281.

80 *Chng Bee Kheng* [2013] 2 SLR 715 at [52]–[53].

governing the interpretation of documents. The court may have regard to a wider category of evidence, such as the parties' subsequent conduct.[81] In *Rahman* v. *Chase Bank*,[82] the court admitted ex post facto evidence regarding the manner in which the trust was administered as evidence of parties' intentions. For example, if terms of the trust are ignored and the trust is treated as the settlor's 'personal money box' notwithstanding the terms of the trust, the trust will be considered to be a sham.[83]

The common intention must generally belong to both the settlor and the trustee. The beneficiary's intention is not important unless looking at the situation where a beneficiary's intention subsequent to the formation of a trust may transform what was a properly constituted trust which was not *ab initio* a sham into a sham. In such a case, all beneficiaries must join together with the trustee in the sham purpose.[84] In *Mehzprom Bank* v. *Pugachev*, the court found a subtle form of sham on the facts of the case.[85] The true intention was for Mr Pugachev to have ultimate ownership and control of assets while claiming to only be a discretionary beneficiary with limited powers as protector. A possible extension from *Pugachev* is that creditors can argue that the trusts are shams where the debtor has retained extensive powers under the trust instrument.[86]

If a trust is considered to be a 'sham', the trust would be set aside and be void and unenforceable. The trustee would be stripped of its power and the beneficiaries would lose their beneficial interest to the trust property.[87] The trust property will be treated as still belonging to the settlor since the beneficial interests still belongs with the settlor.

There is a higher probability of finding a sham when the trust is administered without professional advice. This is even more likely when the trustee is a PTC and decisions are being taken by non-professionals who do not receive proper advice.[88] Also, the risk is increased if all the decision-makers are family members who listen to the settlor, who typically is the chairman of the PTC Board of Directors. There may be no independent directors on the PTC, and even if there is one, he or she

81 ibid at [54]–[55].

82 *Rahman* v. *Chase Bank* [1991] JLR 103.

83 Christopher McKenzie, 'Private Trust Companies: The Best of All Worlds' (2008) 14(2) *Trusts & Trustees* 99.

84 *Chng Bee Kheng* [2013] 2 SLR 715 at [55]–[56]. Also see See 'Revisiting Sham Trusts'.

85 *Mehzprom Bank* v. *Pugachev* [2017] EWHC 2426.

86 Tim Akkouh and Christopher Lloyd, '"Trust-Busting"' after *JSC Mezhdunarodniy Promyshlenniy Bank v Pugachev* [2017] EWHC 2426 (Ch)' (2018) 24(2) *Trusts & Trustees* 151, 155.

87 J. Dash, 'Nevis: A Foundation for Privacy – The Ownership and Management of a Private Trust Company by a Multiform Foundation' (2011) 17(6) *Trusts & Trustees* 586.

88 The mere fact that a trustee had acted on legal advice would not automatically result in relief being granted under s. 60 of the Trustees Act 1967. It is also important to have regard to the size of the trust fund and the circumstances of the trustee in light of the advice received. Efforts to recoup the loss are also required. See *Re Evans* [1999] 2 All ER 777; *National Trustees Co of Australasia* v. *General Finance Co of Australasia* [1905] AC 373.

may be easily outnumbered in a vote. It is argued that separating the ownership between the PTC and settlor limits the possibility that the PTC may held to be a sham.[89] PTC shares should be held by the trustees of a purpose trust which has no beneficial owner.[90]

### 6.2 *Illusory Trusts*

The idea of an illusory trust was raised in the New Zealand case of *Clayton* v. *Clayton* as being formed where there is no true trust involving a separation of legal and beneficial ownership created by the terms of the deed of trust.[91] At the Family Court, Munro J adopted the 'irreducible core' approach and found the trust was 'illusory' as the husband had total control over the trust without the need to account to the beneficiaries, and to the extent that he might revoke the trust in his favour at any time. The irreducible core included the duty of trustees to act honestly and in good faith for the benefit of the beneficiaries, but did not include the duties of skill and care, prudence and diligence.[92] On the facts, the duty to act honestly and in good faith for the benefit of beneficiaries did not exist as: (1) the trustees had absolute unfettered discretion not to consider the beneficiaries' interest and were relieved of any liability for acting in conflict and (2) the trustees also had the power (with the consent of the husband) to vary, amend, revoke or enlarge any provisions of the trust deed 'concerning the management and administration' of the trust.

In the High Court, Hansen J relied on a different basis to find that the trust was illusory, relying on the 'no sufficient disposition approach': 'whether on a proper construction of the deed [the husband] retained such control that he did not intend to give or part from control over the property sufficient to constitute a trust'.[93] It was found that the provisions of the trust gave the husband 'unfettered power to distribute the income and the capital of the trust to himself if he wishes and to bring the trust to an end at any time he pleases'. It was found that the husband, 'through his delegates exercises, in a practical sense, the powers of ownership', resulting in a situation where the reality was that the husband 'is able to deal with trust property just as he would if the trust had never been created'.[94]

The Supreme Court did not come to a conclusion as to whether the trust was illusory but did find there to be a distinction between a sham and illusory trust.[95] The court did hold, however, that there was no value in the label 'illusory'; if there is

[89] McKenzie, 'Private Trust Companies'.
[90] ibid, 105.
[91] *Clayton* v. *Clayton* [2013] NZHC 301, [2013] 3 NZLR 236.
[92] *Armitage* v. *Nurse* [1998] Ch 241.
[93] G. Young, 'Sham and Illusory Trusts – Lessons from *Clayton* v. *Clayton*' (2018) 24(2) *Trusts & Trustees* 194.
[94] *Clayton* [2013] 3 NZLR 236 at [90].
[95] *Clayton* v. *Clayton* [2016] 1 NZLR 551.

no valid trust, that is all there needs to be said.[96] The judgment in *Clayton* raises the possibility that a valid trust may subsequently arise when different people occupy the relevant offices – an emerging trust. In so doing the Supreme Court has also left open the possibility that an initially valid trust may become invalid if the offices are initially occupied by different people but one person comes to occupy them all – emerging invalidity.[97] Questions also arise as to what would be the position if there are different people, but all of whom are accustomed to following the wishes of one person although recent judicial sentiment suggests that such a trust would subsequently become a sham.[98]

In *Pugachev*, the concept of an illusory trust was held to be unhelpful.[99] Instead, the court was to consider the powers and duties under the trust deed as a whole to determine realities of its operation. Accordingly, the court may find the powers retained by the settlor-beneficiary to be sufficiently wide and unfettered to have retained control and ownership of the assets.[100] Arguably, the 'true effects' analysis in *Pugachev* was based on the powers given to Mr Pugachev as protector and the manner in which they could be exercised for his benefit. Moving forward, it will be important to consider the extent of any retained powers and whether appropriate limitations on their exercise should be incorporated into the deeds of the PTC to avoid problems.[101]

More recently, in *Webb* v. *Webb*,[102] the Court of Appeal of the Cook Islands similarly held that there is a distinction between sham trusts and illusory trusts. While both sham and illusory trusts are invalid, a sham trust turns on the subjective intention of the parties involved.[103] In contrast, for illusory trusts, the 'ultimate question is whether the powers reserved to the respondent-settlor were inconsistent with an intention to irrevocably relinquish a beneficial interest'.[104] If the settlor had retained uncontrolled power to recover the property, there is 'objective nullity' and the trust would be invalid. On the facts, the respondent retained the power to, inter alia, make a distribution of capital and income to himself, vest trust property in himself, and nominate himself as sole beneficiary.[105] Thus, if settlors of PTCs retain broad powers for themselves, the trust may be invalid.[106]

96 ibid at [123].

97 Young, 'Sham and Illusory Trusts', 194–204.

98 A v. A [2007] EWHC 99 (Fam) at [44].

99 *Mehzprom Bank* v. *Pugachev* [2017] EWHC 2426 at [169].

100 ibid at [161]–[167].

101 G. Hogan, '*Mezhprom Bank* v. *Pugachev* [2017] EWHC 2426 (Ch)' (2018) 24(2) *Trusts & Trustees* 212, 215.

102 *Webb* v. *Webb* [2017] CKCA 4. The findings of the Court of Appeal were upheld by the Privy Council in *Webb* v. *Webb* [2020] UKPC 22.

103 *Webb* [2017] CKCA 4 at [56].

104 *Webb* [2017] CKCA 4.

105 ibid at [61]–[63].

106 Also see P. W. Lee, 'Remedying the Abuse of Organizational Forms: Trusts and Companies Considered' (2019) 13 *Journal of Equity* 211, 222.

## 7 FAMILY GOVERNANCE FOR FAMILY OFFICES AND PTCs

From the governance perspective, PTCs and Family Offices (focusing on SFOs in this section) share a commonality in terms of the single family they serve and the fact that both entities tend to be controlled by that family. This creates similar issues concerning family dynamics that business-owning families face. As much ink has been spilled on the topic of family governance as it relates to family businesses, this chapter will focus on aspects of family governance particularly relevant to Family Offices and PTCs. Issues such as respecting the requirements that will enable the entities to achieve the objectives they were set up for, addressing issues of conflicts of interest, and incentives to create the desired behaviour of family members involved in the decision-making and management of the Family Office and/or PTC.

In essence, much of the solutions to these concerns revolve around establishing proper family governance to clarify expectations and ensure that the family fully understands: (1) what they have set up and why (especially for future generations who may not know the founder and yet have to manage the Family Office and/or PTC), (2) their roles and responsibilities in the future management of the entities; and most crucially, (3) how decisions will be made pertaining to the Family Office and/or PTC, by whom, and (4) how future disagreements will be handled.

Family Offices and PTCs could benefit from the following common elements of family governance being put in place:

(1) Clarifying Objectives: Good family governance starts with having the objectives of the Family Office and/or PTC clearly set out in the respective constitutional documents but also ideally in the family constitution itself. The family constitution serves as the overarching governance framework for the family's decision-making processes, documenting the key values of the family, guiding and informing all family activities and decisions, and establishing a code of expected conduct for the family members' interactions with each other and with the various family enterprises (the family business, the Family Office and/or PTC, trusts, etc).[107] The relevant objectives include: confirming the priority of the family as a whole or the individual or family branch; priority of wealth preservation or wealth creation; and anti-forced heirship planning or asset protection (which would serve to highlight the need to comply with established protocols designed to maintain trust integrity). It is crucial to document these objectives to manage the expectations of future generations and serve as a permanent sign-post reminder to inform future decisions when disagreements inevitably erupt over time.

(2) Regular Meetings of the Family Board: Family tensions are often exacerbated by lack of clarity and communication among family members and heightened

[107] The Stephens Report, 4.

by the stresses of the family business for those working in the enterprise (which are not faced or understood by family members not employed in the enterprise). Regular family meetings allow for the continued discussion of both business issues and family wealth issues in a structured manner by providing a formal forum for family members to air their concerns and to be heard,[108] and serving as a source of information for the less involved family members. Importantly, this serves to keep family matters at the Family Board level where they belong, and out of the corporate board room.

(3) Selection and Succession of Directors: Good family governance also governs the way families decide whom to appoint to the boards of the Family Offices and/or PTCs. All directors, whether family members or not, should be subject to clear qualification criteria, a fair nomination and selection process, adequate training, and a renewal process that should be aligned to the family constitution. The appointments need to be clear and transparent from the outset, with due consideration given to the engagement and sophistication of any family members appointed to the board, particularly in relation to the competency and public position (such as in the case of a politically exposed person who may warrant additional anti-money laundering measures). A strong and proactive board of directors can steer the strategic direction of the Family Office and/or PTC while managing the interests of all family members to mitigate conflict during intergenerational wealth transfer.[109] Having trusted non-family professionals on the board is also beneficial, as they often bring relevant skills to resolving issues that a Family Office and/or PTC may face.[110] Further, they are able to provide an alternative objective viewpoint to family members who may hold opposing views[111] and serve as an independent mediator to aid in dispute resolution.[112]

(4) Define Operating Policies and Processes: Good governance involves documenting key policies and decision-making processes of the Family Office and/or PTC and ensuring that they are aligned (and remain aligned) to the family constitution and other family wealth arrangements. This includes policies governing the employment of family members in the Family Office and/or PTC and specifying the hiring criteria, performance appraisal, and remuneration of family employees. Ultimately, the constitutional documents of the Family Office and/or PTC as well as the family constitution should be continually reviewed to ensure they remain relevant to the family across the generations.[113]

108 Rosplock, *The Complete Family Office Handbook*, p. 273.

109 Ernst & Young, 'EY Family Office Guide', 24.

110 The Stephens Report, 4.

111 L. Pigorini, Family Office Magazine (Summer, 2017), p. 3, <www.familyofficemag.com/_files/ugd/cf7a10_ebf78249649c41eb9ee0a9929836d6af.pdf> last accessed 15 June 2022.

112 The Stephens Report, 4.

113 Rosplock, *The Complete Family Office Handbook*, p. 275.

(5) Continued Education and Training: A key element of family governance involves educating all family members on the nature of ownership of their shared enterprises and understanding the responsibilities of such ownership. Family members and independent directors should also continually be trained to respect the governance structures and protocols set in place, and the potential consequences of failure to comply. For instance, the long-running litigation involving a very large Family Office in Singapore has demonstrated the risks of failure to maintain crystal clear accounts and of co-mingling funds of the Family Office (that which belongs to the whole family) with a family member's personal funds.[114]

## 8 FAMILY GOVERNANCE PARTICULARLY FOR PTCs

As many of the challenges faced by a PTC outlined earlier are inherent to its structuring, these may be pre-emptively mitigated through proper planning and communication. Some examples of behaviour that families should avoid that may jeopardise the effectiveness of the PTC include the following:

(1) Trust as a Personal Money Box: Treating the trust account like a bank account or 'personal money box', could result in the trust being deemed void. In event of divorce or bankruptcy, treating the trust as a financial resource risks eroding the asset protection feature of the trust. While the PTC board of directors acting as trustees could temporarily exclude the soon-to-be divorced or bankrupt family member as a beneficiary until the situation has been resolved, the affected person may strongly resist this decision for fear of not being reinstated later. Having confidence that the family has clear transparent governance policies and processes in place will go a long way to assuring the affected family member that he or she will be treated fairly in the long term, and facilitate the trustees' desired action. Nonetheless, it is best that family members be well aware to avoid behaviour that could jeopardise the sanctity of the trust in the first instance.

(2) Failing to Understand Trustee Duties and to Avoid Conflict of Interest: All PTC board members hold at least two roles as trustee and as director, which differ in duties, powers, responsibilities, and liabilities. Family members working in the family business whose shares are held in trust by the PTC as trustee and who serve on the PTC board, potentially wear even more hats and hence must be ever vigilant with regards to possible conflicts of interest. In principle, however, nothing precludes a trustee from waiving such conflicts of interest by *ex ante* informed consent. As such, special regard should be given to the independent decision-making ability of any family member appointed to the

[114] *Ernest Ferdinand Perez De La Sala v. Compañia De Navegación Palomar, SA* [2018] 1 SLR 894 at [3].

board of a PTC, and the candidate's aptitude to avoid making decisions that run the risk of a breach of trust or fiduciary duty.

(3) Accountability in Decision-making: At all times, the PTC must resist deference of decision-making to the founder, settlor, or family head. Governance must be exercised with accountability. Trustee decision-making processes must be transparent and properly documented, following the methodology outlined and agreed with the rest of the family. Clear reporting and updated accounts should be maintained in compliance with local trust laws, regulations, and reporting requirements. Regular board meetings, both internal and with the relevant trust company service providers, should also be encouraged to lay out a clear agenda and direction for the PTC to proceed in and to facilitate the disclosure of interests in the decision-making process as they arise.

Voting controls are another important factor that must be managed carefully to ensure that decisions involving the management and control of the company are swiftly and efficiently made. It is recommended that specific categories of different matters should have different requirements for threshold voting, with fundamental matters requiring unanimous votes to proceed. This recognises the importance of both major and minor representation in voting and encourages careful consideration of the specific issues faced by the PTC. Age requirements for different matters can be factored in as well.

As for Family Offices, it is beneficial to have proper administrative procedures dictated in the family constitution to ensure that all family members understand their position in relation to the PTC and the rest of the family. This facilitates the determination of the scope of services the PTC is expected to provide and ensures that the necessary expertise (whether in-house or outsourced) is employed to execute such functions. As a general rule, it is recommended that at the very minimum, matters regarding applicable jurisdictions and other complex legal or restructuring matters should be outsourced to the relevant professional specialists.

(4) The Role of the Licensed Trust Company (in the Singapore context): In the Singapore regulatory context, licensed trust companies that perform trust administration services for anti-money laundering purposes for PTCs should ideally be brought on board as early as possible, preferably before the trust deed is drafted. This is to ensure that proper systems to manage accountability in decision-making are established and any conflicts of interest are declared and mitigated.

## 9 CONCLUSION

While many issues relating to family dynamics and trust integrity can arise in the structuring and operation of Family Offices and PTCs, these problems can be resolved with proper planning and establishing effective family governance. This chapter has proposed several solutions alongside family governance measures, focusing on the importance of proper administration, board selection, succession planning, and employing professionals with good trust experience to assist in management. Many of these issues are more easily resolved if measures are put in place to deal with them at an early stage of the structuring. Thus, the importance of engaging a skilled and experienced professional to assist in the setting up of Family Offices and/or PTCs cannot be overstated.

# PART II

# The Changing Legal Context

# 9

# Trusts of Cryptoassets

*Kelvin F. K. Low*[*]

## 1 THE RISE OF CRYPTOMANIA

Amidst the Great Recession of 2008, when trust in governments was at its nadir, an idea was borne of a person(s) known only as Satoshi Nakamoto.[1] If centralised authorities could not be trusted, could the trust necessary to facilitate transactions between strangers be secured instead by an algorithm? The consensus algorithm that lay at the heart of the bitcoin blockchain leveraged game theory to compel strangers to cooperate in the absence of trust. It employed a 'proof-of-work' algorithm, whereby users that engage in updating the ledger, called 'miners,' are required to solve a computationally difficult puzzle in order to win the right to add a new block of transactions to the blockchain. By doing so, falsifications of the ledger can be easily detected. The high energy and computational cost involved in 'mining', in conjunction with an algorithmic rule to 'mine' on the longest chain, ensure the integrity of the blockchain in most situations. Initially, the preserve of cypherpunks,[2] the Great Recession provided fertile ground for bitcoin to flourish once wider access was provided by the launch of cryptoasset exchanges in 2010, most famously Mt Gox. Instead of 'mining' bitcoins, exchanges provided access to as much bitcoins as a cryptomaniac could desire so long as they could afford them. Combined with the increasing use case of bitcoins for illicit transactions on the dark web,[3] owing to its pseudonymous[4] nature, demand exploded. This led to bitcoin

* Faculty of Law, National University of Singapore. This chapter was first published in (2020) 34 *Trust Law International* 191 but has been updated to take into account of developments since its initial publication. I thank the Editorial Board of *Trust Law International* for permission to reprint it here.

1 A. O'Hagan, 'The Satoshi Affair', *London Review of Books* <www.lrb.co.uk/the-paper/v38/n13/andrew-o-hagan/the-satoshi-affair> last accessed 31 July 2020.

2 Cryptography enthusiasts advocating the use of cryptography for social and political change. See further L. Swartz, 'What was Bitcoin, what will it be? The technoeconomic imaginaries of a new money technology' (2018) 32 *Cultural Studies* 623, 625–626.

3 Particularly on the online black market known as the 'Silk Road' set up by Ross Ulbricht.

4 Pseudonymity is not anonymity. Cf. A. Greenberg, 'Prosecutors Trace $13.4m in Bitcoins from the Silk Road to Ulbricht's Laptop', *Wired* <www.wired.com/2015/01/prosecutors-trace-13-4-million-bitcoins-silk-road-ulbrichts-laptop/> last accessed 31 July 2020.

prices rising, which in turn drew other 'investors' to bitcoin in a manner, not unlike a Ponzi scheme, whereby growth feeds further growth, leading to the inflation of 'the mother and father of all bubbles'.[5] Since its collapse from a then all-time high price of almost US$20,000 per bitcoin in 2017, the price of bitcoin struggled through most of 2020 to even overcome the US$10,000 barrier,[6] though it rapidly scaled new heights to reach US$65,000 in early 2021[7] before collapsing yet again. Its remarkable volatility has attracted both traders, who value volatility over any other attribute, and investors starved of returns in a low to no and in some cases even negative interest rate environment.

Some among these circling investors hungry for returns are trustees, which raise a range of questions about the role that cryptoassets may play in relation to 'the greatest and most distinctive achievement performed by Englishmen in the field of jurisprudence'.[8] First, can cryptoassets even be the subject-matter of a trust? Secondly, if so, how would traditional trust law rules, such as the rules on certainty of intent and subject-matter, apply to cryptoassets? Thirdly, can trustees of pre-existing trusts invest in cryptoassets? Finally, assuming it is permitted, what are the considerations trustees should bear in mind in deciding whether to invest? This article considers these issues.

## 2 CRYPTOASSETS AS TRUST PROPERTY

### 2.1 *Can Cryptoassets Be Held on Trust?*

The question of whether cryptoassets can be held on trust appears initially to translate to the question of whether cryptoassets are property, an approach adopted by the UK Jurisdiction Taskforce's ("the Taskforce") *Legal Statement on Cryptoassets and Smart Contracts* ("the *Legal* Statement").[9] The *Legal Statement* was intended to clarify the status of cryptoassets, which adoption some perceived to have been hindered by legal uncertainty.[10] This may be doubted since provided the innovation

5 N. Roubini, Testimony to the US Senate Committee on Banking, Housing, and Urban Affairs on 'Exploring the Cryptocurrency and Blockchain Ecosystem' <www.govinfo.gov/content/pkg/CHRG-115shrg34525/html/CHRG-115shrg34525.html> last accessed 31 July 2020.

6 O. Godbole, 'First Mover: Bitcoin at Last Passes $10K, but Why Has It Struggled While Gold Shone?', *Coindesk* <www.coindesk.com/first-mover-bitcoin-at-last-passes-10k-but-why-has-it-struggled-while-gold-shone> last accessed 31 July 2020.

7 E. Szalay, 'Bitcoin: Too Good to Miss or a Bubble Ready to Burst?', *Financial Times* <www.ft.com/content/be796d33-a5e7-4753-98a8-b586f1680d58> last accessed 1 July 2021.

8 F. W. Maitland, 'The Unincorporate Body', in H. A. L. Fisher (ed), *The Collected Papers of Frederic William Maitland*, vol. III (Cambridge 1911), pp. 271–272.

9 UK Jurisdiction Taskforce, *Legal Statement on Cryptoassets and Smart Contracts* <https://35z8e83m1ih83drye280o9d1-wpengine.netdna-ssl.com/wp-content/uploads/2019/11/6.6056_JO_Cryptocurrencies_Statement_FINAL_WEB_111119-1.pdf> last accessed 31 July 2020.

10 Sir G. Vos, 'Cryptoassets as Property: How Can English Law Boost the Confidence of Would-be Parties to Smart Legal Contracts?' <www.judiciary.uk/wp-content/uploads/2019/05/Sir-Geoffrey-Vos-Chancellor-of-the-High-Court-speech-on-cryptoassets.pdf> last accessed 31 July 2020.

met some unserved need, legal uncertainty usually provided little hindrance to adoption. Nevertheless, it is arguable that cryptoassets are different in that legal uncertainty is more inimical where property rather than contract is involved. The latter tends to be inclusionary, as evidenced by the general rule that no particular form is required for a legally binding contract. The former, on the other hand, tends to be exclusionary, as evidenced by the *numerus clausus* principle.

Even in the absence of authority, scholars were unanimously of the view that cryptoassets were property,[11] for different reasons. The most common approach, adopted by the Taskforce, to divining proprietary status was to search for so-called indicia of property,[12] which inevitably leads to Lord Wilberforce's famous definition of property in *National Provincial Bank* v. *Ainsworth*:[13]

> Before a right or an interest can be admitted into the category of property, or of a right affecting property, it must be definable, identifiable by third parties, capable in its nature of assumption by third parties, and have some degree of permanence or stability.

The Taskforce concluded that 'cryptoassets possess all the characteristics of property set out in the authorities'.[14] So too did the Singapore International Commercial Court ('SICC') in *B2C2 Ltd* v. *Quoine Pte Ltd*,[15] as well as the English High Court in AA v. *Persons Unknown*,[16] and the New Zealand High Court ('NZHC') in *Ruscoe* v. *Cryptopia Ltd (in liq)*.[17] Although the SICC's conclusion was not confirmed on appeal,[18] neither was it reversed by the Singapore Court of Appeal ('SGCA').

The resort to *Ainsworth* is highly problematic. First, the scathing criticism that the test is 'riddled with circularity'[19] remains unanswered, likely because it is unanswerable. It seems unlikely that the courts are unaware of these criticisms yet they are repeatedly ignored and *Ainsworth* is frequently cited as if its test is uncontroversial.

Secondly, in addition to the vice of circularity, the requirement of 'some degree of permanence or stability' is both vague and incompatible with the common law.

[11] K. F. K. Low and E. Teo, 'Bitcoins and Other Cryptocurrencies as Property?' (2017) 9 *Law, Innovation & Technology* 235; D. Fox, 'Cryptocurrencies in the Common Law of Property' in D. Fox and S. Green (eds), *Cryptocurrencies in Public and Private Law* (Oxford 2019), p. 139.

[12] Taskforce, *Legal Statement*, [49]–[58].

[13] *National Provincial Bank* v. *Ainsworth* [1965] 1 AC 1175 at 1248.

[14] Taskforce, *Legal Statement*, [57].

[15] *B2C2 Ltd* v. *Quoine Pte Ltd* [2019] SGHC(I) 3, [2019] 4 SLR 17.

[16] AA v. *Persons Unknown* [2019] EWHC 3556 (Comm). See also *Vorotyntseva* v. *Money-4 Ltd, t/a Nebeus.com* [2018] EWHC 2598 (Ch); *Liam David Robertson* v. *Persons Unknown* (unreported 15 July 2019).

[17] *Ruscoe* v. *Cryptopia Ltd (in liq)* [2020] NZHC 728 at [75], [102]–[121].

[18] *Quoine Pte Ltd* v. *B2C2 Ltd* [2020] SGCA(I) 2.

[19] K. Gray and S. F. Gray, *Elements of Land Law*, 5th ed. (Oxford 2009), p. 97.

It arguably imports antithetical Roman civil law concepts of permanence in ownership[20] to the common law. It bears remembering that the largest estate known to the common law, the freehold fee simple, was time limited in its original feudal conception. Although freehold fee simple estates are today conceived of as lasting in perpetuity,[21] this is the result of the Statute of Wills 1540[22] and Tenures Abolition Act 1660[23] authorising the devise of all land as well as provisions for their passing upon intestacy. Prior to these developments, freehold fee simple land would escheat to the immediate lord when a tenant died without heirs.[24] Freehold estates can thus be regarded as distinct from leasehold estates, after the latter came to be reified in the fifteenth century,[25] by the manner in which time is measured. Freehold estates are measured in time by human lives – the tenant's and his heirs' – which are uncertain in duration. Leasehold estates must be certain in duration[26] and so are measured by days, weeks, months, and years though in theory, it is difficult to see what beyond commercial practicality stands in the way of a lease for hours, minutes, or seconds. The requirement also sits particularly uneasily with the common law concept of a tenancy at will.[27] The addition of 'some degree' merely heaps ambiguity upon alienness.

Finally, the *Ainsworth* test is simply misguided as a test in the context of determining what property may be the subject-matter of trusts.[28] *Ainsworth* was concerned with the possible *in rem* character of the 'deserted wife's equity' so that 'property' here means *in rem* right. The test is in effect devised to dress up, in the invisible threads of obfuscatory circularity, the process of segregation of *in rem* wheat from *in personam* chaff. But property in the common law is a messy concept.[29] Unlike some civilian systems, which ruthlessly segregate 'property' in the *in rem* sense of the word from 'property' in the wider asset sense through the use of different

20 Cf. W. W. Buckland and A. D. McNair, *Roman Law and Common Law, a Comparison in Outline* (Cambridge: 1936), p. 70.

21 Most obviously in the curious Singapore 'estate in perpetuity': see Tang H. W. Tang and K. F. K. Low, *Tan Sook Yee's Principles of Singapore Land Law*, 4th ed. (Singapore 2019), pp. 44–45.

22 Which permitted the devise of socage land and most land held by knight service.

23 Which converted all land held by knight service to socage.

24 Even if the Crown is the ultimate beneficiary via bona vacantia in an intestacy, there are important distinctions in consequences between escheat and bona vacantia.

25 R. Megarry and H. W. R Wade, *The Law of Real Property*, 5th ed. (London 1984), pp. 1156–1157.

26 *Lace* v. *Chantler* [1944] KB 368; *Prudential Assurance Co Ltd* v. *London Residuary Body* [1992] 2 AC 386; *Mexfield Housing Co-operative Ltd* v. *Berrisford* [2012] 1 AC 955.

27 S. Bridge, E. Cooke, and M. Dixon, *Megarry & Wade: The Law of Real Property*, 9th ed. (London 2019), pp. 741–742.

28 K. F. K. Low, '*Quoines* in *Cryptopia*: When (If Ever) Are Cryptoasset Exchanges Trustees?' [2020] *Conveyancer* 70; J. Lau, 'That New Chestnut – The Proprietary Status of Bitcoins' [2020] *Lloyd's Maritime and Commercial Law Quarterly* 378. Cf. M. Solinas, 'Investors' Rights in (Crypto) Custodial Holdings' (2021) 84 *Modern Law Review* 155, 160.

29 B. McFarlane and S. Douglas, 'Property, Analogy, and Variety' (2021) 42 *Oxford Journal of Legal Studies* 161.

vocabulary,[30] common lawyers muddle along with a single ambiguous word, often shifting between meanings carelessly.[31] If the *Ainsworth* test is determinative of whether a right may be the subject-matter of a trust, then *in personam* contractual rights would not be capable of being held on trust, contrary to authority.[32] It would render nonsensical Lord Shaw's oft-cited exhortation in *Lord Strathcona Steamship Co Ltd* v. *Dominion Coal Co Ltd* that:[33]

> The scope of the trusts recognised in equity is unlimited. There can be a trust of a chattel or of a chose[34] in action, or of a right or obligation under an ordinary legal contract, just as much as a trust of land.

The requirement of transferability would also invalidate both *Don King Productions Inc* v. *Warren (No 1)*[35] and *Swift* v. *Dairywise Farms Ltd (No 1)*,[36] both of which held that non-transferable property could nevertheless be held on trust.

Although *Ainsworth* regards property synonymously with rights *erga omnes*, such a view of property is both too narrow and ahistorical for common law systems. The original thing in action that the common law recognised as a form of personal property was none other than the *in personam* contractual right. Property turns not on exigibility[37] but on exclusivity.[38] Where a resource is tangible, exclusivity can only be secured by rights *erga omnes* since anything short of that would not secure exclusive control of the *res* in question. But even here, the genius of equity cheated strict adherence to logic. The institution of the trust permitted indirect rights to be infinitely replicable to save as against equity's darling, in effect fashioning a simulacrum of property in the *in rem* sense.[39] Where the resource is intangible, any reference to rights *erga omnes* breaks down. Intangible property is ideational and abstract. Right and *res* are inseparable. Exclusivity is thus secured by means other than widespread exigibility, although certain abstractions may require *erga omnes* effect. Thus, in common law systems, we see rights of varying exigibility all classified as things in action

30 Cf. K. F. K. Low and Y. C. Wu, 'The Characterization of Cryptocurrencies in East Asia' in Fox and Green (eds), *Cryptocurrencies in Public and Private Law*, p. 199.

31 Cf. P. W. Lee, 'Inducing Breach of Contract, Conversion and Contract as Property' (2009) 29 *Oxford Journal of Legal Studies* 511. Contra S. Douglas, *Liability for Wrongful Interferences with Chattels* (Oxford 2011), p. 18; A. Goymour, 'Conversion of Contractual Rights' [2011] *Lloyd's Maritime and Commercial Law Quarterly* 67.

32 *Paul* v. *Constance* [1977] 1 WLR 527.

33 *Lord Strathcona Steamship Co Ltd* v. *Dominion Coal Co Ltd* [1926] AC 108 at 124.

34 In this article, unless within a quote, the modern English 'thing' is preferred over the French 'chose'.

35 *Don King Productions Inc* v. *Warren (No 1)* [2000] Ch 291. But see A. Tettenborn, 'Trusts of Unassignable Agreements' [1998] Lloyd's Maritime and Commercial Law Quarterly 498; A. Tettenborn, 'Trusts and Unassignable Agreements Again' [1999] *Lloyd's Maritime and Commercial Law Quarterly* 353.

36 *Swift* v. *Dairywise Farms Ltd (No 1)* [2000] 1 WLR 1177.

37 Cf. P. Birks, 'Before We Begin: Five Keys to Land Law' in S. Bright and J. Dewar (eds), *Land Law: Themes and Perspectives* (Oxford 1998), pp. 457, 473.

38 Cf. K. Gray, 'Property in Thin Air' (1991) 50 *Cambridge Law Journal* 252.

39 S. F. C. Milsom, *Historical Foundations of the Common Law*, 2nd ed. (London 1981), p. 6.

from purely personal rights (contractual things in action) to rights enforceable against a limited but varying and fluctuating class (company shares) to rights *erga omnes* (many intellectual property rights). In each instance though, exclusivity is secured in precisely the same fashion, whether the right is *erga omnes* or *in personam*.[40]

How then are courts to determine whether some new resource is capable of being property? In truth, judicial recognition of new forms of property has slowed if not ceased for decades if not centuries. Most modern innovations in terms of property, such as shares and intellectual property, are creatures of statute. One man's right necessarily impinges upon another's liberty. The conceptual certainty of this tension is also demonstrated by Hohfeld's fundamental legal conceptions.[41] Granting a claim right/privilege/power/immunity to one man necessarily imposes its cognate correlate upon another/others. Where the right is exclusive and the resource precious, the exercise becomes a highly political affair,[42] increasingly unsuited to unelected judges in modern democracies. It is rare for modern courts to recognise a novel form of property right.[43] How is it then that the reification of cryptoassets is so uncontroversial? First, it accords with the practices of users of cryptoassets, corresponding to Humean conceptions of property.[44] But more importantly, properly conceptualised as a narrow right to have the unspent transaction output ('UTXO') of a cryptoasset locked to a holder's public address on a blockchain,[45] it is difficult to conceive how such a right would interfere with any legitimate liberty of any stranger. The only instance where a legitimate concern could arise would be if an innocent stranger purchased some cryptoasset in good faith in circumstances when the transfer is impugned but this is precisely the sort of balancing exercise that property law's priority rules are well adapted to deal with.

There were also concerns as to whether cryptoassets could fit within the common law's traditional twofold classification of personal property, as set out by Fry LJ in *Colonial Bank* v. *Whinney*:[46] 'All personal things are either in possession or in action. The law knows no tertium quid between the two.' The poor fit supposedly led the Taskforce to endorse the recognition of an intangible tertium quid. Although this issue is really a 'red-herring',[47] the argument bears airing:[48]

40 For an elaboration, see K. F. K. Low, 'Trusts of Cryptoassets' (2020) 34 *Trust Law International* 191, 195.
41 W. N. Hohfeld, 'Fundamental Legal Conceptions as Applied in Legal Reasoning' (1917) 26 *Yale Law Journal* 710.
42 Cf. B. McFarlane, *The Structure of Property Law* (Oxford 2008), pp. 4–5.
43 *Regency Villas Title Ltd* v. *Diamond Resorts (Europe) Ltd* [2019] AC 553. Cf. *Hunter* v. *Canary Wharf Ltd* [1997] AC 655.
44 Cf. J. Waldron, 'To Bestow Stability upon Possession' in J. Penner and H. E. Smith (eds), *Philosophical Foundations of Property Law* (Oxford 2013), p. 1.
45 Cf. Low and Teo, 'Bitcoins as Property?', 252–254.
46 *Colonial Bank* v. *Whinney* (1885) 30 Ch D 261 at 285.
47 *Cryptopia* [2020] NZHC 728 at [123].
48 Taskforce, *Legal Statement*, [67]–[68].

> A cryptoasset is not a thing in possession because it not tangible and so cannot be possessed. [...]
>
> Whether a cryptoasset is a thing in action is more debatable. The term is generally used to mean a right of property that can be enforced by court litigation, or action, such as a debt or contractual right. A cryptoasset would not normally be a thing in action on that definition.

Assuming that the Taskforce endorses this narrow definition will colour one's reading of its conclusion 'that the fact that a cryptoasset might not be a thing in action on the narrower definition of that term does not in itself mean that it cannot be treated as property'.[49] By assuming that the Taskforce endorsed the 'narrower definition', Bryan J in AA v. *Persons Unknown* reasoned from their conclusion that 'it is fallacious to proceed on the basis that the English law of property recognises no forms of property other than choses in possession and choses in action'.[50]

But Bryan J reads too much into the Taskforce's conclusion, which means exactly what it states, 'that the fact that a cryptoasset *might* not be a thing in action *on the narrower definition* of that term does not in itself mean that it cannot be treated as property [emphasis added]'.[51] It does not endorse the narrower definition of thing in action nor does it conclude that cryptoassets are intangible tertium quid. In their discussion of *Colonial Bank* v. *Whinney*, the Taskforce explicitly noted that Fry LJ 'attributed a *very broad meaning* to things in action [emphasis added]'.[52] A more accurate reading of the Taskforce's *Legal Statement* should, therefore, be that cryptoassets are preferably regarded as things in action but if this is not possible for some reason, they may still be accommodated as a form of intangible tertium quid. The former view was preferred in *Ruscoe* v. *Cryptopia (in liquidation)*.[53]

Save perhaps for patents in England, which are statutorily excluded[54] as things in action for reasons that are obscure,[55] it is not entirely clear what purpose is served by adopting the narrower definition of things in action. As Bridge et al observed:[56]

> [S]uch a view of things in action both overemphasises the necessity of a right of action and underestimates the panoply of remedies available to a modern court. As to the former, the right of action serves the purpose of securing performance and in the vast majority of cases, things in action, even in the limited sense, are enjoyed in their performance rather than by way of action. [...] As to the latter, the availability of declaratory and quai timet injunctive relief also severely blunts the force of criticisms that no rights of action exist prior to infringement.

49 Taskforce, *Legal Statement*, [84].
50 ibid, [58].
51 ibid, [84].
52 ibid, [75]. See also [76].
53 *Cryptopia* [2020] NZHC 728 at [75], [102]–[121].
54 Patents Act 1977, s. 30.
55 M. Bridge et al, *The Law of Personal Property*, 3rd ed. (London 2022), p. 251.
56 ibid, p. 175.

The irony of permitting legal *actions*, with accompanying remedies, in respect of intangible property that has specifically been rejected as things in *action* seems to have eluded the English court.[57]

Few cases endorse a *tertium quid*. The most well-known instance is the Privy Council decision of *Attorney-General of Hong Kong* v. *Daniel Chan Nai-Keung*,[58] which held that export quotas for textiles fell within the Hong Kong Theft Ordinance as property was defined therein as including 'things in action and other intangible property'. A single sentence summed up both the reasoning and conclusion. 'Their Lordships have no hesitation in concluding that export quotas in Hong Kong although not "things in action" are a form of "other intangible property."'[59] No reasons are offered as to why export quotas are not things in action, nor is *Colonial Bank v Whinney* cited. Given the threadbare reasoning, it is best regarded as decided per incuriam. *Armstrong DLW GmbH v Winnington Networks Ltd*,[60] another decision of the High Court, is also often cited for the proposition that carbon credits are a tertium quid, as the Taskforce did in its *Legal Statement*.[61] However, Stephen Morris QC actually concluded that a carbon credit was '*not a chose in action in the narrow sense*, as it cannot be claimed or enforced by action. However to the extent that the concept encompasses wider matters of property, then it could be so described [emphasis added]'.[62] On the other hand, the Court of Appeal has rejected the tertium quid in *Allgemeine Versicherungs-Gesellschaft Helvetia v Administrator of German Property*[63] and *Your Response v Datateam Business Media*.[64] The grant of remedies by the courts necessarily entails the recognition of legal rights between (at least) the litigants and it is not obvious why such rights are less properly regarded as things in action than contractual debts, rights between shareholders, or intellectual property rights (less patents). It is true that the task of delimiting and defining the precise rights involved is contentious but this is preferable to the tempting alternative 'to first determine if an intangible asset meets the criteria of property and then adapt the rules of tangible property to it'.[65] Such rule adaptation typically entails the application of a metaphorical version of the tort of conversion. However, 'the metaphor is broken since conversion primarily protects against physical interferences with a

57 Cf. Taskforce, *Legal Statement*, 41, endnote 34.

58 *Attorney-General of Hong Kong* v. *Daniel Chan Nai-Keung* [1987] 1 WLR 1339.

59 ibid at 1342.

60 *Armstrong DLW GmbH* v. *Winnington Networks Ltd* [2013] Ch 156, noted in K. F. K. Low and J. Lin, 'Carbon Credits as EU Like It: Property, Immunity, TragiCO2medy?' (2015) 27 *Journal of Environmental Law* 377.

61 Taskforce, *Legal Statement*, [82].

62 ibid, [61].

63 *Allgemeine Versicherungs-Gesellschaft Helvetia* v. *Administrator of German Property* [1931] 1 KB 672 at 704.

64 *Your Response* v. *Datateam Business Media* [2014] EWCA Civ 281, [2015] QB 41.

65 Low, '*Quoines* in *Cryptopia*', 80.

tangible *res* and such interferences are, by definition, impossible in relation to that which is intangible'.[66]

### 2.2 *Certainty of Intention*

The question of whether a trust structure is intended is ultimately one of fact and one of the key issues that cloud the nature of the legal relationship between a cryptoasset exchange and its customers. Most investors in cryptoassets purchase their holdings of cryptoassets through an exchange rather than 'mine' them personally. Unfortunately, many cryptoasset exchange agreements are poorly drafted and contain contradictory indications as to whether a trust or a debt is intended.[67] Clearly drafted cryptoasset exchange agreements, such as that which featured in *Ruscoe v Cryptopia*, are uncommon. Fortunately, a body of case law is beginning to build up that will provide better guidance to future courts faced with this thorny question.

The *Quoine* cases in Singapore concerned seven trades of bitcoin and ether. The trades were purportedly between three customers of Quoine Pte Ltd ('Quoine') the defendant cryptoasset exchange operator – (i) B2C2 Ltd ('B2C2'), the plaintiff, on the one part and (ii) Pulsar Trading Capital ('Pulsar') and (iii) Yu Tomita ("Tomita") as counterparties to B2C2. Pulsar and Tomita engaged in margin trading facilitated by Quoine, who also operated its exchange as a 'market-maker,' actively placing buy and sell orders on its system and engaged in futures trading, which necessarily entailed trading in cryptoassets it did not own. Like Quoine, its customers were also market makers rather than passive investors. In the trades, B2C2 sold ether and bought bitcoin whereas Pulsar and Tomita sold bitcoin and bought ether. A mistake in Quoine's software led B2C2's own algorithmic trading software offer to sell ether at 10 and 9.99 bitcoins per ether, which were filled by Quoine's malfunctioning software to complete the margin calls on Pulsar and Tomita. These trades overvalued ether by a measure of approximately 250 times its then market value. Following the trades, approximately 3092.5 bitcoins were credited by Quoine and 309.25 ether were debited from B2C2's account with it. When Quoine became aware of these trades the following morning, they were immediately reversed, which triggered the dispute between B2C2 and Quoine. Although the case focused primarily on contractual liability,[68] our interest is limited to the question of whether the 3092.5 bitcoins credited to B2C2 was intended by Quoine to be held on trust for B2C2.

66 ibid.

67 Cf. Low and Teo, 'Bitcoins as Property?', 264–267.

68 Noted in K. F. K. Low and E. Mik, 'Lost in Transmission: Unilateral Mistakes in Automated Contracts' (2020) 136 *Law Quarterly Review* 563 and A. Loke, 'Mistakes in Algorithmic Trading of Cryptocurrencies' (2020) 83 *Modern Law Review* 1343.

At first instance, the SICC concluded that Quoine had held the 3092.5 bitcoins credited to B2C2 on trust. On appeal, the SGCA reversed the finding of an intention to create a trust, ostensibly for two reasons. First, because there was no actual segregation of cryptoassets by Quoine on the facts.[69] Secondly, because part of clause 9 of the Risk Disclosure Document indicated that Quoine did not take client safety measures such as depositing clients' assets with a trust bank.[70] Both reasons are unconvincing but before addressing them, it is necessary to understand how cryptoassets are 'held'. This requires a clear understanding of three different concepts: (i) cryptoasset public addresses, (ii) cryptoasset 'wallets', and (iii) notional cryptoasset exchange accounts. A holder of cryptoassets possesses a public address and a private key. The public address is often regarded as serving a similar function to a bank account number, which is necessary in order to receive cryptoassets. Like a bank account, it is possible to have as many public addresses as one can be bothered to create. In order to transfer cryptoassets out of the address, however, one needs both the address and its matching private key. Although sometimes considered the equivalent of a password, the private key is mathematically linked to the public address by cryptography so that it is not possible to change the private key, unlike a conventional password. One creates this mathematically matched pair of data strings by first choosing a private key, which is ideally randomly generated. This randomly generated private key is then fed to an algorithm to generate a mathematically linked public address. The public address is intended to be freely shared whereas the private key is kept secret and the latter is regularly described metaphorically as a digital signature. As both data strings are often a random jumble of characters, it is impractical to commit them to memory alone so a means of storing them securely is often necessary.

This is where cryptoasset wallets feature. Such wallets are often divided into five main types. They are (i) paper wallets, (ii) hardware wallets, (iii) desktop wallets, (iv) mobile wallets, and (v) online wallets. Although it is sometimes said that cryptoassets are stored in such 'wallets', in truth, they merely 'store' the private–public key pair. Paper wallets are simply pieces of paper on which the private–public key pair are printed, often in the form of QR codes for convenience. As they are permanently offline, they cannot be hacked but cryptoassets can be 'stolen' if a stranger manages to glean the information contained therein.[71] Hardware wallets are devices, typically thumb drives, that store the same information, but with some form of added security, including PIN, password, and/or biometric. Similar to paper wallets, they are mostly offline, reducing the risks of hacking. Some of them also come with

[69] *Quoine* [2020] SGCA(I) 2 at [146].

[70] ibid at [148].

[71] L. Coleman, 'Researcher Has Bitcoin Stolen Off His Back in a Public Experiment', *Crypto Coins News* <www.cryptocoinsnews.com/researcher-bitcoin-stolen-off-back-public-experiment> last accessed 31 July 2020.

so-called recovery seeds, which are a list of words in a particular order that can be used to recover data lost through either loss or damage of the device. Although generally regarded as the most secure of all 'wallets', they are alas expensive. Moreover, although recovery seeds may help with recovery of cryptoassets if a hardware wallet is lost/damaged, they risk the loss of cryptoassets if compromised. Desktop wallets are software installed on desktop PCs or laptops which provide some measure of security beyond simply storing the private–public key pair in an unencrypted file on the same device. Obviously, any compromise in the device, whether through hacking or otherwise, could result in a loss of cryptoassets. Mobile wallets are similar to desktop wallets except that the device is a mobile phone. Online wallets are a service provided by a service provider in the cloud, providing advantages similar to those offered by cloud computing more generally – access to the same service from multiple devices and multiple locations. However, just as it is true that cloud computing does not actually happen in a cloud but in actual terrestrial servers, so too any private–public key pair 'stored' in an online wallet will actually be stored in a server (or multiple servers).

Wallets are also generally categorised into hot or cold varieties. Hot wallets are wallets connected to the Internet whereas cold wallets are not. Hot wallets are generally regarded as riskier than cold wallets as they can be hacked. Whilst some wallets will be almost permanently hot (online wallets) and others permanently cold (paper wallets), most can be connected to and disconnected from the Internet as necessary.[72] Most cryptoasset exchanges would, as a cautionary measure, store most of the cryptoassets that it holds in cold wallets and only keep sufficient cryptoassets in hot wallets to meet customer demands.[73] As these 'wallets' store private–public keys rather than cryptoassets per se, the same data strings can be stored in multiple wallets since information is non-rivalrous. Indeed, it is generally advisable to do so. This also means that cryptoasset wallets must be irrelevant for the purposes of cryptoasset segregation. Unlike their physical cousin, it is possible to 'store' private–public key pair A together with private–public key pair B in one wallet whereas another wallet could 'store' private–public key pair A together with private–public key pair C. Cryptoasset 'wallets' therefore matter less to segregation than public addresses, which can obviously be used to segregate cryptoassets since property in cryptoassets is best conceived in terms of exclusive rights to the UTXO associated with a particular public address.[74] Like 'wallets', notional accounts should also be regarded as irrelevant for purposes of segregation since they are purely notional and may not be actually backed by any underlying cryptoasset at all.[75]

[72] *Cryptopia* [2020] NZHC 728 at [22](f).

[73] ibid at [22](c), observing that Cryptopia held 75% of its cryptoassets in cold wallets and 25% in hot wallets.

[74] Low and Teo, 'Bitcoins as Property?', 252–254.

[75] See text accompanying nn 90–92.

The absence of actual segregation in *Quoine* is related to the absence of segregation by either public address or wallet. The latter should be irrelevant, the former at best equivocal. It is important to establish why there was no actual segregation. Was it because the parties agreed that segregation was unnecessary or was it because Quoine promised to segregate but failed to do so? Even if the parties agreed that segregation was unnecessary, this does not preclude a trust.[76] Clause 9 of the Risk Disclosure Document in full clause appears to suggest the opposite conclusion to the SGCA's finding:[77]

> *The Company may receive deposits of money or virtual currency from customers, but the assets deposited by customers will be managed separately from the Company's assets.* The Company does not, however, take client fund safety measures such as depositing them in an account with a trust bank, etc. regarding these assets, so if the Company goes bankrupt, the Company will not be able to return customer assets, and customers may suffer losses ... [emphasis added].

By citing only the unitalicised part of the clause, a wrong impression is created. The italicised (and omitted) part of the clause clearly envisages segregation of assets. Moreover, surely the absence of the use of a trust bank merely precludes a sub-trust (whereby the trust bank holds on trust for the exchange which holds on sub-trust for its clients) rather than a trust per se?

*Cryptopia* concerned the hacking of the eponymous cryptoasset exchange. Although the scale of the hack, where cryptoassets valued at NZ$30m was 'stolen', paled in comparison to the worst hacks of all time,[78] it sufficed to force Cryptopia into liquidation. *Cryptopia* was essentially an application by its liquidators for directions on the legal status of the remaining cryptoassets held by Cryptopia: were the 'unhacked' cryptoassets held on trust for its accountholders? Leaving these aside, Cryptopia's available assets for distribution in the liquidation was a mere NZ$5.4m. This contrasted with the estimated value of all creditors' claims at NZ$12.7m. The liquidators had no personal interest in whatever outcome was reached by the court so that the tussle was effectively one between the creditors of Cryptopia and its account holders. Unlike Quoine, Cryptopia did not engage in market making or futures trading, nor did its customers. Naturally, the documentation of the exchange played an important role in the NZHC concluding that a trust was intended. *Cryptopia*, by highlighting the significance of market making and futures trading, provides some useful guidelines for future courts that may be faced with more muddled drafting.

Although not highlighted by Gendall J, it appears that Cryptopia did not segregate its own beneficially owned cryptoassets from those that it held for its customers,

[76] See text accompanying nn 95–98.

[77] The full clause can be found in Annex 2 of the SICC judgment, *B2C2* v. *Quoine* [2019] 4 SLR 17 at [104].

[78] See text accompanying nn 149–150.

nor did it segregate the cryptoassets of different customers, except by way of its own notional, and hence irrelevant, accounts. Despite Cryptopia having a 'beneficial interest in its own personal cryptocurrency as an accountholder,'[79] this did not deter Gendall J from concluding that a trust was intended. This conclusion is consistent with the law since segregation is merely indicative of and not necessary to demonstrate the requisite intent.[80] It is also trite law that a trustee can have a beneficial interest in trust assets.[81] It is suggested that, as a matter of policy, a clear preference for a presumption of a trustee–beneficiary relationship for cryptoasset exchanges is desirable since the absence of interest payments, a hallmark of debt,[82] in practically all such agreements is highly suggestive.

### 2.3 *Certainty of Subject-Matter*

But for an elementary error made by the SICC in *Quoine*,[83] which elided the question of whether property can be held on trust with the quite separate question of certainty of subject-matter, it would not have been necessary to emphasise their distinctness. Needless to say, the SICC cannot be correct. The leading cases on certainty of subject-matter, *Re London Wine Co (Shippers) Ltd*,[84] *Hunter* v. *Moss*,[85] and *Re Goldcorp Exchange Ltd (in receivership)*,[86] concerned wine, shares, and gold bullion, respectively. All of those 'property' were indubitably capable of being held on trust. Yet they gave rise to fierce debates over whether there was sufficient certainty of subject-matter on the facts of those cases. Conversely, arguably the most controversial case on the susceptibility of 'property' to trust holding is that of *Swift* v. *Dairywise Farms Ltd*,[87] on EU milk quota, which raised no question of certainty of subject-matter at all.

There was almost certainly no trust in *Quoine* in favour of B2C2 of the disputed 3092.5 bitcoins Quoine had mistakenly credited to it. First, as the bitcoins represented one-half of a trade between B2C2 on the one part and Pulsar and Tomita on the other, it seems obvious that any trust intended by Quoine should be impressed upon bitcoins beneficially owned by Pulsar and Tomita rather than bitcoins it personally beneficially owned. In this respect, there was one insurmountable hurdle: 'the available [bitcoin] balances in Pulsar's and Tomita's accounts were insufficient

79 *Cryptopia* [2020] NZHC 728 at [165](d)(iii).

80 *R* v. *Clowes (No 2)* [1994] 2 All ER 316 at 325. Cf. *South Australia Insurance Co* v. *Randell* (1869) LR 3 PC 101; *Henry* v. *Hammond* [1913] 2 KB 515 at 521.

81 The only prohibition is against a trustee holding the equitable interest for himself exclusively: *Re Selous* [1901] 1 Ch 921 at 922. See also *Re Cook* [1948] Ch 212.

82 Cf. *Ex parte Plitt* (1889) 60 LT 397.

83 *Quoine* [2019] 4 SLR 17 at [142].

84 *Re London Wine Co (Shippers) Ltd* [1986] PCC 121.

85 *Hunter* v. *Moss* [1994] 1 WLR 452.

86 *Re Goldcorp Exchange Ltd (in receivership)* [1995] 1 AC 74.

87 *Swift* [2000] 1 WLR 1177.

to meet B2C2's orders'.[88] A trust cannot be impressed upon non-existent property.[89] Even the question of a trust in respect of the bitcoins *actually* beneficially owned by Pulsar/Tomita is also clouded by the issue of priority between competing claims. Presumably, these were held by Quoine on behalf of Pulsar/Tomita under the same terms as with B2C2. If these terms would give rise to trust, then Pulsar/Tomita would have pre-existing equitable interests in these bitcoins. Since the transaction was concluded only on account of the software malfunction, it seems doubtful that Quoine would be, vis-a-vis Pulsar/Tomita, authorised to transfer their equitable interests to B2C2. If so, any declaration of trust by Quoine in favour of B2C2 over assets it already holds on trust for Pulsar/Tomita must be subject to the equitable maxim *qui prior est tempore, potior est jure*[90] so that B2C2's equitable title to the bitcoins that actually exists must rank behind that of Pulsar/Tomita.

Provided the necessary cryptoassets exist, it is likely that a declaration of trust of part of a holding locked to a single public address will be treated in the same way as a declaration of trust of part of a single holding of shares.[91] Like shares,[92] fungibility of cryptoassets may be effectively irrelevant if the entire 'issue' of cryptoassets, for example, all 21 million bitcoins, are regarded as a single asset. Alternatively, if each unit of bitcoin, the smallest being a satoshi, is regarded as a separate asset, they should be regarded as fungible if, like bitcoin and ether, they were intended to serve as an alternative form of money.[93] Naturally, segregation will put matters beyond doubt but provided the requisite intent is clear, segregation is unnecessary, as *Cryptopia* suggests. Segregation is unlikely[94] so far as cryptoasset exchanges are concerned because segregation would make trading in cryptoassets unnecessarily cumbersome and expensive. The sale to or purchase from a customer of cryptoassets would require a transfer on the relevant blockchain from one public address to another. This is impractical for two reasons. First, it is costly. Whilst bitcoin was heralded in the early days for its ability to facilitate cross-border fund transfers at a low cost, this was a function of the high levels of newly 'mined' bitcoins awarded by the system to 'miners' for 'mining' new blocks of transactions. As mining rewards have fallen, transfer fees have increased and many proposed transactions have not

88 *Quoine* [2019] 4 SLR 17 at [75].

89 *Holroyd* v. *Marshall* (1862) 10 HL Cas 191 at 220.

90 Where the equities are equal, the first in time prevails.

91 *Hunter* [1994] 1 WLR 452; *Re Harvard Securities Ltd* [1997] 2 BCLC 369; *Re CA Pacific Finance Ltd* [2000] 1 BCLC 494; *White* v. *Shortall* [2006] NSWSC 1379.

92 R. Goode, 'Are Intangible Assets Fungible?' [2003] *Lloyd's Maritime and Commercial Law Quarterly* 379.

93 T. Cutts and D. Goldstone QC, 'Bitcoin Ownership and its Impact on Fungibility', *Coindesk* <www.coindesk.com/bitcoin-ownership-impact-fungibility/> accessed 31 July 2020.

94 M. Solinas, 'Bitcoiners in Wonderland: lessons from the Cheshire Cat' [2019] *Lloyd's Maritime and Commercial Law Quarterly* 433, 447. Cf. Solinas, 'Investors' Rights in (Crypto) Custodial Holdings', 156, 162.

been selected by miners, giving rise to tens of thousands of unconfirmed transactions in the mempool.[95] Secondly, cryptoasset transfers on the blockchain are slow. As most cryptoassets rely on a 'proof-of-work' consensus algorithm, new transactions are added in blocks only in set intervals when the 'proof-of-work' puzzle is solved by a 'miner'. Although blocks so added supposedly acquired 'immutability' as a result, 'blockchain immutability is not an absolute concept but rather more 60 blocks/shades of grey'.[96] A transaction gets increasingly immutable as more blocks are added to the blockchain so that on initial addition, a transaction contained in a brand new block is surprisingly susceptible to erasure. For bitcoin, the general advice is to wait for six blocks of confirmation before treating a transaction as final. Given that a new block is only added roughly every ten minutes, this is almost a full hour. Any cryptoasset exchange that adopts a business model which segregates its own cryptoassets from those of its customers will find itself uncompetitive vis-a-vis its peers.

## 3 INVESTING IN CRYPTOASSETS

### 3.1 *Are Cryptoassets an Authorised Investment?*

Although it is clear that cryptoassets may be held on trust, it is an entirely different question altogether whether traditional private trusts can/ought to invest in cryptoassets as part of their investment strategy. Two questions arise. First, are the trustees of a particular trust even authorised to invest in cryptoassets? Secondly, if so, should they do so? The former is dependent on the terms of the trust and its governing law. The latter requires an understanding of the peculiar risks involved in holding cryptoassets as well as how they work.

It is convenient to first dismiss the objection to investment in cryptoassets on the basis that they generate no income. Although the traditional meaning of 'invest' is 'to apply money in the purchase of some property from which interest or profit is expected and which property is purchased in order to be held for the sake of the income which it will yield,'[97] a more modern perspective of investment regards the 'acquisition of property for the sake of income *or capital profit*, or a combination of both, can count as an "investment" [emphasis added]'.[98] Accordingly, even the absence of express authorisation of non-income producing property should not prevent trustees from investing in most cryptoassets provided it otherwise falls within the

95 A contraction of memory pool, which has been likened to a waiting area for unconfirmed transactions. See I. Kaminska, 'The Currency of the Future has a Settlement Problem', *Financial Times* <https://ftalphaville.ft.com/2017/05/17/2188961/the-currency-of-the-future-has-a-settlement-problem/> accessed 31 July 2020.

96 Low and Mik, 'Pause the Blockchain Legal Revolution,' 144.

97 *Re Wragg* [1919] 2 Ch 58 at 65.

98 L. Tucker et al, *Lewin on Trusts*, 20th ed. (London 2020), [35–18].

scope of an investment power.[99] Thus, for the purposes of trust law, most cryptoassets *are* an asset class in that they can be held on trust provided the terms of an investment power are sufficiently wide. The only exception to this analysis may well be stablecoins.

There are broadly four types of stablecoins:[100] (i) fiat-collateralised stablecoins, (ii) crypto-collateralised stablecoins, (iii) commodity-collateralised stablecoins, and (iv) non-collateralised stablecoins, also known as algorithmic stablecoins. As their name suggests, stablecoins are cryptoassets designed with price stabilisation in mind.

The most well-known and significant (by market capitalisation) of stablecoins is Tether, a cryptoasset supposedly backed by US dollar deposits and hence an exemplar of fiat-collateralised stablecoins. Tether is an extremely controversial stablecoin in that the true extent of its reserves has been doubted and it is believed to be used to manipulate bitcoin prices.[101] But on the assumption that it truly is fully backed by fiat currency, then it would not amount to an investment unless the US dollar happens to be a foreign currency for a particular trust. However, even in such a situation, it would be difficult to justify an investment in Tether, except perhaps as a means of then using it to invest in non-stablecoin cryptoassets, since a traditional investment in US dollars, whether through the purchase of bonds or a bank deposit, would at least earn interest payments, however, low those may be.

Crypto-collateralised stablecoins operate on similar principles to those backed by fiat currencies except that the collateral used is another cryptoasset rather than fiat currency. Accordingly, they are an even poorer 'investment'. Not only is there no capital appreciation potential, as they are pegged to traditional fiat currencies, there is arguably a risk of depreciation. As the collateral for such stablecoins are other volatile cryptoassets, it is said that 'this type of stablecoins is often "overcollateralized."'[102] Often, unfortunately, is not the same as always, and sharp drops in the prices of the underlying cryptoasset collaterals may leave them undercollaterised.

Commodity-collateralised stablecoins are rare. As their name suggests, they are backed neither by fiat currency nor cryptoassets but commodities. The most infamous example of a commodity-collateralised stablecoin is the petro, issued by a Venezuelan government facing crippling sanctions and a plummeting currency. It has been described as 'the most obviously horrible investment ever [...] The petro

[99] *Marson* v. *Morton* [1986] 1 WLR 1343 at 1350; *Harries* v. *Church Commissioners for England* [1992] 1 WLR 1241 at 1246; *Cook (Inspector of Taxes)* v. *Medway Housing Society Ltd* [1997] STC 90 at 98.

[100] M. Mita et al, 'What Is Stablecoin? A Survey on Its Mechanism and Potential as Decentalized Payment Systems' 2019 *8th International Congress on Advanced Applied Informatics (IIAI-AAI)*, Toyama, Japan, 2019, 60.

[101] J. M. Griffin and A. Shams, 'Is Bitcoin Really Untethered?' (2020) 75 *The Journal of Finance* 1913.

[102] A. R. Zhang et al, 'The Regulation Paradox of Initial Coin Offerings: A Case Study Approach' (2019) 2 *Frontiers in Blockchain* 2, 8.

is about creating something useless – that's why only foreigners can buy them, but only Venezuelans can spend them'.[103]

Instead of using another asset to stabilise its price, non-collateralised or algorithmic stablecoins do so through algorithms, either in their protocol or applications layers, adjusting supply to ensure long-term price stability. One of the most successful stablecoin proposals in terms of fundraising is Basis, which raised US$133m through private placement for their project.[104] It envisaged ensuring price stability of its Basis token, which is being pegged to a fiat currency, through the issue of two other types of tokens: (i) bond tokens, and (ii) share tokens.[105] Despite funding success, the Basis project is now defunct,[106] and it has been suggested that its price stability algorithm, dubbed the seignorage share model,[107] is fundamentally flawed:[108]

> [...] incentives to buy bonds are based on a circular dependency: people will buy the bonds if they think Basis will climb up, but Basis will only climb up if people buy the bonds. This assumption will inevitably break in free markets.

It is thus not clear that algorithmic stablecoins will be able to ensure price stability in the face of sharp market sell-offs.[109]

In most Commonwealth jurisdictions, apart from stablecoins, cryptoassets will be an authorised investment owing to statutory expansions of trustees' investment powers to an unlimited class of assets, moving away from the old statutory list of authorised trustee investments,[110] unless the statutory power is either excluded or restricted. In some common law jurisdictions, such as Hong Kong, which retains the statutory list of authorised trustee investments,[111] whether or not cryptoassets are an authorised investment class will turn instead on the express powers of investment within the trust deed (if any). A general power of investment should suffice but more

[103] M. O'Brien, 'Venezuela's cryptocurrency is one of the worst investments ever', *Washington Post* <www.washingtonpost.com/news/wonk/wp/2018/03/05/venezuelas-cryptocurrency-is-one-of-the-worst-investments-ever/> last accessed 31 July 2020.

[104] N. Al-Naji, J. Chen, and L. Diao, 'Basis: A Price-Stable Cryptocurrency with an Algorithmic Central Bank' <www.basis.io/basis_whitepaper_en.pdf> last accessed 31 July 2020.

[105] For an elaboration, see Low, 'Trusts of Cryptoassets', 206.

[106] N. Al-Naji, 'Letter to the Basis Community' <www.basis.io/> last accessed 31 July 2020.

[107] R. Sams, 'A Note on Cryptocurrency Stabilisation: Seigniorage Shares' <https://blog.bitmex.com/wp-content/uploads/2018/06/A-Note-on-Cryptocurrency-Stabilisation-Seigniorage-Shares.pdf> last accessed 31 July 2020.

[108] Q. Wang, *Twitter* <https://twitter.com/QWQiao/status/998213027097989120> accessed 31 July 2020.

[109] Mita et al, 'What Is Stablecoin?', 66.

[110] New Zealand (Trustee Amendment Act 1988, No 119); the Northern Territory (Trustee Amendment (No 2) Act No 60 of 1995); South Australia (Trustee (Investment Powers) Act 1995); Victoria (Trustee and Trustee Companies (Amendment) Act 1995 (No 104/1995)); New South Wales (Trustee Amendment (Discretionary Investments) Act No 102 of 1997); Queensland (Trustee (Investments) Amendment Act No 69 of 1999); Tasmania (Trustee Amendment (Investment Powers) Act 1997); Western Australia (Trustees Amendment Act 1997); Australian Capital Territory (Trustee Amendment Act No 28 of 1999); England and Wales (Trustee Act 2000); Singapore (Trustees Act (Cap 337, 2005 Rev Ed)).

[111] See Schedule 2, Trustee Ordinance (Cap 29).

limited powers of investment may not. Thus, a power to invest in such securities as the trustees thought fit[112] is arguably not sufficiently wide to permit investment in cryptoassets given the controversies over whether they are securities or not. Given that investment clauses are to be construed strictly,[113] statements such as those by regulators expressing the view that some cryptoasset offerings are securities offerings[114] may not be persuasive as courts may take the view that the definition of securities for regulatory purposes may be wider than that for trustee investment purposes. This is because a wider regulatory definition would better protect the public from initial coin offering scams, whereas a narrower definition may be preferable from a trustee investment perspective since cryptoassets do not resemble traditional securities. They do not generate income like ordinary securities, carry completely different risks in ownership, and exhibit price volatility on an altogether different scale.

### 3.2 *Understanding the Risks*

Even on the assumption that cryptoassets are an authorised investment under the terms of a particular trust, the question remains as to whether the trustees ought to invest in cryptoassets. This requires trustees to be familiar with the risks and consequences that investments in cryptoassets entail. These may be broadly classified into four categories: (i) hacks and scams, (ii) insurance, (iii) volatility, and (iv) ethics, and environmental considerations.

#### 3.2.1 Hacks and Scams

It has been suggested that the first duty of trustees is to acquire control over trust property.[115] Once under their control, trustees are under a duty to ensure their safe custody. Despite cryptoassets being marketed as 'secure', supposedly as a result of their reliance upon the vaunted blockchain, cryptoassets are actually remarkably insecure. Much is often made of the indisputable, mathematical link between the private keys and public addresses that holders use to receive and transfer cryptoassets, but little is said of the absence of a similar link between a private key and its user.[116] After all, the blockchain consensus protocol cannot differentiate between an end user using his private key and his dog doing the same.[117] Accordingly,

[112] Cf. *Re Smith* [1896] 1 Ch 71; *Re McEachern's Settlement Trusts* [1939] Ch 858.

[113] *Re Maryon-Wilson's Estate* [1912] 1 Ch 55; *Re Harari's Settlement Trusts* [1949] WN 79.

[114] See, e.g. U.S. S.E.C. Chairman Jay Clayton, 'Statement on Cryptocurrencies and Initial Coin Offerings' <www.sec.gov/news/public-statement/statement-clayton-2017-12-11> last accessed 31 July 2020.

[115] *Wyman* v. *Paterson* [1900] AC 271 at 288.

[116] C. Ellison and B. Schneier, 'Ten Risks of PKI: What You're Not Being Told about Public Key Infrastructure' (2000) 16 *Computer Security Journal* 1, 2.

[117] Cf. P. Steiner, 'On the Internet, Nobody Knows You're a Dog' (cartoon caption), *The New Yorker*, 5 July 1993. See also S. Mason and T. S. Reiniger, '"Trust" between Machines? Establishing Identity

cryptoasset holders are only as secure as they are able to secure their private keys. Blockchains provide '*zero* protection [to end users] from [...] hacking, which is not only possible but commonplace'.[118] Individuals can be targeted[119] just as easily as cryptocurrency exchanges.[120] The threat extends beyond cyber-intrusion. Mere sight of paper wallets can lead to loss.[121] Other forms of cold wallets, including thumb drives unconnected to the Internet, are like all tangible property susceptible to theft. Physical threats of violence have also been used to divest a cryptomaniac of their cryptoassets.[122]

Lest it appears that trustees need only concern themselves with securing trust cryptoassets from dishonest interlopers, the challenge is complicated by the risk of loss of the private key, highlighted by the curious case of QuadrigaCX. Although revealed to be a case of fraud,[123] the original headlines highlighted the risks of maintaining only a single copy of the private key. After the sudden death in India of Gerald Cotten, the co-founder and CEO of QuadrigaCX, then Canada's largest cryptoasset exchange, QuadrigaCX announced that it had lost access to the cryptoassets it held for its customers because 'Cotten was the only person with the cryptographic keys to access $137 million of cryptocurrencies kept in "cold" storage to mitigate the risk of hacks'.[124] This has since been revealed to be merely an excuse to hide the fact that QuadrigaCX was essentially run as a Ponzi scheme[125] but through the cautionary tale proved false, the lesson of the parable is very real. Other cautionary tales exist of the great lengths that cryptoasset holders had to go through to recover their 'lost' cryptoassets when they lost access to sole copies of their private keys.[126] For every

between Humans and Software Code, or Whether You Know It Is a Dog, and If So, Which Dog?' (2015) 21 *Computer and Telecommunications Law Review* 135.

118 K. F. K. Low and E. Teo, 'Legal Risks of Owning Cryptocurrencies' in David Lee Kuo Chuen and Robert Deng (eds), *Handbook of Blockchain, Digital Finance, and Inclusion, Vol 1: Cryptocurrency, FinTech, InsurTech, and Regulation* (Singapore 2017), pp. 225, 236.

119 N. Popper, 'Identity Thieves Hijack Cellphone Accounts to Go After Virtual Currency', *The New York Times* <www.nytimes.com/2017/08/21/business/dealbook/phone-hack-bitcoin-virtual-currency.html> last accessed 31 July 2020.

120 Many hacks have targeted Asian cryptocurrency exchanges because of higher rates of adoption of cryptocurrency in Asia: see Low and Wu, 'Characterisation of Cryptocurrencies in East Asia'.

121 Coleman, 'Researcher Has Bitcoin Stolen off His Back'.

122 N. Popper, 'Bitcoin Thieves Threaten Real Violence for Virtual Currencies', *The New York Times*, <www.nytimes.com/2018/02/18/technology/virtual-currency-extortion.html> last accessed 31 July 2020.

123 Ontario Securities Commission, 'QuadrigaCX: A Review by Staff of the Ontario Securities Commission' (14 April 2020).

124 G. Barber, 'A Crypto Exchange CEO Dies—With the Only Key to $137 Million', *Wired* <www.wired.com/story/crypto-exchange-ceo-dies-holding-only-key/> last accessed 31 July 2020.

125 Ontario Securities Commission, 'QuadrigaCX', 3.

126 M. Frauenfelder, '"I Forgot My PIN": An Epic Tale of Losing $30,000 in Bitcoin', *Wired* <www.wired.com/story/i-forgot-my-pin-an-epic-tale-of-losing-dollar30000-in-bitcoin/> last accessed 31 July 2020; Z. Hines, 'My $200,000 Bitcoin Odyssey', *Engadget* <www.engadget.com/2017-12-05-how-not-to-store-your-bitcoins.html> last accessed 31 July 2020.

triumphant story of recovery, innumerable tales of woe go unreported.[127] In 2018, a digital forensics firm estimated that at least 2.3m bitcoins are lost and a further 1.5m are likely to be lost,[128] representing more than 22 per cent of bitcoins then in existence. Trustees who invest in cryptoassets must thus maintain a delicate balance between guarding against inadvertent loss of their private keys and securing the same against prying third parties. The former dictates that multiple copies be kept as the loss of the only copy of a private key is disastrous whereas the latter implores against multiplicity since each additional copy is an additional point of failure.

Trustees confident in their ability to sail between the Scylla of fraud and the Charybdis of loss must still contend with risks at the network level. 'Proof-of-work' blockchains are only secure so long as a majority of users by network hash rate (i.e. total computing processing power) are honest. They are thus susceptible to what is called the 51 per cent attack, in which persons who control(s) 51 per cent of the network hash rate could rewrite earlier blocks and effectively invalidate previously valid transactions.[129] The 51 per cent attack has since transitioned from theoretical possibility to worrisome reality for a handful of smaller blockchain networks,[130] so trustees must avoid investing in cryptoassets with small networks. Any bugs in the blockchain code may also spell disaster. On 20 September 2018,[131] it was revealed that the bitcoin code contained a bug, which would have allowed malicious miners to artificially inflate bitcoin's theoretically finite supply,[132] defeating one of its raison d'êtres.

Where a cryptoasset's blockchain includes so-called 'smart contract' functionality, these carry additional security concerns. 'Smart contracts', no more than 'self-executing ledger-modification instructions',[133] are code used to automate a particular change of state within the relevant blockchain ledger. There is nothing fundamentally wrong with automation or with code but marrying that supreme human frailty – mistake – with blockchain immutability is a recipe for disaster, as demonstrated by the Decentralized Autonomous Organisation ('DAO') disaster.[134]

[127] L. Matsakis, 'How WIRED Lost $100,000 in Bitcoin', *Wired* <www.wired.com/story/wired-lost-bitcoin/> last accessed 31 July 2020.

[128] 'Bitcoin's $30 billion sell-off' <https://blog.chainalysis.com/reports/money-supply> accessed 31 July 2020.

[129] S. Jimi, 'Blockchain explained: how a 51% attack works (double spend attack)' <https://blog.goodaudience.com/what-is-a-51-attack-or-double-spend-attack-aa108db63474> last accessed 31 July 2020.

[130] A. Hertig, 'Blockchain's Once-Feared 51% Attack Is Now Becoming Regular' <www.coindesk.com/blockchains-feared-51-attack-now-becoming-regular/>accessed 31 July 2020; J.I. Wong, 'Every cryptocurrency's nightmare scenario is happening to Bitcoin Gold', *Quartz* <https://qz.com/1287701/bitcoin-golds-51-attack-is-every-cryptocurrencys-nightmare-scenario/> last accessed 31 July 2020.

[131] See CVE-2018-17144 Full Disclosure <https://bitcoincore.org/en/2018/09/20/notice/> last accessed 31 July 2020.

[132] Fixed at 21 million bitcoins. Note that there is no cap for ether.

[133] Low and Mik, 'Pause the Blockchain Legal Revolution', 165.

[134] For an elaboration, see Low, 'Trusts of Cryptoassets', 209–210.

The incident exposed the risks of smart contracts, particularly among novice coders attracted to the crypto-community's libertarian ideals, who fail to appreciate the exactitude that coding demands.[135] According to a leading text, '[i]ndustry average experience is about 1-25 errors per 1000 lines of code for delivered software'.[136] For Ethereum 'smart contracts', the industry average was 100 bugs per 1000 lines of code in 2016.[137] Many of the investors in the DAO who lost their ether were able to 'recover' them as the hack affected so many investors that a majority of users of Ethereum supported rolling back the Ethereum blockchain to its pre-hack state,[138] a decision so controversial that it caused a fork in the blockchain when a small core of users refused to do so.[139] Should trustees face a similar loss, there can be no assurance that a majority of users of the relevant cryptoasset would support a wholesale reversal of that cryptoasset's blockchain so as to allow them to recover their lost cryptoasset.

The view is also increasingly shared that many cryptoasset launches in the form of initial coin offerings (ICOs) are inadequately regulated[140] so that even if none of the above risks eventuate, the cryptoasset itself is either simply a scam or a poorly thought out venture.

### 3.2.2 Insurance

Although there is some authority suggesting that trustees are under no duty to insure trust property,[141] this view has been doubted by no less than the Law Commission.[142] The absence of insurance may be excusable in certain situations because it is impracticable because the costs implications are enormous, such as where the trust estate comprises paintings, works of art, antique furniture, or other chattels of substantial value. In such cases, 'it would go too far to say that trustees must sell some of the chattels in order to fund the insurance of the rest'.[143] However, it is obvious

135 ibid, 173.

136 S. McConnell, *Code Complete*, 2nd Ed (Redmond 2004), p. 521.

137 P. Vessenes, 'Ethereum Contracts Are Going to Be Candy for Hackers' <https://vessenes.com/ethereum-contracts-are-going-to-be-candy-for-hackers/> last accessed 31 July 2020.

138 J. I. Wong and I. Kar, 'Everything You Need to Know about the Ethereum "Hard Fork"', *Quartz* <http://qz.com/730004/everything-you-need-to-know-about-the-ethereum-hard-fork/> last accessed 31 July 2020.

139 A. van Wirdum, 'Rejecting Today's Hard Fork, the Ethereum Classic Project Continues on the Original Chain: Here's Why', *Bitcoin Magazine* <https://bitcoinmagazine.com/articles/rejecting-today-s-hard-fork-the-ethereum-classic-project-continues-on-the-original-chain-here-s-why-1469038808> last accessed 31 July 2020.

140 A. Gurrea-Martínez and N. Remolina, 'The Law and Finance of Initial Coin Offerings' in C. Brummer (ed), *Cryptoassets: Legal, Regulatory, and Monetary Perspectives* (Oxford University Press 2019), p. 117; C. Brummer, T. I. Kiviat, and J. Massari, 'What Should Be Disclosed in an Initial Coin Offering?' in C. Brummer (ed), *Cryptoassets: Legal, Regulatory, and Monetary Perspectives* (Oxford University Press 2019), p. 157. Cf. K. Yeung, 'Regulation by Blockchain: The Emerging Battle for Supremacy between the Code *of* Law and Code *as* Law' (2019) 82 *Modern Law Review* 207, 210.

141 *Re McEachern* (1911) 103 LT 900 at 902.

142 Law Commission and Scottish Law Commission, *Trustees' Powers and Duties* (LC 260; SLC 172).

143 *Lewin on Trusts*, [34–75].

from the context that this relaxation of the duty to insure relates to the trust estate in its original form, not new investments made by trustees out of trust funds, for which the availability of insurance must surely be an important consideration in deciding if it is an appropriate investment.

In this respect, the necessity of insurance is even more important because of the risks previously considered.[144] Already generally regarded as necessary for most trust assets, the case for insurance of cryptoassets must surely be a fortiori. Unfortunately, insurance coverage for cryptoassets is scarce. Although Aon was recently reported to have insured a major cryptoasset exchange, Coinbase, to the tune of US$255m,[145] there are many hurdles to insuring cryptoassets which have deterred many other insurers from doing so. Cryptoasset exchange hacks have not abated despite the industry being subject to regulation.[146] After suffering the most infamous cryptoasset exchange hack in 2014 with the Mt Gox hack,[147] the Japanese Financial Services Agency began to regulate the industry. However, in spite of the regulation, another Japanese exchange, Coincheck, was hacked in 2018 in an even worse hack, bestowing Japan with the dubious honour of having hosted the two worst cryptoasset exchange hacks of all time.[148] It is not obvious that more regulation will resolve this risk. Hacking presents challenges to law enforcement that have proven remarkably resilient as it usually crosses national boundaries. 'Existing mechanisms for international police cooperation are expensive and slow – designed to catch the occasional fugitive murderer, but not for dealing with millions of frauds at a cost of a few hundred dollars each.'[149] The pseudonymous nature of cryptoassets exacerbate the challenges to law enforcement agencies, as does their transaction modality. Although transferees are advised to wait for multiple blocks before treating a transaction as finalised, it is effectively beyond the control of the transferor from the moment the transaction is added to the blockchain. Any subsequent reversal of the transaction is a matter of chance rather than choice, making hacks of cryptoassets less readily reversible than hacks of bank money.[150] The extreme volatility of cryptoasset prices also makes it challenging to set appropriate premiums. Although '[c]ertain insurers are willing to deploy capital and create bespoke insurance solutions for digital asset companies, many remain conservative given the evolving nature of the underlying blockchain technology,' it is thus not surprising that 'a number

[144] See Section 3.2.1.

[145] P. Martin, 'On Insurance and Cryptocurrency' <https://blog.coinbase.com/on-insurance-and-cryptocurrency-d6db86ba40bd> last accessed 31 July 2020.

[146] For a list of cryptoasset exchange hacks, see 'A Comprehensive List of Cryptocurrency Exchange Hacks' <https://selfkey.org/list-of-cryptocurrency-exchange-hacks/> last accessed 31 July 2020.

[147] R. McMillan, 'The Inside Story of Mt Gox, Bitcoin's $460 Million Disaster', *Wired* <www.wired.com/2014/03/bitcoin-exchange/> last accessed 31 July 2020.

[148] L. Lewis and R. Harding, '"Crypto crazy" Japanese mystified by virtual heist', *Financial Times* <www.ft.com/content/7010982c-0800-11e8-9650-9c0ad2d7c5b5> last accessed 31 July 2020.

[149] T. Moore, R. Clayton, and R. Anderson, 'The Economics of Online Crime' (2009) 23 *Journal of Economic Perspectives* 3, 16.

[150] Low and Teo, 'Legal Risks of Owning Cryptocurrencies'.

of the larger, established insurers have taken a hard line and do not participate in the crypto sector at all'.[151] Thus far, the few insurance products that exist appear to be available only to large entities within the crypto-community such as cryptoasset exchanges and the adequacy of coverage is concerning. Coinbase's coverage with Aon only extends to its hot wallets, not its cold wallets, which whilst less susceptible to hacks, is not impervious to loss. Furthermore, Coinbase boasts of responsibility for the custody of more than US$20 billion of cryptoassets,[152] so that Aon's coverage amounts to little more than 1.2 per cent of total assets under management.

### 3.2.3 Volatility

The extreme volatility of cryptoassets is both an attraction (when prices rise) and a concern (when prices collapse).[153] The famed investor Warren Buffett has christened bitcoin as 'rat poison squared,'[154] explaining in an interview:[155]

> Cryptocurrencies basically have no value and they don't produce anything. [...] It can't do anything. And what you hope is that somebody else comes along and pays you more money for it later on. But then that person's got the problem. But in terms of value, uh, zero.

Cryptoasset volatility[156] resembles atrial fibrillation in an electrocardiogram, marked as it is by irregular irregularity. Although their volatility has been defended on the basis of their comparatively low volume of trade,[157] trustees are understandably concerned with 'raw' volatility rather than volume-normalised volatility. The low volume of trades[158] also arguably makes cryptoassets more susceptible to price manipulation,[159] of which evidence is rife.[160] Given these circumstances, only

[151] J. Shawdagor, 'Crypto Insurance a Promising Sector Despite Caution of Major Players' <https://cointelegraph.com/news/crypto-insurance-a-promising-sector-despite-caution-of-major-players> last accessed 31 July 2020.

[152] S. McIngvale, 'Coinbase Custody Is Officially Open for Business' <https://blog.coinbase.com/coinbase-custody-is-officially-open-for-business-182c297d65d9> last accessed 31 July 2020.

[153] For an elaboration, see Low, 'Trusts of Cryptoassets', 212.

[154] K. Burgess, 'The Jabberwocky World of Bitcoin', *Financial Times* <www.ft.com/content/167cbec4-5f73-11e8-ad91-e01af256df68> last accessed 31 July 2020.

[155] Interview with *CNBC Squawk Box* <www.youtube.com/watch?v=JvEas_zZ4fM> last accessed 31 July 2020.

[156] Cryptoasset volatility is tracked by the Crypto Currencies Index at <https://cci30.com/> accessed 31 July 2020. See also J. C. Gerlach, G. Demos, and D. Sornette, 'Dissection of Bitcoin's Multiscale Bubble History from January 2012 to February 2018' (2019) 6 *Royal Society Open Science* 180643.

[157] S. Sapuric and A. Kokkinaki, 'Bitcoin Is Volatile! Isn't That Right?' in W. Abramowicz and A. Kokkinaki (eds), *Business Information Systems Workshops. BIS 2014. Lecture Notes in Business Information Processing, vol 183* (Cham 2014), pp. 255, 262–264.

[158] Cf. D. McCrum, 'Bitcoin Passes $1,000 but Only Number That Matters Is Zero', *Financial Times* <www.ft.com/content/b5d66ed8-d1b3-11e6-b06b-680c49b4b4c0> last accessed 31 July 2020.

[159] Cf. R. K. Aggarwal and G. Wu, 'Stock Market Manipulations' (2006) 79 *The Journal of Business* 1915.

[160] Griffin and Shams, 'Is Bitcoin Really Untethered?'; J. Kamps and B. Kleinberg, 'To the Moon: Defining and Detecting Cryptocurrency Pump-and-Dumps' (2018) 18 *Crime Science* 7; N. Gandal

a foolhardy trustee would invest without securing the consent of all beneficiaries[161] since investments 'which are attended with hazard'[162] are to be avoided. It would be difficult to justify even a modest holding of cryptoassets in a large portfolio[163] without such consent given its speculative nature and concerns over manipulation.

### 3.2.4 Ethics and the Environment

Although the scope for considering ethical concerns remains limited for most private trusts,[164] some trustees, such as pension fund trustees in England,[165] may set out and take into account such concerns in a statement of investment principles. A settlor could also direct trustees of a private trust to take into account ethical considerations. As we transition clearly into the Anthropocene,[166] environmental concerns are increasingly likely to feature in both types of trusts. Such trusts must avoid investing in any cryptoassets that employ 'proof-of-work' consensus algorithms, which is to say many cryptoassets. 'Proof of work' consensus requires enormous amounts of energy[167] to solve the cryptographic puzzle involved in mining so as to ensure that their blockchains are immutable. At the time of writing, according to the *Digiconomist*, a single transaction on the bitcoin blockchain carried the equivalent carbon footprint of 627,716 Visa transactions at 251.09 kg of carbon dioxide and consumed 528.60 kilowatt-hours of electricity, which is the equivalent power consumption of an average US household over 17.86 days. Despite these alarming numbers, the bitcoin blockchain is only capable of processing about 4.6 transactions per second as compared to the average of 1,700 transactions per second on Visa's centralised network.[168] A world that transacted on 'proof-of-work' blockchains would find that global warming is no longer an urgent problem because it is now a hopeless one.

et al, 'Price Manipulation in the Bitcoin Ecosystem' (2018) 95 *Journal of Monetary Economics* 86. See also A. Kessler, 'Behind the Bitcoin Bubble', *Wall Street Journal* <www.wsj.com/articles/behind-the-bitcoin-bubble-11612125537> last accessed 1 February 2021.

161 Which would serve as a defence to a claim in breach of trust.

162 *Learoyd* v. *Whiteley* (1887) 12 App Cas 727, HL at 733.

163 Cf. Lord Nicholls of Birkenhead, 'Trustees and Their Broader Community: Where Duty, Morality and Ethics Converge' (1995) 9 *Trust Law International* 71, 76.

164 *Cowan* v. *Scargill* [1985] Ch 270.

165 Occupational Pension Schemes (Investment) Regulations 2005 (SI 2005 No. 3378), reg 2(3)(b)(vii).

166 S. L. Lewis and M. A. Maslin, 'Defining the Anthropocene' (2015) 519 *Nature* 171.

167 A. de Vries, 'Bitcoin's Growing Energy Problem' (2018) 2 Joule 801; C. Stoll, L. Klaaßen, and U. Gallersdörfer, 'The Carbon Footprint of Bitcoin' (2019) 3 *Joule* 1647. For the latest information on Bitcoin energy consumption, see <https://digiconomist.net/bitcoin-energy-consumption> last accessed 31 July 2020.

168 K. Li, 'The Blockchain Scalability Problem & the Race for Visa-Like Transaction Speed' <https://hackernoon.com/the-blockchain-scalability-problem-the-race-for-visa-like-transaction-speed-5cce48f9d44> accessed 31 July 2020.

## 4 CONCLUSION

Although there is much interest in cryptoassets, the conclusions to the four questions posed at the outset of this article may be summarised as follows. First, cryptoassets are capable of being the subject-matter of a trust. Secondly, being preferably regarded as things in action, trust law rules that have developed in relation to such property can be readily applied to trusts of cryptoassets so that despite the absence of segregation, most cryptoasset exchanges should be regarded as trustees of their cryptoasset holdings in relation to their customers. Thirdly, provided a general power of investment exists, most cryptoassets, save for stablecoins, would be an authorised investment for such trustees. Finally, even if cryptoassets are an authorised investment, the vast majority of trustees should avoid investing in them.

# 10

# Pragmatic Modernisation? Judicial Directions in Trusts and Wealth Management

*James Lee*[*]

## 1 INTRODUCTION

This chapter analyses recent decisions on trustees and fiduciaries from several appellate courts in the common law world and identifies how the courts pragmatically innovate to tackle modern problems. Professor Hanbury, writing in 1929, observed:[1]

> there is continuity throughout the whole history of equity. Equity is employed by the Property Acts of 1925 for new purposes, purposes possibly undreamed of by its early pioneers, but yet the root principles are the same.

Nearly 100 years later, modern pioneers of equity continue to find new purposes for its application. The complexity of modern trust and wealth management practices can pose challenges for traditional understandings of the trust as an institution and the obligations it involves.[2] We find differing approaches in respect of how to adopt (and adapt) in a way which leaves future directions open to interpretation: illustrations of what Lady Arden has called 'the capacity of equity to develop to meet new challenges'.[3] That capacity must still be harnessed in a way that promotes coherence, rooted in principle, and the cases considered below all demonstrate the difficulties with setting appropriate limits.

The assessment here is timely for two reasons. First, the reasoning in these three recent cases demands analysis. This chapter first examines the Privy Council decision in *Webb* v. *Webb*,[4] on the reservation of powers and effective alienation of

* Professor of English Law, The Dickson Poon School of Law, King's College London; Associate Academic Fellow of the Inner Temple. I benefited from presenting a paper at the conference which gave rise to this collection. I am grateful to Jamie Glister, Adam Walton, Tang Hang Wu, Goh Yihan, and Man Yip for helpful discussions. Any errors, and all views, are my own.

1 H. G. Hanbury, 'The Field of Modern Equity' (1929) 45 *Law Quarterly Review* 196, 203.

2 D. Clarry, 'Fiduciary Ownership and Trusts in a Comparative Perspective' (2014) 63 *International & Comparative Law Quarterly* 901, 902–903.

3 *The Children's Investment Fund Foundation (UK)* v. *Attorney General* [2020] UKSC 33, [2020] 3 WLR 461 at [43] ('*CIFF*').

4 *Webb* v. *Webb* [2020] UKPC 22.

ownership in the creation of a trust. We then consider aspects of the trust once up and running,[5] examining *Zhang Hong Li* v. *DBS Bank (Hong Kong)*[6] from the Hong Kong Court of Final Appeal. I argue that the courts' approach in these cases should be best understood as grounded in respecting (or attempting to respect) the integrity of the trust as an institution.[7] The debates around these cases also demonstrate the limits of judicial development of the law. The final substantive section turns to recent authority on fiduciaries, in particular the UK Supreme Court decision in *The Children's Investment Fund Foundation (UK)* v. *Attorney General*,[8] addressing the status and supervision of members of a charitable company, a vehicle for philanthropic giving. Although only *CIFF* is an English authority, it is argued that the approaches in *Webb*[9] and *Zhang Hong Li* represent the current state of English law.

The second reason for considering this theme now is the prospect of legislative reform. In 2017, the Law Commission of England and Wales proposed, as part of its Thirteenth Programme of Law Reform, projects that broadly met two aims: to 'boost Global Britain and help enhance the UK's competitiveness as we leave the EU'[10] and 'improve the way in which the law works for the individual or businesses'.[11] One of those projects is entitled 'Modernising Trust Law for a Global Britain'. This project would review the law of trusts

> with a view to modernising trust law to enhance the competitiveness of this jurisdiction's trust services in a global market. The general law of trusts has not been comprehensively reviewed since 1925. In contrast, many other 'onshore' and 'offshore' jurisdictions – including Scotland, Jersey, New Zealand, and Singapore – have updated their trust law and been creative in maintaining a healthy trust market.[12]

The Commission has not yet been able to commence its project,[13] but I argue that the courts are already engaged in modernisation efforts. In the absence of legislation, it falls to courts to determine how traditional principles apply to new

5 In the nice phrase of J. E. Penner, *The Law of Trusts*, 11th ed (Oxford: Oxford University Press), title of ch 10.

6 *Zhang Hong Li* v. *DBS Bank (Hong Kong)* [2019] HKCFA 45.

7 J. Palmer, 'Controlling the Trust' (2011) 12 *Otago Law Review* 473.

8 *CIFF* [2020] UKSC 33.

9 M. Bennett, 'The Illusory Trust Doctrine: Formal or Substantive?' (2020) 51 *Victoria University of Wellington Law Review* 193, 219.

10 Law Commission, Announcement of 13th Programme of Law Reform <www.lawcom.gov.uk/project/13th-programme-of-law-reform/> last accessed 5 July 2021.

11 Law Commission, Announcement of 13th Programme of Law Reform.

12 Law Commission, *Thirteenth Programme of Law Reform* (Law Com No 377, 2017), para. 2.24 (an errant apostrophe is corrected from original). The Commission is referring to the programme of legislative reforms including the Law of Property Act 1925 and the Trustee Act 1925 (as mentioned in Hanbury, 'The Field of Modern Equity'). For an overview of the New Zealand reforms implemented by the Trusts Act 2019 (NZ), see an article by the responsible Law Commissioner, G. McLay, 'How to Read New Zealand's New Trusts Act 2019' (2020) 13 *Journal of Equity* 325.

13 The Commission remains committed to it, and it will be 'rolled over' to the Law Commission's 14th Programme of Law Reform, which at the time of writing, is open for consultation.

developments. What we shall see is an attempt to construct an understanding of contemporary practices and to develop the law in response, in the period since the Law Commission proposed its project. Features of offshore trust practices in the area of private client and wealth management may eventually drift onshore.[14]

Much may be made of the creativity of lawyers and wealth managers in devising ways to develop private law architecture, but the cases also reveal that judges are capable of innovating too. The choices being made by the courts considered here, however, show 'creativity' but are not necessarily in line with policies that might be adopted by legislative reform seeking to maintain a 'healthy trust market'. A similar question arises in the case of fiduciaries, where the Supreme Court recently chose a pragmatic path that results in greater scope for inventive judicial intervention.[15] Yet, a pragmatic approach can only take the law so far without affecting certainty and coherence: the mode of reasoning in the cases does not always afford lower courts with sufficient direction.[16]

## 2 POLICIES AND REFORMS

As chapters in this collection show,[17] the sophistication[18] of modern trusts can involve considerable complexity. For trusts, the matrix of powers and duties may be structured in such a way as to limit the role of the trustees, whether by settlor design or trustee preference, and to confer powers on others, including the settlor or their chosen appointee.[19] Competing interests and policies are thus engaged and a balance must be struck.[20] On the one hand, there is the desire to offer flexibility in trust structures and to respect settlor autonomy: the Law Commission described trust law as 'an important global legal export bringing a range of business to the UK for

[14] L. Smith, 'Massively Discretionary Trusts' (2017) 70 *Current Legal Problems* 17, 54; republished in R. C. Nolan, K. F. K. Low, and H. W. Tang (eds), *Trusts and Modern Wealth Management* (Cambridge: Cambridge University Press 2018), chapter 5 (citations here are to the Current Legal Problems version); R. C. Nolan, '"The Execution of a Trust Shall Be under the Control of the Court": A Maxim in Modern Times' (2016) 2 *Canadian Journal of Comparative and Contemporary Law* 469.

[15] My focus here is on 'private' wealth contexts, but my argument benefits from previous collaborative work with Man Yip on the commercial context: M. Yip and J. Lee, 'The Commercialisation of Equity' (2017) 37 *Legal Studies* 647.

[16] Hon Justice Stephen Kos (President of the Court of Appeal of New Zealand), 'A Short History of the Trust' Keynote Address, Law Society Trusts Conference, June 2019, 1 'Perhaps in equity more than any other part of our law, one drives ahead safely with one eye on the rear vision mirror'.

[17] See, in particular, Chapters 2 (Lady Arden), 3 (Gallanis), 7 (Yip and Tang), 8 (Ooi and Chan), 14 (Palmer), and 15 (Virgo).

[18] Cf. 'Sophistry in conceptualization [...] may dazzle the admirer of doctrine, but it suggests loopholes to those concerned with their own interests': D. Waters, 'Settlor Control – What Kind of a Problem Is It?' (2009) 15 *Trusts & Trustees* 12, 16.

[19] L. Ho, 'Breaking Bad: Settlors Reserved Powers' and R. C. Nolan, 'Trustees and Third-Party Powers', in R. C. Nolan, K. Low, and H. W. Tang (eds), *Trusts and Modern Wealth Management*; Smith, 'Massively Discretionary Trusts'.

[20] N. Peart, 'Intervention to Prevent the Abuse of Trust Structures' [2010] *New Zealand Law Review* 567.

lawyers, accountants, banks and trust companies'.[21] On the other hand, permitting too much flexibility risks undermining the need to maintain trustee accountability and to protect beneficiaries. There must be some limits to how far flexibility for the settlor and their ability to continue to exercise influence or control can go before the arrangements are no longer properly characterised as a trust. As Professor Smith has pithily put it, '[i]f you want people to hold property without being accountable to beneficiaries, then you don't want a trust'.[22]

The future Law Commission project will thus be an opportunity to consider the policies and principles in the modern context. There are instructive lessons from a previous Law Commission project, which engaged similar considerations but focused on the specific issue of trustee exemption clauses.[23] The Commission in its consultation paper initially proposed legislation to restrict the ability of professional trustees to rely on exclusion clauses for breach of trust arising from negligence, and that the court should have the power to disapply duty modification clauses or extended powers clauses.[24] The broad concern over exemption/exclusion clauses was that they may be included by trustees in the standard terms of trust deeds, without the settlor appreciating the consequences. *Armitage* v. *Nurse*[25] held that trustees may rely on an exclusion clause except in cases where their duty is to act honestly and good faith: they may thus exclude liability for negligence.[26] Millett LJ conceded that 'the view is widely held that these clauses have gone too far,'[27] especially in the case of professional trustees, but if such clauses were 'to be denied effect, this should be done by Parliament'.[28]

The proposal to enable courts to disapply clauses was considered necessary because otherwise the trust could be structured so as to avoid the putative legislative restriction on exclusion clauses: if as a trustee I am not permitted to exclude liability for breach of a particular duty, I might rather require the duty itself to be modified from the outset so that I cannot incur the potential liability in the first place.

In its final Report, the Commission rowed back from its provisional proposal of legislative intervention. Responses to its consultation caused the Commission to reconsider its approach. Its revised principles included that 'reform should not impinge on settlor autonomy unless absolutely necessary,'[29] while observing that there was 'a general distaste for the wide and sometimes indiscriminate inclusion of

21 Law Commission, Thirteenth Programme of Law Reform, para. 2.23.

22 Smith, 'Massively Discretionary Trusts', 54.

23 Law Commission, *Trustee Exemption Clauses* (CP 171, 2003) ('Exemption Clauses CP') and Law Commission, *Trustee Exemption Clauses* (Law Com No 301, 2006) ('Exemption Clauses Report').

24 See, for example, Exemption Clauses CP, Executive Summary at viii–ix and Parts IV & V.

25 *Armitage* v. *Nurse* [1998] Ch 241; see also *Spread Trustee Company Ltd* v. *Hutcheson (Guernsey)* [2011] UKPC 13.

26 *Armitage* [1998] Ch 241 at 253–254.

27 ibid at 256.

28 ibid at 256.

29 Exemption Clauses Report, para. 1.13(2).

trustee exemption clauses in trust instruments'.[30] The Commission was not able to overcome the difficulties posed by extended powers and duty modification clauses, 'other than by creating a system with even greater potential adverse impact'.[31] Given the number of obstacles to statutory intervention,'[32] the ultimate proposal was instead a rule of professional practice for paid trustees, that required them to take reasonable steps to draw the settlor's attention to the meaning and effect of any exclusive clause.[33]

The Commission described the analysis of extended (and extensive) powers and duty modification clauses as 'an area of formidable difficulty where the tension between settlor freedom and beneficiary protection is very great'.[34] These problems are writ large in the judicial examinations below, and have not proved any easier for the courts to resolve than they were for the Law Commission. As the Commission observed:[35]

> Trustee exemption clauses operate within a complex economic system in which the interests of the three principal players (settlor, trustee, and beneficiary) are not always coincidental.[36]

The exemption clauses project was thus a microcosm of the broader themes facing modern trusts practice and law that we examine here. The Commission may have better prospects for confronting the issues and deciding on the appropriate policy and balance between competing interests as part of a more comprehensive project. But in the absence of legislation, it is through litigation that this area of formidable difficulty is being explored.

## 3 RESERVATIONS ABOUT TRUSTS: *WEBB V. WEBB*

*Webb* v. *Webb* invited the Privy Council to determine when a trust with extensive reserved powers may not be a trust. The case was a matrimonial dispute which raised numerous issues,[37] but the key points concerned the validity of two trusts, in respect of which powers had been reserved by Mr Webb, the settlor. The parties were married and had a daughter, Bethany, while Mr Webb had a son, Sebastian, from his previous marriage. Mr Webb was a businessman who used a 'complex

30 ibid, para. 1.6.

31 ibid, para. 1.18 and 5.57–5.96.

32 ibid, para. 1.7.

33 See an article by the then Law Commissioner: S. Bridge, 'Better Regulation of Trustee Exemption Clauses' (2006) 156 *New Law Journal* 1589.

34 Exemption Clauses CP, para. 4.95. See further, Exemption Clauses Report, para. 5.46ff.

35 Exemption Clauses Report, para. 1.15.

36 ibid.

37 Including the relevance of a New Zealand tax liability and its enforceability, and the position to be adopted where a spouse fails to disclose relevant information. Lord Wilson dissented, but only in respect of the tax liability point, not the analysis of the trusts, which is our focus here.

structure of companies and trusts' to manage his affairs.[38] After the parties married, Mr Webb had set up a family trust – the Arorangi Trust – in order to acquire interests in land in the Cook Islands: he appointed himself trustee, with Sebastian and Mr Webb as beneficiaries. Mr Webb later appointed a business associate, a Mr Tauber, as co-trustee, and Mr Tauber's children added as beneficiaries. That position did not last as Mr Webb and Mr Tauber fell out and Mr Tauber retired as trustee and his children were removed. Mr and Mrs Webb separated in 2016. Mr Webb began a new relationship and appointed himself and his new partner, a Ms Dixon, as trustees of a new trust – The Webb Family Trust. Mr Webb, Sebastian and Bethany were beneficiaries of this Trust. At Mr Webb's direction, the Arorangi Trust transferred some of its assets to the Webb Family Trust for nominal consideration.

The trust deed provided for the appointment of a 'Consultant', who could remove and appoint trustees, request early vesting of the property of the trust with any beneficiary, and consent to variations of the deed. Mr Webb appointed himself the Consultant. The trustee was permitted via clause 14.1(c) 'to exercise all of the Trustee's powers and discretions notwithstanding that [...] the interests or duty of the Trustee in any particular matter may conflict with his duty to the Trust Fund or any Beneficiary'.[39]

Mrs Webb argued that the two trusts were invalid on the bases that they 'lacked the irreducible core of obligations necessary for a trust to exist; they were shams; and the settlor of each trust did not intend to relinquish control of the beneficial interest in the trust property'.[40] She therefore claimed that the assets held under the trusts were available for division under the relevant matrimonial legislation.

At first instance, Potter J rejected the challenges to the validity of the trusts. The Court of Appeal allowed Mrs Webb's appeal and held that the trusts were invalid because they did not involve an effective alienation of the beneficial interest in the relevant assets. Both courts rejected the challenges that the trusts were shams or lacked the 'irreducible core of obligations'[41] identified in *Armitage* as necessary for a trust. The Privy Council considered the question of when the reservation of powers under a trust can mean that the settlor's relationship to the trust property is 'tantamount to ownership'.[42]

In some cases,[43] the purported trust structure may be deemed to be a sham where the court concludes that there was no serious, genuine intention to create a trust in the first place. The reservation of various powers to the settlor may be indicative of

38 *Webb* [2020] UKPC 22 at [1] (Lord Kitchin).
39 By clause 14.1(c).
40 *Webb* [2020] UKPC 22 at [10].
41 See *Armitage* [1998] Ch 241 at 253G-254 (Millett LJ).
42 *Webb* [2020] UKPC 22 at [77]: 'It has long been recognised that a completely general power of appointment, such that the holder of the power can appoint the subject matter of the power to himself, may be tantamount to ownership.'
43 Such as *JSC Mezhdunarodniy Promyshlenniy Bank* v. *Pugachev* [2017] EWHC 2426 (Ch).

ulterior motives. However, in *Webb*, the Privy Council endorsed the lower courts' conclusion that the trusts were not shams, yet that there had been no effective alienation of the relevant beneficial interests. Mr Webb had challenged this conclusion as inconsistent. Lord Kitchin disagreed:[44]

> Acceptance that Mr Webb intended to create trusts does not in any way preclude a finding that he reserved such broad powers to himself as settlor and beneficiary that he failed to make an effective disposition of the relevant property.

Potter J had found that Mr Webb operated the trusts in 'cavalier fashion',[45] but she did not find that the trusts were set up as a pretence. If the trusts were not shams, how exactly ought the court to determine whether Mr Webb had failed to dispose of the property effectively? Lord Kitchin endorsed the Court of Appeal's approach that there were two alternatives in terms of analysing the powers. One was whether the powers were so extensive that he had never effectively disposed of the property; the other was to ask whether his extensive powers meant that equity would regard him as having rights tantamount to ownership. In addressing the facts in *Webb*, Lord Kitchin preferred to focus on the substantive question whether

> Mr Webb's powers under each of the trust deeds were such that, in equity and in all of the circumstances of this case, he can be regarded as having had rights in the trust assets which were indistinguishable from ownership. In my view he plainly can. Mr Webb had the power at any time to secure the benefit of all of the trust property to himself and to do so regardless of the interests of the other beneficiaries. [...] The bundle of rights which he retained is indistinguishable from ownership.[46]

Although framing one's case in more than one way can help as a forensic tactic, it is not quite clear how distinct or distinctive these two approaches are[47]: are there situations where the answer to one question could be 'yes' while the other 'no'?

The decision is marked by relatively limited consideration of pertinent authority: the Board refers to its previous decision in *Tasarruf Mevduati Sigorta Fonu* v. *Merrill Lynch Bank & Trust Co (Cayman) Ltd*[48] and somewhat cursorily to the New Zealand Supreme Court analysis in *Clayton* v. *Clayton*.[49] Completely omitted is

[44] *Webb* [2020] UKPC 22 at [87].

[45] *Webb* v. *Webb* [2017] CKHC 31 at [56]: 'On any account, it is clear Mr Webb operated the Arorangi Trust in a cavalier fashion. At times, he exercised de facto control over the assets, perhaps using the trust as his alter ego. The record keeping is poor; and even if these records were maintained by the Honk Group before 2013, trust records from after this time are patchy and less than coherent.'

[46] *Webb* [2020] UKPC 22 at [89].

[47] S. Agnew, 'The Reservation of Powers by Settlors: Intention and Illusion' (2021) 80 *Cambridge Law Journal* 18, 20, noting also that Lord Kitchin's reasoning is 'brief and in places a little opaque'.

[48] *Tasarruf Mevduati Sigorta Fonu* v. *Merrill Lynch Bank & Trust Co (Cayman) Ltd* [2011] UKPC 17, [2012] 1 WLR 1721 ('*TMSF*').

[49] *Clayton* v. *Clayton* [2016] NZSC 29, [2016] 1 NZLR 551. The case is mentioned by Lord Wilson in *Webb* [2020] UKPC 22 at [79], as an application of *TMSF*.

*JSC Mezhdunarodniy Promyshlenniy Bank* v. *Pugachev*,[50] in which Birss J offered the leading English consideration of the interplay between the concepts of 'sham trusts' and 'illusory trusts'.[51] Lady Arden, who was not on the panel in *Webb*, has described *Pugachev* as a 'landmark case' on the point,[52] and the Court of Appeal of the Cook Islands had referred to it.[53] Assessment of *Pugachev* would have been valuable in *Webb* because Birss J offered substantive engagement with the relevant doctrines, in a significant judgment which has yet to be scrutinised at appellate level.[54] It would also have afforded an opportunity to consider whether the reservation of powers by the settlor are to be determinative even in cases where the settlor is not also the sole trustee or even a trustee.[55]

Nor is there any consideration of the extensive academic literature in this area:[56] in particular, there is no assessment of the 'illusory trust' doctrine (since counsel in the High Court had not framed submissions on that basis).[57] The illusory trust doctrine allows a finding that 'despite the use of the language associated with the creation of a trust, the legal arrangement created is not in fact a trust.'[58] Although the court should be cautious in developing too many independent doctrines,[59] it would still have been beneficial for there to be judicial interrogation of the limits of alternative analyses, as it would have provided further scope for understanding the boundaries of the limiting approach to trust validity.

50 *Pugachev* [2017] EWHC 2426 (Ch); C. Strachan, 'Whither the "Illusory Trust"?' (2021) 137 *Law Quarterly Review* 206, 212.

51 *Pugachev* [2017] EWHC 2426 (Ch); R. J. Turner, 'Is the Power to Appoint a Trustee a Fiduciary Power in the Hands of a Non-fiduciary?' (2018) 32 *Trust Law International* 163.

52 See Chapter 2 (Lady Arden).

53 *Webb* v. *Webb* [2017] CKCA 4 at [53]–[56].

54 J. Davies, 'New Developments in Settlor Reserved Powers' [2017] *Conveyancer and Property Lawyer* 175.

55 See further Agnew, The Reservation of Powers, 19–20.

56 The literature is plentiful, but see, for example, J. Palmer, 'Dealing with the Emerging Popularity of Sham Trusts' (2007) *New Zealand Law Review* 81; M. Conaglen, 'Sham Trusts' (2008) 67 *Cambridge Law Journal* 176; S. Douglas and B. McFarlane, 'Sham Trusts' in H. Conway and R. Hickey (eds), *Modern Studies in Property Law: Volume* 9 (Oxford: Hart Publishing 2017); M. Bennett, 'Competing Views on Illusory Trusts: The *Clayton v Clayton* Litigation in Its Wider Context' (2017) 11 *Journal of Equity* 48; Y. K. Liew, '"Sham Trusts" and Ascertaining Intentions to Create a Trust' (2018) 12 *Journal of Equity* 237; J. Wall, 'Taking the Bundle of Rights Seriously' (2019) 50 *Victoria University of Wellington Law Review* 733. See also J. Glister and J. Lee, *Hanbury and Martin: Modern Equity*, 22nd ed (London: Sweet & Maxwell, forthcoming 2021), para. 4-004.

57 *Webb* [2017] CKHC 31 at [55] (Potter J): 'I also record that Mr Hikaka did not base his submissions on the more controversial "emerging sham" or "illusory trust" doctrines'.

58 Bennett, 'The Illusory Trust Doctrine', 207.

59 See the thorough analysis in Pey-Woan Lee, 'Remedying the abuse of organisational forms: Trusts and companies considered' (2019) 13 *Journal of Equity* 211 and P. W. Lee, 'Form, substance and recharacterisation' in A. Robertson and J. Goudkamp (eds), *Form and Substance in the Law of Obligations* (Oxford: Hart Publishing, 2019); and Law Commission (New Zealand), *Review of the Law of Trusts: A Trusts Act for New Zealand* (NZ Law Com No 130, 2013), p. 9 and at paras 3.25–3.33.

While tax legislation may mean that reservation of powers in English law is less of a concern than with offshore trusts,[60] the cases raise points of principle for trusts lawyers to determine. In some instances, the exact resolution will depend upon the provisions of relevant legislation, particularly, for example, the extent to which matrimonial legislation permits the court to look past the initial structure of the trust. Indeed, in such a context, it was observed by a Court of Appeal panel including Wilson LJ (who later sat in *Webb*) that, when considering whether assets under a trust can be attributed to (e.g.) a party's resources:[61]

> it is essential for the court to bring to [that enquiry] a judicious mixture of worldly realism and of respect for the legal effects of trusts, the legal duties of trustees and, in the case of off-shore trusts, the jurisdictions of off-shore courts.

While recognising the different statutory contexts in different jurisdictions, the New Zealand Supreme Court in *Clayton* endorsed this 'need for worldly realism' when approaching such cases.[62]

Beyond the resolution of the instant appeal, *Webb* reveals the potential for greater judicial intervention in trust structures (or apparent ones). The Board dispels the idea that it was necessary to find a sham in order to conclude that there had not been an effective alienation of the property.[63] Beyond that, however, we are left wanting further guidance in terms of when, beyond sham cases, the court can reach such a determination, because the Board eschewed the academic rationales for different analyses and suggested that the different approaches can all be reduced to a broad test of whether 'in equity and in all of the circumstances of this case,'[64] Mr Webb's powers meant that rights in the trust assets which were indistinguishable from ownership.[65] The test thus seems avowedly impressionistic, placing more emphasis on Wilson LJ's 'worldly realism' limb than 'respect for the legal effects of trusts'. A greater focus on whether the proposed arrangement is compatible with a proper respect for the integrity of the institution of the trust would offer a clearer guide. As it is, the Privy Council's judgment invites future judicial consideration of the complex web of powers and duties that make up modern trusts to determine the legal effect of their creation.

60 Waters, Settlor control, 16; Bennett, 'The Illusory Trust Doctrine', 226.

61 *Charman* v. *Charman* [2007] EWCA Civ 503 at [57] (considering whether assets under the relevant discretionary trust amounted to 'financial resources' under s.25(2)(a) of the Matrimonial Causes Act 1973); see also the opening of Lord Wilson's partially dissenting judgment in *Webb* [2020] UKPC 22 at [110].

62 *Clayton* [2016] NZSC 29 at [78]; *Charman* was adopted for Hong Kong in *Kan Lai Kwan* v. *Poon Lok To Otto* [2014] HKCFA 66, [2014] 17 HKCFAR 414. See P. G. O'Hagan, 'Reserved Powers and Illusions' [2017] *Conveyancer and Property Lawyer* 380.

63 See also *Clayton* [2016] NZSC 29 at [123].

64 *Webb* [2020] UKPC 22 at [89].

65 ibid.

## 4 MODERN TRUSTS IN ACTION: *ZHANG HONG LI*

We have just seen examples of extensive settlor-reserved powers, and that *Webb* recognises some limits to settlor autonomy in choosing the precise arrangement, if it is still to amount to a valid trust. But if a trust is held to be valid in such cases, how does this balance between settlor autonomy and beneficiary protection bear on the trust once up and running,[66] particularly in the light of the complexities identified by the Law Commission?[67]

An example of modern practice concerns the obligations on trustees where a trust holds sufficient shares to have a degree of control in a company, which are the duties identified in *Bartlett* v. *Barclays Bank Trust Co Ltd*.[68] Broadly, these duties provide that the trustees cannot simply leave it to the directors of the company to run the organisation as they see fit,[69] but must keep themselves informed and be ready to act: the trustees must act as 'a prudent man of business [...] in such manner as is necessary to safeguard his investment'.[70] These duties are significant, and trustees themselves may not have the requisite expertise or experience to carry out the supervision. The trust deed may therefore provide for the restriction or negation of these duties in the form of an 'anti-*Bartlett*' clause, an example of which the Law Commission gave when illustrating exemption clauses.[71] Such clauses may be included as a matter of practice by a professional trustee in their standard terms, or it may be a specific choice by the settlor to restrict the trustees' interference in the decisions of a company over which the settlor has control or influence.

In *Zhang Hong Li* v. *DBS Bank (Hong Kong)*,[72] the Hong Kong Court of Final Appeal offered guidance on the proper scope of such clauses in a trust document. The parties had settled shortly before judgment was to be handed down, but the CFA determined that the case involved issues of sufficiently general importance that their reasons should still be published.[73]

66 Palmer, 'Controlling the Trust', 108.

67 Section 2.

68 *Bartlett* v. *Barclays Bank Trust Co Ltd* [1980] Ch 515, [1980] 2 WLR 430. See generally L. Tucker, N. Le Poidevin QC, and J. Brightwell, *Lewin on Trusts*, 20th ed (London: Sweet & Maxwell, 2020), paras. 34-056–34-061; and M. Yip, 'Trust-Owned Companies: Understanding the Trustee's Duties' (2017) 31 *Trust Law International* 185.

69 See also *Re Lucking's Will Trusts* [1968] 1 WLR 866 at 874 (Cross J).

70 *Bartlett* [1980] Ch 515 at 532.

71 *Exemption Clauses CP*, para A3, citing *Butterworth's Encyclopaedia of Forms and Precedents* (5th ed, 2001 Reissue), p. 462.

72 *Zhang Hong Li* [2019] HKCFA 45; R. Lee and M. Yip, 'Exclusion of Duty and the Irreducible Core Content of Trusteeship: A Re-assessment' (2020) 14 *Journal of Equity* 131.

73 *Zhang Hong Li* [2019] HKCFA 45 at [1]–[6], adopting for the Hong Kong jurisdiction the approach of Lord Neuberger of Abbotsbury MR in *Barclays Bank plc* v. *Nylon Capital LLP* [2011] EWCA Civ 826. Lord Neuberger sat in *Zhang Hong Li* itself on the appeal as a Foreign Non-Permanent Judge. The same approach was taken by the New Zealand Supreme Court in giving judgment in *Clayton* [2016] NZSC 29 at [3] 'given the importance of the issues they raise', although the court declined to resolve all issues possibly raised on the facts (at [127]).

The facts concerned a trust which was to be governed by Jersey Law. That company was used as an investment vehicle in financial products by customers of a private bank. The settlors were wife (Ji) and husband (Zhang). The original trustee was DBS Trustee HK (Jersey) Ltd. The beneficiaries were the couple and their two children. When the trust was established, the single share in a British Virgin Islands company, Wise Lords, was transferred to the Trustee. Ji was appointed as the company's investment advisor, and in addition, the settlors issued a letter of wishes which stated that DBS Trustee 'should always consult [Ji] in the first place with regards to all matters and her recommendation should be final'.[74]

Significant sums were lost during the course of Wise Lords' investment activities, following a shift in investment strategy by Ji from mutual funds to foreign exchange transactions. The claimants pursued various claims against those associated with the trust during the relevant period, but by the time of argument before the CFA, only the claims against the trustees were live. The claims for breach of trust were found to be established by the judge at first instance and affirmed by the Court of Appeal.

The First Schedule of the Trust Deed in *Zhang Hong Li* had a number of relevant provisions: the authorisation of the 'acquisition of any investment of a speculative nature'; that the trustees were under no duty to diversify investments; and that the trustees were not under any duty to see the value of the fund preserved or enhanced.[75] It also included anti-*Bartlett* clauses, which were set out in paragraphs headed 'Trustees Not Bound to Interfere in Business of Company in which Settlement is Interested' and 'Trustees Not Bound to Obtain Information Regarding Company in which Settlement is Interested'.[76] These provided that the trustees were not under any duty nor were they bound to interfere in the 'administration, management or conduct' of any company in which the settlement had an interest; instead, they were to leave such matters to directors, officers and other persons authorised (except in cases of dishonesty). Similarly, the trustees were not obliged to seek information in respect of the management of the company. They were to 'assume at all times' that the business and affairs of the company were being 'carried on honestly, diligently and in the best interests of the Trustees' unless they had actual knowledge to the contrary.

The claimants argued that, notwithstanding the wording of the relevant clauses, the Trustees nevertheless retained a 'high level supervisory duty'. The court unanimously held that there was no such duty. As we have seen, the terms of the Trust Deed disapplied any duties to interfere in or otherwise supervise the management of the company.

The CFA emphatically rejected the argument that either a 'high level supervisory duty' or a residual obligation[77] could be found where no reasonable trustee could

[74] *Zhang Hong Li* [2019] HKCFA 45 at [10].
[75] Paragraph 2 of the First Schedule.
[76] Respectively, paragraphs 4 and 5 of the First Schedule.
[77] There was some difference in emphasis in the analysis on this point at first instance and in the Court of Appeal.

refrain from intervening (notwithstanding the exclusions in the Deed): to recognise such a duty would be 'to introduce an amorphous and ill-defined basis for undermining a legitimate arrangement consciously adopted by the parties, exposing the trustees to unanticipated risks of liability and sowing confusion as to the extent of their duties'.[78] That reference to 'consciously adopted by the parties' is pertinent here, since the trust in *Zhang Hong Li* is contractual with a professional trustee.

Accepting counsel's submission, the CFA held that the trustees were 'consistently being told to keep their noses out of the company's business and to leave those having conduct of the same free to manage it without interference'.[79] The relevant clauses therefore disapplied the very duties contended for.[80] Furthermore, the relevant powers which the Trustees were alleged to have exercised to interfere in the company's business were not available to the trustees.[81] The CFA also held that in any event, the trustees could not be said to have been grossly negligent, given the terms of the trust in authorising the relevant risks taken.[82]

Although these observations were obiter given its findings on liability, the CFA further disagreed with the lower courts' approach to equitable compensation, examining the principles applicable to claims for compensation for breach of fiduciary duty in *Libertarian Investments* v. *Hall*,[83] where 'it was emphasised that the duties owed by fiduciaries are variable in nature and it may be important to ascertain the nature of the breach in question and the impact of that breach on any trust property'.[84] Within Hong Kong, Sin argues, the court 'is sending a message, in no uncertain terms, that it will not allow a carefully and meticulously-drafted anti-*Bartlett* clause to be emasculated by artful advocacy'.[85] As commentators have noted,[86] the case raises important issues for other common law jurisdictions, as such clauses have yet to be considered at the highest level: the editors of Lewin consider *Zhang Hong Li* to represent English Law,[87] which must be correct.

Rebecca Lee and Man Yip have argued ingeniously that a better way of rationalising the alleged 'high level' duty is to frame it as aspect of the irreducible core of

78 *Zhang Hong Li* [2019] HKCFA 45 at [64]; see also R. Davern, 'Trustee Residual Obligation: Is There a Basis for It?' (2019) 25 *Trusts & Trustees* 285 (writing in respect of the Court of Appeal decision in *Zhang Hong Li*).

79 ibid at [77].

80 ibid at [83].

81 ibid at [79].

82 ibid at [90].

83 *Libertarian Investments* v. *Hall* [2014] 1 HKC 368.

84 *Zhang Hong Li* [2019] HKCFA 45 at [115].

85 I. Sin, '*Bartlett* Duty and "Anti-*Bartlett*" Clauses: Resolving Controversies' (2021) 137 *Law Quarterly Review* 50.

86 ibid; S. Y. C. Leung, 'The Approach for Ascertaining a Trustee's Duties and Liabilities, Effectiveness of Anti-*Bartlett* Provisions, and Equitable Compensation for Breach of Trust or Fiduciary Duty' (2020) 26 *Trusts & Trustees* 235.

87 Tucker, *Lewin on Trusts*, 34-059(7).

the trustee's obligations:[88] 'a trustee's duty of good faith requires him to act in a fair-minded, serious and rational manner in his administration of the trust'.[89] However, given the matrix of powers and duties found in modern trusts, there is a difficulty in addressing individual elements, rather than assessing the trust in the round. There will be, as we saw above in *Webb*, some 'trusts' where the arrangement is held to be tantamount to ownership. But in cases such as *Zhang Hong Li* where the trust is found to be valid in the first place, isolating certain clauses may imbalance the architecture of the trust and its overall integrity. The CFA emphasised this in arguing that the supposed residual obligation was 'not to be equated with the "irreducible core of obligations"',[90] as those obligations 'do not operate to override express terms of a trust. They provide a touchstone for deciding whether the minimum requirements for constituting a trust have been met'.[91] There is a separate argument that could be made as to the desirability of reinforcing the responsibility of trustees in this respect: however, such a change should be consciously adopted by the legislature, rather than introduced by the courts as an addition to the irreducible core.

This point is further demonstrated by the approach of the CFA to the allegations of gross negligence by the trustees in respect of speculative investments (including is exposure to the Australian Dollar): the relevant provisions of the trust deed deemed 'speculative investments to be authorised and relieves the trustees of any duty to diversify the trust fund's investments'.[92] The authorisation of 'investments of a speculative nature' does not of course require that such investments should be made, but the overall framework of powers and duties under the specific trust here suggests that it is difficult to conceive of the remaining scope for trustees to act. Indeed, the Law Commission in its Trustee Exemption Clauses Consultation Paper considered the example of a clause where the trustees could speculate freely with the trust assets as illustrative of the inherent difficulties.[93]

*Zhang Hong Li* fits our theme here because it demonstrates the limits and consequences of modernised structures where settlor-beneficiaries seek to maximise their own control. In this case, the settlor-beneficiaries sought to establish liability on the part of the trustees should things go wrong. The flexibility of asset management and investment powers for the settlors had its corollary in the absence of specific or generalised duties on the part of the trustees to intervene or interfere: a consequence of successfully creating the institution of the trust in the terms desired by the settlors. Respecting the integrity of the trust requires respecting the balance of the benefits and

88 Lee and Yip, 'Exclusion of Duty and the Irreducible Core Content of Trusteeship', 138ff. See also Joyman Lee, 'The irreducible core of trustee duties in East Asian trusts' (2021) *Trusts & Trustees* (Advance Access) 1.

89 Lee and Yip, 'Exclusion of Duty and the Irreducible Core Content of Trusteeship', 147.

90 *Zhang Hong Li* [2019] HKCFA 45 at [65].

91 *Zhang Hong Li* [2019] HKCFA 45.

92 ibid at [45](f).

93 Exemption Clauses CP, para. 4.94.

limitations of the structure adopted: active settlors such as the couple in *Zhang Hong Li* cannot have it both ways.[94] 'Choices of legal forms have to have consequences'.[95] In the wider policy context, the case shows that reasoning which emphasises settlor autonomy does not always result in outcomes which favour the settlors in any given case. As the Law Commission found in its Exemption Clauses project, it is important to appreciate the interconnectedness of the powers and duties within a trust.

## 5 FIDUCIARIES, PRINCIPLES, AND EXCEPTIONS: *CHILDREN'S INVESTMENT FUND FOUNDATION*

In both *Webb* and *Zhang Hong Li*, the relevance of the trustees' fiduciary status was examined. For Mr Webb, it was argued that the breadth of his powers to act in his own interest was tempered by his fiduciary duties as trustee. In *Zhang Hong Li*, the high-level supervisory duty was argued to be a feature of the fiduciary relationship owed by DHJ Management as director of Wise Lords, even though it had granted authority to Ji. In both cases, the role and scope of the irreducible core of obligations central to the trust was important in resolving the points of principle. In this section, we shall consider the status of fiduciaries,[96] and the court's ability to supervise and to intervene in the exercise of a fiduciary's discretion. As with the cases above, the judgments struggle with issues over when, how, and why the court's intervention can be sought.

Coulson LJ has recently observed that 'the expression "fiduciary" is freighted with a good deal of legal baggage':[97] the decision in *The Children's Investment Fund Foundation (UK)* v. *Attorney General ('CIFF')*[98] is a weighty addition to that baggage.

The facts concerned a charitable company,[99] The Children's Investment Fund, which had more than $4bn worth of assets. The Fund is a charity and a company limited by guarantee – it therefore has a governance structure with directors, who are trustees, and then members of the company. The Fund was established by a married couple, Jamie Cooper and Sir Christopher Hohn, who were the original members of the charitable company, along with a third member, Dr Lehtimäki. Following the breakdown of the couple's relationship, the governance of the charity became difficult, and so the proposed solution was that the Fund would make

94 Or 'have their cake and eat it too', see Lee and Yip, 'Exclusion of Duty and the Irreducible Core Content of Trusteeship', 137.

95 McLay, 'How to Read New Zealand's New Trusts Act 2019', 328.

96 On the uncertainty of 'fiduciary', see P. Birks, 'Equity in the Modern Law: An Exercise in Taxonomy' (1996) 26 *Western Australian Law Review* 1, 17; see also Lee, 'Form, Substance and Recharacterisation', 73.

97 *Secretariat Consulting Pte Ltd* v. *A Company* [2021] EWCA Civ 6 at [64].

98 *CIFF* [2020] UKSC 33; J. Picton, '*Lëhtimaki v Cooper*: Duty and jurisdiction in charity law' (2021) 84 *Modern Law Review* 383.

99 For consideration of why a company or trust structure might be adopted for a charity, see Trustee Exemption Clauses CP, paras. 2.74–2.79.

a grant of $360m to 'Big Win Philanthropy', a new charity founded by Ms Cooper, who would resign as a member and trustee of the Fund. The payment of the Grant therefore constituted 'a payment for loss of office' to Ms Cooper, and thus required approval by resolution of members of the Company (under ss. 215 and 217 of the Companies Act 2006). Since both Sir Christopher and Ms Cooper were conflicted, Dr Lehtimäki's vote would be determinative of the matter.

There was emphasis on how exceptional a case it was thought to be. Lady Arden said that 'the facts and circumstances of this case are most unusual';[100] while at first instance, Sir Geoffrey Vos C (as he then was) said 'the present position has not arisen before [and] it may never arise again'.[101] Although the case was regarded as exceptional in many ways by the judges who decided it, I shall argue that it coheres with wider patterns of decision-making in this area.

Vos C found that the trustees had surrendered their discretion to the court over whether to make the Grant; Dr Lehtimäki had not surrendered his discretion as a member. Vos C then held that Dr Lehtimäki was a fiduciary and could be directed to vote in favour of the grant. The Court of Appeal agreed on the fiduciary conclusion, but allowed Dr Lehtimäki's appeal on the basis that the court could not direct him in the exercise of his discretion. The Supreme Court unanimously restored Vos C's original decision, albeit via a distinct rationale as to the justification for the court's direction.

The case decides two key points for this essay: first, that a member of charitable company is a fiduciary, owing their duties to the charitable purposes.[102] The second point is that in some circumstances, the court can intervene to direct a fiduciary to exercise his discretion in a particular way, even where the fiduciary has not surrendered his decision to the court. We consider each point in turn. The panel included three of the Court's then judges with experience of the Chancery Division.[103] The first judgment in the Supreme Court was given by Lady Arden, although on the second point, it was Lord Briggs' reasoning that commanded a majority of the Court.

### 5.1 *Recognising and Extending Fiduciary Obligations*

Lady Arden conducted an analysis of the context in which charitable companies operated and also offers a significant discussion of how fiduciary duties may arise.[104]

[100] *CIFF* [2020] UKSC 33 at [144].

[101] *Children's Investment Fund Foundation (UK)* v. *Attorney General* [2017] EWHC 1379 (Ch), [2018] Ch 371 at [155].

[102] *CIFF* [2020] UKSC 33 at [50].

[103] Of the twelve Justices of the Supreme Court at the time of writing, five were judges of the Chancery Division. Lord Briggs of Westbourne was appointed in October 2017; Lady Arden of Heswall and Lord Kitchin in October 2018; Lord Sales in January 2019 and Lady Rose of Colmworth in April 2021. Compare the position previously, in 2012–2017 as addressed in Yip and Lee, 'The Commercialisation of Equity', 649–652.

[104] Compare, for example, *Tan Yok Koon* v. *Tan Choo Suan* [2017] SGCA 13, [2017] 1 SLR 654 at [188]–[211]; T. Barkley, 'Conceptions of the Fiduciary in Trust Law' (2019) 13 *Journal of Equity* 23, writing about the position in what is now section 13 of the Trusts Act 2019 (NZ).

Her Ladyship concluded that *Liverpool and District Hospital for the Diseases of the Heart* v. *Attorney General*[105] 'was an important decision because it set the direction of travel. Slade J gave precedence to the fact that a member had agreed to become a member of a charity'.[106] The fiduciary duties owed are tailored by the company's memorandum and articles, as well as the framework provided by statute and position in equity.[107] As noted in *CIFF*:[108]

> the law allows the duties of a fiduciary to be fashioned to a certain extent by the arrangements between the parties. In the case of a member of a charitable company this means that the duties of a member can be fiduciary even if the memorandum and articles of association impose restrictions which mean that he cannot discharge all the obligations which a fiduciary would have under the general law.

It was not necessary for the member to owe 'the full range of fiduciary duties which a fiduciary might owe'.[109] It is also relevant to note, given what we have seen in earlier sections, that Lady Arden stated the court did not need at that stage to consider whether 'if the duties were reduced below the irreducible minimum, the court could in any circumstances declare that reduction to be ineffective'.[110]

Much is left open in the decision as to the scope and content of the fiduciary obligations owed by the newly found fiduciary member. 'The precise circumstances in which the member of a charitable company has fiduciary duties in relation to the charitable purposes and the content of those duties will have to be worked out when they arise'.[111] Similarly, although stating that the principles 'apply to charitable companies large or small',[112] her Ladyship left open the position in respect of mass membership charitable companies,[113] rather than considering that the potential complications for such charities was a reason to be reticent about recognising fiduciary obligations in the first place. There is thus a problem with the scope of *CIFF*: the decision sets out 'an initial framework for the fiduciary duties of the members of charitable companies, but many issues are left unresolved'.[114]

More generally, this is a clearly instrumental and teleological approach to fiduciary status, as shown by Lady Arden's reasoning:[115]

[105] *Liverpool and District Hospital for the Diseases of the Heart* v. *Attorney General* [1981] Ch 19.
[106] *CIFF* [2020] UKSC 33 at [80]. On fiduciary duties arising in the context of voluntary undertakings, see J. Edelman, 'When Do Fiduciary Duties Arise?' (2010) 126 *Law Quarterly Review* 302.
[107] ibid.
[108] ibid at [79].
[109] ibid at [83].
[110] ibid.
[111] ibid at [101].
[112] ibid at [105].
[113] ibid.
[114] Picton, '*Lëhtimaki v Cooper*: Duty and Jurisdiction in Charity Law', 389.
[115] *CIFF* [2020] UKSC 33 at [93]. See also at [91]: 'to hold that a member is a fiduciary is consistent with the "special" and "beneficent" treatment which the law gives to charities'.

> If Dr Lehtimäki is a fiduciary, then a well-known set of rules and remedies come into play. It will be easier for the court to exercise its inherent jurisdiction over charities, and the law of charities will be more internally coherent.

The Justices' view was that it was desirable for the court to be able to direct Dr Lehtimäki how to vote, but in order to be able to do so, it was necessary to find that he is a fiduciary.

### 5.2 *Exceptions to Non-intervention*

Having decided that Dr Lehtimäki was a fiduciary, the Court unanimously held that he could and should be directed to vote in favour of the grant. The Justices did, however, adopt significantly different bases for the court's ability to make that direction. Lady Arden and Lord Briggs gave separate judgments on this issue; Lords Wilson and Kitchin agreed with Lord Briggs. Lord Reed, dubitante, concurred with the outcome, without indicating his view as to the preferred approach.

Lady Arden took in a broad historical survey of the court's powers of intervention.[116] Her Ladyship's solution rested on 'an exceptional jurisdiction which goes beyond breach of duty':[117]

> the Chancellor was entitled to conclude that this was one of the cases in which the court can exceptionally intervene irrespective of any breach of duty, alleged or found, by any fiduciary. That is because an impasse is threatened in the performance of the trust if Dr Lehtimäki is unable to reach the same conclusion as the Chancellor has done.[118]

Lady Arden considered that this was not inconsistent with *Pitt* v. *Holt*, which her Ladyship described as the 'leading authority on the non-intervention principle',[119] where Lord Walker had said, '[a]part from exceptional circumstances (such as an impasse reached by honest and reasonable trustees) only breach of fiduciary duty justifies judicial intervention'.[120] That 'hard-won'[121] focus on breach of duty in *Pitt* provides clarity as to when, and why, the court can intervene. With respect to this, the allowance for the possibility of exceptions in statements of principle does not absolve the court from explaining the rationale for and limits of the recognition of any such principle.

[116] Lord Briggs observed that his approach 'depends upon no deep consideration of the law of trusts and charities of the type which both the parties and my Lady have considered it necessary to undertake': ibid at [205].

[117] ibid at [129].

[118] ibid at [137].

[119] ibid at [121]. Interestingly, Lord Briggs saw a 'useful parallel' for his own approach in the case of deadlocked trustees at [219].

[120] *Pitt* v. *Holt*, *Futter* v. *Futter* [2013] UKSC 26, [2013] 2 AC 108 at [73].

[121] J. A. W. Grower, 'What Does It Mean to Be a Fiduciary?' (2021) 80 *Cambridge Law Journal* 21, 24.

Lord Briggs, by contrast, held that Dr Lehtimäki could be directed on how to vote on the basis of 'a simple although unusual reason'.[122] The trustees had surrendered their discretion to the court, and the court had decided that it was in the best interest of the charity for the grant to be made. In Lord Briggs' view, it would

> be a plain breach of fiduciary duty for a relevant fiduciary of the charity to [vote] otherwise, a fortiori to exercise a fiduciary power so as in effect to veto the very transaction which the court has decided should proceed in furtherance of the charity's purposes.[123]

Lord Briggs' view therefore rests on a 'threatened breach of duty':[124] Dr Lehtimäki never indicated which way he intended to vote, but resisted being directed to vote in favour of the grant. Although the subjective decision-making[125] of the fiduciary is in principle respected by Lord Briggs' approach, nonetheless the outcome is that there has been an objective determination of what that judgment should be.

> [T]here will, very occasionally, be decisions of great difficulty, sometimes of great controversy, with which the court is there to assist, in its general supervisory role over charity. That this is just such a case is the foundation of Lady Arden's judgment as much as it is of mine.[126]

Nevertheless, despite their disagreements as to the approach, the outcome is the same. Principles are clear, except, perhaps, when they are not. Beyond being satisfied with the facts that *CIFF* was an exceptional case, the rationale for that exception varied. The way is open for the court to determine that future cases are themselves 'exceptions' or 'particular'[127] such as to justify intervention.[128] Lady Arden set the threshold as 'if the circumstances attain a sufficient level of exceptionality and seriousness'.[129] The example is given of an impasse being reached, but from the language of her Ladyship's judgment, that is merely an example of when the exception is available. It does not take much judicial imagination to distinguish one set of facts from another,[130] and so potentially to find another exception. Although differently

122 *CIFF* [2020] UKSC 33 at [205].

123 ibid at [208].

124 ibid at [227].

125 L. Smith, 'Fiduciary Relationships: Ensuring the Loyal Exercise of Judgement on Behalf of Another' (2014) 130 *Law Quarterly Review* 608, 611–612.

126 *CIFF* [2020] UKSC 33 at [234].

127 *In re Beloved Wilkes's Charity* (1851) 3 Mac & G 440 at 448 (Lord Truro).

128 Grower, 'What does it mean to be a Fiduciary?'; for a more favourable view of the decision, see J. de Lacey, 'Trusts: A Single-Minded Loyalty' [2021] *Private Client Business* 85.

129 *CIFF* [2020] UKSC 33 at [123].

130 Hanbury, 'The Field of Modern Equity', 203: 'equity cases generally contain very complicated facts, and the facts of one case may be at first sight exactly similar to those of another, and yet, on closer examination, reveal just one little element which will prevent the complete coincidence of the two cases. It is the business of the jurist to examine all the cases minutely, to range each one on its proper side of the line, and so to define in which that line consists'.

formulated, Lord Briggs' approach to threatened breaches of duty, which have not yet happened, is speculative and can give rise to uncertainty in pre-empting the respect for the fiduciary's decision-making domain.

In this context, the one-paragraph judgment from Lord Reed, the Court's President, is interesting:[131]

> With some reluctance, as I found the judgment of the Court of Appeal more persuasive than have your Ladyship and your Lordships, but in deference to the unanimity of the other members of the court as to the outcome of this appeal, and bearing in mind that the facts of this case seem unlikely ever to be replicated, I concur in the order proposed.

Lord Reed therefore concurred with the order but did not take a view on the significant differences between the other Justices, being content that 'the facts of this case seem unlikely ever to be replicated'. Yet, as has been argued, the decision has wider implications: it involves the extension of fiduciary obligations by recognising a new category of fiduciary relationships, without setting boundaries. The aim of that extension was to bring Dr Lehtimäki within the reach of the court's supervision, but the case then required a further extension in order to cover this case, without adequately setting the boundaries of the novel approaches.

While *CIFF* may represent a pragmatic response to a specific problem in the case, and the judgments focus on the peculiar position of members of charitable companies, the reasoning generates uncertainty beyond that narrow sphere. As we saw in earlier sections, fiduciary status, and the court's supervision of fiduciaries, is significant in constructing and understanding wealth management structures. A broader approach to fiduciaries may then in turn feed back into judgments and judgments in respect of trusts and trustees. *CIFF* therefore represents a significant expansion of the court's ability to intervene, even if framed as exception: a new direction for giving directions.

## 6 CONCLUSIONS

This chapter has identified and reflected upon a pattern of creative reasoning in recent authorities grappling with contemporary trust and commercial practices. In *Webb*, we saw the Privy Council emphasise substance over form in concluding that the settlor's relationship to the trust property, given his powers, was tantamount to ownership, rather than the effective alienation required for a trust. In *Zhang Hong Li*, the Hong Kong Court of Final Appeal denied an attempt by settlors to establish a safety net of a high-level duty when they had enjoyed control of asset management powers during good times. In *CIFF*, the Supreme Court extended both the reach of fiduciary obligations and the reach of equitable jurisdiction to intervene in fiduciary decision-making.

[131] *CIFF* [2020] UKSC 33 at [236].

There are various challenges in seeking to adopt a pragmatic modernisation agenda through judicial decision-making. Chief among them is the problem of certainty. In a recent case on the remedy of forfeiture, Lord Briggs described it as

> one of those equitable remedies which plays a valuable role in preventing the unconscionable abuse of strict legal rights for purposes other than those for which they were conferred. But it needs to be constrained with principled boundaries, so that the admirable certainty of English law in the fields of business and property is not undermined by an uncontrolled intervention of equity in any situation regarded by a judge as unconscionable.[132]

It is the perimeter of these principled boundaries to equitable interventions which the courts need to maintain. Rhetoric about the importance of certainty is offset by a progressive willingness to intervene. We have seen that the cases raise further questions, particularly with respect to the scope of novel framing of doctrines, the offering of yet-to-be-reconciled alternative analyses, or the creation of exceptions with wider implications. This pattern is unsatisfactory.[133]

The courts are responding to what is going on in practice, as Smith has noted:[134]

> As in many fields of the common law, there has been a gradual evolution, over long years, in styles of trust drafting. This kind of gradual evolution may make it more difficult for judges to notice when a line has been crossed, from what is acceptable to what is impossible.

That gradual evolution has been some time in the making. The Law Commission observed that the 'general law of trusts has not been comprehensively reviewed since 1925'[135]; while this may be a justifiable claim on a particular definition of 'comprehensive review', we have seen that the judicial development of the law has travelled a long way. We saw at the outset of this essay that the Law Commission's future project for reform would be 'with a view to modernising trust law to enhance the competitiveness of this jurisdiction's trust services in a global market' and to 'a healthy trust market'.[136] Yet, the choices that might be expected in promoting such goals via legislative reform may vary from the interventionist position which has been analysed above. Doctrines such as those found in *Webb* or *CIFF* incentivise litigation[137] rather

[132] *The Manchester Ship Canal Company Ltd* v. *Vauxhall Motors Ltd* [2019] UKSC 46, [2020] AC 116 at [2]; see also his Lordship's extra-curial observations in Lord Briggs of Westbourne, 'Equity in Business' (2019) 135 *Law Quarterly Review* 567. Compare Lady Arden, in the same case, at [63]: 'Equity serves to finesse rules of law in deserving cases. It thus makes the system of law in England and Wales one which is more likely to produce a fair result than would be possible if equity did not exist. This must surely be one of the reasons why the law of England and Wales is held in high regard in the world.'

[133] S. Worthington, 'Four Questions on Fiduciaries' (2018) 32 *Trust Law International* 22, 23.

[134] Smith, 'Massively Discretionary Trusts', 53.

[135] Law Commission, Thirteenth Programme of Law Reform.

[136] ibid.

[137] Picton, '*Lëhtimaki v Cooper*: Duty and Jurisdiction in Charity Law', 393: 'Once gaps emerge in the law, there is normally litigation to fill them.'

than the creation of trusts and the settlement of property within a jurisdiction. One *could* define a 'healthy trusts market' as one in which there is such uncertainty about principles relating to trusts that one has to go to court to determine them, but that would be at best a counter-intuitive case for any reform.

In addition, any legislative reform would need to consider the extent to which equitable doctrines and jurisdictions would intersect:[138] the potential for the courts to find, for example, that a protector owes fiduciary duties, or the reach of the 'exceptional' jurisdiction in *CIFF*, could cut across a statutory scheme. Ingenuity should not be underestimated, especially when 'litigants continue to agitate for more robust judicial remedies against alleged abuses of entity shielding'.[139] A focus on respecting the integrity of the trust and fiduciary status would act as a check on an excessive willingness to intervene.[140]

My aim here has been to identify the pattern of reasoning within the cases, which risk engendering uncertainty. It is necessary 'to better calibrate the balance between party autonomy and beneficiary protection based on the precise application of the trust'[141]; adopting an approach that responds to modern practice need not involve one-way traffic. Striking that balance also needs to be done in a way which promotes certainty, with an open confrontation of the policy choices. Judges, if they are to devise solutions, should be conscious of the implications. The need for a 'judicious mixture of worldly realism and of respect for the legal effects of trusts'[142] applies whether it is judicial or legislative consideration of modern trust principles.[143]

[138] Such points were considered by the New Zealand Law Commission, for example: *Review of the Law of Trusts: A Trusts Act for New Zealand* (NZ Law Com No 130, 2013), paras. 3.25–3.33; paras. 4.15–4.17. Kos, 'A Short History of the Trust', 14.

[139] Lee, 'Form, Substance and Recharacterisation', 236.

[140] N. Peart, 'Intervention to Prevent the Abuse of Trust Structures' [2010] *New Zealand Law Review* 567; Palmer, 'Controlling the Trust', 495.

[141] Lee and Yip, 'Exclusion of Duty and the Irreducible Core Content of Trusteeship', 201.

[142] *Charman* [2007] EWCA Civ 503.

[143] 'None of this means that there can be no development. It is part of the lawyer's interpretative expertise to be creative. An inert interpreter is a bad interpreter. There is and always will be a pragmatic flexibility in the law, but it is not due to any 'sea change' in the nature of equity, much less to equity's special concern with justice': Birks, 'Equity in the Modern Law', 24.

# 11

# Decision-Making in Trusts

## Applying *Wednesbury* Reasonableness after *Braganza*

*David Pollard*[*]

### 1 INTRODUCTION

Trustees under express trusts have a number of powers and discretions and decisions that need to be made.[1] The exercise (or non-exercise) of these decision-making powers are subject to review by the courts. Trustees will want to know what they need to do in order to exercise a relevant discretion properly, and others affected (e.g. beneficiaries or third parties) will want to know when they can successfully challenge a decision in a court.

There are obvious similarities between decision-making by trustees and decision-making by public bodies. Both have discretions (conferred by the trust instrument or legislation) that they do not (in the main) exercise in their own interest and owe duties to others. The question arises as to whether the legal review of relevant decision-making is then the same, or similar in some respects, as between trustees and public authorities.

A number of decisions have, over the years, indicated that there are similarities, particularly in applying to trustees the long-standing public law *Wednesbury*[2] test (in its two limbs, considering factors that ought to be considered and not reaching a decision that is perverse in the sense that no reasonable decision-maker could reach it). Or if not applying *Wednesbury* expressly, at least apply a very similar test.

In 2013, in *Pitt* v. *Holt* ('*Pitt*'), a seven judge bench in the Supreme Court dealt with legal review of two decisions made by fiduciaries, including trustees.[3] Lord

* Barrister, Wilberforce Chambers, Lincoln's Inn, London.
This chapter is based on extracts from David Pollard, *Pensions, Contracts and Trusts: Legal Issues on Decision Making: Applying Braganza* (Bloomsbury Professional, 2020), but focusing on the position of trustees and the *Braganza* tests alone.

1 In practice, such discretions are much more limited for a custodian or bare trustee. They are also much less relevant in non–express trusts (e.g. constructive or resulting).

2 *Associated Provincial Picture Houses Ltd* v. *Wednesbury Corpn* [1948] 1 KB 223, CA.

3 *Pitt* v. *Holt*, *Futter* v. *Futter* [2013] UKSC 26, [2013] 2 AC 108. *Pitt* v. *Holt* involved a receiver appointed under the Mental Health Act 1983. The linked case, *Futter* v. *Futter*, involved an exercise of discretion by trustees.

Walker, giving the only judgment, clarified that a breach of trust needed to be shown in order to invalidate a decision and that there would be no breach of trust if the decision-maker had taken 'apparently competent advice'. Lord Walker also echoed criticism that had been made by the Court of Appeal earlier in the case about the use of public law.

However, a little under two years later, in 2015 in *Braganza* v. *BP Shipping* ('*Braganza*'),[4] a five-judge bench in the Supreme Court had to consider what review standard should apply to an exercise of a factual determination provision in a contract of employment. All five judges held that both limbs of the public law *Wednesbury* test should apply to the exercise of a private law discretion. Two of the judges in the Supreme Court then took a different view from the majority as to whether that review standard had in the case been met.

This chapter considers the impact of *Pitt* and *Braganza* on the tests applied by a court in relation to a decision by trustees and reaches the conclusion that, following *Braganza*, the two-stage public law *Wednesbury/Braganza* reasonableness tests apply to legal review of decisions made by trustees and indeed others with roles under a trust (e.g. protectors and, in a pension trust, employers).

This chapter deals with the laws of England and Wales. But the common law (and equitable) position does not seem to differ much in the other major common law jurisdictions (e.g. Australia, New Zealand, Singapore, Hong Kong, or Ireland).[5]

## 2 LEGAL REVIEW OF POWERS AND DISCRETIONS

*Braganza* broadly confirmed a trend to apply (in appropriate cases) a similar test in private law cases to the *Wednesbury* reasonableness test as developed in the public law case of *Associated Provincial Picture Houses Ltd* v. *Wednesbury Corporation* ('*Wednesbury*').[6] In *Braganza*, the Supreme Court applied both limbs of the public law *Wednesbury* test to the contractual decision-making power held by BP Shipping as employer to determine the cause of death at sea of its employee, Mr Braganza.

4 *Braganza* v. *BP Shipping Ltd* [2015] UKSC 17, [2015] 4 All ER 639.

5 The position may differ where there has been statutory intervention – particularly in those jurisdictions (e.g. Jersey and Bermuda), which have enacted legislation with the aim of reversing the part of the decision of the UK Supreme Court in *Pitt* [2013] 2 AC 108 dealing with there being a need for a breach of duty.

6 *Wednesbury Corpn* [1948] 1 KB 223, CA. It is perhaps ironic that in public law cases, the test of *Wednesbury* unreasonableness may be having a lesser role in recent years in public law cases. Richard C. Nolan made this point in 'Controlling Fiduciary Power' [2009] 68 (2) *Cambridge Law Journal* 293, 302. See also Lord Carnwath (extra judicially) 'From rationality to proportionality in the modern law' (2014) 44 *Hong Kong Law Journal* 447. *Wednesbury* is making a comeback in public law outside fundamental EU rights – see *R (Plan B Earth)* v. *Secretary of State for Transport* [2020] EWCA Civ 214 at [75] and [79]. *Wednesbury* was also cited on appeal, *R (Friends of the Earth Ltd)* v. *Heathrow Airport Ltd* [2020] UKSC 52 at [119].

*Braganza* concerned a factual determination being made by an employer, but the decision has been cited and followed in many later cases outside the employment or pensions context, both in England and Wales and other jurisdictions (notably Australia and New Zealand). Much of the case law considers the application of the *Braganza* test in other contexts (e.g. leases, share options) and *Braganza* itself expressly noted that its application and 'intensity' are context specific. It seems clear that the *Braganza* test will usually apply to most decisions and discretions of employers and principal companies under occupational pension schemes. There seems no reason why the *Braganza/Wednesbury* test should not apply, by analogy with public law, to decisions and discretions of trustee boards and other trustees as well (despite comments to the contrary in *Pitt*).[7]

### 2.1 *Trustee Decisions and Discretions*

Such decision-making powers can be of either: (a) a factual nature (e.g. is, in the view of the decision-maker, a factual situation met?) – these tend to be more binary (i.e. is the fact situation met or not) or (b) a more discretionary nature (e.g. how are assets invested, can an amendment power be exercised?).[8] These can more often allow for a range of potential outcomes.

Trusts, such as private sector pension schemes in the United Kingdom, include many powers and discretions held by various parties. In UK pension trusts, this can be the employer, a principal company,[9] the trustee board, or indeed an advisor such as the actuary. In other trusts, third parties may have roles – for example, protectors. Such decision-makers will want to make sure that they make the right decisions consistent with their powers and duties under the contract or scheme and in line with any tests implied by law.

Conversely others, affected by the decision (or potential decision), may want to challenge a decision or stop it from being carried out or claim for loss or damage flowing from the decision. Courts will generally respect decisions made within powers by a decision-maker or trustee board.[10] If the trust or contract expressly gives the power/discretion to (say) the employer or trustee, then there is in general no right of appeal to the courts – no general merits review.

7 *Pitt* [2013] 2 AC 108 at [11].

8 Categorising a power as discretionary or just fact determinative can be difficult, see *Carty* v. *Croydon LBC* [2005] EWCA Civ 19 and, in Australia, *Dwyer* v. *Calco Timbers Pty Ltd* [2008] HCA 13 and *Finch* v. *Telstra Super Pty. Ltd.* [2010] HCA 36, (2010) 242 CLR 254. Discussed in Pollard, *Pensions, Contracts and Trusts*, ch 8. Binary (yes or no) fact determinations are in practice more intensively scrutinised by a court compared to more discretionary decisions; see *Braganza* [2015] UKSC 17 at [57] (Lord Hodge).

9 Who may or may not also be (or have in the past been) an employer of members in the scheme.

10 The position may differ for charities: *Lehtimäki* v. *Cooper* [2020] UKSC 33.

Some powers or discretions may be absolute and unfettered and not subject to general judicial review (absent fraud or dishonesty). These are most likely to arise when a power or discretion is not held by a fiduciary and is linked to a property right or would otherwise in its context be problematic to be reviewable.[11] But clearly in some cases, there can and should be some review by the courts. For trustees, this is likely to apply to all decisions and discretions. In *Scott* v. *National Trust*, Walker J held that 'trustees must act in good faith, responsibly and reasonably. They must inform themselves, before making a decision, of matters which are relevant to the decision'.[12]

Walker J cited the decision of the House of Lords in *Dundee General Hospitals Board of Management* v. *Walker* where Lord Reid said that even where trustees are expressed to have an absolute discretion:[13]

> If it can be shown that the trustees considered the wrong question, or that, although they purported to consider the right question they did not really apply their minds to it or perversely shut their eyes to the facts or that they did not act honestly or in good faith, then there was no true decision and the court will intervene.

Different rules may apply if trustees ask the court to approve a major decision – for example, *MNRPF*,[14] but even this is moving towards applying *Braganza* style rationality tests.[15]

Unlike (say) decisions made by a court, there is no general right of appeal or rehearing to the courts generally on the merits of a decision made under a trust (such as a pension scheme) or a contract or articles of association of a company. The relevant instrument provides that the decision in relation to the discretion or power is held by the relevant person. The courts will not rewrite the provision to allow the court a right of general review – for example, if it would have made a different decision on the relevant facts.[16] Partly this reflects respect for the terms of the contract

[11] See Pollard, *Pensions, Contracts and Trusts*, ch 9.

[12] *Scott* v. *National Trust for Places of Historic Interest or Natural Beauty* [1998] 2 All ER 705 at 717g (Robert Walker J). An unreserved judgment. Later approved by Lord Walker (as he had then become) in *Pitt* [2013] 2 AC 108 at [10].

[13] *Dundee General Hospitals Board of Management* v. *Walker* [1952] 1 All ER 896, HL at 905 (Lord Reid).

[14] *Merchant Navy Ratings Pension Trustees Ltd* v. *Stena Line Ltd* [2015] EWHC 448 (Ch) (Asplin J). Citing *Public Trustee* v. *Cooper* [2001] WTLR 901 (Hart J) and *Cotton & Moore* v. *Earl of Cardigan* [2014] EWCA Civ 1312. See Daniel Clarry, *The Supervisory Jurisdiction over Trust Administration* (Oxford University Press, 2018), ch 4.

[15] *Airways Pension Scheme Trustee Ltd* v. *Fielder* [2019] EWHC 3027 (Ch) at [5] (Zacaroli J), citing *MF Global UK Ltd* [2014] EWHC 2222 (Ch). This applies even if relevant litigation has previously been authorised by a court order under the Beddoes jurisdiction: *Airways Pension Scheme Trustee Ltd* [2019] EWHC 3032 (Ch) at [20] (Zacaroli J).

[16] See *Braganza* [2015] UKSC 17 at [18]–[19] (Lady Hale). This is long standing in public law – see, for example, the comments of Lord Greene MR in *Wednesbury Corpn.* [1948] 1 KB 223 at 228. Statute can sometimes include a more general review power – for example, under the Pensions Act 2004,

(or trust) and partly an acknowledgement in some cases that the decision-maker has an expertise that the court does not possess. But there are often limits to this judicial restraint. Even in contract cases, the courts may well find that decision-makers' decisions are reviewable at the extremes, even absent fraud or an absence of good faith. This is similar to the role of the courts in the well-trodden area of public law when reviewing decisions of public authorities.

The extent of this review leads to two issues:

(1) For the decision-maker, how does he, she, or it make a proper (and unchallengeable) decision? What are the extent of its duties? What does it need to do to make a proper decision?
(2) For the non-decision-maker, what are the circumstances when a decision can be challenged (and what is the nature of that challenge)? And other parties may be expected to act on the basis of the relevant decision – when are they expected to only so act if the decision is not challengeable?

### 2.2 *Nature of Decision*

A decision-making power or duty under a trust or contract can be of various forms, including:

(a) A full discretion – that is with a range of various potential outcomes. For example, how much to pay under a discretionary trust, whether a trustee should agree to a scheme amendment and the form of the amendment.
(b) A binary fact discretion – for example, 'in the opinion of the trustee' is a relevant test met – is the person a child of the settlor, is a member incapacitated?

This need for a decision can be distinguished from the position where a person (e.g. a trustee) is directed to do something if a particular fact is satisfied – for example, pay a child of the settlor when she reaches age 21 or pay a pension when a pension scheme member reaches age 65. In this case, there is no discretion given to the trustee – the payment must be made if the facts are proved (if disputed as the court may decide).[17]

Despite the general desire to respect the terms of the contract or trust and to leave the relevant decision to the relevant decision-maker, the courts will still review a decision and allow a challenge in a number of ways.

there is a right to refer some decisions of the determinations panel of the Pensions Regulator to the Upper Tribunal for a rehearing (not an appeal).

17 See *British Telecommunications Plc v. BT Pension Scheme Trustees Ltd* [2018] EWCA Civ 2694, [2019] Pens LR 10 at [24]–[25] (Asplin LJ) on whether or not an index 'becomes inappropriate' with no decision-maker expressly stated.

### 2.3 *Ground of Challenge: General*

Despite the general desire to respect the terms of the contract or trust and to leave the relevant decision to the relevant decision-maker, the courts will still review a decision and allow a challenge in a number of ways. Set out below is a brief list of some of the major ways in which decisions can be challenged. This chapter focuses on the application of the *Braganza* tests to trustees.

The decision in *Braganza* (applying *Wednesbury*) provides two grounds for review:

(1) *Proper process*: usually acting with due consideration (e.g. considering relevant factors) – this is the first, process, limb of *Braganza/Wednesbury*.
(2) *If a decision is fully irrational (or perverse)*: a decision that no reasonable decision-maker could have reached. This is a (stiff) outcome test and the second limb of *Braganza/Wednesbury*.

### 2.4 *Who Is Making the Decision*

Who is making the relevant decision is also relevant to the issue of what legal review is appropriate. A decision being made by a trustee or other fiduciary is likely to be more intensely reviewed.

The type of decision being made is also relevant. In a trust or contractual context, there seems to be at least three types of decision: one that involves an 'absolute' discretion (and so is not reviewable at all) – in a pensions context, this is most likely to arise in relation to an employer discretion; a decision as to a matter of fact; or a general discretion about whether or not to do something. This is flagged in the Supreme Court decision in *Braganza* itself, saying that the test is context specific.

It seems clear that a factual decision (in *Braganza* itself it was whether or not an employee had committed suicide) is considered more reviewable than a general discretion, for example, whether or not to amend the scheme, whether or not to close the scheme, whether or not to increase or reduce benefits and whether or not to give a bonus or pay rise or not. An 'absolute' discretion may not be reviewable at all under either of the *Braganza* limbs. Examples in a commercial context may be whether or not to terminate a contract for breach.[18]

## 3 LEGAL REVIEW OF DECISIONS: MAJOR TESTS

It is helpful to look at the two limbs of the *Braganza* test in context, by briefly considering the other legal review tests that can apply. A whole range of tests have been developed by the courts as part of the process of controlling discretionary

[18] See 'Intensity of review' in Pollard, *Pensions, Contracts and Trusts*, ch 45.

powers and decision-making, particularly (but not exclusively) when exercised by fiduciaries, such as trustees or directors.[19] Where a power or discretion is held under a contract or trust (or company constitution), a number of factors come into play if the decision is challenged in the court – that is if the courts are asked to review the decision.

At one end of the scale is that the relevant structure gives the decision-making power to the relevant decision-maker: not to the courts and not subject to a general right of appeal to the courts. At the other end of the scale is a need for some limits and reviews on the process. The parties will often be intended not to confer an absolute untrammelled and unconstrained power to the decision-maker to make whatever decision he/she or it thinks fit, with no judicial control. This was analysed by Lady Hale in *Braganza* (see below).

But in some circumstances, the courts may well find that a decision is not intended to be limited – in a contractual setting, this may well depend on factors such as whether there is a potential conflict of interest or whether the parties have a particular need for speed. The intensity of review may well depend also on the size and resources of decision-maker (e.g. as in *Braganza*).[20]

There are five major tests for a decision-maker when exercising a discretion or making a decision under a trust:

(1) act honestly (i.e. good faith);
(2) within the terms of the power: by the specified person, in the specified way and at the specified time;
(3) for a proper purpose;
(4) no unauthorised conflicts (fiduciary only);
(5) with due care and skill, which includes undertaking the process with due consideration and considering the reasonably discoverable and relevant factors; and ensuring the outcome is not perverse, capricious or fully irrational.

The case law in both Britain and Australia does seem to be inching towards a coherent structure. The nature of these tests is important, as each is formed by and its scope is determined by reference to the others. Note that it is better to consider that there is no (or at least not literal) overarching 'act in best interests' test in the UK – (part of proper purpose test in Test (3) instead).[21]

The aim of the list is to give a useful checklist for those making decisions (and those advising them). It suffers from necessarily being relatively high level – some of

[19] See Newey J (extrajudicially) 'Constraints on the exercise of trustees' powers' in PG Turner (ed), *Equity and Administration* (Cambridge University Press, 2016) and Nolan, 'Controlling Fiduciary Power'.

[20] See Pollard, *Pensions, Contracts and Trusts*, ch 45.

[21] See Pollard, 'The Short-Form 'Best Interests Duty'; Mad, Bad and Dangerous to Know' (2018) 32 *Trust Law International* 106, 176

the points made in the case law (e.g. on delegation or making decisions at the right time) or in some commentary get into more detail,[22] but these seem to flow as a matter of logic from the higher level tests.

### 3.1 *Good Faith and Trusts*

Clearly, the courts will review a decision made by a fiduciary in bad faith – that is if there is dishonesty or fraud. For example, if there is deceit (see the example mentioned by McGarvie J in *Karger* v. *Paul*).[23] The courts of equity being founded on conscience, this is an obvious control. Where there are impacts on third parties, fraudulent acts may in some cases not be overturned.[24] Some of the older case law indicates that lack of good faith or honesty may be the only control; for instance, that trustees acting honestly and in good faith cannot have their decisions overturned.[25]

Thus in 1877 in *Gisborne* v. *Gisborne*,[26] where the decision was at the trustees' 'discretion and of their uncontrollable authority', it was held by the House of Lords that a bona fide exercise will not be reviewed by the court. But the court considered the exercises of the discretion in question to be a reasonable exercise.[27] And in the next decade, the House of Lords moved to a more stringent duty of care based on (at least) prudence and 'the ordinary prudent man of business'.[28]

In present times, good faith, at least in the context of trusts, is better considered now as meaning the same as honesty.[29] The use in the older cases of a potential wider meaning of 'good faith' should be regarded as seeking to encapsulate what has

22 See, for example, the lists in relation to trustees in Tucker, Le Poidevin and Brightwell, *Lewin on Trusts* (20th ed, Sweet & Maxwell, 2020), 29-033 (listing four grounds of review) and Hayton, Matthews and Mitchell, *Underhill and Hayton: Law of Trusts and Trustees* (Lexis Nexis UK, 2016), 57.1. See also *Karger* v. *Paul* [1984] VR 161 (McGarvie J) and *Kowalski* v. *MMAL Staff Superannuation Fund Pty Ltd (No 3)* [2009] FCA 53 at [22] (Finn J).

23 *Karger* [1984] VR 161 at 175.

24 *Fairfield Sentry Ltd* v. *Migani* [2014] UKPC 9. Contrast an internal transaction: *Skandinaviska Enskilda Banken AB (Publ)* v. *Conway and another (as Joint Official Liquidators of Weavering Macro Fixed Income Fund Ltd)* [2019] UKPC 36 at [19].

25 *Re Beloved Wilkes's Charity* (1851) 3 Mac & G 440, 42 ER 330 (Lord Truro LC); *Duke of Portland* v. *Topham* (1864) 11 HLC 32. See also *Re Londonderry's Settlements* [1965] 1 Ch 918, CA, *Whishaw* v. *Stephens; Re Gulbenkian's Settlement Trusts* [1970] AC 508 at 518, and *Hartigan Nominees Pty Ltd* v. *Rydge* (1992) 29 NSWLR 405 at 427, 428–429.

26 *Gisborne* v. *Gisborne* (1877) 3 App Cas 300.

27 ibid at 309 (Lord Penzance); 311 (Lord O'Hagan).

28 See *Speight* v. *Gaunt* (1883) 9 App Cas 1 at 19 (Lord Blackburn), approving Jessel MR in the Court of Appeal (1882) 22 Ch D 727 at 739–740 and *Re Whiteley* (1886) 33 Ch D 347, CA at 355 (Lindley LJ), on appeal *Learoyd* v. *Whiteley* (1887) 12 App Cas 727, HL. The concept of 'prudence' is itself not very clear and is probably now better seen as being the same as 'reasonableness' (see e.g. the Law Commission, *Fiduciary Duties of Financial intermediaries* (Law Com No 350, 2014), para. 3.72, discussing the Trustee Act 2000 and Pollard, 'The prudence test for trustees in pension scheme investment' (2021) 34 *Trust Law International* 215).

29 See *Karger* [1984] VR 161 at 164 (McGarvie J) and *Medforth* v. *Blake* [2000] Ch 86, CA at 103.

now become the other grounds of review outlined below (e.g. proper purpose and due consideration).[30]

It can be argued that the terminology of 'bad faith' or 'mala fides' under *Gisborne* (and later cases) in a trustee context could extend to include perversity.[31] But good faith (or bad faith) seems to be better seen (in a trustee context at least) as involving a subjective standard (similar to dishonesty). David Maclean in '*Trusts and Powers*' commented that a decision can be (say) perverse without being made in bad faith, [32] citing *Tabor* v. *Brooks*[33] and that 'Mala fides is not constituted by honest blundering, carelessness or even gross negligence'.[34]

Some of the case law treats bad faith (or lack of good faith) as being a subjective test, effectively involving dishonesty or at least intentional impropriety. An example is *Medforth* v. *Blake*[35] a case on the duties of a receiver appointed by a mortgagee. The concept of 'good faith' is tricky.[36] It appears in various areas of the law, in each case with a 'distinct body of authority as to its meaning and application'.[37]

It seems to be clearer to move away from a good faith/bad faith test as being the only grounds of review, rather than trying to construe bad faith as encompassing irrationality or perversity (e.g. as attempted in *Jacobs' Law of Trusts in Australia*),[38] unless perhaps a deliberate and wilful refusal to carry out due consideration. Good faith is referred to in both *Dundee General Hospitals*[39] and *Scott* v. *National Trust*.[40] Some of the modern case law uses the term 'good faith' in a wider sense (beyond just honesty) to include a lack of arbitrariness etc., in effect applying

30 See, for example, *Re Marsella (No 2)* [2019] VSC 65 at [36] (McMillan J).

31 See Ashdown, *Trustee Decision Making* (Oxford University Press, 2015), 3.36. See also *Marsella* v. *Wareham* [2019] VSC 733 at [37] (McMillan J): 'In this context a lack of good faith, or mala fides, encompasses more than fraud. It may include the taking account of irrelevant considerations and a refusal to take into account relevant considerations.' Mere carelessness or honest blundering' will not amount to mala fides: *Jones* v. *Gordon* (1877) 2 AC 616 at 628.

32 D. M. Maclean, *Trusts and Powers* (Sweet & Maxwell, 1989), p. 58.

33 *Tabor* v. *Brooks* (1878) 10 ChD 273 (Malins V-C).

34 Citing *Jones* v. *Gordon* (1877) 2 App Cas 616 at 628–629 and *Karger* [1984] VR 161 at 164. See also to the same effect *Royal Brunei Airlines* v. *Tan* [1995] 2 AC 378 at 389 and *Marsella* [2019] VSC 733 at [37] (McMillan J), citing *Jones* (1877) 2 App Cas 616 at 628.

35 *Medforth* v. *Blake* [2000] Ch 86, CA at 103B-D (Scott V-C). Discussed in relation to an exoneration clause in a trust in *Barnsley* v. *Noble* [2014] EWHC 2657 at [265]–[267] (Nugee J) (decision upheld by the Court of Appeal [2016] EWCA Civ 799).

36 See Richard C. Nolan and Matthew Conaglen, 'Good Faith: What Does It Mean for Fiduciaries and What Does It Tell Us about Them?' in Elise Bant and Matthew Harding (eds), *Exploring Private Law* (Cambridge University Press, 2010); Lusina Ho, 'Good Faith and Fiduciary Duty in English Law' (2010) 4 *Journal of Equity* 19 and Charles Mitchell 'Good Faith, Self-denial and Mandatory Trustee Duties' (2018) 32 *Trust Law International* 92.

37 *Service Station Association Ltd* v. *Berg Bennett & Associates Pty Ltd* [1993] FCA 638, 45 FCR 84 at [31] (Gummow J).

38 J. D. Heydon and M. J. Leeming, *Jacob's Law of Trusts in Australia* (8th ed, LexisNexis, 2016), [16-09].

39 *Dundee General Hospitals Board of Management* [1952] 1 All ER 896 at 905 (Lord Reid).

40 *Scott* [1998] 2 All ER 705 at 717 (Robert Walker J).

one or both limbs of the *Braganza* tests. In *Hayes* v. *Willoughby*,[41] Lord Sumption commented on a meaning of good faith as encompassing a 'logical connection' between the evidence and the reason for a decision and this meaning an absence of arbitrariness, etc.

### 3.2 *Public Law Analogy in Private Law Discretions?*

Some aspects of private law, particularly those involving review of discretions, are clearly similar to public law in many respects. This is particularly true in relation to decisions and actions of trustees and other fiduciaries (e.g. directors). Similar to public officials, trustees are not usually acting for their own benefit, but instead for a relevant purpose, usually the benefit of a structure or third party.

The two areas have tended to borrow from each other over the years (and in some cases, public officials are seen as being fiduciaries in a similar role to trustees). It may therefore be appropriate to look at how the 'no unlawful fetter' rules have been applied in public law cases.[42] But public law is different from private law. The issue is how different. It is clear that not all public law concepts should be imported and applied in a private law context. In a private trust case, *Re Barr's Settlement Trusts, Abacus Trust Co (Isle of Man)* v. *Barr*,[43] Lightman J identified three important differences: the discretionary nature of relief on judicial review, a different approach to nullity, and strict time limits.

But, following the decision in *Braganza* particularly, it is appropriate to have a selective borrowing in this area – at least the two limbs of the *Wednesbury* review of decisions. There is an example of this (before *Pitt*) in *Byng* v. *London Life Association Ltd*,[44] where the Court of Appeal applied proper purposes and public law *Wednesbury* tests to a review of decisions by a chair of a shareholder meeting.

Before *Pitt*, various trust cases, including the pension cases *Harris* v. *Lord Shuttleworth*,[45] *Edge* v. *The Pensions Ombudsman*,[46] and *Wild* v. *Pensions*

41 *Hayes* v. *Willoughby* [2013] UKSC 17 at [14] (Lord Sumption). Cited by Lady Hale in *Braganza* [2015] UKSC 17 at [23] and the Court of Appeal in *IBM United Kingdom Holdings Ltd* v. *Dalgleish* [2017] EWCA Civ 1212 at [227].

42 This is suggested by Geraint Thomas, *Thomas on Powers* (2nd ed, Oxford University Press, 2012), 10.74 and by P. Finn, *Fiduciary Obligations* (Sydney, Law Book Co, 1977), [62].

43 *Re Barr's Settlement Trusts, Abacus Trust Co (Isle of Man)* v. *Barr* [2003] Ch 409 at [29]. Cited in *Pitt* [2013] 2 AC 108 at [11] (Lord Walker).

44 *Byng* v. *London Life Association Ltd* [1990] Ch 170, CA at 189B (Browne-Wilkinson V-C) and 194C (Mustill LJ).

45 *Harris* v. *Lord Shuttleworth* [1994] ICR 991, [1995] OPLR 79, CA at 999G (Glidewell LJ).

46 *Edge* v. *The Pensions Ombudsman* [2000] Ch 602, CA at 627–630 (Chadwick LJ). Cited on this in later cases, including *Merchant Navy Ratings Pension Fund Trustees Ltd* v. *Chambers* [2002] ICR 359, [2001] OPLR 321 at [7] (Blackburne J) and *Stena Line* [2015] EWHC 448 (Ch) at [16] and [161] (Asplin J).

*Ombudsman*,[47] had looked at a review of decisions on a very similar basis to *Wednesbury* and in some cases had expressly drawn an analogy with public law review on *Wednesbury* grounds. The analogy with public law had also been made in other areas – for example, the Court of Appeal in *Socimer International Bank Ltd* v. *Standard Bank London Ltd*[48] referred to various cases on when a contractual discretion in a contract could be challenged, referring to the public law *Wednesbury* test.

In the pension case, *IBM*, on an implied duty of trust and confidence as a limit on employer powers (called the 'Imperial duty'), at first instance Warren J followed this:[49]

> Although one must heed Lord Hoffmann's warning in *O'Neill* v. *Phillips* [1999] 1 WLR 1092 (the well-known case concerning unfair prejudice petitions in a company law context) about importing concepts from one area of law to another in an inappropriate way, I do not see any difficulty in using the concepts of irrationality and perversity, as developed in the context of public law, to identify the test for establishing the scope of the Imperial duty.

### 3.3 *Public Law:* Braganza *and Trustees*

For trustees, there was a fairly clear warning away from applying public law by the Court of Appeal in *Pitt*, although slightly less clear by Lord Walker in the Supreme Court. But two years later in *Braganza*, the Supreme Court unanimously decided that the public law *Wednesbury* test (in both limbs) is the right one to apply in a private law context. In effect, *Pitt* should be treated as impliedly overturned on this point by *Braganza*. There is no express overturning in *Braganza*, in which *Pitt* was not cited either by counsel or by the judgments (Lord Neuberger and Lady Hale did sit in both cases).

Following *Braganza*, it is clearly right to apply the public law *Wednesbury* irrationality test (in both limbs) to appropriate private law decisions as well, but that there still needs to be caution in the use of other public law concepts. For example, issues on voidness of decisions, who may claim, and on no implied 'natural justice' rule seem still not to be appropriate. It could perhaps be argued that *Braganza* (and the public law *Wednesbury* test) is limited to contractual discretions and not to family trusts (such as those involved in *Pitt* v. *Holt*), leaving more commercial trusts (such as a pension scheme or unit trust) still to be categorised. But *Braganza* has already

47 *Wild* v. *Pensions Ombudsman* [1996] OPLR 129 at 135 (Carnwath J). See also *Telstra Super Pty Ltd* v. *Flegeltaub* (2000) 2 VR 276 at [33] (Batt JA) noting that 'a decision of a superannuation fund trustee [...] is different in kind from, and arises in a context different from that of, the exercise of a discretion by a trustee of a trust for bounty or charity.'

48 *Socimer International Bank Ltd* v. *Standard Bank London Ltd* [2008] EWCA Civ 116, [2008] Bus LR 1304, CA at [66] (Rix LJ).

49 *IBM United Kingdom Holdings Ltd* v. *Dalgleish* [2014] EWHC 980 (Ch) at [442] (Warren J).

been treated as applying in many commercial contexts[50] and, given the existing references to 'relevant factors' and 'no reasonable trustee' in many previous trust cases, it seems right that *Braganza* will be applied to trustee decisions as well.

It is also noticeable that the three 'important differences' noted by Lightman J in *Barr*[51] and cited by Lord Walker in *Pitt*, namely 'the discretionary nature of relief on judicial review, a different approach to nullity, and strict time limits' are all procedural differences and do not relate to the substantive review of the relevant decision.

### 3.4 *Public Law* Wednesbury *Test Applied*

A 'relevant/irrelevant factors' test, is, of course, derived from the similar *Wednesbury* test applied in the review of decisions by public administrative bodies following the 1948 decision of the Court of Appeal in *Wednesbury*.[52]

Nearly twenty years before *Pitt* v. *Holt*, Sir Robert Walker (as he then was) extra-judicially in a talk in Cambridge had made the point that there is an important balance to be struck here between the procedure of perfectly informed decision-making – and the need for practical certainty. [53] Having said that, it now appears that it is appropriate to apply the *Wednesbury* test to private law situations. In *Braganza*, all five justices in the Supreme Court were happy to apply the full *Wednesbury* test to a decision being made by an employer in relation to a death benefit (the dissenting two JSCs considered that the employer had satisfied the standard required, but the other three JSC's held that it had not and so invalidated the employer's decision). In *Braganza*, Lady Hale (giving the main decision of the majority) addressed this full on (although not referring to *Pitt*).[54]

*Braganza* was a case involving the review of a contractual discretion. But the Supreme Court held that *Wednesbury* principles should apply, partly driven by the situation involving a discretion exercisable by an employer. If an employer is subject to the full *Wednesbury* test, it is difficult to see that a fiduciary, such as a trustee board should be subject to any lesser review standard.

### 3.5 *Absolute Powers*

Seemingly a statement in the relevant trust (or contract) that the decision is 'absolute, final and unchallengeable' may be enough to exclude or modify review by the

[50] See Pollard, *Pensions, Contracts and Trusts*, ch 44. And in a fairly private context, a decision about whether a dog was allowed to stay in a flat under a lease: *Victory Place Management Company* v. *Kuehn* [2018] EWHC 132 (Ch) (Vos C).

[51] *Re Barr's Settlement Trusts* [2003] Ch 409 at [29] (Lightman J).

[52] *Wednesbury Corpn* [1948] 1 KB 223, CA.

[53] Robert Walker, 'Some Trust Principles in the Pensions Context', in A. J. Oakley (ed), *Trends in Contemporary Trust Law* (Clarendon Press, 1996), ch 5.

[54] *Braganza* [2015] UKSC 17 at [19]–[32].

courts.[55] Conversely, some of the cases look at trusts where the trustee's decision is stated to be 'final'. Despite this, the courts reviewed the decision on the irrationality basis. See, for example, Glidewell LJ in *Lord Shuttleworth*:[56]

> The trustees shall be empowered conclusively to determine all matters, questions, and disputes touching or in connection with the fund's affairs and all claims thereon [...] every such determination shall be conclusive and binding on all parties.

In *Saffil*,[57] the trust deed provided that 'the decision of the Trustees shall be final'. Despite this, in both cases, the courts reviewed the decision on the irrationality basis. Merely describing a power or discretion in the relevant contract or trust as 'absolute' or 'sole and absolute' may well not be enough to exclude the *Braganza* irrationality tests. There are a number of decisions where a power or discretion has been described as 'absolute' in the relevant instrument, but the courts have still applied review concepts.[58]

Conversely, if a discretion is not described as 'absolute' or 'uncontrollable', a court may be 'more willing' to intervene'.[59] In practice, there may be a higher level of intensity of review (similar to the different levels of intensity described above for factual determinations). In the share option case, *Mallone* v. *BPB*,[60] Rix LJ held that a discretion was reviewable for being fully irrational even though it was described as absolute.

In *Equitas Insurance Ltd* v. *Municipal Mutual Insurance Ltd*,[61] a case on discretions under a reinsurance contract, Males LJ held that the fact that the contract referred to an absolute discretion was not determinative of this point. He held that whether the perversity test applied was a matter for a process of construction which takes account of the characteristics of the parties, the terms of the contract as a whole and the contractual context. Similarly in *British Telecommunications plc*

55 See Jonathan Morgan, 'Resisting Judicial Review of Discretionary Contractual Powers' (2015) *Lloyd's Maritime and Commercial Law Quarterly* 483, 487, noting the argument by Richard Hooley in 'Controlling Contractual Discretion' (2013) *Cambridge Law Journal* 65, 81, that any exclusion should not be allowed on public policy grounds or should require a 'clear and unmistakeable exclusion'. In appropriate cases, the consumer legislation could apply to such an exclusion (e.g. the Consumer Rights Act 2015 or the Unfair Contract Terms Act 1977, but note that those Acts do not apply to trusts or employment contracts).

56 *Lord Shuttleworth* [1995] OPLR 79, CA at 86B (Glidewell LJ). Cited in *Trustees of the Saffil Pension Scheme* v. *Curzon* [2005] EWHC 293 (Ch), [2005] OPLR 113 at [23] (Park J).

57 ibid.

58 For example, see *TJH and Sons Consultancy Ltd* v. *CPP Group plc* [2017] EWCA Civ 46 at [16], *Socimer* [2008] EWCA Civ 116, and *Wellington City Council* v. *Local Government Mutual Funds Trustee Ltd* [2017] NZHC 2901 at [165] and [168] (Collins J).

59 *Esso Australia Ltd* v. *Australian Petroleum Agents' & Distributors Association* [1999] 3 VR 642 at 652 and *Ying Mui Pty Ltd* v. *Frank Kiang Ngan Hoh (No 6)* [2017] VSC 730 at [409] (Vickery J). See now on appeal *Hoh* v. *Ying Mui Pty Ltd* [2019] VSCA 203. See also Thomas, *Thomas on Powers*, [11.12].

60 *Mallone* v. *BPB Industries Ltd* [2002] EWCA Civ 126, [2002] ICR 1045 at [12] and [40].

61 *Equitas Insurance Ltd* v. *Municipal Mutual Insurance Ltd* [2019] EWCA Civ 718, [2020] 1 All ER 16. See also Leggatt LJ at [152]–[155] referring to the construction test.

v. *Telefónica O2 UK Ltd*, Lord Sumption (with whose judgment the other Justices agreed) said this was a construction test.[62]

## 4 BRAGANZA

### 4.1 *Later Cases*

The Supreme Court judgment in *Braganza* was given in March 2015. There are now over fifty decisions in England and Wales on Westlaw referring to it. There have also been decisions referring to *Braganza* in Singapore,[63] Scotland,[64] Australia,[65] New Zealand,[66] Hong Kong,[67] and Jamaica.[68]

### 4.2 *Papers on* Braganza

There have been a number of useful papers[69] on *Braganza*, but mainly focusing on its application outside trusts or pensions.

62 *British Telecommunications Plc* v. *Telefónica O2 UK Ltd* [2014] UKSC 42 at [37].

63 *Leiman, Ricardo* v. *Noble Resources Ltd* [2018] SGHC 166 (George Wei J). At least three earlier decisions in Singapore on discretions followed similar lines and cited the English cases on which *Braganza* is based, including both *Wednesbury Corpn* [1948] 1 KB 223, CA and *Socimer* [2008] EWCA Civ 116: *MGA International Pte Ltd* v. *Wajilam Exports (Singapore) Pte Ltd* [2010] SGHC 319 at [105], *Edwards Jason Glenn* v. *Australia and New Zealand Banking Group Ltd* [2012] SGHC 61, and *ABN AMRO Clearing Bank NV* v. *1050 Capital Pte Ltd* [2015] SGHC 271 at [73]–[80] (George Wei J).

64 *Teoranta* v. *Opito Ltd* [2018] CSOH 10.

65 In particular, *Mineralogy Pty Ltd* v. *Sino Iron Pty Ltd (No 6)* [2015] FCA 825, 329 ALR 1 at [1011] (Edelman J); and *Bartlett v Australia & New Zealand Banking Group Ltd* [2016] NSWCA 30. *Hannover Life Re of Australasia Ltd* v. *Jones* [2017] NSWCA 233 referred to, but did not apply, the *Braganza* test (on the grounds that in Australia decisions of insurers are subject to a different general reasonableness review). *Braganza* was also mentioned by Edelman J in the High Court of Australia in a public law review case, *Minister for Immigration and Border Protection* v. *SZVFW* [2018] HCA 30 at [133]. *Braganza* and *Mineralology* were considered by Lee J in two contractual cases: *Avenia* v. *Railway & Transport Health Fund Ltd* [2017] FCA 859 at [215] and *Bupa HI Pty Ltd* v. *Andrew Chang Services Pty Ltd* [2018] FCA 2033 at [120].

66 For example, *Peregrine Estate Ltd* v. *Hay* [2017] NZCA 496, [2018] 2 NZLR 345 and *Wellington City Council* [2017] NZHC 2901. See also the contract case: *L&M Coal Holdings Limited* v. *Bathurst Resources Limited* [2018] NZHC 2127 at [197] and [202] (Dobson J) and a case on the power of an airline to refuse to carry a person: *Sharma* v. *Air New Zealand Ltd* [2020] NZHC 230.

67 *FWD Life Insurance Co (Bermuda) Ltd* v. *Poon Cindy* [2019] HKCA 697 at [34]–[35] (Lam VP, Cheung and Chu JJA), *Chok Kin Ming* v. *Equal Opportunities Commission* [2019] HKCFI 755, *Global Gaming Philippines LLC* v. *Deutsche Bank AG, Hong Kong Branch* [2019] HKCFI 405, *Pa Sam Nang* v. *The Hongkong and Shanghai Banking Corporation Ltd* [2016] HKCFI 409 and briefly in *Invest Gain Ltd* v. *Novel Good Ltd* [2019] HKCFI 1633.

68 *Williamson* v. *Port Authority of Jamaica* [2019] JMCA Civ 8, (2019) 94 WIR 466.

69 See, for example, Michael Bridge 'The exercise of contractual discretion' (2019) 135 *Law Quarterly Review* 227; Ernest Lim and Cora Chan 'Problems with Wednesbury Unreasonableness in Contract Law: Lessons from Public Law' (2019) 135 *Law Quarterly Review* 88; Jason Varuhas 'Judicial Review beyond Administrative Law: *Braganza v BP Shipping Ltd* and Review of Contractual Discretions'

Lord Sales has recently commented (extrajudicially) that he is 'critical of attempts to use the *Wednesbury* decision as an appropriate model, for which there appears to be something of a vogue at the moment'.[70] But this seems to be in the context of its application to contractual discretions (rather than those under trusts). He points to the use of proper purposes (fraud on a power) and interpretation as potential public law analogies. This does not seem to divert from the principles outlined in this chapter in relation to trustees (who will be subject to those concepts as well).

One incredibly useful (but fortuitous) feature of the *Braganza* decision is that it makes later cases citing it very easy to find using a simple word search.

## 4.3 *The Decision*

*Braganza*[71] is a key decision of the Supreme Court looking at a challenge to a contractual determination, in that case involving a decision made by an employer about how an employee had died (and hence whether or not a lump sum death benefit was payable under the employment contract). The five members of the Supreme Court in the case unanimously agreed that it was appropriate to use the public law *Wednesbury* test when deciding whether or not a decision by the employer, BP, was challengeable.

However, when applying that test to the actual facts of the case, the Supreme Court split: three of the judges held that the decision should be overturned on the basis of a failure to comply with the first limb (consideration of relevant factors): Lady Hale, Lord Hodge, and Lord Kerr; the minority (Lord Neuberger and Lord Wilson) applied the same legal test but would have decided that the decision should not be overturned.

This meant that of the nine judges who heard the case, five of them (two in the Supreme Court and three in the Court of Appeal) would have upheld BP's decision and only four (three in the Supreme Court and Teare J at the first instance) decided to overturn it. However, because the majority in the Supreme Court held that it should be overturned, the views of the four judges prevailed.

U.K. Constitutional Law Blog (31 May 2017) <https://ukconstitutionallaw.org/tag/braganza-v-bp-shipping-ltd/> accessed 20 May 2021; Peter Susman, 'Braganza and beyond: Judicial review of the exercise of contractual discretion in private law' (2017) 5 *Journal of International Banking & Financial Law* 280; Wayne Courtney 'Reasonableness in contractual decision-making' (2015) 131 *Law Quarterly Review* 552; David Foxton, 'A Good Faith Goodbye? Good Faith Obligations and Contractual Termination Rights' (2017) *Lloyd's Maritime and Commercial Law Quarterly* 360.

70 Philip Sales, 'Use of Powers for Proper Purposes in Private Law' (2020) 136 *Law Quarterly Review* 384. See also the comments on Lord Sales article by Sarah Worthington in 'Powers' in William Day and Sarah Worthington (eds), *Challenging Private Law: Lord Sumption on the Supreme Court* (Hart Publishing, 2020), ch 16.

71 *Braganza* [2015] UKSC 17. Noted in Wayne Courtney, 'Reasonableness in contractual decision-making' (2015) 131 *Law Quarterly Review* 552.

### 4.4 *The Facts*

Mr Braganza, the chief engineer on board a ship, *MV British Unity*, was lost at sea one night. He simply went missing. The ship turned around when it was noticed that he was no longer there but could not find him. On reaching port, a report was commissioned by BP to try and find out what had happened to Mr Braganza.

Mr Braganza's employment contract included a specific lump sum death in service benefit payable by his employer, BP. However, the contract expressly provided in clause 7.6.3[72] that the lump sum:

> shall not be payable if, in the opinion of the Company or its insurers, the death [...] resulted from amongst other things, the Officer's wilful act, default or misconduct whether at sea or ashore.

It is noticeable that this is not a pure general discretion as to whether or not to pay the death benefit. Instead, the death benefit is payable unless BP reaches the relevant factual decision. This can be seen as having an impact on the ultimate decision in the case – it seems tantamount to mean that BP had the onus to show that the death resulted from a wilful act.[73] In light of the report, BP concluded that Mr Braganza had indeed committed suicide and so no lump sum was payable. Mr Braganza's wife brought a claim in tort against BP in negligence (under the Fatal Accidents Act 1976) and (presumably as Mr Braganza's executor) under the contract for the payment of the death lump sum. The negligence claim was dismissed by Teare J at first instance, but he upheld the contractual lump sum claim. BP appealed and the Court of Appeal (unanimously) allowed the appeal and upheld BP's decision on the lump sum.

### 4.5 *The Supreme Court*

Mrs Braganza appealed to the Supreme Court, which allowed her appeal (by a three-two majority), holding: (unanimously) the public law *Wednesbury* test should apply (in both limbs); and (by a majority) three (Lady Hale, Lord Hodge, and Lord Kerr) to two (Lord Neuberger and Lord Wilson): applying this test, BP had acted irrationally (under the first limb of *Wednesbury*) in reaching its decision. The majority held that BP had not considered all relevant factors. Mr Braganza was a Roman Catholic, so this (according to the majority) meant suicide was more unlikely.

BP's decision was not considered to be irrational under the second *Wednesbury* limb based on the outcome – that is it was not considered to be one that no reasonable

[72] See *Braganza* [2015] UKSC 17 at [1] (Lady Hale).

[73] Ibid at [14] (Lady Hale).

decision-maker could have reached.[74] Nor was it challenged as having been made for an improper purpose.

Lord Kerr agreed with Lord Hodge, who agreed[75] with the bulk of Lady Hale's judgment that there had to be cogent evidence of suicide.[76] Lord Hodge went on to discuss in more detail the implication of this being a discretion in a contract of employment, ultimately concluding that, although BP had acted in good faith and not unfairly:[77]

> I do not think that the report of the investigation team gave [BP, the decision maker] the evidential basis for forming the positive opinion that Mr Braganza had committed suicide.

BP had already conceded that, if its decision was overturned, then the lump sum would be paid. This, in effect, meant that there was no question of the Supreme Court (or the earlier courts) referring the decision back to BP itself to redecide the question based on the proper test.[78]

## 4:6 *The Rationality Test*

The finding in *Braganza* was that the decision in that case must be exercised rationally (and consistent with its contractual purpose). Rational in the public law (*Wednesbury*) sense has the two limbs previously mentioned – process and outcome.[79] The Supreme Court was clear that the Court is not substituting its own decision on what is reasonable.[80]

This use of the two-limb test is not new in private law, but until *Braganza*, the use of the public law test in relation to a private law instrument had not been expressly approved in these terms by the Supreme Court.[81] The express application in *Braganza* of the public law *Wednesbury* concepts looks to be directly contrary to the reservations expressed two years earlier in *Pitt* on their use in relation to trustee discretions.

In the public law area, the classic principle was that laid down in *Wednesbury* by Lord Greene MR:[82]

74 *Braganza* [2015] UKSC 17 at [42] (Lady Hale). Perhaps just as well given that five judges (three in the Court of Appeal and two in the Supreme court) would have upheld the decision. Described on this point as 'reassuring' by Foxton, 'A good faith goodbye? Good faith obligations and contractual termination rights', 368.

75 *Braganza* [2015] UKSC 17 at [52] and [53] (Lord Hodge).

76 ibid at [61] (Lord Hodge).

77 ibid at [63].

78 ibid at [14] (Lady Hale).

79 ibid at [24] and [30]; [103] (Lord Neuberger).

80 Although on the facts and the 3-2 split on application of the public law *Wednesbury* test, the final decision came close to doing just that.

81 Although equivalent concepts of rationality had been mentioned in various cases – for example, trustees in *McPhail* v. *Doulton* [1971] AC 424 at 449C (Lord Wilberforce) and employers in *UC Rusal Alumina* v. *Miller* [2014] UKPC 39 at [51] and [55].

82 *Wednesbury* [1948] 1 KB 223, CA at 233–234.

> The court is entitled to investigate the action of the local authority with a view to seeing whether they have taken into account matters which they ought not to take into account, or conversely, have refused to take into account or neglected to take into account matters which they ought to take into account. Once that question is answered in favour of the local authority, it may still be possible to say that, although the local authority have kept within the four corners of the matters which they ought to consider they have nevertheless come to a conclusion so unreasonable that no reasonable authority could ever have come to it.

Thus, as already mentioned, there are two limbs of *Wednesbury* unreasonableness, which can be flagged as being 'process' and 'outcome':[83]

(1) *Process*: 'The first limb focusses on the decision-making process – whether the right matters have been taken into account in reaching the decision.'
(2) *Outcome*: 'The second focusses upon its outcome – whether even though the right things have been taken into account, the result is so outrageous that no reasonable decision-maker could have reached it.

Lady Hale commented that the outcome limb is 'often used as a shorthand for the *Wednesbury* principle, but without necessarily excluding the [process limb]'.[84] And went on to state:[85]

> For my part, I would include both limbs of the *Wednesbury* formulation in the rationality test. Indeed, I understand Lord Neuberger (at para 103 of his judgment) and I to be agreed as to the nature of the test.

## 5 TRUSTEE CASES ON *WEDNESBURY/BRAGANZA* TYPE REVIEW

Many trustee cases[86] before *Braganza* had raised the principles, seemingly similar to that applicable in public law under *Wednesbury*, that trustees should comply with both limbs of the test. They 'must take into account all relevant but no irrelevant factors' and must not reach a decision that no reasonable trustee would make.

The relevant factors limb (effectively the first part of the *Braganza* test) is the effect of the whole line of cases based on the rule in *Re Hastings-Bass*, culminating in the 2013 decision of the Supreme Court in *Pitt*.[87] Effectively this rule looked at setting aside a decision made by trustees because they had not considered properly a relevant matter (e.g. tax).

83 *Braganza* [2015] UKSC 17 at [24] (Lady Hale).
84 ibid.
85 ibid at [30].
86 See, generally, Thomas, *Thomas on Powers*, [10.75][10.145], although note that this book predates the decisions of the Supreme Court in both *Pitt* [2013] 2 AC 108 and *Braganza* [2015] UKSC 17. It does however refer to the decision of the Court of Appeal in *Pitt* [2011] EWCA Civ 197.
87 *Pitt* [2013] 2 AC 108.

In 1991 in *Stannard* v. *Fisons Pensions Trust Ltd*,[88] the Court of Appeal upheld the overturning of a decision by pension trustees about the amount of a bulk transfer payment to another scheme. The decision was overturned because they had not considered the increase in value of the fund over the interim since the relevant valuation. They had not given 'properly informed consideration' to the discretion they had to exercise.[89]

In 1993 in a pensions case concerning an ill-health retirement, *Lord Shuttleworth*, Glidewell LJ approved the reasoning of Judge Moseley QC at first instance[90] and held that trustees:[91]

> must not arrive at a perverse decision, i.e. a decision to which no reasonable body of trustees could arrive, and they must take into account all relevant but no irrelevant factors.

The two-limb approach was applied by Scott V-C at first instance[92] and by Chadwick LJ in the Court of Appeal in *Edge*.[93] Scott V-C held:[94]

> It is the trustees' discretion that is to be exercised. Except in a case in which the discretion has been surrendered to the court, it is not for a judge to exercise the discretion. The judge may disagree with the manner in which trustees have exercised their discretion but, unless they can be seen to have taken into account irrelevant, improper or irrational factors, or unless their decision can be said to be one that no reasonable body of trustees properly directing themselves could have reached, the judge cannot interfere.

Later in *Edge*, dismissing the appeal, Chadwick LJ cited Glidewell LJ in *Lord Shuttleworth* and held that on the facts in *Edge* that 'the decision cannot be challenged on the ground of manifest irrationality'.[95] Chadwick LJ went on to say that 'the trustees' decision can be set aside if it can be shown that they failed to consider matters which were relevant, or took into account matters which were irrelevant'.[96]

88 *Stannard* v. *Fisons Pension Trust Ltd* [1992] IRLR 27, [1991] Pens LR 225, CA. Lord Walker commented on this decision in *Pitt* [2013] 2 AC 108 at [34], noting that the scale of the change is crucial.

89 *Fisons Pension Trust Ltd* [1992] IRLR 27 at [37] (Dillon LJ).

90 *Lord Shuttleworth* [1992] OPLR 151 at 159 (Judge Moseley QC), citing Denning LJ in the valuation case, *Dean* v. *Prince* [1954] Ch 409 at 418.

91 *Lord Shuttleworth* [1994] ICR 991 at 999G. Followed in Australia in a unit trust case, *Ying Mui Pty Ltd* [2017] VSC 730 at [408] (Vickery J).

92 *Edge* v. *Pensions Ombudsman* [1998] Ch 512. Cited by the Singapore Court of Appeal in *Foo* v. *Foo* [2012] SGCA 41, [2012] 4 SLR 339 at [59], going on to comment at [61] that the danger of an extension of public law considerations into the duties of trustees 'could be many-fold'.

93 *Edge* [2000] Ch 602, CA. On a perversity or 'no reasonable trustee' test, see *PNPF Trust Co Ltd* v. *Taylor* [2010] All ER (D) 251 (Jun) at [684] (Warren J), *Independent Schools Council* v. *Charity Commission* [2012] 1 All ER 127 at [220] (approved by the Court of Appeal in *Children's Investment Foundation Fund (UK)* v. *Attorney General* [2018] EWCA Civ 1605, [2019] Ch 139 at [61]) and *Thales UK Ltd* v. *Thales Pension Trustees Ltd* [2017] EWHC 666 (Ch), [2017] Pens LR 15 at [152] (Warren J).

94 *Edge* [1998] Ch 512 at 534B.

95 *Edge* [2000] Ch 602, CA at 631.

96 ibid at [633].

### 5.1 *Administrative or Dispositive Powers?*

It is sometimes commented that any due consideration/relevant factors review (*Braganza* 1 or formerly *Hastings-Bass*) of decisions by trustees only applies to dispositive powers, but not to administrative powers.[97] But this seems an unnecessary distinction (the cases predate *Braganza*).

### 5.2 *Public Law Analogies with Trustee Duties before* Pitt v. Holt

In 1993, in *Lord Shuttleworth*, the Court of Appeal adopted a 'no perversity and relevant factors' test for trustees.[98] Cases after *Lord Shuttleworth* went on to expressly make the connection with the public law tests in *Wednesbury*. In 1996, in another pensions case, *Wild*,[99] the comments in *Lord Shuttleworth* were adopted and followed by Carnwath J (as he then was) observing that, to a public lawyer, those words were virtually identical to the *Wednesbury* principles.

And later, in 1999 in the pensions case *Edge*,[100] the Court of Appeal adopted a public law analogy with enthusiasm (including because of the reasons for entrusting decisions to the relevant decision-makers: *Edge* at 630).[101]

### 5.3 *Public Law:* Braganza *and Trustees*

As previously mentioned, there was a clear warning away from applying public law in trustee cases by the Court of Appeal in *Pitt*, although slightly less clear by Lord Walker in the Supreme Court. But two years later in *Braganza*, the Supreme Court unanimously decided that the public law *Wednesbury* test (in both limbs) is the right one to apply in a private law context. As commented above, in effect, *Pitt* should be treated as impliedly overturned on this point by *Braganza*.

97 *Re Duxbury's ST* [1995] 1 WLR 425, CA at 427–428 (Rattee J) at first instance had held the rule does not apply to statutory power to appoint new trustees; and *Donaldson* v. *Smith* [2006] EWHC B9 (Ch), [2007] WTLR 421 (David Donaldson QC). Cited in J. Hudson and C. Mitchell, 'Legal consequences of the flawed exercise of pension scheme powers' in C. Mitchell, S. Agnew and P. Davies (eds), *Pensions: Law, Policy and Practice* (Hart Publishing, 2020), but also noting that Cayman and Jersey courts have taken a broader view of the rule's application: *Barclays Private Bank and Trust (Cayman) Ltd* v. *Chamberlain* (2005) 9 ITELR 302; *Re Howe Family No 1 Trust* [2007] JRC 248, [2009] WTLR 419.

98 *Lord Shuttleworth* [1995] OPLR 79, CA. Followed in Australia in a unit trust case, *Ying Mui Pty Ltd* [2017] VSC 730 at [408] (Vickery J).

99 *Wild* [1996] OPLR 129 at 135 (Carnwath J).

100 *Edge* [2000] Ch 602, CA at 627–630 (Chadwick LJ). Cited on this in later cases, including *Chambers* [2002] ICR 359 at [7] (Blackburne J) and *Stena Line* [2015] EWHC 448 (Ch) at [16] and [161] (Asplin J).

101 See Jonathan Evans 'Challenging trustee decisions' (2012) *Trust Law International* 55. See also Newey J (extrajudicially) in 'Constraints on the exercise of trustees' powers' in P. G. Turner (ed), *Equity and Administration* (Cambridge University Press, 2016), pp. 50–56.

The decision in *Braganza* on this public law analogy is an incursion into the more wide-ranging comments against the use of a public law analogy in *Pitt* by Mummery LJ and Lord Walker. As mentioned above, the public law *Wednesbury* test analogy clearly applies by analogy to decisions of employers under pension schemes (*Braganza* and *IBM*). There seems little reason not to apply the same tests to decisions by trustees as well, in particular in relation to trustees of commercial trusts, such as pension schemes.

### 5.3.1 Wellington City Council

*Braganza* has been applied in New Zealand to the trustee of a commercial trust.[102] This involved a commercial trust under which local authorities contributed to a trust fund, called 'Riskpool', on the basis that the trustee had a discretion to use the funds to meet claims on the local authority for damages for 'water ingress' in buildings. Wellington Council made a claim and (several years later) the trustee rejected it.

On a challenge to that rejection, Collins J referred to *Braganza* and applied the irrationality test, holding that '[n]o material differences were identified between the claims based on breach of contract and those that alleged that [the trustee] had breached its fiduciary duties to the council'.[103]

## 5.4 *Other Public Law Concepts?*

It seems right to apply public law *Wednesbury* irrationality (in both limbs) to appropriate private law decisions as well, but that there may still need to be caution in the use of other public law concepts. For example, issues on voidness of decisions, who may claim, no implied 'natural justice' rule seem still not to be appropriate. Mummery LJ's comments (in particular the last sentence cited above on the 'conceptual difference') in the Court of Appeal in *Pitt* seem to be wider and inconsistent with *Braganza* (which unanimously applied both limbs of '*Wednesbury* rationality' in a private law context).

It could perhaps be argued that *Braganza* (and the public law *Wednesbury* test) is limited to contractual discretions and not to family trusts (such as those involved in *Pitt*), leaving more commercial trusts (such a pension scheme or unit trust) still to be categorised. But *Braganza* has already been treated as applying in many commercial contexts[104] and, given the existing references to 'relevant factors' and 'no reasonable trustee' in many previous trust cases, it seems right that *Braganza* will be applied to trustee decisions as well.

[102] *Wellington City Council* [2017] NZHC 2901.
[103] ibid at [167] and [170].
[104] See Pollard, *Pensions, Contracts and Trusts*, ch 44.

It is also noticeable that the three 'important differences' noted by Lightman J in *Barr*[105] and cited by Lord Walker in *Pitt*, namely 'the discretionary nature of relief on judicial review, a different approach to nullity, and strict time limits' are all procedural differences and do not relate to the substantive review of the relevant decision.

## 6 WHERE ARE WE NOW?

The vast bulk of the case law applies both limbs of the *Braganza/Wednesbury* test to decisions of trustees. Clearly since *Braganza*, it is appropriate to apply such a public law test in relation to employer discretions in relation to death benefits in contracts and, since *IBM* to employer discretions under pension schemes. It would be perverse not apply a similar test to decisions by trustees as well. Indeed, it would be odd to have a lower standard applying to fiduciaries such as trustees as compared to employers.

The comments to the contrary in *Pitt*, both at the Court of Appeal and (somewhat elliptically) in the Supreme Court must be regarded as not now applying, given the clear contrary decision of the unanimous Supreme Court in *Braganza*. *Braganza* itself did not refer to *Pitt*, but must be regarded as clarifying that some aspects of public law can indeed be applied in private law. This should apply to trustee decisions.

[105] *Re Barr's Settlement Trusts* [2003] Ch 409 at [29] (Lightman J). A cautious approach to the use of public law analogies was stated in Singapore in the private trust case *Foo* [2012] SGCA 41 at [64].

# 12

# Trustee Decision-Making in the Australian Superannuation Context

*Tobias Barkley*[*]

## 1 INTRODUCTION

In 1992, the Australian Labor government introduced a superannuation scheme where employers were required to contribute to a superannuation account for every employee.[1] The intention was for 'ordinary Australians [to] be able to build a decent nest-egg for their retirement' so that people 'on average weekly earnings will be able to retire on an income twice the old age pension'.[2] At commencement, employers were required to contribute 3 per cent of an employee's earnings; this has now risen to 9 per cent and is legislated to rise to 12 per cent by 2027.[3] The scheme has grown into a complex system of 166 large funds operated by 104 licensed trustees and nearly 600,000 small funds[4] holding $3 trillion Australian dollars.[5] It is estimated that this system holds about 20 per cent of Australian wealth.[6]

The system was designed as a privatised system of retiree welfare. It was intended to support the government-run pension system, including tax incentives, but was outsourced to the private sector. As such it was built on the law of trusts. Every employee became beneficiary of a superannuation trust. This meant that private corporations were to be key decision-makers with control over a large segment of Australian wealth. This raises the question, recently explored in detail by M Scott Donald, of whether trust law is suitable for this purpose.[7]

* Lecturer at La Trobe University, Australia.

1 Superannuation Guarantee Charge Act 1992 (Cth); Superannuation Guarantee (Administration) Act 1992 (Cth).

2 Commonwealth, *Parliamentary Debates* (House of Representatives, 25 June 1992), pp. 3956–3957 (Paul Keating, Prime Minister).

3 Kenneth Hayne, *Royal Commission into Misconduct in the Banking, Superannuation and Financial Services Industry*, 2 vols (Final Report, February 2019) vol 1, p. 220.

4 Large and small means those with more or less than four members.

5 Australian Prudential Regulation Authority (APRA), *Quarterly Superannuation Performance: December 2020* (Statistics Report, 2 March 2021).

6 Australian Bureau of Statistics, *Household Income and Wealth: Australia 2017–2018* (Statistics Report, Cat No 6523.0, 12 July 2019).

7 M. Scott Donald, 'The Pension Trust: Fit for Purpose?' (2019) 82 *Modern Law Review* 800.

This chapter builds on Donald's work by examining how decision-making is regulated in two areas: distribution and investment. The chapter starts with a survey of the superannuation system and the different types of funds that it contains. Second, it analyses three layers in the legal structure that regulates trustee decision-making: mandatory covenants, a dispute resolution process, and traditional trust law principles. Third, it examines how distributive discretions are subject to more intensive scrutiny in the superannuation context. Fourth, it examines how the structure of conflicts affects investment decisions. Finally, the experience of superannuation law raises some questions about the suitability of trust law in other contexts.

## 2 THE AUSTRALIAN SUPERANNUATION SYSTEM

The Australian superannuation system is governed by a complex system of legislation. There are no fewer than forty-five principal[8] federal Acts currently in force that include 'Superannuation' in the title. In this complex system, decision-making power is granted to numerous individuals and bodies. Several distinctions in the types of superannuation trusts and the different funds they operate are important to understand the structure of trustee decision-making.

The superannuation sector can be into five types of funds. *Self-managed superannuation funds* ('SMSFs') allow wealthier individuals to retain control and management of their funds, while receiving the same tax benefits. They include less than 5 per cent of accounts but hold 25 per cent of assets under management.[9] *Corporate funds* are provided by large corporations, like Telstra, Qantas, and the big banks, exclusively for their own employees. They are largely legacies from prior to the compulsory superannuation system and contain only 1 per cent of accounts but 2 per cent of assets. *Retail funds* are offered as a service by financial institutions and are open to any employees. They contain a third of member accounts and 21 per cent of assets. *Industry funds* were historically set up by trade unions to provide superannuation to employees in certain industries.[10] They now compete with retail funds but are distinguished by ongoing connections to trade unions and employer associations, and by a not-for-profit, or profit-for-members, structure. They contain

[8] Not including Acts that primarily amend other legislation. Other legislation also governs the superannuation sector, such as the Corporations Act 2001 (Cth) Part 7.10A that regulates superannuation complaints.

[9] Australian Prudential Regulation Authority, *Annual Superannuation Bulletin: June 2015 to June 2020* (Bulletin, 29 January 2021). Individuals may have more than one superannuation account as a new default account will be created with each new job if the employee does not engage. Reforms have been undertaken to consolidate the number of accounts, especially those inactive or incurring fees. Over the five years to 2020 the number of accounts reduced from 28.9 to 23.3 million: Australian Prudential Regulation Authority, *Annual Superannuation Bulletin Highlights: June 2020* (Bulletin, 29 January 2021), p. 6.

[10] See, for example, Hostplus, 'About Us' <hostplus.com.au/super/about-us> last accessed 22 March 2021.

26 per cent of assets under management but 46 per cent of member accounts.[11] Finally, *public sector funds* include government funds for public employees. They contain 15 per cent of accounts and 24 per cent of assets.[12] The line between the public sector and industry funds has become blurred as many public sector funds have opened to all applicants and there has been a process of mergers. Like industry funds, they are not-for-profit and retain ties with unions.[13]

The entitlements offered to members by different funds may be accumulation accounts or defined benefit accounts. In both cases, the member's contributions are pooled and invested. In an accumulation scheme, the member is credited with an individual account that accumulates the value of contributions along with investment earnings or losses.[14] In the defined benefit scheme, the member is entitled to a defined income upon retirement.[15] In the latter, risk is taken on by the employer, who guarantees the promised benefits if the pooled investments are insufficient. In the former, the member takes on the risk that the investment return is reduced.[16] In Australia, most defined benefit schemes have been phased out or are not open to new members.[17] This has reduced the difficulty identified by David Pollard of trustees being obliged to balance the interests of the employees and the employers.[18]

Another distinction is between choice and default funds. While most employees are free to choose a superannuation fund when they start employment,[19] more than two-thirds make no active choice.[20] In such cases, employers are obliged to pay their contributions to a default fund, which is nominated by the employer, alone or in an industrial relations agreement.[21] This has raised significant concerns about employers not making choices in their employees' interests.[22] Government attempted to limit

11 APRA, 'Annual Superannuation Bulletin'.

12 ibid.

13 See, for example, VisSuper, 'VicSuper's History' <www.vicsuper.com.au/about-us/our-history> last accessed 23 March 2021.

14 Australian Securities and Investments Commission, 'Accumulation Fund' <moneysmart.gov.au/glossary/accumulation-fund> last accessed 23 March 2021.

15 Australian Securities and Investments Commission, 'Defined Benefit Fund' <moneysmart.gov.au/glossary/defined-benefit-fund> last accessed 23 March 2021.

16 Productivity Commission, *Superannuation: Assessing Efficiency and Competitiveness* (Productivity Commission Inquiry Report No 91, 21 December 2018), p. 85.

17 See, for example, Superannuation Act 1990 (Cth), s. 6(4).

18 David Pollard, 'Application of the Proper Purpose Test to Pension Schemes' (2016) 30 *Trust Law International* 159.

19 There are some exceptions where employees are bonded to a particular superannuation fund through collective employment agreements. For example, university employees' contributions must be paid to UniSuper.

20 Productivity Commission, Superannuation, p. 82; Jeremy Cooper, *Super System Report: Final Review* (Final Report, 30 June 2010), p. 11.

21 Superannuation Guarantee (Administration) Act 1992 (Cth), s. 32C(2).

22 Productivity Commission, Superannuation, p. 344.

the impact of this problem by regulating default funds as 'MySuper' products. The Cooper review in 2010 proposed this 'libertarian paternalism' approach, in which the system ought to be designed for disengaged members as well as engaged.[23] MySuper default funds are simpler and have lower fees.[24] The Productivity Commission ('PC') found that MySuper products had better investment performance than choice products, although the analysis may be affected by selection bias.[25]

## 3 STRUCTURE AND REGULATION OF DECISION-MAKING

Understanding these different types of funds is important to understanding the structure of who makes decisions, the legal duties that apply to those decisions, and how those duties are enforced. Decisions in SMSFs are usually controlled by the beneficiary, who must be a trustee or director of the trustee.[26] The primary regulation of SMSF decisions is by the Australian Taxation Office, which polices compliance with the terms of the trust, particularly the requirement that SMSFs exist for the exclusive purpose of benefiting the member after retirement or death.[27] In the corporate, retail, industry and public funds, decisions are made by professional trustee corporations. They are primarily regulated by the Australian Prudential Regulation Authority ('APRA'), except for some exempt public sector funds regulated by specific legislation.[28] The Australian Securities & Investments Commission also plays a role, with a focus on disclosure obligations and licensing.[29]

The legal structure regulating trustee decisions can be understood as three layers. Two are found in legislation, and the third is supplied by the ordinary principles of equity. The latter applies because, even though the legislation refers to funds, schemes, and trusts,[30] they are all intended to be trust relationships.[31] The different layers may raise issues of jurisdiction between the state and federal courts.[32] While state courts are vested with jurisdiction to decide all federal matters, the reverse is

[23] Cooper, Super System Report, pp. 8–11.

[24] Superannuation Industry (Supervision) Act 1993 (Cth), Part 2C; Superannuation Legislation (MySuper Measures) Amendment Regulation 2013 (Cth). The simplicity of MySuper products is that they all provide a single diversified investment strategy with common characteristics: Hayne, Royal Commission: Final Report, p. 223.

[25] Productivity Commission, Superannuation, pp. 124–126.

[26] Superannuation Industry (Supervision) Act 1993 (Cth), s. 17A.

[27] ibid, s. 62. See *Deputy Commissioner of Taxation* v. *Lyons* (2014) 100 ATR 130 at [36].

[28] Hayne, Royal Commission: Final Report, pp. 219–220.

[29] Superannuation Industry (Supervision) Act 1993 (Cth), ss. 4–6.

[30] ibid, s. 10 'beneficiary'.

[31] See *Edington* v. *Board of Trustees of State Public Sector Superannuation Scheme* [2015] QSC 245 at [33]–[40].

[32] *Jeffcoat* v. *Queensland Coal & Oil Shale Mining Industry (Superannuation) Ltd.* [2000] FCA 655 at [22].

not true.[33] The Constitution only allows federal courts to decide non-federal claims that are part of the same 'matter' that raises a federal claim.[34] However, given the broad duties in federal legislation, it is likely that most matters would be included.

### 3.1 *Statutory Regulation of Decision-Making*

The statutory structure regulating trustee decision-making has two layers. First, there are legislated mandatory covenants that incorporate some standard trustee duties, such as honesty and reasonable care. Second, there is a distinct procedure that allows some decisions to be reviewed for fairness and reasonableness.

The Superannuation Industry (Supervision) Act 1993 (Cth) prescribes covenants that must be included in every superannuation trust deed.[35] They were intended to incorporate the standard trust duties, not to expand them.[36] They include duties: to act honestly; to exercise the care, diligence, and skill of a prudent superannuation trustee;[37] and to act in the best interests of the members. The duty of impartiality is included as the duty to act fairly in dealings both between classes of members and within the classes. The standard fiduciary duty against being in a position of conflict, which is typically modified in trust deeds,[38] was left out of the original provision. In 2013, amendments introduced a mandatory duty to manage conflicts to prioritise members' interests.[39] All the mandatory covenants apply to directors of trustees,[40] which eliminates the 'dog-leg' claim problem.[41]

Remedies for breaches of these duties include a unique cause of action for loss, civil and criminal penalties,[42] and actions by the trustee on behalf of the fund for compensation and recovery of profits.[43] A civil penalty order may result in a fine[44] or compensation of any amount paid to the trustee,[45] which possibly includes punitive damages.[46] The Act states twice that breach does not result in the invalidity of

33 *Re Wakim* (1999) 198 CLR 511.
34 ibid at [135]–[140] (Gummow and Hayne JJ).
35 Superannuation Industry (Supervision) Act 1993 (Cth), s. 52.
36 *Manglicmot* v. *Commonwealth Bank Officers Superannuation Corporation Pty. Ltd.* (2011) 282 ALR 167 at [110]–[121].
37 This higher standard of care replaced a simple prudent person standard in 2013: Superannuation Legislation Amendment (Trustee Obligations and Prudential Standards) Act 2012 (Cth).
38 See, for example, *Hostplus Trust Deed* (Trust Instrument, 5 April 2013) cl. 13.3 <hostplus.com.au/super/about-us/governance-and-disclosures> accessed 23 March 2021.
39 Superannuation Industry (Supervision) Act 1993 (Cth), s. 52.
40 ibid, s. 52A.
41 Thomson Reuters, *Ford and Lee: The Law of Trusts* (online looseleaf, accessed 15 January 2021) at [8.055], [17.11010].
42 Superannuation Industry (Supervision) Act 1993 (Cth), s. 54B.
43 ibid, s. 218.
44 ibid, s. 196(3).
45 ibid, s. 215.
46 ibid, ss. 196(5), 222.

a transaction,[47] which rules out voidness but is ambiguous as to voidability.[48] The Act does allow exemption of liability for a breach, apart from dishonesty or recklessness, but *APRA* v. *Kelaher* found that this does not apply to the statutory action for loss.[49] JC Campbell argues that general law duties continue to provide alternative remedies alongside the statutory duties.[50]

Enforcement of these statutory duties can be litigated by members, trustees, and APRA in the courts. APRA has a significant extrajudicial role in supervising the licensing of trustees. Trustees must report any breaches of the conditions of their licenses, which provides APRA with an opportunity to recommend alternative action.[51] An example of this is found in *APRA* v. *Kelaher* where one reason APRA could not establish its case is that, following pressure from APRA, the trustees did not implement the decisions that APRA alleged were a breach of duty.[52]

The second layer of regulation is a dispute resolution ombudsman service provided by the Australian Financial Complaints Authority ('AFCA'). It applies to decisions that affect an individual member, rather than the fund as a whole.[53] AFCA has more of a dispute resolution role than the previous Superannuation Complaints Tribunal ('SCT'), but is still empowered to make final determinations.[54] In the 2019–2020 financial year, 35 of 578 death benefit complaints resulted in a determination.[55] This dispute resolution is more accessible than the courts in both cost and convenience, but has a restrictive 28-day time limit from the notification of a decision.[56] It is likely that this excludes many genuine disputes, but there is little evidence that they are finding their way to the courts.

AFCA does not directly apply traditional trust principles. In contrast to the traditional trustees' immunity from giving reasons,[57] trustees must supply AFCA

47 ibid, ss. 54B(4), 54C(3).

48 See generally Jessica Hudson and Charles Mitchell, 'Legal Consequences of the Flawed Exercise of Scheme Powers' in Sinéad Agnew, Paul S. Davies, and Charles Mitchell (eds), *Pensions: Law, Policy and Practice* (Oxford: Hart Publishing, 2020).

49 *APRA* v. *Kelaher* (2019) 138 ACSR 459 at [20]–[22].

50 See J. C. Campbell, 'Obligations and Powers of Superannuation Trustees Concerning Situations of Actual or Possible Conflict' (2020) 49 *Australian Bar Review* 1.

51 Superannuation Industry (Supervision) Act 1993 (Cth), s. 29JA.

52 *APRA* (2019) 138 ACSR 459 at [264]–[268], [686]. Jagot J found that an unimplemented decision could not, as a matter of principle, be a breach of the trustees' duties because that would amount to a 'thought-crime': ibid at [706]. This reasoning is questionable as trustees' decisions are legal actions, unlike thoughts.

53 AFCA, *Complaint Resolution Scheme Rules* (Rules, 2018), rule C.1.5.

54 Corporations Act 2001 (Cth), s. 1055.

55 Total complaints reported: AFCA, *Annual Review 2019–2020* (Report, November 2020), p. 38 <www.afca.org.au/about-afca/annual-review> last accessed 23 March 2021. The number of determinations derived from death benefit decisions are searchable <www.afca.org.au/about-afca/annual-review> last accessed 23 March 2021. Determinations must be given in writing: Corporations Act 2001 (Cth), s. 1055A. They are published publicly at <www.afca.org.au/what-to-expect/search-published-decisions/public-reporting-of-determinations> last accessed 23 March 2021.

56 Corporations Act 2001 (Cth), s. 1056(2).

57 *Mandie* v. *Memart Nominees Pty. Ltd.* (2014) 42 VR 325 at [94].

with written reasons.[58] Rather than apply trust duties, AFCA determines whether a trustees' decision was 'fair and reasonable in all the circumstances'.[59] This requires AFCA to stand in the shoes of the trustee[60] and decide the range of fair and reasonable outcomes.[61]

Interestingly, this means that only the merits of the outcome are considered. Unlike judicial review, the process of decision-making is irrelevant. Thus, evidence of an improper purpose or irrelevant consideration does not matter if the outcome remains fair and reasonable.[62]

### 3.2 *Karger* v. *Paul* Principles

The mandatory covenants do not explicitly include some trustee duties that have been developed in relation to discretionary powers: the proper purpose and genuine consideration duties. They may be implicitly included under the duty to exercise powers in the best interests of the members, which was intended to incorporate the general law.[63] In Australia, these duties are known as the *Karger* v. *Paul* principles,[64] as stated in that case:[65]

> the effect of the authorities is that, with one exception, the exercise of a discretion in these terms will not be examined or reviewed by the courts so long as the essential component parts of the exercise of the particular discretion are present. Those essential component parts are present if the discretion is exercised by the trustees in good faith, upon real and genuine consideration and in accordance with the purposes for which the discretion was conferred. The exception is that the validity of the trustees' reasons will be examined and reviewed if the trustees choose to state their reasons for their exercise of discretion.

The *Karger* v. *Paul* principles are particularly important in relation to certain types of discretions that are not subject to the duties of reasonable care. Outside of superannuation, these include distributive discretions, such as powers of appointment, which trustees do not need to exercise reasonably or wisely.[66] The original reason that a duty of care was not imposed on these powers was that their terms purported to exclude judicial control by giving unfettered or absolute discretion to trustees.[67] In contrast, other discretions, such as powers of investment, were subject to a general

58 Superannuation Industry (Supervision) Act 1993 (Cth), s. 101.
59 Corporations Act 2001 (Cth), s. 1055(3).
60 *Ievers* v. *Superannuation Complaints Tribunal* (2016) 160 ALD 96 at [70].
61 ibid at [20].
62 *Stock* v. *NM Superannuation Pty. Ltd.* [2015] FCA 612 at [42].
63 *Commonwealth Bank Officers Superannuation Corp Pty. Ltd.* v. *Beck* (2016) 334 ALR 692 at [136]–[139].
64 *Finch* v. *Telstra Super Pty. Ltd.* (2010) 242 CLR 254 at [28].
65 *Karger* v. *Paul* [1984] VR 161 at 163–164.
66 *A-G (Cth)* v. *Breckler* (1999) 197 CLR 83 at [7].
67 *Gisborne* v. *Gisborne* (1877) 2 App Cas 300.

duty of care.[68] Exclusionary terms in distributive powers are no longer given much weight; for example, the leading United Kingdom Supreme Court decision on the equivalent of the *Karger* v. *Paul* principles did not even mention the terms of the discretion.[69] However, the duty of reasonable care has not been reapplied to these powers because distributive and administrative powers are now seen as distinct categories that naturally attract different regulations.[70]

Thus, the effect of the *Karger* v. *Paul* principles is to protect trustees by displacing duties to take reasonable care in exercising powers.[71] This fits with the courts' 'traditional reluctance' to interfere in trustees' discretions[72] and enthusiasm for protecting trustees from having to justify their decisions with reasons.[73] One case, *Curwen* v. *Vanbreck Pty Ltd*, is often cited as authority that a trustee is even entitled to 'stand mute' and have no adverse inference drawn from their silence.[74] While the Victorian Court of Appeal did refuse to make an adverse inference,[75] this was because the allegation of improper reasons had not been put to the trustee in cross-examination.[76] Nevertheless, the *Karger v Paul* principles are not static but continue to develop in the general law. For example, the United Kingdom Supreme Court recently summarised them as a duty of adequate deliberation,[77] which includes taking into account relevant, but not irrelevant, considerations.[78]

Until *Finch* v. *Telstra Super Pty. Ltd.*, it was widely assumed that these restrictive principles applied in the superannuation context.[79] However, in that case, the High Court of Australia held that there were several reasons why the context must qualify their application: the fact that superannuation entitlements constitute a large share of most people's wealth, the fact that benefits are obtained not gratuitously but as part of remuneration in an employment relationship, the compulsory nature of contributions, the public importance of superannuation trusts, and the size of the sector, all militate in favour of members' legitimate expectations that trustees will make sound decisions.[80]

[68] *Speight* v. *Gaunt* (1883) LR 9 App Cas 1.

[69] *Pitt* v. *Holt* [2013] 2 AC 108.

[70] See *Lewis* v. *Tamplin* [2018] EWHC (Ch) 777 at [47]–[52].

[71] See *Finch* (2010) 242 CLR 254 at [59]–[60]; *Foreman* v. *Kingstone* [2004] 1 NZLR 841 at [89].

[72] *Re Whitehouse* [1982] Qd R 196 at 583; *Burns* v. *Burns* [2008] QSC 173 at [32].

[73] See *Hartigan Nominees Pty. Ltd.* v. *Rydge* (1992) 29 NSWLR 405 at 436 (Mahoney JA), 442 (Shelley JA); *Breakspear* v. *Ackland* [2009] Ch 32 at [54]–[58]; *Erceg* v. *Erceg* [2017] 1 NZLR 320 at [36].

[74] *Mandie* (2014) 42 VR 325 at [92]–[93].

[75] *Curwen* v. *Vanbreck Pty Ltd* (2009) 26 VR 335 at [25].

[76] ibid at [26]–[31].

[77] *Pitt* [2013] 2 AC 108 at [73].

[78] ibid at [60]. See also *Esso Australia Ltd.* v. *Australian Petroleum Agents' and Distributors' Association* [1999] 3 VR 642 at [38]–[41]. Contra *Telstra Super Pty. Ltd.* v. *Flegeltaub* (2000) 2 VR 276 at [33] (Batt JA).

[79] *Finch* (2010) 242 CLR 254 at [64].

[80] *Finch* (2010) 242 CLR 254 at [33]–[36].

Unfortunately, the High Court did not set out what qualifications should be placed on the *Karger* v. *Paul* principles. First, the High Court decided that the type of decision under consideration – concerning a total permanent disability ('TPD') benefit – was not a discretion but a strict trust.[81] The decision was whether an employee was 'in the opinion of the Trustee [...] unlikely ever to engage in any gainful Work,'[82] which was a factual evaluation that would determine entitlement to a fixed TPD benefit rather than a true discretion.[83] Second, the Court was able to dispose of the case by finding that the first instance judge applied the *Karger* v. *Paul* principles correctly. Therefore, the Court was not obliged to decide how they should be qualified.[84] However, the Court did hold that, while all trustees have a duty to give 'properly informed consideration' to exercises of power, it is more intense in superannuation trusts.[85] The Court indicated that increased intensity was required in the specific case of TPD benefits because they are strict trusts, but also hinted that the intensity of review applies more broadly because of the public importance of superannuation members' interests.[86]

The current situation is that 'the law seems to be in a state of development'.[87] In relation to TPD decisions, thus far it is the trustee's duty to make properly informed decisions including a 'high' and 'more intense' duty to initiate any inquiries that may be necessary.[88] For example, this duty cannot be satisfied solely by asking the member to provide information.[89] In relation to non-TPD discretionary decisions, *Finch* v. *Telstra* provides little guidance on how the *Karger* v. *Paul* principles ought to be qualified. No court has yet taken up the question left open in *Finch* v. *Telstra* as to whether the standard applicable in the AFCA jurisdiction – fairness and reasonableness – ought to replace the *Karger* v. *Paul* principles.[90]

The resolution of this open question that is most consistent with the statute would be accepting that the mandatory covenant to exercise the care, diligence, and skill of a prudent superannuation trustee applies, as s. 52(2)(b) says, 'to all matters affecting the entity', including the exercise of all discretions.

## 4 DISTRIBUTION DECISIONS

One of the rare areas where superannuation trustees exercise a distributive discretion similar to those that gave rise to the *Karger* v. *Paul* principles is the distribution

81 ibid at [66].
82 ibid at [7].
83 ibid at [29]–[37].
84 ibid at [37], [65].
85 ibid at [66].
86 ibid.
87 *Edington* [2015] QSC 245 at [45].
88 *Alcoa of Australia Retirement Plan Pty. Ltd.* v. *Frost* (2012) 36 VR 618 at [57].
89 ibid at [58].
90 *Finch* (2010) 242 CLR 254 at [62], [65].

of benefits on the death of a member.[91] Unlike TPD benefits, this does not involve a factual evaluation, but a true discretion. It also involves the core of trust law, which is at heart a relationship about the distribution of assets.

On a member's death, her superannuation interest does not pass to her estate.[92] Instead, the deceased's retirement entitlements are replaced with a discretion in the trustees.[93] The trustee has the discretion to choose to distribute the deceased's accumulated funds, and any death benefits arising from insurance,[94] to their personal representative or dependants. For example, the Hostplus trust deed states:[95]

> Subject to the Relevant Law, upon the death of a Member or Beneficiary who had Dependants, the Trustee shall:
>
> (1) pay or apply the Benefit of one or more of the Member's or Beneficiary's Dependants (including any Nominated Beneficiaries) and Legal Personal Representative in such proportions, form, manner and at such times as the Trustee shall from time to time in its discretion determine [...].

'Dependants' always include the deceased's legal or de facto spouse, children and those with whom the deceased live with in a close, personal, 'interdependency relationship'.[96] The class may also be expanded by the trust deed, for example, to include those who were financially dependent on the deceased.[97] The discretion can be excluded by the member's binding nomination.

On its face, this broad discretion is radical and gives superannuation trustees enormous power over many people's largest asset. My experience teaching trust law in Australia suggests that it is not widely understood. However, as we shall see, AFCA's jurisdiction and the *Karger* v. *Paul* principles, as ambiguously qualified by *Finch* v. *Telstra*, significantly limits the scope of the trustee's discretion in this context. Both layers of regulation contribute to a more intensive regulation of distributive decisions than is typical in traditional trust law.

91 Another area is the distribution of trust fund surpluses: see *Edge* v. *Pensions Ombudsman* [2000] Ch 602. Although often the discretion is vested in the employer: see *Lock* v. *Westpac Banking Corporation* (1991) 25 NSWLR 593.

92 See *Stock* [2015] FCA 612 at [16].

93 Superannuation Industry (Supervision) Regulations 1994 (Cth), r 6.22.

94 Most accounts, including MySuper accounts, provide death insurance as an opt-out benefit: Superannuation Industry (Supervision) Act 1993 (Cth), s. 68AA.

95 Hostplus Trust Deed, cl. 23.1.

96 Superannuation Industry (Supervision) Act 1993 (Cth), ss. 10, 10A. This definition can, and has been, modified in small ways by regulation: Superannuation Industry (Supervision) Regulations 1994 (Cth), reg. 1.04AAAA.

97 Hostplus Trust Deed, cl. 1.

### 4.1 *Courts*

A rare example of the *Karger* v. *Paul* principles being applied to the death benefit discretion is the decision by a SMSF trustee in *Re Marsella (No 2)*.[98] Because SMSF trustees are not subject to AFCA's dispute resolution process,[99] the complaint could only be brought to court.

In this case, the trustee–beneficiary of a SMSF died leaving her daughter as sole surviving trustee. The dependants who were objects of the death benefit discretion were the daughter, her brother, and the mother's husband of thirty-two years. The daughter exercised the death benefit discretion to appoint the entire fund to herself. When the husband sought review, McMillan J cited and applied the *Karger* v. *Paul* principles.[100] She found there was no breach of the proper purpose duty because the daughter was an eligible object of the discretion and had not disclosed any reasons.[101] Even suspicious timing of the distribution, two weeks before mediation, might have had a justifiable explanation, so could not be impeached without exposing the trustee's reasons.[102] Nevertheless, McMillan J did find a breach of the genuine consideration and good faith duties. She found the decision was so unreasonable that the outcome alone demonstrated a lack of genuine consideration.[103] Failure to take into account relevant considerations was evidenced by the husband's relationship and financial position being 'ignored', which must mean placing no weight on them.[104] The trustee's own written record that the interests of all dependants had been considered before the discretion exercised was dismissed by McMillan J as formulaic.[105] These findings are significant departures from the non-interventionist approach seen outside of the superannuation context.

Moreover, McMillan J's consideration of conflicts of interest raises a marked contrast with *Karger* v. *Paul*. The latter involved two co-trustees who appointed the entire fund to one of them.[106] However, the conflict between the trustee's duty and his interest as an object was simply not mentioned by the judge, presumably because the settlor appointing the trustee implicitly authorised the conflict. McMillan J agreed the conflict in *Re Marsella (No 2)* was authorised.[107] However, she found

98 *Re Marsella (No 2)* [2019] VSC 65.
99 Corporations Act 2001 (Cth), s. 1053(4)(a).
100 *Curwen* (2009) 26 VR 335 at [34]–[42].
101 *Re Marsella* [2019] VSC 65 at [63].
102 ibid at [64].
103 ibid at [51].
104 ibid at [52].
105 ibid at [55].
106 *Karger* [1984] VR 161.
107 *Re Marsella* [2019] VSC 65 at [66].

it remained relevant and demanded heightened vigilance from the trustee.[108] The trustee failed to meet this standard through her lack of appreciation of her role or the other's interests – an 'ill-informed arbitrariness' – which evidenced lack of genuine consideration and amounted to bad faith.[109]

### 4.2 *Australian Financial Complaints Authority*

The indirect approach in *Re Marsella (No 2)* can be compared with the directly interventionist approach taken in disputes under the AFCA jurisdiction, which determines what was 'fair and reasonable in all the circumstances'.[110]

When determining what qualifies as a fair and reasonable distribution, the SCT and AFCA have adopted a rather rigid approach, driven by purpose. Many determinations recite the same paragraph:[111]

> The purpose of superannuation is to provide retirement benefits for a superannuation member and his or her spouse in retirement. In the event of death, a superannuation death benefit is to provide for anyone who was financially reliant on or had an expectation of ongoing financial support from the superannuation member, had the member not died.

This fixed approach to purpose is justified to the extent that it means that spouses and minor children are given priority.[112]

The purposive approach allows detailed interference with the trustee's discretion. In one instance, a trustee had distributed 80 per cent to the deceased's de facto partner and 20 per cent to his parents who were in an interdependency relationship with him. The SCT decided that the parents' share did not adequately reflect the deceased's reliance on his parents during his illness and increased it to 40 per cent.[113]

The strict purposive approach does result in some uncomfortable outcomes. It means that dependants always benefit before personal representatives, regardless of the circumstance. A telling case is *Ievers* v. *SCT*, where the deceased tragically died of suicide. The trustee decided to distribute the entire fund to her mother as personal representative. The only other potential object was the deceased's boyfriend. The main dispute was whether he had stopped being a dependant due to the deceased ending the relationship the day before her death, which the SCT decided in his favour. The SCT concluded that in those circumstances, there was

[108] ibid at [48].
[109] ibid at [56]–[57].
[110] Corporations Act 2001 (Cth), s. 1055(3).
[111] AFCA *Determination 601401* (7 February 2019) at [2.2] <www.afca.org.au/what-to-expect/search-published-decisions> last accessed 23 March 2021.
[112] *Stock* [2015] FCA 612 at [37].
[113] *D18-19-187* [2019] SCTA 87 (21 May 2019).

no rational basis to distribute anything to the mother because the boyfriend was the only dependant with the right to look to the deceased for financial support.[114] The reasonably contestable status of that relationship was not a relevant factor. Even more problematically, the mother and trustee pointed to forceful evidence of escalating domestic violence and controlling behaviour by the boyfriend against the deceased,[115] which was acknowledged by the Federal Court.[116] The SCT's rigid approach, which was confirmed by the Federal Court, meant that this evidence was not considered relevant to the exercise of discretion. If ever there were a strong case for a trustee to prefer a personal representative over a dependant, it would be when the latter was engaged in escalating domestic violence towards the deceased.

This last case demonstrates how AFCA's jurisdiction is applied to significantly limit the freedom of the trustee's discretion. This increases certainty for dependants, but it also means other important considerations are not being taken into account.

## 5 INVESTMENT MANAGEMENT DECISIONS

Investment decisions are not regulated primarily by the *Karger* v. *Paul* principles but by the duty of care found in the mandatory covenants. There is also an investment covenant that requires trustees to set and review investment strategies for the whole fund and each investment option offered.[117] Apart from one test case, discussed below, we have little insight into investment decisions from litigation.[118] Investment decisions are excluded from AFCA's jurisdiction along with other decisions that concern the management of a fund as a whole.[119] Fortunately, the work of two commissions provides great insight into this area.

### 5.1 *Productivity Commission*

In 2018, the PC completed a report on the efficiency and competitiveness of superannuation. This included much economic analysis of investment performance in different funds. The PC found a large variation in performance with the best MySuper options delivering annual net returns between 2005 and 2017 over 4 per

114 *Ievers* (2016) 160 ALD 96 at [32].
115 ibid at [27].
116 ibid at [59].
117 Superannuation Industry (Supervision) Act 1993 (Cth), s. 52(6).
118 One private test case about managing the financial risk of climate change resulted in a successful public settlement where the trustee agreed to manage its investments in accordance with the current standard of net zero emissions by 2050: Michael Slezak, 'Rest Super Fund Commits to Net-zero Emission Investments after Brisbane Man Sues', Australian Broadcasting Corporation (3 November 2020) <www.abc.net.au/news/2020-11-02/rest-super-commits-to-net-zero-emmissions/12840204> last accessed 23 March 2021.
119 *Employers First* v. *Tolhurst Capital Ltd.* (2005) 143 FCR 356 at [74]; AFCA, Complaint Resolution Scheme Rules, rule C.1.5.

cent greater than the worst performers,[120] and an even greater range in choice options.[121] This difference in performance can cause an extraordinary difference to the individual. The PC's modelling found that a person with an average salary with a superannuation fund in the median top quartile of returns would retire with more than twice the funds ($1.2 million) than if her fund was in the bottom quartile of returns ($560,000).[122] Differences in fund performance allow insight into investment decision-making because of structural differences between retail and not-for-profit funds.

The PC found a systematic performance divide between retail and not-for-profit funds. The difference was large: not-for-profit funds delivered average returns of 7.1 per cent from 2005 to 2017, while retail trusts delivered returns of 5.1 per cent.[123] The divide also appeared in analysis according to fund types and asset classes.[124] In the long tail of funds that underperformed industry benchmarks, 77 per cent of member accounts and 72 per cent of assets were in retail funds.[125]

The PC tackled the question of what caused the underperformance in retail funds. Possible ascertainable causes were taxation, investment fees, trustee administration fees, and allocation between asset classes. On tax and reported investment fees, it was found that retail funds actually outperformed not-for-profits by 0.52 per cent. However, administration fees were twice as high in retail funds, reducing returns by 0.40 per cent, which almost cancels out the outperformance. Retail funds tended to invest in more conservative asset classes, which explained a further 0.15 per cent. The PC's conclusion was that none of these factors explained the 1.92 per cent lower returns in retail funds.[126] Economies of scale did not appear to be a decisive factor. For example, while the largest industry funds did outperform smaller industry funds, large retail funds performed as poorly as smaller ones.[127] Unreported investment fees might contribute to the performance difference, but other analysis suggested the contribution would be small. The PC concluded that the most likely cause was the trustees' selection of assets within classes.[128]

Assuming the PC's identification of the cause is correct, the critical question for investment decision-making is this: why does the average for-profit trustee choose investments that return nearly 2 per cent less than the investments chosen by the average not-for-profit trustee? Why does the average not-for-profit trustee appear

[120] Productivity Commission, Superannuation, p. 136.
[121] ibid, p. 149.
[122] ibid, p. 139.
[123] ibid, pp. 126–128.
[124] ibid, pp. 129–130.
[125] ibid, p. 139.
[126] ibid, pp. 131–132. The PC's analysis set different benchmarks for the two types of funds to account for the different in asset class allocation.
[127] Productivity Commission, Superannuation, p. 137.
[128] ibid, pp. 118, 130–133, 137.

nearly 40 per cent better at investment decisions than the average retail trustee? Some answers to these questions are found in the *Royal Commission into Misconduct in the Banking, Superannuation and Financial Services Industry* ('RC'), that commenced during the PC's investigation.

### 5.2 *Royal Commission*

As part of the RC investigation, Commissioner Kenneth Hayne undertook detailed case studies into a number of different funds: retail funds owned by large banks (National Australia Bank, Commonwealth Bank, ANZ, and Westpac); retail funds owned by large financial services groups (AMP, IOOF, Suncorp, Aon Group, Mercer); industry funds jointly owned by employer groups and unions (Hostplus, AustralianSuper, Cbus, Sunsuper, CSF, and Energy Super); and a public sector fund (QSuper).[129] While Hayne's findings regarding QSuper were entirely laudatory,[130] and those regarding many of the industry funds were positive or neutral, he found significant misconduct in relation to many of the retail funds.

One of Hayne's findings that must contribute to the underperformance of retail funds is the evidence some trustees are simply not acting with the care, diligence, and skill expected of a prudent superannuation trustee. For example, lack of diligence was shown by the repeated issue of members being charged fees for a service that they had not received.[131] Another repeated issue was trustees' lack of diligence in monitoring other entities to whom they delegated responsibility. One example is NM Superannuation Pty Ltd, a trustee in the AMP group, which exercised its delegation powers to outsource its investment and administrative functions to other members of the AMP group. The only functions it retained were approval of high-level strategy (such as business plans, investment policies, financial statements, and amendments to trust deeds) and ultimate responsibility for the outsourcing arrangements.[132] AMP accepted that it had breached the duty of care when some members' cash investment options were receiving negative returns: less than what would have been received with an ordinary AMP bank account.[133] The trustees had completely failed to consider the performance of the fund from the perspective of members and had not considered the total return including fees and taxes.[134] Moreover, the monitoring system was structured so that investment underperformance could continue for up to five years before being reported to the trustee.[135] In

[129] Hayne, Royal Commission: Final Report, vol 2.

[130] Hayne praised the trustee's attempts to identify remote and indigenous Australian members, inform them of their interests and help them engage with the system: ibid, pp. 203–209.

[131] ibid, pp. 50–55, 71–73, 92, 261–262.

[132] ibid, pp. 107–108.

[133] ibid, p. 121.

[134] ibid, pp. 119, 123.

[135] ibid, p. 115.

these examples, it is not lower returns alone that indicate a lack of care – even skillful and prudent trustees may fail to beat the market. However, the discrete instances of a lack of care in these cases did lead to lower returns.

The deeper issue that helps explain the care and skill deficit in relation to retail funds is incentives. It appears obvious that, where a superannuation service is provided by a retail group on a for-profit basis, trustee decisions may be influenced by a profit incentive. As the PC found in 2017, out of $1.6 billion extracted from members as fees for advice, 90 per cent was in ten retail funds.[136] And, as there is no necessary alignment between the retail groups' profit and the members' profit, the former may generate a serious conflict of interest.

The conflict rules in the mandatory covenants are not the traditional fiduciary rules. First, fiduciary conflict rules may be excluded by a trust instrument, and express trusts almost always do this.[137] Prior to the 2013 amendments, the standard position applied to superannuation trusts. However, since 2013, s. 52 of the Superannuation Industry (Supervision) Act 1993 (Cth) has imposed mandatory conflict rules that cannot be excluded.[138] Second, in traditional trust law, where the conflict rules are not excluded, they have a strict operation that strips all profits from the fiduciary[139] and allows the transaction to be rescinded.[140] Section 52 imposes a very different duty that contemplates ongoing conflicts. Where a conflict arises[141] the trustee's duties are:

(1) to give priority to the duties to and interests of the beneficiaries over the duties to and interests of other persons;
(2) to ensure that the duties to the beneficiaries are met despite the conflict;
(3) to ensure that the interests of the beneficiaries are not adversely affected by the conflict; and
(4) to comply with the prudential standards in relation to conflicts.

The prudential standards determined by APRA prescribe more detail about developing, implementing, and reviewing a conflicts management policy, and identifying and maintaining a register of duties and interests.[142] A summary of the conflicts management policy and the register must be publicly disclosed.[143]

The case studies undertaken in the RC provided repeated evidence that these conflicts of interest have a highly detrimental effect on trustee decisions. The extreme is the above example of AMP, where the trustee itself did not extract profit

[136] Productivity Commission, Superannuation, p. 175.
[137] See, for example, Hostplus Trust Deed, cl. 13.3.
[138] See also s. 7.
[139] *Keech* v. *Sandford* [1726] Sel Cas T King 61, 25 ER 223.
[140] *Maguire* v. *Makaronis* (1997) 188 CLR 449.
[141] That is, an actual rather than potential conflict: *APRA* (2019) 138 ACSR 459 at [78]–[79].
[142] APRA, Prudential Standard SPS 521 (2012, No. 7).
[143] Superannuation Industry (Supervision) Regulations 1994 (Cth), r 2.38(2)(l)-(m)

from the members, but outsourced all trustee functions to related parties in the same corporate group that profited from fees.[144] Of the Commonwealth Bank case study, Hayne concluded:[145]

> One broad theme ran throughout each part of this case study: for each way in which the trustees' conduct was examined, their conduct appeared to be calculated to generate or retain, or weighted in favour of generating or retaining, fees from members, for the trustee's or a related party's own use, in circumstances where that generation or retention was not in members' best interests.

Related-party conflicts not only allow fee extraction by related parties but also affect where funds are invested. An example is the RC case study on ANZ's relationships with third-party investment providers. ANZ offered its superannuation members a platform through which members could select from a menu of options, which included third-party-managed investment schemes.[146] However, for a third party's offerings to be included in the platform a fee had to be paid. Thus, ANZ made $13.7 million from presenting third parties as options for their superannuation members. Hayne identified that this conflict of interest may well have influenced the trustee's choices about what options to include in the platform, which may not have been the best investment options available.[147] Opportunities for fee extraction likely negatively influence minds considering the question of what investments are best for members.

Commissioner Hayne's conclusions on retail fund trustees was damning. He found that trustees generally did not understand what it meant to have a duty to act in the best interests of members and never sought to avoid conflicts of interest, only to manage them, which they did ineffectively.[148] While he concluded that it was not impossible for retail funds to comply with their duties while profit-seeking, he strongly condemned their failure in practice. Frameworks for conflict management that might look effective on paper, and be approved by APRA, were not applied to prioritise members' interests.[149] Hayne determined that (1) disclosure of related-party conflicts was not sufficient, (2) trustees needed to take active measures to ensure that members' interests were prioritised over those of other parties in the corporate group, and (3) the regulators needed to more closely scrutinise the effectiveness of conflict management frameworks.[150]

The damning evidence uncovered in the RC about the behaviour of retail funds does not mean that not-for-profit funds were better at managing conflicts of interest.

144 Hayne, Royal Commission: Final Report, vol 2, pp. 103–159.
145 ibid, p. 101.
146 Hayne, Royal Commission: Final Report, vol 2, p. 251.
147 Hayne, Royal Commission: Final Report, vol 2, pp. 255–257.
148 ibid, vol 1, pp. 225–228.
149 ibid, vol 2, pp. 255–257.
150 ibid, vol 1, pp. 231–232.

Hayne considered examples where conflicts could arise between the interests of members and the interests of the trustee or their shareholder union and employer organisations. For example, Hostplus might not have acted in the best interests of disengaged members when it encouraged them to stay in Hostplus by offering a chance to win a prize.[151] An earlier Royal Commission had found that the Construction, Forestry, Mining and Energy Union had influenced which construction businesses were offered work by their associated Cbus fund.[152] The employer's role in choosing default funds has also incentivised trustees to spend trust funds competing for the employer's nomination, such as by providing sporting tickets and corporate hospitality,[153] which has drawn a legislative response.[154]

What the work of the RC and the PC demonstrates is that the nature of conflicts of interest matters as much as, or more than, their management. The types of conflicts of interest that occur in for-profit funds appear to be more serious and divert more financial value away from the members to other parties.

### 5.3 *APRA* v. *Kelaher*

We have seen that the PC provides evidence of trustee breaches in the aggregate. The RC provides evidence of trustee breaches sufficient for a royal commission. However, these were not legal findings because the purpose of the RC was to identify systemic causes of misconduct rather than remedy particular breaches[155] The final question is whether this evidence can be translated into legal remedies and deterrents. Hayne recommended that the regulators engage in more strategic litigation to enforce the trustees' duties.[156] However, thus far, the key litigation associated with the RC investigations is *APRA* v. *Kelaher*,[157] which demonstrates the difficulty of legal solutions.

In this case, APRA sought the disqualification of corporate trustees, directors, and responsible officers of retail superannuation funds promoted by the IOOF group.[158] The structure of the group included most of the features that had been criticised by Hayne in the RC. First, the two trustee companies were dual-regulated as they also

[151] ibid, vol 2, p. 217.

[152] Dyson Heydon, *Royal Commission into Trade Union Governance and Corruption*, 6 vols. (Final Report, December 2015) vol 3, pp. 467–469.

[153] Productivity Commission, Superannuation, pp. 425, 453–454.

[154] Treasury Laws Amendment (Improving Accountability and Member Outcomes in Superannuation Measures No. 1) Act 2019 (Cth), sch. 9.

[155] Kenneth M. Hayne, *Royal Commission into Misconduct in the Banking, Superannuation and Financial Services Industry*, 2 vols. (Interim Report, 28 September 2018) vol 1, 2.

[156] Hayne, Royal Commission: Final Report, vol 1, p. 234.

[157] *APRA* (2019) 138 ACSR 459.

[158] Other reported cases involving the disqualification of superannuation trustees have been brought by the ATO against SMSF trustees: see, for example, *Re Fitzmaurice and Commissioner of Taxation* (2019) 165 ALD 400.

acted as the responsible entities of distinct managed investment funds, in which the superannuation funds were invested.[159] Hayne recommended complete prohibition of this practice.[160] Second, the directors of the trustees were also directors of other members of IOOF group; they did not even hold separate meetings for the different group entities.[161] Third, the trustees outsourced all their trustee administrative functions, including the employment of responsible officers, to related parties such as IOOF Service Co.[162] Jagot J accepted that this vertically integrated model allowed IOOF group to generate fees at every level.[163]

APRA's case focused on four administrative errors that shared several commonalities.[164] First, the errors occurred in the outsourced administrative operations, including investment management.[165] For example, the Pursuit error involved an undetected fault in an IT platform administered by IOOF Service Co that meant reinvestment instructions were not carried out for some members, leaving their funds in low-return cash accounts.[166] Second, there were delays in detecting the errors, ranging from seven years to two weeks.[167] Third, when noticed, the trustees decided to remedy the errors through compensation from a fund of trust monies reserved to meet operational risks and not to pursue difficult claims against the related parties.[168] Fourth, in response to pressure from APRA, and a whistle-blower,[169] IOOF group either abandoned the compensation plans or replenished the trust reserve funds.[170]

In a scathing decision, Jagot J found APRA had presented a completely inadequate case. It had failed to adduce evidence that a prudent superannuation trustee would have detected the errors earlier, or that there were reasonably arguable cases against related parties that a prudent trustee would have pursued. Several factors contributed to these findings. First, she decided that res ipsa loquitur did not apply so APRA needed to establish exactly how the errors occurred.[171] For example, the Sweep error occurred through IOOF Service Co not implementing the transfer of

159 *APRA* (2019) 138 ACSR 459 at [84].
160 Hayne, Royal Commission: Final Report, vol 1, pp. 228–229.
161 *APRA* (2019) 138 ACSR 459 at [86].
162 ibid at [90], [95].
163 ibid at [85].
164 A fifth allegation did not involve an administrative error but the trustee's refusal to consider the exercise of a discretion to transfer members to a different fund at the request of their employer. This was essentially a claim that acting in the best interests of the members includes a duty to consider transferring those members to another fund: ibid at [798]–[872].
165 ibid at [172]–[183], [469], [662]–[664], [745].
166 ibid at [469]–[485].
167 ibid at [183], [481]–[482], [717], [745].
168 *APRA* (2019) 138 ACSR 459 at [230]–[231], [528]–[529], [697]–[698], [748]
169 ibid at [242].
170 ibid at [391]–[393], [610], [686], [723], [751].
171 ibid at [5].

clients' investment instructions (to 'sweep' cash accounts into investments) alongside the transfer of their accounts to a new investment fund. Although there was evidence that the reinstatement of the sweep instructions had been left off project task lists, the fact that there was no evidence about how this happened was understood as no evidence of a lack of care.[172] Second, she criticised APRA's reliance on IOOF group's internal compliance documentation, which acknowledged breaches, because their conclusions of law were neither admissions nor probative, and their conclusions of fact were too general and assumed knowledge of IOOF's systems that had not been proved.[173] Third, she concluded that APRA sought to disqualify the directors because of decisions that had not been implemented, which was tantamount to complaining of a 'thought-crime'[174] – even though it was APRA's pressure that had halted the implementation. Fourth, regarding APRA's prudential standard on conflicts,[175] in contrast to Hayne's focus on its direction to avoid conflicts where possible,[176] Jagot J's focus was its definition of a conflict as something that had 'significant impact'.[177]

Although APRA's case may well have been deficient, there are several aspects of the decision that are concerning. First, Jagot J dismissed any possibility that IOOF group may have been motivated by profit by referring to the fact that $3.4 million paid in compensation was an exceedingly small fraction of the total members' funds.[178] This is strange as the more relevant comparison would be with IOOF group's profits. Moreover, even if the sum is small, the profit motive could still have a significant impact on decisions as cost-cutting imperatives exist at all levels of corporate management. Second, Jagot J found the decisions not to pursue compensation claims against the related parties were in the best interests of the members because those claims were exceedingly complicated. However, the reason they were so complicated is that, as admitted by the respondents themselves, 'the nature of the contractual obligations is such as to make it inherently difficult to assign responsibility as between the parties to the contract'.[179] However, it was the IOOF group, including trustees, that set those terms. This gives the impression that the trustees escaped accountability by arranging their affairs so that there were no clear lines of responsibility,[180] which itself would not be in the best interests of the members.

[172] *APRA* (2019) 138 ACSR 459 at [682]–[692].
[173] ibid at [4].
[174] ibid at [706].
[175] APRA, Prudential Standard SPS 521.
[176] Hayne, *Royal Commission: Final Report*, vol 1, pp. 227–228.
[177] *APRA* (2019) 138 ACSR 459 at [71], [79].
[178] ibid at [141], [731].
[179] ibid at [111].
[180] ibid at [109].

In conclusion, although this case is unusual given the judge's aversion to how it was pleaded, it does indicate the difficulty that even a dedicated government regulator has in bringing claims against trustees to hold them accountable.

## 6 CONCLUSION

The Australian superannuation system establishes a complex regime for the management of a significant proportion of wealth in Australia. The system has both public and private elements: the state compels the payment of individuals' income to corporate trustees in the private sector, which are regulated by both public agencies and members' private actions. A critical part of this wealth management system is the regulation of trustee decision-making. The examples of death benefit distributions and investment management demonstrate how superannuation law provides more intensive regulation of trustee decisions than standard trust law. Distributive discretions are reviewed under qualified *Karger* v. *Paul* principles that provide heightened accountability controlled by the statutory purpose of aiding those who would have been supported by the deceased's retirement. Investment management is subject to ongoing monitoring and compliance by APRA under the terms of trustees' licences.

The study of wealth management in the superannuation system raises two questions for wealth management through traditional trust law. First, there is a question about the accountability of discretionary trustees. Second, there is a question about the ability of legal duties to ensure positive outcomes for members.

Regarding the first question, superannuation law is an example where trustees are granted a broad discretion over the distribution of benefits with a serious expectation of accountability in how they exercise it. The result is that trustees must exercise the power in close accordance with the purpose for which it was granted. In contrast, those creating domestic discretionary trusts usually do not have this expectation. Settlors typically intend to retain effective control over the trustee's distribution of benefits[181] and to limit accountability to the members.[182] The primary purpose of including discretions is the proprietary consequences – the separation of those intended to benefit from taxable and executable fixed beneficial interests.[183] However, it is the trustee's supposed accountability to the beneficiaries that justifies the proprietary consequences. The question raised by the death benefit discretion is whether genuine accountability, which we can see is possible, ought to be a precondition to the desired proprietary consequences.

181 See Donovan Waters, 'Trusts: Settlor Reserved Powers' (2006) 25 *Estates, Trusts & Pensions Journal* 234.

182 See Adam S. Hofri-Winogradow, 'The Stripping of the Trust: A Study in Legal Evolution' (2015) 65 *University of Toronto Law Journal* 1.

183 See *Schmidt* v. *Rosewood Trust Ltd.* [2003] 2 AC 709 at [34].

Regarding the second question, the analysis of investment management suggests that there are limits on the effectiveness of legal duties in achieving positive outcomes for beneficiaries. The difficulty of enforcing general duties, such as to exercise the care, skill, and diligence of a prudent trustee, demonstrated by *APRA* v. *Kelaher*, suggests that the best that can be expected from them is the avoidance of negative outcomes, not the achievement of positive outcomes. Instead, the difference in outcomes between retail and not-for-profit superannuation trusts suggests that regulatory choices about who can be a trustee, and what incentives they are subject to, may be much more effective at achieving positive outcomes for beneficiaries.

These conclusions suggest that trust law generally should pay more attention to the traditional wisdom that humans are more swayed by self-interested incentives than duty.[184] This is particularly relevant to discretionary trusts where a trustee is the object, like in *Re Marsella (No 2)* and *Karger* v. *Paul*. To impose *Karger* v. *Paul* duties upon a person in such a position of conflict is farcical. Either the trustee should be automatically removed in recognition that compliance with those duties is impossible in such a position of conflict, or it must be concluded that the settlor never intended that duties were to limit the trustee's ability to benefit themselves. As Hayne concluded, 'experience shows that conflicts between duty and interest can seldom be managed; self-interest will almost always trump duty'.[185]

Note: After this chapter was written, the Australian government passed legislation to reform investment governance in two respects.[186] First, APRA has been charged with making annual performance assessments of funds against benchmarks and publishing the results on a public website.[187] If a fund fails to achieve the prescribed standard of performance, they must notify the members.[188] If a fund fails two years consecutively, it must stop enrolling new members.[189] Second, the duty to act in the best interests of members has been amended to the best financial interests and has been specifically stated to apply to payments to third parties.[190] Moreover, in a departure from traditional trust law, trustees are now presumed to have not acted in the best interests of the members until they satisfy an evidential onus.[191] These reforms are promising, but their effectiveness may be limited by their accompanying regulations. First, as allowed by the legislation,[192] the draft regulations prescribe

[184] *Bray* v. *Ford* [1896] AC 44 at 51–52.
[185] Hayne, Royal Commission: Final Report, vol 1, p. 3.
[186] Treasury Laws Amendment (Your Future, Your Super) Act 2021 (Cth).
[187] Superannuation Industry (Supervision) Act 1993 (Cth), s. 60C (as amended).
[188] ibid, s. 60E.
[189] ibid, s. 60F.
[190] ibid, ss. 52(2)(c), 52(3A).
[191] ibid, s. 220A.
[192] ibid, s. 60D(3).

a performance test that measures returns net of administration fees.[193] This means that funds with higher fees, typically retail funds, will be benefited over funds that provide better total returns. Second, the reforms do not apply to all superannuation funds, but only MySuper funds and those prescribed by regulation. For example, the draft regulations specifically exclude funds where the trustee offers members investment products managed by third parties,[194] which are typically retail funds. If the draft regulations come into force, there is a possibility that underperforming retail funds will continue to fail their members.

193 Australian Government Treasury, Exposure Draft: Treasury Laws Amendment (Your Future, Your Super – Addressing Underperformance in Superannuation) Regulations 2021 <treasury.gov.au/consultation/c2021-162375> last accessed 24 June 2021.

194 ibid, reg. 9AB.2(6).

# 13

# Trusts and UWOs

## *Unpacking the 'Holding' Requirement Puzzle*

*Simone Wong*[*]

### 1 INTRODUCTION

In the past few years, there have been significant changes to the law as part of the UK's drive to combat money laundering. The fourth Money Laundering Directive, that is, Directive (EU) 2015/849 (the 4AMLD),[1] of the European Union ('the EU') has been transposed into UK law as the new Money Laundering, Terrorist Financing, and Transfer of Funds (Information on the Payer) Regulations 2017 ('the Money Laundering Regulations 2017'). More recently, the British government has been working on cleaning up UK's reputation as a haven for laundered money. Steps taken include introducing new laws to help strengthen the powers of law enforcement authorities to tackle money laundering as well as their capabilities in recovering the proceeds of crime. No sooner had EU Member States implemented the 4AMLD, amendments were being made by the EU to update the 4AMLD. The new fifth Money Laundering Directive, that is, Directive (EU) 2018/843 ('the 5AMLD'), came into force on 30 May 2018.[2]

Some of the key changes implemented by the 5AMLD undoubtedly affect the trustees and beneficiaries of express trusts. In particular, the increasing call for greater transparency of beneficial ownership information has predictably led to greater alignment of corporate entities and trusts (or similar legal arrangements) under the 5AMLD. One of the key changes brought in by the 5AMLD is the

* Kent Law School.

1 Council Directive (EU) 2015/849 of the European Parliament and of the Council of 20 May 2015 on the prevention of the use of the financial system for the purposes of money laundering or terrorist financing, amending Regulation (EU) No 648/2012 of the European Parliament and of the Council, and repealing Directive 2005/60/EC of the European Parliament and of the Council and Commission Directive 2006/70, OJ 2015 No.L141, 5 June 2015.

2 Council Directive (EU) 2018/843 of the European Parliament and of the Council of 30 May 2018 amending Directive (EU) 2015/849 on the prevention of the use of the financial system for the purposes of money laundering or terrorist financing, and amending Directives 2009/138/EC and 2013/36, OJ 2018 No. L156, 19 June 2018.

requirement for the establishment of a public register of the 'beneficial ownership' of trusts.[3] This reflects the current trend towards greater transparency which promotes increased access to and the sharing of 'beneficial ownership' information by law enforcement and supervisory authorities as well as members of the public with a 'legitimate interest', such as investigative journalists and civil society organisations (e.g. Transparency International and Tax Justice Network).[4] A key argument for transparency is that it will necessarily assist in identifying corrupt and fraudulent individuals who have thus far been able to hide their ill-gotten gains through opaque forms of beneficial ownership in corporate and/or trust structures.

Notwithstanding that the UK left the EU on 31 January 2020, the 5AMLD was implemented in the UK through the enactment of the Money Laundering and Terrorist Financing (Amendment) Regulations 2019 which came into force on 10 January 2020. Even prior to the 5AMLD, a trust that is liable for tax in the UK is required to be registered with HM Revenue and Customs but that register is not accessible to the public. The 2019 Regulations makes no change to that position and there is, at least for the time being, no move to provide public access to any such beneficial ownership register of trusts. Aside from transparency issues of beneficial ownership, a further problem that often plagues money laundering investigations is the lack of evidence. A recent development in the UK that will address this evidential dilemma in part is the introduction of Unexplained Wealth Orders ('UWOs').

The UK added UWOs to its anti-money laundering armoury as part of a broader fight against corruption and money laundering when the Criminal Finances Act 2017 came into force on 31 January 2018. Organisations, such as, Transparency International, have been strong advocates for the introduction of UWOs in the UK. UWOs are intended to be investigative tools which law enforcement authorities may use alongside other civil recovery powers (e.g. the powers of confiscation and seizure of assets provided in the Proceeds of Crime Act 2002) to strip individuals of assets which are the proceeds of their alleged crimes. UWOs enable law enforcement authorities to gather evidence from individuals who may be suspected of benefitting from being involved in or associated with persons who are involved in criminal activities.

As UWOs are governed by civil rather than criminal law, they have the lower evidentiary threshold of 'balance of probabilities' and are therefore potentially powerful

3 The statutory definition of 'beneficial owner' adopted by the 4AMLD has a much wider meaning and includes a person who owns or controls a party on whose behalf a transaction or activity is being conducted: see 4AMLD, Art. 3(6). In the case of trusts, the 'beneficial owner' extends to not only the beneficiaries of an express trust but also the trustee, the settlor, the protector (if any), and other third parties who are able to exercise direct or indirect control over the trust. The latter can therefore include, for example, a donee of a power of appointment.

4 5AMLD, Art. 31(4)(c).

weapons for law enforcement authorities in their fight against crime and money laundering. The lower evidentiary threshold for the grant of UWOs raises in turn the question of how concerned, if at all, trusts should be with the use of UWOs by UK law enforcement authorities. Given the wide scope of UWOs, trustees should be aware of the implications of UWOs on trusts, whether located in or outside of the UK, as well as the potential issues that may arise. Some issues for trusts include, for example, the wide range of persons connected with a trust against whom a UWO may potentially be made, and the extent to which access to – and disclosure of – information relating to the trust are readily available to a UWO respondent in order to provide a satisfactory response to the UWO. The need to provide a satisfactory response to the income requirement may potentially give rise to conflicts relating to the disclosure of confidential trust information and the trustee's obligation to balance the interests of beneficiaries. The disclosure of information may be further complicated by trusts being located offshore where there are stricter confidentiality rules.

This chapter will focus on the amendments made to Proceeds of Crime Act 2002 by the Criminal Finances Act 2017 which are applicable to UWO applications in England and Wales. Due to constraints of space, the paper considers the implications of the inclusion of a 'beneficiary (actual or potential)' within the definition of someone 'holding' trust property under the Criminal Finances Act 2017. The inclusion of not only an actual but also a potential beneficiary suggests the application of the UWOs regime to beneficiaries can be extremely wide. All beneficiaries are potentially caught by the definition of 'hold', regardless of whether or not they have an existing interest in the trust assets. The chapter considers the specific issue of the scope and effect of the holding requirement for trusts, particularly discretionary trusts. The chapter will argue that greater clarity is needed on the meaning of 'beneficiary (actual or potential)' and will make some suggestions for the interpretation of 'hold' in relation to discretionary beneficiaries so that the making of UWOs does not become over-inclusive and impracticable.

## 2 CRIMINAL FINANCES ACT 2017 AND UWOs

### 2.1 *Scope and Nature of UWOs*

The Criminal Finances Act 2017 was enacted to plug gaps in the Proceeds of Crime Act 2002 which often left law enforcement authorities unable to recover or freeze assets suspected of being the proceeds of criminal activity, despite there being reasonable ground to believe specific assets were linked to such nefarious activities. As the Explanatory Notes to the Criminal Finances Act 2017 sets out[5]:

5 Explanatory Notes: Criminal Finances Act 2017, para. 1 <www.legislation.gov.uk/ukpga/2017/22/notes> last accessed 30 May 2019.

> The Criminal Finances Act 2017 makes the legislative changes necessary to give law enforcement agencies new capabilities and powers to recover the proceeds of crime, and to tackle money laundering, corruption and terrorist financing.

By virtue of s. 1 of the Criminal Finances Act 2017, Chapter 2 of Part 8 of the Proceeds of Crime Act 2002 was amended by the insertion of new provisions which include powers to, for example, request information (through UWOs),[6] and ensure money laundering and asset recovery powers extend to investigations under the Terrorism Act 2000 and the Proceeds of Crime Act 2002.[7] Two new corporate offences of failing to prevent tax evasion were also created.[8]

UWOs may be made by the court on the application of a relevant law enforcement authority[9] and are targeted at two particular groups of individuals (the 'UWO respondent'). The first covers someone who is a foreign Politically Exposed Person (PEP).[10] A PEP is defined by s. 362B(7) of the Proceeds of Crime Act 2002 as a person who is or has been entrusted with 'prominent public functions' by an international organisation or a State other than the UK or other European Economic Area State, or a family member of such a person.[11] A PEP also includes a person who is closely associated or connected with such a person. A person would be a close associate of a PEP where he or she has joint beneficial ownership (as defined by the 4AMLD) in legal entities or legal arrangements (e.g. a trust) or any other close business relations with the PEP, or has sole beneficial ownership in legal entity or legal arrangement set up for the de facto benefit of the PEP.[12] The target of UWOs therefore appears to be individuals who are high-net worth foreign PEPs who may be, for instance, kleptocrats who have (mis)used their powers and positions as senior political figures in order to enrich and benefit themselves, their family members and/or those closely associated or connected with them.

The second group of potential UWO respondents are those suspected of being involved in or connected with someone involved in serious crime, whether committed in or outside of the UK.[13] 'Serious crime' includes, for example, the trafficking of drugs, people, and arms; money laundering; fraud; corruption; and bribery.[14] The

6 Criminal Finances Act 2017, Part 1.

7 ibid, Part 2.

8 ibid, Part 3.

9 Proceeds of Crime Act 2002, s. 362A(1). The law enforcement authorities include: the National Crime Agency (NCA); HM Revenue and Customs (HMRC); the Financial Conduct Authority (FCA); the Director of Serious Fraud Office (SFO); and the Director of Public Prosecutions (for England and Wales) and Director of Public Prosecutions for Northern Ireland (for Northern Ireland): see Proceeds of Crime Act 2002, s. 362A(7).

10 ibid, s. 362B(4)(a).

11 'Family member' would include the spouse, children and spouses of the children, and the parents of a PEP: see Proceeds of Crime Act 2002, s. 362B(8); 4AMLD, Art. 3(10). Guidance is further provided on determining whether a person is a close associate in Art. 3(11) of the 4AMLD.

12 4AMLD, Art. 3(11).

13 Proceeds of Crime Act 2002, s. 362B(4)(b).

14 Serious Crime Act 2007, sch 1.

Criminal Finances Act 2017 adopts the same interpretation of 'connected persons' as in s. 1122 of the Corporation Tax Act 2010. One key, and arguably controversial, difference between the two groups is that, in the case of a PEP, there is no requirement for the PEP to be involved in any criminal activity. The potential for UWOs to be made against foreign PEPs is thus status-based.

Once the PEP/serious crime requirement is met, the court has jurisdiction to grant a UWO if it is satisfied that three further requirements provided in the Proceeds of Crime Act 2002 (as amended by the Criminal Finances Act 2017) are also met. First, the court is satisfied that there is reasonable cause to believe that the UWO respondent 'holds' the property ('the holding requirement'). Second, the value of the property (and not the respondent's interest in the property) is £50,000 or more ('the value requirement').[15] Third, there must be reasonable grounds for suspecting that the UWO respondent's known sources of lawfully obtained income would have been insufficient to enable him or her to obtain the property ('the income requirement').[16] The income requirement includes taking into consideration any mortgage, charge or security that may reasonably be available to the respondent for the purposes of obtaining the property and that the property was obtained for market value.[17] UWOs may be granted against property that is either solely owned or jointly held by the UWO respondent with others.[18] The UWO must specify or describe the property in respect of which the order is sought.[19] This suggests that some level of generality is permissible in the description of the property. However, UWOs cannot be used as fishing expeditions to enquire into unidentified assets of the UWO respondent.

The UWO effectively shifts the burden onto the UWO respondent to provide a satisfactory explanation of the origin of the funds used to obtain the property in question. In doing so, the investigative burden of law enforcement authorities is reduced. In addition, the grant of UWOs is non-conviction based, that is, a UWO may be granted without the respondent having been convicted of any criminal wrongdoing or being subject to ongoing criminal proceedings. It follows that UWOs have potentially far-reaching geographical scope. They may be served on overseas companies and trusts,[20] and even where neither the UWO respondent nor the property is in the UK.[21] The orders may be applied retrospectively to property obtained

[15] Proceeds of Crime Act 2002, s. 362B(2). Where the property comprises more than one item of property, the value requirement is met if the combined value of the items of property is more than £50,000.

[16] ibid, s. 362B(3).

[17] ibid, s. 362A(6).

[18] ibid, s. 362B(5)(a).

[19] ibid, s. 362A(2)(a).

[20] ibid, s. 362H(5) (corporate entities incorporated in or outside of the UK); s. 416(7ZA) and Income Tax (Trading and Other Income) Act 2005, s. 620 (meaning of 'settlement' includes settlements wherever made).

[21] The Proceeds of Crime Act 2002 applies to property that is outside of the UK: see Proceeds of Crime Act 2002, ss. 326(9) and 414.

prior to the Criminal Finances Act 2017 coming into force. The court further has jurisdiction to grant interim freezing orders where the law enforcement authorities are able to satisfy the court of the necessity of preventing the respondent or any other person from dealing with the property if it may frustrate any recovery order that may subsequently be made.[22]

UWOs are still in their infancy in the UK and we have not seen a large volume of UWO applications being made by law enforcement authorities since the Criminal Finances Act 2017 came into force. As of December 2018, only three UWOs had been granted in the UK,[23] of which two have been successfully pursued. More UWOs were granted by the High Court in 2019. One case involved UWOs granted in May 2019 in relation to three residential properties in London worth a total of more than £80 million.[24] Another related to the UWOs granted against a Leeds businessman, Mansoor Mahmood Hussain, who the National Crime Agency ('NCA') suspects of being involved in money laundering for major criminal gangs in northern England.[25] It would seem that, as UWOs become more established, law enforcement authorities will gradually be making greater use of them.[26] Although a UWO may be made against PEPs without their being involved in any criminal activity, it is more likely that in most cases the PEPs who are targeted with UWOs will be high-net worth ones who are reasonably suspected of being either directly or indirectly linked to some element of criminal activity (e.g. corruption, fraud, and/or tax evasion).

A case in point is that of Mrs Zamira Hajiyeva.[27] Two UWOs granted in 2018 were made against Mrs Hajiyeva on the basis that she is a PEP, that is, spouse of Mr Hajiyev. Her husband, Jahangir Hajiyev, was the former Chairman of the International Bank of Azerbaijan and is currently serving a fifteen-year prison

[22] Proceeds of Crime Act 2002, s. 362J.

[23] United Kingdom Anti-Corruption Strategy 2017–2022: Year 1 Update, published in December 2018 <www.gov.uk/government/publications/anti-corruption-strategy-year-1-update> last accessed 27 February 2021.

[24] Barney Thompson, 'London properties worth £80m targeted in "dirty money" probe' (Financial Times, 29 May 2019). The three UWOs granted against the respondents in relation to those London properties were on the basis of their being persons 'connected' with a foreign PEP. All the properties were acquired through a network of offshore companies. On appeal by the respondents, the UWOs were discharged on the grounds that the holding, PEP/serious crime and income requirements were not met. See *National Crime Agency* v. *Baker & ors* [2020] EWHC 822 (Admin). As at the time of writing this paper, the NCA said that they would be appealing against the High Court's decision to discharge the three UWOs.

[25] Hussain has since reached a settlement with the NCA to surrender a vast portion of his properties, amounting to £10 million in value: see Dominic Casciani, 'Unexplained Wealth Orders: Suspected money launderer gives up £10m of property' (BBC, 7 October 2020).

[26] Transparency International have identified at least five other cases ripe for the grant of UWOs: see Transparency International, 'Unexplained Wealth Orders: Here's at least 5 cases the Police should consider today!' (31 January 2018) <www.transparency.org.uk/uwo-consider-today/> last accessed 30 May 2019.

[27] *National Crime Agency* v. *Hajiyeva* [2018] EWHC 2534 (Admin), [2018] 1 WLR 5887 (*Hajiyeva*).

sentence for embezzlement, abuse of office, fraud, and other offences. Mrs Hajiyeva received two UWOs, one in respect of a house near Harrods and the other, a golf club in Berkshire. The total purchase price of the two properties is said to be in the region of £22 million. In addition, her conspicuous and extravagant consumption (in)famously included a Gulfstream private jet and a £16 million spending spree in Harrods over a ten-year period. She does not seem to have any, or at least significant, sources of income of her own with which she would have had the means to obtain the properties in question or to maintain her luxurious lifestyle in the UK. The two properties and the private jet were obtained through a network of onshore and offshore companies which, according to the court documents, reveal that her husband is the person who has significant control.[28]

### 2.2 *To Respond or Not to Respond: Consequence of (Non-)Compliance*

Once a UWO is granted by the court, the UWO respondent will be required to explain and provide evidence of the origin of his or her assets which appear to be disproportionate in value to his or her known income.[29] The respondent is required to respond within the period specified in the UWO (the response period)[30] and provide a statement in the form and manner specified in the UWO.[31] The information that the respondent will usually be expected to disclose includes[32]:

1. the nature and extent of his or her interest in the property;
2. how he or she obtained the property;
3. the details of the trust settlement where the property is held by a trustee under such a settlement; and
4. any other information relating to the property as may be specified by the UWO.

Notwithstanding that UWOs are not to be used as fishing expeditions, the respondent may be further required to provide information or documentation to prove the legitimacy of the funds used to obtain the property.

The respondent is not deemed to have complied with the UWO unless all of the requirements imposed by the UWO are complied with.[33] A significant

[28] For more background on the UWO made against Mrs Hajiyeva, see, e.g. Dominic Casciani, 'Zamira Hajiyeva: How the wife of a jailed banker spent £16m in Harrods', BBC, 28 May 2019. Mrs Hajiyeva's appeal against the UWO on the grounds that her husband is not a PEP and that, by definition, she too is not a PEP, was unsuccessful. See *Hajiyeva* v. *National Crime Agency* [2020] EWCA Civ 108.

[29] Proceeds of Crime Act 2002, s. 362A(3) and (5).

[30] ibid, s. 362C(4).

[31] Proceeds of Crime Act 2002, s. 362A(4).

[32] ibid, s. 362A(3)(a)-(d).

[33] Proceeds of Crime Act 2002, s. 362D(7). There is an added point that may be useful to note but is beyond the scope of this paper. Given the focus of the Criminal Finances Act 2017 on foreign PEPs, there is the question of whether PEPs in the foreign diplomatic service who enjoy personal and/or

consequence of the respondent's non-compliance is that it raises the presumption that the property is 'recoverable property' in any subsequent civil recovery proceedings. In other words, the property is deemed to be the product of criminal activity and therefore vulnerable to civil recovery proceedings.[34] In addition, the Criminal Finances Act 2017 imposes criminal liability on a UWO respondent who makes false or misleading statements, or recklessly makes false or misleading statements, when purportedly complying with the requirements of the UWO.[35]

Upon compliance with a UWO, the law enforcement authority has to determine whether any further enforcement or investigatory proceedings are to be taken. If an IFO is in place, that determination has to be made within sixty days of compliance. If the relevant authority decides that no further proceedings are to be taken, the authority is required to notify the court of its decision as soon as reasonably practicable, and in any event by the end of the sixty-day period.[36] Where no IFO has been made, a decision by the law enforcement authority to take any further enforcement or investigatory proceedings may be taken at any time. In other words, a decision not to take further enforcement or investigatory proceedings does not prevent such proceedings being taken subsequently where new information comes to light.[37]

## 3 UWOs AND THE 'HOLDING' REQUIREMENT: ISSUES FOR TRUSTS

Of the three requirements needed for the grant of a UWO (viz., the holding requirement, the value requirement, and the income requirement), the holding requirement may raise particular concerns for trusts. Given the broad definition of 'hold' adopted by the Criminal Finances Act 2017, the holding requirement has the potential to capture a wide range of persons who have very different types of interests in the trust. A deeper analysis of the meaning of 'holding' trust property for the purposes of UWOs – and, more particularly, what it means to 'hold' and when one can be taken to 'hold' trust property – is therefore needed. Relatedly, construing 'potential' beneficiaries as 'holding' property may be problematic in the context of a discretionary trust. Clearer guidance is thus needed on the meaning of 'beneficiary (actual or potential)' so that there is greater clarity of when UWOs may be made and against whom. This section will separate out the analysis of the holding requirement into three components, namely, the 'who', 'what', and 'when' of 'holding' trust

functional immunity will be able to claim such immunity as a way of avoiding compliance with a UWO. The issue did not arise in the *Hajiyeva* case since neither Mrs Hajiyeva nor her husband enjoyed personal or functional immunity but the immunity point may need further clarification in the Criminal Finances Act 2017.

34 Proceeds of Crime Act 2002, s. 362C.

35 ibid, s. 362E(1) and (2). The offence is punishable on conviction to imprisonment up to two years and/or a fine.

36 ibid, s. 362D(2)-(4).

37 ibid, s. 362D(5)-(6).

property. The aim is to provide some tentative conclusions about the sort of guidance that may be useful to the interpretation of a 'potential' beneficiary in the case of discretionary trusts.

### 3.1 *The 'Who' of Holding Trust Property*

For the purposes of UWOs, the Criminal Finances Act 2017 uses the term 'hold' instead of other terms, such as, 'own', to describe the types of interest-holder one has to be. The 2017 Act goes on to clarify that the situations in which a person (P) is taken to 'hold' property include the following[38]:

1. where P has effective control over the property;
2. where P is the trustee of a settlement in which the property is comprised;
3. where P is a beneficiary (whether actual or potential) in relation to such a settlement.

The above clarification indicates that there is scope for treating persons who do not have any formal rights but who can exercise control over specific trust assets and/or the operation of the trust, particularly the trustee's decision-making, in relation to such assets as an indication of 'holding' that property for the purposes of UWOs.[39] This suggests that having formal proprietary rights in the property is not a prerequisite and that the holding requirement takes a more pragmatic approach to determining whether the property in question is or is not within the de facto control of an individual. 'Effective control' over the property is not specifically defined in the Criminal Finances Act 2017 but it may be reasonably assumed that the courts will adopt a broad interpretation. In the context of a trust, 'effective control' is likely to refer to a person's ability to exercise direct or indirect control over an asset in terms of, for instance, allocation, possession or use of the asset. Indirect control may be exercised through having control over the exercise of a trustee's discretion and powers under the trust. To help provide a better understanding of the notion of 'control', we may further draw assistance from regulation 6(2) of the Money Laundering Regulations 2017 which provides that, in relation to a person who has control over the trust[40]:

> 'control' means a power (whether exercisable alone, jointly with another person or with the consent of another person) under the trust instrument or by law to—
>
> a) dispose of, advance, lend, invest, pay or apply trust property;
> b) vary or terminate the trust;

[38] Proceeds of Crime Act 2002, s. 362H(2)(a)-(c).
[39] ibid, s. 362H(2)(a).
[40] The Money Laundering, Terrorist Financing and Transfer of Funds (Information on the Payer) Regulations 2017 (SI 2017 No. 692).

c) add or remove a person as a beneficiary or to or from a class of beneficiaries;
d) appoint or remove trustees or give another individual control over the trust;
e) direct, withhold consent to or veto the exercise of a power mentioned in sub-paragraphs (a) to (d).

Given the broad notion of 'control', someone like the settlor may be treated as 'holding' the trust property where he has effective control of the trust by reserving powers to himself under the trust or using letters of wishes to control the trustee's decision-making.[41] Likewise, there is potential for others, such as, a protector and a donee of a power of appointment, to be caught even though they do not have any legal or equitable proprietary interest in the trust assets.

'Holding trust property' also extends to those with equitable rights under the trust, regardless of whether the equitable rights have vested or not, or interests tantamount to proprietary interests in the trust property. There are parallels between the above clarification and the statutory definition used in other anti-money laundering legislation, such as, the Money Laundering Regulations 2017, for reporting beneficial ownership information of a trust. The rationale for including trustees and beneficiaries under the umbrella of 'beneficial owners' is to ensure that anti-money laundering legislation, including the Criminal Finances Act 2017, apply not only to those with legal but also equitable interests in the trust assets.[42] The upshot is that there is a conflation of the rights of trustees and beneficiaries as 'beneficial owners' who 'hold' trust property for the purposes of a UWO application. From a policy perspective, one can appreciate the reason for the Criminal Finances Act 2017 adopting a wide interpretation of 'beneficiary'. A wide interpretation will avoid the problem of under-inclusion and will enable the net to be cast as wide as possible in order to prevent PEPs and those involved in criminal activities from hiding their interests in property behind the veil of trusts, particularly discretionary trusts.

However, the conflation of actual and potential beneficiaries in relation to trust assets for the purposes of the holding requirement in the Criminal Finances 2017 Act is problematic. It fails to appreciate the differences between the rights that actual and potential beneficiaries have under the trusts and in relation to the trust assets. For the purposes of this chapter, I focus on the beneficiaries of a discretionary trust ('the discretionary beneficiary'). While the discretionary beneficiaries may have equitable rights under the trust, they are not normally treated as having any

41 For a fuller discussion of the issues arising from the use of reserved-powers trusts and concerns about settlors' control over such trusts, see L. Ho, '"Breaking Bad": Settlors' Reserved Powers', in R. C. Nolan, K. F. K. Low, and H. W. Tang (eds), *Trusts and Modern Wealth Management* (Cambridge: Cambridge University Press, 2018), p. 34.

42 Proceeds of Crime Act 2002, s. 362H.

equitable proprietary interest in the trust property until the trustee exercises his or her discretion to distribute the trust property to them.[43] In the light of this, it is necessary to gain a better understanding, if not clarity, of the nature of the beneficiary's equitable interest in the trust property in order for the holding requirement to be met. We should probe deeper as to what rights exactly a beneficiary holds, or should at least hold, in relation to the trust property in order to justify making a UWO. More careful analysis and clarification is needed, especially when non-compliance with a UWO attracts severe penalties, such as, imprisonment. In the case of discretionary trusts, merely being a member of a class of objects who may potentially benefit is arguably over-inclusive and should not be enough to meet the holding requirement. Given the very nature of a discretionary trust is the discretion given to the trustee in the distribution or allocation of trust assets, that discretion may not necessarily be exercised in favour of a particular beneficiary. There should be a sufficient nexus between the discretionary beneficiary and a particular piece of trust property before the beneficiary may appropriately be subject to a UWO, which we turn to in the next section.

### 3.2 *The 'What' of Holding Trust Property*

As legal title to the trust property vests in the trustee, it is uncontroversial that the trustee may be treated as 'holding' trust property for the purposes of UWOs. This is notwithstanding that the trustee is not entitled to the benefit of all the rights relating to the assets as a legal owner. The inclusion of a beneficiary as a person who 'holds' the property may not, at first blush, seem controversial either. This may be no more than a reiteration of the principle that a beneficiary has equitable rights under the trust. The concept of 'holding property', however, seems to suggest that there should be some proprietary nexus to, or at least some benefit derived from, the trust assets. By providing that a beneficiary, whether actual or potential, will be taken to 'hold' property, the Criminal Finances Act 2017 treats the nature of the equitable interests of *all* beneficiaries as similar regardless of the type of trust in question. Put differently, beneficiaries of, say, a fixed, discretionary or protective trust, are taken to hold exactly the same rights as equitable (proprietary) owners of the trust assets. In doing so, the rights of beneficiaries are placed on a similar footing with not only the rights of trustees as legal owners but also inter se regardless of the type of trust in question. While some aspects of the beneficiary's equitable interest may be described as being proprietary in nature, it is quite another matter to equate that interest to ownership. Given the wide scope for UWOs to apply to beneficiaries of both fixed and discretionary trusts, the issue of what exactly the beneficiary 'holds' for the purposes of making a UWO needs to be probed further so that the grant of UWOs can be made in a principled manner.

43 See *Gartside* v. *IRC* [1968] AC 553; *Sainsbury* v. *IRC* [1970] Ch 712.

Where property is held on trust, the law clearly recognises that the beneficiary has an equitable interest in the trust property. As Aitkens LJ states in *Williams* v. *Central Bank of Nigeria*[44]:

> [I]n English law an express trust is created when a person (the settlor) directs that certain identified property (the trust property) will be held either by him or by others (as trustees) under a legal obligation which binds the trustees to deal with that property, which is owned by them as a separate fund, for the benefit of another (the beneficiary) who has an *equitable proprietary interest* in the trust property and its fruits from the moment it is created. [emphasis added]

Notwithstanding that the beneficiary's interest is often loosely described as an equitable proprietary one, the exact nature of that equitable interest is harder to pin down since it cannot be neatly classified as being either proprietary or personal in nature. Labelling the beneficiary as 'beneficial owner', as the statutory definition does in, for instance, the Money Laundering Regulations 2017, does not mean that all beneficiaries, actual and potential, have a proprietary interest in the trust property and even when they do, that they have the same rights to property as those of a legal owner.[45]

In some cases, the beneficiary's equitable interest is considered as giving rise to rights that are personal in nature, for example, the right to ensure proper administration of the trust, and the right to trust documents. Maitland, for instance, has characterised the beneficiary's interest under the trust as being personal rather than proprietary in nature.[46] Contemporary academic commentators take a less rigid view of the beneficiary's equitable interest. Virgo, for example, states that it is preferable to see the beneficiary's equitable interest as 'a compendium of rights relating to a particular asset [the trust property]'.[47] The beneficiary's interest in the trust therefore refers to the legal relations that the beneficiary has with the trustee and the trust property. Virgo adds that these legal relations provide the beneficiary with some interest in the trust, more particularly, the economic benefit of the trust property. That interest in turn gives rise to certain rights and obligations. In a similar vein, Nolan describes the equitable interests of beneficiaries as a 'repackaging and bundling of rights' and that these rights include the 'rights to benefit from assets, hopes of so benefitting, rights to recover misappropriated assets and rights to enjoy trustees' management of trusts assets'.[48]

44 *Williams* v. *Central Bank of Nigeria* [2013] EWCA Civ 785 at [37].

45 S. Wong, 'The New EU Anti-Money Laundering Directive: Farewell to transparency of UK trusts' (2018) 31(3) *Trust Law International* 137.

46 F. W. Maitland, *Equity – Also the Forms of Action in Common Law - Two Courses of Lectures* (Cambridge: Cambridge University Press, 1929), Lectures IX – XI.

47 G. Virgo, *The Principles of Equity and Trusts* (3rd ed, Oxford: Oxford University Press, 2018), pp. 44–45.

48 R. C. Nolan, 'Equitable Property' (2006) 122 *Law Quarterly Review* 232 at 254.

Penner, on the other hand, argues that the beneficiary's interest in the trust takes the form of a chose in equity, which means that: 'the [beneficiaries] have no direct ownership of the trust fund: they have rights *in personam* against the trustee that he carry out the terms of the trust so that the benefits of the trust property are distributed to them accordingly'.[49] However, unlike the purely personal nature of a legal chose in action, Penner acknowledges that there are proprietary elements to the beneficiary's chose in equity.[50] These proprietary elements have from time to time been acknowledged in case law.[51] A notable example of the proprietary aspect of the beneficiary's equitable interest is the restriction placed on a trustee, albeit the legal owner, in not being able to use the trust property for his own benefit or purposes. Another is that the trust property must also be kept separate from the rest of the trustee's estate and is not available to his creditors. A beneficiary further has a general right to use the trust property and, correspondingly, to exclude non-beneficiaries from using or having access to the trust property. There is abroad consensus that a beneficiary's equitable rights may therefore comprise personal and proprietary rights. The more complex issue, however, is whether those proprietary rights are sufficient to make that equitable interest similar to ownership.

The beneficiary's right to exclude others who are non-beneficiaries from drawing any benefit from the trust property or its fruits is one of the key features that makes the beneficiary's equitable interest a property right.[52] As Nolan puts it, the beneficiary's interest is proprietary because of its exclusionary aspects: 'it involves rights both to exclude others from access to assets, whether or not they consented to such exclusion, as well as some claim to possible benefit from such assets'.[53] However, the beneficiary's proprietary rights are distinguishable and different from the rights of ownership as the former is not binding against everyone and is subject to certain exceptions. In particular, the beneficiary's equitable interest does not bind a bona fide purchaser for value without notice.[54] Notwithstanding that beneficiaries are often described as the equitable 'owners' of trust property, they have lesser rights than a legal owner. Virgo aptly describes these 'lesser rights' as 'modified proprietary rights' as they do not have the same characteristics of and are subsidiary to legal proprietary rights of ownership, as reflected by the exceptions that apply to them.[55]

49 J. Penner, *The Idea of Property in Law* (Oxford: Oxford University Press, 1997), p. 134.

50 ibid, p. 135.

51 See, e.g. tracing cases such as *Foskett* v. *McKeown* [2001] 1 AC 102 at 128 where Lord Millett refers to the tracing process as one which enables a beneficiary to trace or follow his 'property'.

52 For a fuller analysis of the 'right of exclusive use' aspect of the beneficiaries' proprietary rights, see Nolan, 'Equitable Property'; Penner, 'The Idea of Property in Law'.

53 Nolan, 'Equitable Property', 236.

54 See G. Virgo, 'The Principles of Equity and Trusts', p. 48; Penner, 'The Idea of Property in Law', p. 137.

55 Virgo, 'The Principles of Equity and Trusts', pp. 50–51.

The extent to which a beneficiary can be said to have equitable proprietary rights in the trust property further depends on the type of trust, that is, whether the trust is fixed or discretionary. In the case of fixed trusts, the orthodox position is that the beneficiary of a fixed trust ('the fixed beneficiary') does have an equitable proprietary interest in the trust property.[56] The nature of the beneficiary's interest under a discretionary trust ('the discretionary beneficiary') is more complicated. The discretionary beneficiary is normally described as having mainly personal rights against the trustee to ensure that the trust is managed properly and in good faith in accordance with the terms of the trust.[57] These personal rights include the proper consideration and exercise of the trustee's discretion and any powers of appointment given to him or her.[58] Consequently, a discretionary beneficiary is no more than a *potential beneficiary* and merely has an equity to be considered by the trustee. He or she cannot be said to have an interest in, or a benefit from, the trust property until the trustee exercises the discretion in his or her favour.[59] A further reason for not treating a discretionary beneficiary's equitable rights as proprietary rights is due to the non-transmissibility of those rights.[60] This is notwithstanding that a discretionary beneficiary's interests in the trust property can provide a sufficient proprietary base to bring a claim against third parties who have misappropriated trust property, which is a characteristic of proprietary rights.[61]

Reference to a 'potential' beneficiary in the definition of 'hold' means that a UWO can technically be made against a discretionary beneficiary even when the trustee has not exercised his discretion in his or her favour and the beneficiary has not received any benefits from the trust property. The discretionary beneficiary's equity to be considered *per se* seems sufficient to make him or her a holder of proprietary rights in the trust assets for the purposes of UWOs. This wider definition of a beneficiary's equitable interest is reinforced by s. 362B(6)(e) of the Proceeds of Crime Act 2002, as inserted the Criminal Finances Act 2017, which provides that:

> where the property is an interest in other property comprised in a settlement, the reference to the respondent obtaining the property is to be taken as if it were a reference to the respondent obtaining *direct ownership of such share in the settled property as relates to, or is fairly represented by, that interest.* [emphasis added]

The wide definition of 'hold' therefore appears to extend beyond situations in which the beneficiary is traditionally seen as having equitable proprietary rights in the trust

56 *Westdeutsche Landesbank Girozentrale* v. *Islington London Borough Council* [1996] AC 669 at 705 (Lord Browne-Wilkinson).

57 *Armitage* v. *Nurse* [1998] Ch 241 at 253 (Millett LJ).

58 Where the trustee fails to exercise their discretion or exercises it in breach of trust, the beneficiaries can apply to the court. See, e.g. *McPhail* v. *Doulton* [1971] AC 424 at 456–457 (Lord Wilberforce).

59 *Gartside* [1968] AC 553; *Sainsbury* [1970] Ch 712.

60 *Schmidt* v. *Rosewood Trust Ltd* [2003] 2 AC 709 at [51]–[52] (Lord Walker).

61 Nolan, 'Equitable Property', 256–257.

property. The potential for UWOs to be made against a discretionary beneficiary in the absence of getting any benefit from the trust assets seems to conflict with cases, which support the view that such a beneficiary does not have an interest in the trust property. As Nolan points out, the beneficiary cannot be seen as holding proprietary rights in the trust assets in relation to the positive right of benefit from assets. This is notwithstanding that the discretionary beneficiary's negative exclusionary right does have proprietary elements in a general sense.[62] Furthermore, identifying what a discretionary beneficiary's equitable proprietary interest is and in what proportions to the trust assets can be further complicated by the size of the class of objects of the discretionary trust, which can be fairly wide.[63] While the UWO regime is still in its infancy, greater clarification of what is meant by 'beneficiary (actual or potential)' for the purposes of the holding requirement is to be welcomed. A possible way of (re)interpreting the meaning of 'hold' is to consider not only 'what' a beneficiary holds but, more importantly, 'when' he or she can be taken to 'hold' property, which we turn to next.

### 3.3 *The 'When' of Holding Trust Property: Some Thoughts*

Given that the use of UWOs is still in its infancy, there is limited case law to assist us in ascertaining the judicial approach to interpreting the holding requirement in the case of a discretionary beneficiary who may potentially but may not necessarily ever receive any benefit under the trust. The case of *Hajiyeva* may shed some insight on how the holding requirement may be interpreted with respect to a discretionary beneficiary. Mrs Hajiyeva's application for the discharge of the UWO had more to do with the issues of whether she fell within the definition of a PEP and had control over the company which owned the properties subject to the UWO. She was further a beneficiary under discretionary trust set up by her husband. In response to the question of Mrs Hajiyeva's rights as a discretionary beneficiary in the trust property, it is useful to note the following comments from Supperstone J:

> merely a member of a class to whom the trustees have a discretion to apply trust capital or income, has no interest [for the purposes of Article 1 of Protocol 1] in the narrow sense. […] and *an object of a discretionary trust has no proprietary interest in the trust assets or capital* [emphasis added].[64]

If a discretionary beneficiary neither 'owns' nor has an interest in the trust assets until the trustee exercises his discretion in favour of that beneficiary, equating the discretionary beneficiary's equitable rights to proprietary rights before such

[62] ibid, 256. *Gartside* [1968] AC 553 is a case in point where the lack of benefit flowing to the discretionary beneficiary led the court to hold that the beneficiary had no interest.

[63] *McPhail* [1971] AC 424 is the classic authority for the possibility of a valid discretionary trust to be set up even when the class of objects is large provided that the objects satisfy the 'is or is not' test and is not so wide as to be administratively unworkable.

[64] *Hajiyeva* [2018] EWHC 2534 (Admin) at [98].

discretion has been exercised is misleading. A proprietary nexus between the discretionary beneficiary and the property in question must be found in order for the holding requirement to be met and for a UWO to be granted.

From a policy perspective, one may argue that a broad approach is needed for anti-money laundering purposes, especially when the trust structure makes it possible for property to be held by trustees for a wide range of individuals or collectivities as beneficiaries. However, that may lead to an over-inclusion of beneficiaries as potential UWO respondents. If, as discussed above, a discretionary beneficiary does not have any proprietary interest in the trust property, it is argued that 'what' the beneficiary 'holds' for the purposes of UWOs should depend on 'when' he or she can be taken to 'hold' property, which may not necessarily mean having proprietary rights in a strict sense. This reasoning builds on Cotterrell's argument that, contrary to the view that only trustees hold power in a trust relationship, beneficiaries are not necessarily wholly passive and that they lack access to property-power.[65]

The main thrust of Cotterrell's thesis is that beneficiaries have property-power which goes unrecognised because the trust form allows for a 'commonsense (ideological) conception of ownership' to be extended beyond the basic bilateral relationship between owner and the thing owned.[66] A description of beneficiaries as 'owners' based on a conventional notion of 'ownership' is inappropriate since it seeks to conceptualise beneficiaries as having direct proprietary rights to the trust assets. The trust in fact enables the nature and range of owners of property and what can be owned to be extended. Cotterrell argues that the trust form enables the fluid nature of equitable interests to mask the indirect equitable rights of beneficiaries, including large collectivities such as discretionary beneficiaries, to the abstract value of the trust assets, rather than in specific assets.[67] The trust form therefore allows the beneficiary to be conceptualised as someone lacking in power and requiring protection against the abuse of the trustee's potential power. The beneficiary's property-power, Cotterrell argues, is in fact reinforced as no obligations are imposed on the beneficiary in relation to the operation and the management of the trust while obligations are owed (principally by the trustee) to the beneficiary because of his or her equitable entitlement.[68]

We might instead re-focus on the power that beneficiaries can potentially exert in the light of their indirect link to the abstract value of the trust assets. The existence of equitable proprietary rights in the assets is thus not a prerequisite. Cotterrell's property-power analysis provides a useful basis for reflecting more critically on the

65 R. Cotterrell 'Power, Property and the Law of Trusts: A Partial Agenda for Critical Legal Scholarship' (1987) 14(1) *Journal of Law and Society* 77.

66 ibid, 85. The commonsense (ideological) conception of property refers to the conceptualisation of a 'person' owning a 'thing' whereby a direct link between owner and assets can be made.

67 Cotterrell, 'Power, Property and the Law of Trusts', 86.

68 ibid, 87–88.

question of when a discretionary beneficiary can be said to exercise sufficient power over the trust (and relatedly, the maintenance and/or use of the abstract value represented by the trust assets) so as to be treated as 'holding' those assets or its fruits. In that respect, it is argued that there are three situations where the discretionary beneficiary may be treated as 'holding' the assets in question for the purposes of UWOs.

The first is when a discretionary beneficiary actually receives benefits from the trust property, for example, a distribution of income or capital, or rent-free use of trust property; he or she should be taken to 'hold' that property. The rationale for this may be drawn from the approach taken in the taxation of payments made to a beneficiary for his or her benefit, or as an allowance at the trustee's discretion, including the rent-free right of occupation of properties held by the trust.[69] In such cases, the discretionary beneficiary's position is similar to a fixed beneficiary. The beneficiary can be taken to have equitable proprietary interests in the property represented by those benefits since a direct nexus can be made between the two. However, the risk in limiting the notion of a discretionary beneficiary 'holding' trust property to these situations may arguably undermine the use of UWOs. There is also an element of tautology since we revert to a discourse of proprietary rights and of the beneficiary having interests in the assets *per se*. One undesired consequence is that criminal proceeds can then be hidden behind discretionary trusts without the fear of a UWO ever being made provided that no benefits from the trust are actually distributed to a discretionary beneficiary.

To counter the concern with under-inclusion, a discretionary beneficiary may be taken to 'hold' property in two other situations due to the beneficiary's ability to exert more direct interference with the management of the trust. 'Holding' of trust property in these situations is based on the combined effect of the beneficiary's equitable rights under the trust and control over the trust. The first is where there is a strong likelihood that the trustee will exercise his discretion in favour of that beneficiary. Here, assistance may be drawn from family law cases where the family court judges have had to grapple with determining the extent to which trust assets can be treated as the financial resources of a spouse who is a discretionary beneficiary. In these family cases, the courts have sometimes treated the trust assets as the discretionary beneficiary's financial resources when the trustee may make distributions to that spouse-beneficiary from time to time and/or is very likely to look favourably upon any request to make a distribution to him or her. The extent to which trust assets may form part of the spouse's financial resources depends on various factors, for example, the trust deed, any letters of wishes given by the settlor to the trustees and the pattern of distribution by the trustees over the years.[70]

69 See *Gartside* [1968] AC 553.

70 *Browne* v. *Browne* [1989] 1 FLR 291; *Thomas* v. *Thomas* [1996] 2 FCR 544; *Charman* v. *Charman (No 4)* [2007] EWCA Civ 503. See also M. Harper and others, *International Trust and Divorce Litigation* (Bristol: Jordans, 2013), p. 129.

The point here is that, notwithstanding that a discretionary beneficiary may not yet receive any benefits from the trust, it is not an obstacle to those trust assets or benefits being treated as the beneficiary's assets which are available for redistribution between the spouses.[71] In these cases, the discretionary beneficiary is often able to exercise power or influence over the trustee's decision-making. This does not necessarily mean that all objects of the discretionary trust will fall within this category. The treatment of trust assets as the financial resources of the discretionary beneficiary hinges on his or her 'reasonable expectation' of receiving a distribution of assets and/or benefits from the trust.[72] The extent to which trust assets should be seen as the financial resources of a discretionary beneficiary so that the beneficiary may appropriately be treated as 'holding' those trust assets will depend on the facts of each case. The treatment of trust assets as financial resources provides space for trust assets to be treated as if they belong to a discretionary beneficiary even when the beneficiary's interests have not been vested and are contingent.[73] A nexus can thus be established between the discretionary beneficiary and the trust assets so that the assets can be said to be held for the de facto benefit of that discretionary beneficiary. The discretionary beneficiary can thus be treated as 'holding' the relevant assets for the purposes making UWOs.

The other possibility of treating a discretionary beneficiary as holding trust assets, even when no benefits have been received from the trust, is where he or she is able to exercise effective control over the trust and the trustee's exercise of discretion. This may include situations where the discretionary trust may be a sham, and the trust assets in fact belong to the discretionary beneficiary absolutely and form part of his or her resources.[74] In other words, the discretionary trust is a 'mere pretence'; it lacks substance or is not what it purports to be.[75] A trust may be a sham when the settlor and the trustee do not intend to act on the terms of the trust, or the trustee is a party to the sham by going along with the settlor's intention of creating a sham trust. Matthews gives two examples of sham trusts.[76] The first is where the settlor's intention is not for the trustee to hold the trust assets for the benefit of the named

71 For further discussion on when trust assets may be treated as financial resources of one of the parties to a marriage, see S. Wong, 'Tapping into Trust Assets for Redistribution upon Divorce in England and Wales' in R. C. Nolan, K. F. K. Low, and H. W. Tang (eds), *Trusts and Modern Wealth Management* (Cambridge: Cambridge University Press, 2018), p. 340.

72 *Charman* [2007] EWCA Civ 503; *A* v. *A* [2007] EWHC 99 (Fam); *SR* v. *CR* [2008] EWHC 2329 (Fam); *Whaley* v. *Whaley* [2012] 1 FLR 735; *Tchenguiz-Imerman* v. *Imerman* [2014] 2 FLR 939.

73 *C* v. *C (Ancillary Relief: Trust Fund)* [2010] 1 FLR 337.

74 For an explanation of the meaning of a 'sham' transaction, see *Snook* v. *London and West Riding Investments Ltd* [1967] 2 QB 786 at 802 (Diplock LJ); *Shalson* v. *Russo* [2003] EWHC 1637 (Ch), [2005] Ch 281; *Prest* v. *Petrodel Resources Ltd* [2013] 2 AC 415. For arguments made about sham trusts, see, for example, *Minwalla* v. *Minwalla and ors* [2004] EWHC 2823 (Fam).

75 Wong, Tapping into Trust Assets, pp. 349–352; P. Matthews, 'The Sham Trust Argument, and How to Avoid It' (2007) 21(4) *Trust Law International* 191.

76 Matthews, 'The Sham Trust Argument, and How to Avoid It'.

beneficiaries but rather for his own benefit or the benefit of other persons nominated by him or her ('sham in fact'). The other is where the trustee holds the trust assets as the settlor's nominee ('partial sham'). In these situations, the intention to create a trust is absent, and the settlor (who may also be a discretionary beneficiary) retains control over the trust and uses the trust structure as a way of obscuring the true beneficial ownership of the trust assets.

A common thread in these three situations is the element of control that the discretionary beneficiary has over the management of the trust and/or the trust assets. Even where the discretionary beneficiary, strictly speaking, has not received any benefits from the trust, the discretionary beneficiary should rightly be treated as 'holding' trust property for the purposes of UWOs where, in reality, he or she is able to exert control over the management of the trust and the distribution of benefits from the trust. In such cases, the discretionary beneficiary is not merely an object of the discretionary trust but rather the de facto beneficiary.

## 4 CONCLUSION

UWOs may raise concerns for trusts due to the wide definition used to describe who may be treated as holding the property for which the UWO is sought. In relation to trusts, the term 'beneficiary (actual or potential)' is in itself a broad description of the different types of beneficiaries who have very different rights in the trust. The notion of a beneficiary's equitable interest in the trust further encompasses a bundle of rights that may be personal and proprietary in nature. The Criminal Finances Act 2017, however, provides little guidance on the meaning of the notion of 'hold'. Thus, it is not particularly clear which precise rights of a beneficiary are essential for the purposes of the holding requirement. One possible construction is that 'hold' refers to a general, if not loose, sense of 'beneficial ownership' (as statutorily defined) of the trust. Another is that involves having some equitable *proprietary* rights in the trust assets. However, both constructions may be problematic for discretionary beneficiaries since they are not traditionally seen to hold proprietary rights to the trust property, at least not until the trustee exercise his or her discretion in their favour.

Policy considerations may dictate that a liberal interpretation of a beneficiary's equitable interest, whether under a fixed or a discretionary trust, is used for the purposes of UWOs. However, it is hard for such a liberal interpretation to be squared with the existing doctrinal understandings of a discretionary beneficiary's interest in the trust property. To do so will lead to greater confusion both at a doctrinal level as well as in the operation of UWOs. It is therefore necessary to clarify when a 'potential' beneficiary (such as, a discretionary beneficiary whose hopes are to get some benefits from the trust) may be treated as having sufficient interest in the trust property and can be said to 'hold' it. This would avoid not only the UWO legislation from being over-inclusive but also concerns of limiting the effectiveness of UWOs as an investigative tool.

One clear case where a discretionary beneficiary may be rightly treated as holding trust property is when he or she in fact has received a distribution or benefits from the trust. The alternative is to focus on substance rather than form in order to determine the exercise of power by a discretionary beneficiary. Two possible situations come to mind. The first situation where the trust assets may be treated as the discretionary beneficiary's assets is when he or she is able to exercise control or influence over the trustee's decision-making, and ensure that that discretion is very likely to be exercised in his or her favour, should a request be made. The other is where the discretionary trust is a sham and the settlor has never genuinely intended the trust to operate in accordance with its terms. In both situations, the main reasons for treating the discretionary beneficiary as 'holding' the trust property are the beneficiary's ability to exercise control over the trust and his or her being the de facto beneficiary

It is presently unclear how the courts are likely to interpret 'beneficiary (actual or potential)' for the purposes of the holding requirement. It may be equally useful for law enforcement authorities, such as Her Majesty's Revenue and Customs and the National Crime Agency, to provide clearer guidance. In the interim, it is hoped that the suggestions made in this chapter will go some way in providing such guidance and enable UWOs to be applied in a more principled manner. Outside of the situations discussed in this chapter, it may be harder to treat the discretionary beneficiary as 'holding' the trust property. In those instances, the better respondent of a UWO may be either the trustee or the person[77] who has 'effective control' as per s. 362H(3) of the Proceeds of Crime Act 2002.

77 For example, the settlor who has reserved powers that allows him or her to effectively control the trust's management and the trustee's decision-making.

# 14

# Constructive Trusts on Express Trusts

## *Principles under Threat*

*Jessica Palmer*[*]

### 1 INTRODUCTION

There has, in modern times, been a growing focus on trust validity, particularly in the light of increasing settlor control.[1] Powers retained by settlors (or bestowed on non-trustee appointors) include, for example, powers to appoint and remove trustees and/or beneficiaries; powers to direct trustees to act; powers to veto trustees' decisions and powers of revocation.[2] While these powers are usually non-dispositive, they are nevertheless significant because of the degree of control they confer on the holder to affect the affairs of the trust. These trusts have been met with a measure of popular suspicion. More often than not, however, when they have been challenged, courts have tended to a formalist approach, preferring a trust's validity in the absence of compelling evidence of an intention to deceive or to construct a facade. Courts have shown a reticence to consider the purpose or object of a trust as relevant to its legitimacy.[3]

This has had particular relevance in New Zealand which features a high number of discretionary trusts and an increasing appetite for drafting into trust deeds mechanisms for the retention of settlor control. With limited statutory look-through provisions currently available to provide recourse for creditors and spouses or de facto partners of the settlor, challenges of two different kinds have been increasingly mounted.

* University of Otago.

[1] *In re Esteem Settlement* [2003] JLR 188, [2004] 1 WTLR 1 (Jersey); *A* v. *A* [2007] EWHC 99 (Fam); *Re AQ Revocable Trust* [2010] 13 ITELR 260 (Bermuda); *Kan Lai Kwan* v. *Poon Lok To Otto* [2014] HKCFA 66, [2014] 17 HKCFAR 414; *JSC Mezhdunarodniy Promyshlenniy Bank* v. *Pugachev* [2017] EWHC 2426 (Ch); *Webb* v. *Webb* [2020] UKPC 22. See also D. Waters, 'Settlor Control – What Kind of Problem Is It?' (2009) 15 *Trusts and Trustees* 12.

[2] For an interesting empirical study of this practice see A. Hofri-Winogradow, 'The Demand for Fiduciary Services: Evidence from the Market in Private Donative Trusts' (2017) 68 *Hastings Law Journal* 931.

[3] See, for example, *Lewis* v. *Condon* [2013] NSWCA 204. Although, see *Webb* [2020] UKPC 22 and *Pugachev* [2017] EWHC 2426 (Ch) for signs of a developing willingness to question a trust's validity.

The first is those directed to the veracity of the trust itself with the intent to have the property treated as that of the settlor or other controlling party. Trusts have been challenged as being shams; or the alter ego of the controlling party; or simply as illusory – a non-trust – because essential trust features are compromised or absent.[4] Few challenges have, however, been successful: for shams, the evidential threshold for the relevant intention is high;[5] the alter ego's narrow focus only on *acts* of control does not equate with ownership of the trust property;[6] and courts have recently expressed some doubt about the illusory trust concept.[7]

Given the present limits on direct challenges, the second type of challenge has instead left the trust intact and turned attention to recognising a property right distinct from the trust property, but which is closely related to the trust property. Two discrete claims fall within this category: first, that powers held by a settlor or protector are capable of being treated in combination as items of property with a value commensurate to the value of the trust property; and, second, that a separate constructive trust in favour of a stranger to the trust may be imposed over part or all of the express trust property on account of interactions and resulting expectations arising between the stranger and one of the trustees (who is usually also the party exerting control over the trust affairs). Both types of claims have been favourably received in the New Zealand appellate courts,[8] notwithstanding their controversy.[9]

The focus of this chapter is on the 'constructive trust on express trust' notion. The particular constructive trust at issue in these cases is said to arise in response to the reasonable expectations of the third-party claimant and the trustees that the claimant would receive an interest in the property in return for various contributions made. Constructive trusts have been recognised despite, in situations of more than one trustee, at least one of the trustees having no knowledge of the expectations and/or the contributions and despite the pre-existing interests of the express

4 *Official Assignee* v. *Wilson* [2008] 3 NZLR 45; *Armitage* v. *Sanctuary Propvest* HC Auckland CIV-2009-404-0852, 11 June 2009; *Rosebud Corporate Trustee Ltd* v. *Bublitz* [2014] NZHC 2018.

5 *Clayton* v. *Clayton* [2016] NZSC 29, [2016] 1 NZLR 551.

6 *Sharrment* v. *Official Trustee* (1988) 18 FCR 449 at 470–471; *Wilson* [2008] 3 NZLR 45 at [70]; *Vervoort* v. *Forrest* [2016] NZCA 375 at [28].

7 *Clayton* [2016] NZSC 29; *Webb* [2020] UKPC 22. I have elsewhere criticised the New Zealand Supreme Court's hesitation to recognise an illusory trust on the facts of that case given it was content to declare that on account of his range of powers, the trustee could distribute property to himself 'unrestrained by fiduciary obligations' (at [58]). If that is the case, it is difficult to see how, with respect, any trust existed: Palmer, 'Equity and Trusts' [2019] *New Zealand Law Review* 365.

8 *Clayton* [2016] NZSC 29; *Murrell* v. *Hamilton* [2014] NZCA 377; *Vervoort* [2016] NZCA 375; *Hawke's Bay Trustee Co Ltd* v. *Judd* [2016] NZCA 397.

9 See, for example, J. Nitikman, '*Clayton v Clayton* in the NZ Supreme Court: It's Hard to Keep a Good Court Down' (2016) 22 *Trusts & Trustees* 1049; G. Young, 'Sham and Illusory Trusts – Lessons from *Clayton v Clayton*' (2018) 24 Trusts & Trustees 194; C. Rickett, 'Instrumentalism in the Law of Trusts: The Disturbing Case of the Constructive Trust upon an Express Trust' (2016) 47 *Victoria University of Wellington Law Review* 463.

trust beneficiaries. In so doing, courts have seen themselves as departing from trust orthodoxy stating that 'traditional rules [...] must bend to the practical realities' and 'the Court's approach to trusts must [...] meet the reality of how property is owned in New Zealand'.[10]

This chapter examines these constructive trust cases and analyses whether they are in fact a departure from trust principles and whether such departure is justified. These scenarios raise questions in relation to the nature of the trustees' powers and the beneficiaries' interest in the property. It is the hypothesis of this chapter that the judicial reasoning so far relied upon to ground these claims is worrying and shows, at best, a concern to address pernicious trusts without careful consideration of the implications for trust principles and, at worst, a misunderstanding and misapplication of orthodox trust principles.

After describing the reasonable expectation constructive trust and the recent authorities that have extended its application to property already subject to an express trust, this chapter will consider two principal objections to these developments; first, that the constructive trust cannot defeat the beneficial interests arising from the express trust; and, second, that the constructive trust is in any case unnecessary to ensure that a contributing third-party recovers value conferred, and only serves to obfuscate the analysis. For these reasons, the notion of a constructive trust upon an express trust ought to be rejected.

## 2 THE REASONABLE EXPECTATIONS CONSTRUCTIVE TRUST

A constructive trust is generally said to arise when a property owner has so conducted herself in relation to another that it would be inequitable or unconscionable for her to deny to the other party a beneficial interest. There are several different contexts in which a constructive trust can arise, and therefore some variation in the relevant elements that must be proved. The particular constructive trust that New Zealand courts have recognised or imposed over property already subject to an express trust is said to arise in response to the reasonable expectations of the parties.[11] It was originally developed in New Zealand in the context of de facto relationship disputes at a time when such relationships were not included in the statutory scheme for sharing property upon dissolution of the relationship.[12] The de facto exclusion has

[10] *Vervoort* [2016] NZCA 375 at [62]–[63].

[11] Other traditional categories in which a constructive trust may arise include, for example, incompletely constituted transfers (*Pennington* v. *Waine* [2002] EWCA Civ 227); secret trusts (*Re Cleaver* [1981] 1 WLR 939; *Brown* v. *Pourau* [1995] 1 NZLR 352); specifically enforceable contracts (*Lysaght* v. *Edwards* (1876) 2 ChD 499); and performance of a pre-existing fiduciary duty (*FHR European Ventures LLP* v. *Cedar Capital Holdings LLC* [2014] UKSC 45).

[12] Property (Relationships) Act 1976 (since amended in 2001); *Gillies* v. *Keogh* [1989] 2 NZLR 327; *Phillips* v. *Phillips* [1993] 3 NZLR 159; *Nash* v. *Nash* (1994) 12 FRNZ 446 (CA). In the United Kingdom, a similar trust developed for the benefit of co-habitees: *Graham-York* v. *York* [2015] EWCA

since been removed. The constructive trust is called upon again now because the property being sought is held on trust and so is excluded from the statutory regime applying to divide relationship property. For this reason, its relevance has expanded beyond de facto relationships.

Crucial to recognition of the constructive trust is the presence of contributions made by the claimant to the property owned by the defendant, coupled with an expectation of an interest in return. In the leading case of *Lankow* v. *Rose* in the Court of Appeal, Hardie Boys J said[13]:

> It is however important that whatever the legal rubric there should be clear criteria for the imposition of constructive trusts in the area of de facto relationships. These will necessarily involve a value judgment, but there is nothing unusual about that. The essential requirement I see to be twofold: that the plaintiff contributed in more than a minor way to the acquisition, preservation or enhancement of the defendant's assets, whether directly or indirectly; and that in all the circumstances the parties must be taken reasonably to have expected that the plaintiff would share in them as a result. Both statements need some amplification. In the first place, by contributions to assets, one is not referring to those contributions to a common household that are adequately compensated by the benefits the relationship itself confers. The contributions must manifestly exceed the benefits. Putting it in conventional estoppel terms, the plaintiff's contributions must have been to his or her detriment; or in Canadian terms, they must have resulted by the end of the relationship in the enrichment of one to the juristically unjustified deprivation of the other. Further, the contributions need not be in money; they may be in services or in any other respect. But there must be a causal relationship between the contributions and the acquisition, preservation or enhancement of the defendant's assets for, as a claim to constructive trust is a proprietary claim, a claim to an interest in property, the contributions must have been made to assets; not necessarily to particular assets but certainly to the defendants' assets in general. The contributions may then be recognised by the imposition of a trust over a particular asset or particular assets, which may in turn be quantified or satisfied by monetary awards.

Subsequent cases[14] have tended to rely upon Tipping J's exposition in *Lankow* v. *Rose* of the elements the claimant must prove, as follows:[15]

Civ 72; *Burns* v. *Burns* [1984] Ch 371. It is possible in these situations to have both a resulting and constructive trust: *Re Densham* [1975] 1 WLR 1519, where a wife, who was not on the title, was entitled to a ninth share on a resulting trust as she had contributed to a ninth of the purchase price and a half share under a constructive trust.

13 *Lankow* v. *Rose* [1995] 1 NZLR 277 at 282.

14 *Raats* v. *Sinclair* (28/7/97, Chisholm J, HC Timaru CP6/94); *McMahon* v. *McMahon* [1996] 3 NZLR 334; *Drever* v. *Rickard* (9/7/98, Doogue J, HC Hamilton A37/98); *Henri* v. *Public Trustee* (27/10/98, Potter J, HC Auckland CP235/98).

15 *Lankow* [1995] 1 NZLR 277 at 294.

(1) contributions by the claimant, direct or indirect, to the property in question;
(2) the expectation by the claimant of an interest in the property;
(3) that such expectation is reasonable; and
(4) that the defendant should reasonably expect to yield the claimant an interest.

It is noted that the expectation of an interest need not be the *only* reason for the claimant's contribution. The Court in *Lankow* v. *Rose* considered there was an essential difference between motive and expectation for the claimant's contributions. In that case, the claimant had stated in her evidence that she undertook work for her de facto partner and his company to save him money and keep his company afloat. The appellant argued that this evidence demonstrated that she had no expectations of an interest in any of his property. Justice Tipping called this a confusion of concepts and it did not follow from the claimant's stated motivation that she had no expectation of an interest.[16]

There are clear similarities between the reasonable expectations constructive trust and the common intention constructive trust found in other common law jurisdictions,[17] albeit that the latter use different terminology: 'common intention' and 'detriment', in contrast to reasonable expectations and contributions, respectively.[18] The requirement that the claimant must have relied on a common intention to its detriment is determined by assessing contributions made, directly or indirectly, to the relevant property. The courts take a broad view of what will count as a contribution in much the same way as do the New Zealand courts.[19] Financial contributions to the property (including mortgage repayments),[20] physical contributions that increase the value of the property,[21] or significant unpaid work which enabled savings to be made and diverted to purchase of other property[22] are all relevant. Contributions, whether financial or non-financial, must be substantial to qualify. Contributions that merely enable the other partner to spend less appear not to be sufficient,[23] nor are the normal domestic duties of running the home,[24] but contributions that enable the other partner to pay the mortgage will usually qualify.[25] A clear and substantial connection to the property is necessary in both forms of the constructive trust.

16 *Lankow* [1995] 1 NZLR 277 at 283 (Hardie Boys J), see also 287 (Gault J).
17 *Stack* v. *Dowden* [2007] UKHL 17; *Allen* v. *Snyder* [1977] 2 NSWLR 685. In Singapore, a resulting trust has been favoured as the default analysis for contributions to property unless the parties' common intention is for a division different from that which accords with their contributions: *Chan Yuen Lan* v. *See Fong Mun* [2014] SGCA 36.
18 *Gissing* v. *Gissing* [1971] AC 886; *Grant* v. *Edwards* [1986] Ch 638 (CA).
19 *Stack* [2007] UKHL 17.
20 *Chan Yuen Lan* [2014] SGCA 36.
21 *Cooke* v. *Head* [1972] 1 WLR 518.
22 *Nixon* v. *Nixon* [1969] 1 WLR 1676.
23 *Nuthall* v. *Heslop* (1995) 13 FRNZ 518.
24 *Burns* [1984] Ch 317; *Lloyds Bank Plc* v. *Rosset* [1991] 1 AC 107.
25 *Gissing* [1971] AC 886.

The requirement for an identifiable common intention may be more demanding than the reasonable expectation standard.[26] In the common intention constructive trust, there will generally need to be some shared understanding or agreement. However, the requisite agreement can be inferred from the claimant's contributions.[27] In the New Zealand cases, the claimant's contributions are usually taken to establish the reasonable expectation of both the claimant and defendant.[28] In addition, the parties' reasonable expectation can arise after the acquisition of the property.

The relationship between the two types of constructive trust was recognised by the New Zealand Court of Appeal recently in *Almond* v. *Read* where Winkelmann J stated[29]:

> Where a contribution is made on the basis of a pre-existing common intention that the contribution will result in a proprietary interest, there will be no difficulty in establishing a reasonable expectation.

Her Honour went on to classify the common intention constructive trust as 'simply [...] one type of situation in which a reasonable expectation will be found to exist'.[30] There are enough similarities between the two such that the judicial attention being paid in New Zealand to the imposition of constructive trusts on property subject to express trusts may very well have relevance beyond New Zealand. In addition, despite their origin, the scope of such trusts is not necessarily limited to the domestic context given that the common intention constructive trust has already been extended to some commercial scenarios.[31]

## 3 THE CONSTRUCTIVE TRUST ON EXPRESS TRUST AUTHORITIES

There are two instances in which a reasonable expectation constructive trust may arise in relation to property subject to an existing express trust. First, factors that establish the elements of the constructive trust may have occurred prior to settlement of the property on express trust. Where qualifying contributions were made and a reasonable expectation of an interest in the property arose *before* it was settled on express trust, the original owner of the property then held the property subject to the constructive trust. The claimant's resulting property right under the constructive trust is simply traced through to the trustees now holding the property, who

[26] *Hayward* v. *Giordani* [1983] NZLR 140 (CA) at 149 (Richardson J); *Irvine* v. *Scaysbrook* [2005] NSWSC 565.

[27] *Grant* [1986] Ch 638 at 654 (CA); *Jones* v. *Kernott* [2011] UKSC 53.

[28] *Gormack* v. *Scott* [1995] NZFLR 289 (CA) at 47–48 (Cooke P.).

[29] *Almond* v. *Read* [2019] NZCA 26 at [69].

[30] ibid at [71].

[31] *Agarwala* v. *Agarwala* [2013] EWCA Civ 1763; *Marr* v. *Collie* [2017] UKPC 17.

are effectively treated as volunteers. The claim in this instance is a vindication of pre-existing equitable rights that arose prior to the settlement of the express trust, the claim being good against all but the bona fide purchaser for value.[32] It is not necessary to establish any knowledge, expectation, or wrongdoing on the part of the trustees. A claim of this sort was affirmed by the High Court in *Marshall* v. *Bourneville*.[33] This chapter is not concerned with this kind of claim.[34]

The second and more significant instance of a constructive trust in this context concerns a claim directly against trustees for contributions made to property while it is owned by the trustees. If a spouse or partner can show that, in the circumstances, the trustees should reasonably expect to yield an interest in the trust property to the spouse or partner, then it is said that a constructive trust will arise. Claims of this sort have been affirmed by the New Zealand Court of Appeal in *Murrell*,[35] *Vervoort*[36] and *Hawke's Bay Trustee Co Ltd*.[37]

Each of the express trusts in the cases was discretionary and had been settled by the claimant's partner prior to forming a co-habiting relationship with the claimant. The beneficiaries were the settlor, his children, and grandchildren. The settlor appointed himself trustee along with an 'independent' trustee who had minimal involvement in the running of the trust. The trust and trust property were effectively controlled by the settlor-trustee. All three cases were claims by the settlor-trustee's de facto partner that contributions she had made to the trust property in the form of maintenance, redecoration, and working around the house enabling her partner to focus on business activities gave rise to a reasonable expectation of an interest in the property, where her partner had not dissuaded her from her belief.

In all three cases, the Court accepted the possibility of a reasonable expectation constructive trust binding the trustees of an already existing express trust. Where the four elements can be made out, a constructive trust is imposed in order that the beneficiaries do not benefit from the value of the claimant's contributions. *Murrell* was

32 *Foskett* v. *McKeown* [2001] 1 AC 102. Although see J. Hudson, 'Who Is Equity's Darling? Recipient Trustees as Bona Fide Purchasers' (2017) 3 *Conveyancer* 195, where the author argues that a recipient who receives property to be held on trust incurs obligations and gives correlating rights to the beneficiary which should be treated as valid consideration thereby engaging the bona fide purchaser defence.

33 *Marshall* v. *Bourneville* [2013] NZCA 271, [2013] 3 NZLR 766.

34 Constructive trusts are also said to arise in relation to express trusts in two further instances: first, where property is transferred on what appears to be the terms of an existing express trust, but in fact the intention of the transferor is that the property is held on a different (implied or constructive) trust (*Robson* v. *Gallaher* [2011] NZCA 459); and, secondly, in earlier cases that accepted the argument that the trust was in fact the alter ego of the settlor before it was discredited (*Prime* v. *Hardie* [2003] NZFLR 481 (HC); *Glass* v. *Hughey* [2003] NZFLR 685 (HC)). However, both of these are situations in which the correct analysis is that no express trust over the relevant property in fact arose. These constructive trust instances are different in kind from the reasonable expectations/common intention constructive trust with which this chapter is concerned.

35 *Murrell* [2014] NZCA 377.

36 *Vervoort* [2016] NZCA 375.

37 *Hawke's Bay Trustee Co Ltd* [2016] NZCA 397.

the first clear affirmation of the constructive trust on an express trust in these circumstances. In the subsequent cases, *Vervoort* and *Hawke's Bay*, two principal arguments were made by the trustees. First, it is not correct to say, it was submitted, that the trustees should reasonably expect to yield an interest to the claimant if they did not all participate in the raising of the claimant's expectation of such an interest. Where one or other of the trustees had not actively participated in the affairs of the trust and therefore there had not been unanimity among the trustees, the expectation could not be said to be shared by the trustees. Second, recognition of the constructive trust would unduly interfere with the beneficiaries' interest in the express trust property.

### 3.1 *Trustee Unanimity and Non-Delegation*

In all three cases, one of the trustees had had little or no involvement in the management of the property and the operation of the trust. In *Murrell*, the Court admonished the independent trustee for having abjured his trustee responsibilities in favour of the settlor-trustee.[38] In *Vervoort*, the other trustee had initially carried out some tasks, but in later years, he was never consulted or asked for his approval of contributions received or purchases made.[39] In *Hawke's Bay*, the corporate trustee had initially been active but had effectively delegated matters of maintenance and upkeep of the house to the settlor-trustee.

Given the presence of an inactive trustee, the trustees in *Vervoort* and *Hawke's Bay* both submitted that the settlor-trustee's actions in giving rise to a reasonable expectation on the part of the claimant of a property interest could not be validly relied upon to justify a constructive trust because his actions were without the required approval of the other trustee. The trustees had failed to act unanimously and were obliged not to delegate their duty to act personally in respect of dispositions. At first instance in *Vervoort*, for example, Ellis J had considered that it would not be equitable to hold the trustees bound to the claimant, given their lack of involvement. To hold otherwise would, her Honour opined, 'violate orthodox trust principles of unanimity and non-delegation'.[40]

The argument is, however, misconceived because the trustees' lack of unanimity does not render any disposition or other interaction between one trustee and parties external to the trust invalid. The lack of unanimity on the part of the non-active trustee is irrelevant to whether a third-party interest arises. Rather, it means that the trustees have breached their personal duty to the beneficiaries to act unanimously. The real objection of the beneficiaries must be that the settlor-trustee was in breach of trust for misappropriating trust property by the engendering of expectations in the claimant and his acceptance of contributions from the claimant. The failure

38 *Murrell* [2014] NZCA 377 at [27].

39 *Vervoort* [2016] NZCA 375 at [33].

40 *Vervoort* v. *Forrest* [2015] NZHC 808 at [81].

of the other trustee to engage in the decision-making process was a breach of duty owed to the beneficiaries, but it was not the causative action on the part of the trustees that could be said to give rise to a claim on the property by the de facto partner.

The Court of Appeal's rejection of the unanimity objection was at once decisive and misplaced. Instead of seeking to explain why the principles of unanimity and non-delegation have little bearing on the constructive trust claim, it is clear that it saw its approach as departing from these principles because of the particular social nuisance of the controlling settlor-trustee[41]:

> [T]hose principles [of unanimity and non-delegation] must bend to the practical realities when one trustee is in absolute control of all trust activities and the other trustees have effectively abdicated their trustee responsibilities. Any other conclusion would mean settlors, who appointed themselves as trustees, would be able to take advantage of their own wrong in failing to ensure the trust is properly administered by all trustees. The trust would get a windfall, not available but for the use of the trust format.

With respect, 'bending' these principles was unnecessary, as neither have very much application to the third-party's assertion of a property interest in trust property, and everything to do with the trustees' personal trust obligations to the beneficiaries. Neither a strict holding to the requirements of unanimity and non-delegation, nor a policy-motivated setting aside of such principles provided the answer to the question whether property subject to an express trust could be made subject to a constructive trust. This was a red herring.

### 3.2 *The Beneficiaries' Pre-Existing Interest*

The issue that required addressing, and which was raised in *Vervoort* and *Hawke's Bay*, was whether a constructive trust can be imposed where to do so adversely affects, if not ignores, the beneficiaries' prior interest in the trust property. The constructive trust in this scenario, it has been argued, effectively validates a trustee's unilateral redistribution of property rights in breach of trust and at the expense of existing beneficiaries.[42]

To recognise an equitable interest on the part of the claimant in the property subject to the express trust raises questions about the extent of permissible interference with the express trust beneficiaries' interest in that property. In response, the Court's view was that the constructive trust was not taking anything from the beneficiaries to which they should otherwise be entitled.[43] As France P said in *Hawke's Bay*:[44]

[41] *Vervoort* [2016] NZCA 375 at [62].

[42] ibid at [66]. See further C. Rickett, 'Instrumentalism in the Law of Trusts: The Disturbing Case of the Constructive Trust Upon an Express Trust' (2016) 47 *Victoria University of Wellington Law Review* 463.

[43] *Vervoort* [2016] NZCA 375 at [67].

[44] *Hawke's Bay* [2016] NZCA 397 at [47], citing *Murrell* [2014] NZCA 377 at [30].

> The concern about the impact of this approach on the property rights that form a key part of the trust concept is understandable. [...] We agree with [counsel's] submission that Ms Judd's successful claim simply reverses or disgorges the benefit of the defendants' enrichment. This Court in *Murrell* made the same point. As the Court put it, the claim means 'a part of the value of the Trust's property which should not accrue to the Trust does not accrue to it'.

The Court did not deal specifically with the issue of the beneficiaries' interest, except to say effectively that their interest should not incorporate the value of the claimant's contributions. The concern appears to be with value and not property rights as such. The Court's approach has implications for the nature of the beneficiaries' interest and the nature of the remedy, both of which will be discussed in more detail in the next section of this chapter. The point to make at this stage is simply that the Court is less concerned with *property rights* and more so with reversing an unjust transfer of *value*. To anticipate my arguments to come, a reversal of unjust enrichment should not on its own justify recognition of a property interest or, more significantly, rejection of a prior property right.

Having outlined the New Zealand Court of Appeal's answer to the question of whether constructive trusts can arise over property of an express trust, this chapter turns to consider what I believe to be the two principal reasons why the Court's approach must be rejected: first, that the constructive trust undermines the beneficial interests extant pursuant to the express trust; and, second, that the remedial objective in these cases is not best achieved by a constructive trust.

## 4 THE BENEFICIAL INTEREST OBJECTION: THE EXPRESS TRUST BENEFICIARY HAS A PRE-EXISTING RIGHT THAT CAN BE ENFORCED AGAINST A THIRD-PARTY

The constructive trust recognises an equitable interest on the part of the claimant. But how does such an interest relate to the prior interest of the beneficiary of the express trust? The Court's response in the New Zealand cases was to focus on why the claimant should be granted an interest, but it failed to really grapple with the effect on the beneficiary's right, except to excuse any interference on the basis that value conferred needed to be returned to the claimant. The relationship between value and proprietary claim will be discussed shortly. But an examination of the proprietary effect of a beneficiary's interest is first required to determine whether property subject to an express trust can also become subject to a constructive trust.

Proponents of a strong proprietary view of the beneficiary's interest would argue that the trust assets are beneficially owned by the beneficiaries and the trustee's rights in those assets are accordingly limited. Given the trustee cannot yield an interest that is not hers to give, she cannot possibly by her conduct yield to the claimant a beneficial interest in the cases discussed here. To do so would be 'unthinkable in the equity jurisdiction'.[45] The trustee has no power to give up a second equity, it has been argued, and so no such interest can thus arise.[46]

The position is however slightly more nuanced than this. As regards the beneficiary, the trustee has duties not to act in relation to the property beyond the bounds of the express trust. Where she so does, the beneficiary may seek relief from her for breach of trust. To the outside world, the trustee has power to act as an absolute owner would, and strangers to the trust may rely on those actions *unless* they have notice of the trust. Third parties take their interest subject to the rights of the beneficiary only if their conscience is so bound.

To explain, it is of course right that the trustee cannot dispose of the beneficiaries' interest; it can only be overridden. In the context of a disposition of shares by the trustee in breach of trust to a bona fide purchaser for value, Lord Mance said in *Akers* v. *Samba Financial Group*[47]:

> [W]here a trust exists, the legal and beneficial interests are distinct, and what affects the former does not necessarily affect the latter. Where an asset is held on trust, the legal title remains capable of transfer to a third party, although this undoubted disposition may be in breach of trust. But the trust rights, including the right to have the legal title held and applied in accordance with the terms of the trust, remain. They are not disposed of. They continue to be capable of enforcement unless and until the disposition of the legal title has the effect under the lex situs of the trust asset of overriding the protected trust rights. If the trust rights are overridden, it is not because they have been disposed of by virtue of the transfer of the legal title. It is because they were protected rights that were always limited and in certain circumstances capable of being overridden by virtue of a rule of law governing equitable rights.

The most obvious rule of law that permits the trust rights to be overridden is the bona fide purchaser for value.[48] This understanding of the reach of the beneficial interest applies whether one views the beneficiary interest as itself a proprietary right[49] or as a personal right upon a right, as has been advocated strongly by some writers in recent years.[50] Lord Mance specifically noted this when his Lordship said

45 C. Rickett, 'Instrumentalism in the Law of Trusts: The Disturbing Case of the Constructive Trust Upon an Express Trust' (2016) 47 *Victoria University of Wellington Law Review* 463, 474.

46 J. Penner, 'The (True) Nature of a Beneficiary's Equitable Proprietary Interest under a Trust' (2014) 27 *Canadian Journal of Law and Jurisprudence* 473, 491.

47 *Akers* v. *Samba Financial Group* [2017] UKSC 6 at [51]. In the case, it was argued that misappropriation of a beneficiary company's interest in the trust property was a disposal in accordance with insolvency legislation and could be clawed back on the liquidation of the company. The Supreme Court rejected the argument because the company's interest was equitable and could not be disposed, only overreached.

48 *Independent Trustee Services Ltd* v. *GP Noble Trustees Ltd* [2012] EWCA Civ 195 at [106] (Lloyd LJ).

49 *Foskett* [2001] AC 102.

50 L. Smith, 'Trust and Patrimony' (2008) 38 *Estates, Trusts and Pensions Journal* 379; B. McFarlane and R. Stevens, 'The Nature of Equitable Property' (2010) 4 *Journal of Equity* 1.

'[the beneficiary's] property, whether it consisted of an equitable proprietary interest or personal rights to have the shares held for its benefit, continued, despite the disposal of the legal title, unless and until that disposal overrode it'.[51] Equitable rights, whether proprietary or personal, are not defeated other than by being overreached.

Misappropriation of property by a trustee does not itself stop the transfer or disposition to a third-party, but the beneficiary can assert his or her right against the property. However, the enforcement of the beneficial interest against a third-party recipient is a question of conscience.[52] It is often said that the beneficial interest is good against all but equity's darling, the bona fide purchaser for value.[53] But this undervalues the importance of conscience and notice. A volunteer is taken to hold property that is subject to a beneficiary's equitable interest on trust to restore to the beneficiary. This appears to be an automatic duty that supports the strong view of the beneficial interest but if the volunteer were to dispose of property before he had notice of the interest, there would be no breach of trust on his part, nor a personal liability to account in knowing receipt.[54] The beneficiary has a persisting right in the trust property or its traceable proceeds but the volunteer comes under a duty only when his 'conscience is affected by knowledge (from whatever source) of the pre-existing trust relationship'.[55] In the same way, the bona fide purchaser is not free of the beneficiary's claim if he had notice of the prior interest at the time of his purchase. The beneficiary's equitable interest gives rise to corresponding duties on the part of the trustee and any third-party recipient on the basis that their conscience is affected.[56] This analysis extends beyond beneficiaries said to have a fixed or vested interest, and includes a discretionary beneficiary who, despite having only a mere hope or expectation in the property itself, is nevertheless entitled to insist that misapplied property is returnable to the trust corpus. The beneficial interest is significant, but not absolute. As Nolan has written, 'conscience and property are entirely compatible concepts.'[57]

Applying these principles, it is therefore possible for a third-party to receive and deal with property from a trustee who was acting in breach of trust, without being under a duty to the beneficiary because her conscience is not affected by notice or

51 *Akers* [2017] UKSC 6 at [54].

52 *Akers* [2017] UKSC 6 at [89] (Lord Sumption).

53 See, for example, J. Glister and J. Lee (eds), *Hanbury & Martin: Modern Equity* (21st ed, Sweet & Maxwell, 2018), 1–039.

54 *GP Noble Trustees Ltd* [2012] EWCA Civ 195.

55 S. Agnew and B. McFarlane, 'The Paradox of the Equitable Proprietary Claim' in B. McFarlane and S. Agnew (eds) *Modern Studies in Property Law Volume 10* (Hart, 2019), p. 306. Although the authors reject the proprietary conception of the beneficial interest, their point about notice stands regardless of which theoretical framework is adopted.

56 The content of the duty will differ, of course. While the express trustee must actively manage the property, the third-party recipient will hold the property on a bare trust to restore it to the beneficial owner: *Akers* [2017] UKSC 6 at [88] per Lord Sumption. See also R. C. Nolan, 'Equitable Property' (2006) 122 *Law Quarterly Review* 232.

57 R. C. Nolan, Dispositions and equitable property' (2017) 133 *Law Quarterly Review* 353, 356.

knowledge of the prior interest at the time of receipt. She will, nevertheless, become bound upon notice to hold the property for the beneficiary (if she remains in possession), unless she is a purchaser.

The next step in the argument is to consider the relevance of the nature of the title being taken by the third-party recipient. In the scenario with which we are here concerned, the claimant is not taken as a legal owner and it is not really apt to say that the property is being disposed of to her. Instead, the constructive trust recognises property as being held on trust for her, albeit that enforcement of that trust will inevitably lead to disposal or transfer of the property to her. A trustee may deal with the legal title to the trust property, but it is also possible that a trustee could deal with the property in such a way as to grant equitable rights to a third-party. It is important to note that the trustee is not giving over the beneficiaries' equitable rights to the third-party because they are not hers to give. Rather, a new and distinct equitable interest is arising in relation to the same property by way of a separate constructive trust on account of the claimant's contributions and the trustee's conduct. Equity will permit two sets of equitable interests in relation to the same property, unless they are in competition. Where the equities are in competition, it is well accepted that the prior equitable interest prevails.[58]

So, in summary, the beneficiary's persisting interest in the trust property does not in itself prevent the third-party from taking an interest in the property. However, if the interest taken is a legal one, the third-party will be bound to a duty to hold it on trust for the beneficiary if the third-party's conscience is affected (at the time of receipt in the case of a purchaser, or at any time while the third-party remains in possession in the case of all other recipients). If the interest conferred is equitable and in competition with that of the beneficiary, the beneficiary's interest will trump as the first in time.

So to consider again the particular context with which this chapter is concerned, the right bestowed on the claimant pursuant to the constructive trust necessarily competes with the interest of the express trust beneficiary in the same property, and must normally therefore concede to the express trust interest. The issue is a competition between interests, rather than a complete denial of any interest taken by the claimant. The trustee's conduct vis-a-vis the claimant does not make the beneficiaries' reliance on their interest inequitable such that they would lose priority.[59]

Were there no special rule regarding competing equities and the claimant's rights treated in the same way as third-party recipients of legal title to the trust property, the claimant should nevertheless still have difficulty resisting the

[58] *Phillips* v. *Phillips* (1862) 4 De G F &J 208; *Fung Ping Shan* v. *Tong Shun* [1918] AC 403.

[59] The beneficiaries' priority is not lost by reason of the claimant's equitable interest under the constructive trust having been brought about by a breach of trust because as between the trustee and beneficiaries, the trustee did not have a power to confer such an interest: *Shropshire Union Railways and Canal Co* v. *The Queen* (1875) LR 7 HL 496; see also Tucker et al, *Lewin on Trusts* (19th ed, Sweet & Maxwell), 33–024.

beneficiaries' interest. It might be possible that the claimant could be treated by equity as a purchaser for value, rather than a volunteer, on the basis that 'purchaser' historically denotes simply someone who takes an interest in property other than by descent,[60] and the requirement of value could be satisfied by the contributions given.[61] However, in most of these cases we are concerned with here, the claimant *knows* of the existence of the trust and therefore has knowledge sufficient to amount to, at least, suspicion of breach by the controlling trustee in their giving rise to an expectation of an interest without the involvement of the other trustees and against the terms of the trust. The threshold for notice is low. The crucial fact, which the claimant must know, is that a pre-existing right exists in respect of the property which may be breached by the way in which the trustee is dealing with the property vis-à-vis the claimant.[62]

In *Papadimitriou* v. *Credit Agricole Corp*,[63] the Privy Council was concerned with a claim of knowing receipt; that is, an action for personal liability on account of the defendant having received property in breach of trust. There has long been confusion as to whether, where the recipient does not have actual knowledge, the level of knowledge sufficient to ground liability must amount to wilful blindness of a prior interest.[64] Lord Clarke, giving the advice of the Privy Council, set the enquiry as whether the facts known to the defendant would give a reasonable person in his position serious cause to question the propriety of the transaction.[65] What is particularly significant for our purpose here is the assimilation of the necessary mental element required for both knowing receipt and notice in a proprietary claim, as noted by Lord Sumption in his concurring judgment:[66]

> [W]hether a person claims to be a bona fide purchaser of assets without notice of a prior interest in them, or disputes a claim to make him accountable as a constructive trustee on the footing of knowing receipt, the question what constitutes notice or knowledge is the same [...] If there are features of the transaction such that if left unexplained they are indicative of wrongdoing, then an explanation must be sought before it can be assumed there is none.

It is not necessary for the third-party recipient to have deliberately or wilfully failed to make enquiries in order to be fixed with notice, so long as a reasonable person

60 Glister and Lee, *Hanbury & Martin*, 1–040.

61 For an example of this wider approach to bona fide purchaser for value, see *GP Noble Trustees Ltd* [2012] EWCA Civ 195, where the Court accepted foregoing the right to claim ancillary relief as part of a divorce settlement amounted to giving value for the purpose of the bona fide purchaser protection.

62 Agnew and McFarlane, 'The Paradox of the Equitable Proprietary Claim', p. 309.

63 *Papadimitriou* v. *Credit Agricole Corp* [2015] UKPC 13.

64 *Baden* v. *Société Générale pour Favoriser le Developpement du Commerce et de l'Industrie en France SA* [1993] 1 WLR 509.

65 *Papadimitriou* [2015] UKPC 13 at [20].

66 *Papadimitriou* [2015] UKPC 13 at [33].

would suspect that there is a serious possibility of an equitable interest.[67] On the facts of all three of the New Zealand cases examined in this chapter, the claimant knew of the existence of the trust and therefore had knowledge sufficient to amount to suspicion of other possible competing interests in the property.

The presence of notice means the claimant's interest in the property is held subject to a duty to preserve the interests of the beneficiaries. But, in addition and perhaps more significantly, it should surely also negate the reasonable expectation element of the constructive trust. How can the claimant reasonably expect an interest if she knows of the prior right? Surprisingly, in my view, the Court did not see this as problematic. In *Hawke's Bay*, it was accepted that the claimant knew of the trust and that she was not a beneficiary. The trustees submitted that this meant she could not have had a reasonable expectation of an interest in the property. The Court's view, however, was that it did not necessarily follow from that knowledge that there could be no reasonable expectation of a share in the property. '[The claimant]'s understanding of the situation that pertained to the Trust did not mean she expected she was to contribute in the way she did but, if the marriage broke up, receive nothing.'[68] Although the Court was there concerned with whether the expectation was reasonable in the circumstances and not with notice in respect of a proprietary claim as such, this would nevertheless seem, with respect, to set the bar unreasonably high for what will amount to notice of a beneficiary's pre-existing right and ought to be rejected.

With respect, there are real problems with the constructive trust upon express trust analysis adopted by the New Zealand Court of Appeal. Primarily, it fails to recognise the beneficiaries' prior and persisting interest in the trust property which is not extinguished or overreached by a trustee's disposition of the property to another in breach of trust. In so doing, it departs from trust principles and undermines the express trust institution. A proper analysis would have determined that, although the claimant could establish the elements of the reasonable expectation constructive trust as against one of the trustees, her equitable property interest pursuant to that trust was either defeated by the earlier competing equitable interest of the beneficiaries of the express trust; or was taken with notice of the beneficiaries' prior right and therefore held subject to the prior right, which in turn defeated her own.

## 5 THE REMEDIAL OBJECTION: THE APPROPRIATE REMEDY IS TO RESTORE VALUE, NOT CONFER A PROPERTY RIGHT

The second objection to the Court's approach lies with the remedy given. The constructive trust finding should ordinarily lead to a property remedy in order that the

[67] D. Hayton, 'Third-Party Liability of Recipients of Trust Property' in P. Devonshire and R. Havelock (eds) *The Impact of Equity and Restitution in Commerce* (2019, Hart), p. 241.

[68] *Hawke's Bay* [2016] NZCA 397 at [36].

claim and relief connect coherently.[69] The claim is to contributions giving rise to a share in the asset. A notable feature of the cases is that the justification for the constructive trust indicated the focus was really on a personal remedy concerned with recognising and reversing the value conferred by the claimant's contributions, rather than a recognition of a property right arising as a result of the contributions. The Court seemed largely uninterested in the proprietary effect of the constructive trust. Indeed, the awards in the two successful cases were not in fact property orders at all.

The remedy ordered was a monetary award and the figures were relatively small. In *Hawke's Bay*, where the property had actually decreased in value over the period of the relationship due to market changes, the claimant had sought 40 per cent of the value of the house, amounting to approximately $350,000. She was awarded $65,000 by the trial judge, of whose 'broad brush approach to quantum' the Court of Appeal referred to approvingly.[70] The Court applied what it called a 'cross-check', noting the award amounted to $200 a week for the course of the marriage and together with not having to pay rent, was *equivalent* to the value of her contributions. This seems to unduly limit the scope of the claimant's property rights if indeed a constructive trust arose. Only in *Murrell* did the award appear to be tagged to the value of the property itself. There, the claimant was awarded 15 per cent of the net value of the sale proceeds of the property after the mortgage had been cleared, which amounted to only $37,000. The percentage was set on the basis of evaluating the extent of the claimant's contribution.[71]

Although slightly different in each, the awards show that a direct property order is uncommon and that the concern is to give relief for the value of the services or contributions rendered, rather than to give effect to any understanding or reasonable expectation between the parties as to what the proportions of ownership were. This was evident in several statements in the judgments. In addition to France P's observation in *Hawke's Bay* quoted earlier in this chapter,[72] Asher J stated in *Vervoort*, in response to the objection that the beneficiaries' interest is being unduly interfered with[73]:

> There is no misappropriation of property in that the beneficiaries of the express trust have no claim in conscience to the increases in value resulting from the contributions. Beneficiaries cannot expect trustees to retain for them an unearned benefit, extracted by expectations engendered by the trustees. The express trust beneficiaries should reasonably expect to yield the third parties an interest.

Similarly in *Murrell*, Wild J explained[74]:

> We emphasise that allowing Ms Murrell's claim does not alienate Trust property, that is it does not take away from the beneficiaries of the Trust something to which

69 A proprietary remedy is of course attractive because it can be used to counter an insolvent trustee.

70 *Hawke's Bay* [2016] NZCA 397 at [32].

71 *Murrell* 2014] NZCA 377 at [40].

72 *Hawke's Bay* [2016] NZCA 397 at [47].

73 *Vervoort* [2016] NZCA 375 at [70].

74 *Murrell* [2014] NZCA 377 at [30].

> they are entitled. Rather, it means a part of the value of the Trust's property which should not accrue to the Trust does not accrue to it. Allowing Ms Murrell's claim averts the unjust enrichment which would otherwise result to the Trust [...].

The concern, inherent in these statements, is clearly with value and not property rights. This does not answer the earlier objection regarding alienation of the beneficiaries' prior interest. It simply raises a different question. The constructive trust is being used as a mechanism to prevent unjust enrichment (in its most general sense). But if that is so, a personal restitutionary order to restore the value conferred is more appropriate than a proprietary claim in the form of a constructive trust. This is a problem for the reasonable expectation constructive trust more generally and not limited only to the present context. Indeed, in the leading reasonable expectation constructive trust case, *Lankow* v. *Rose*, Hardie Boys J acknowledged that the outcome can be 'quantified or satisfied by monetary awards'.[75] And in *Vervoort*, Asher J noted that the reasonable expectation constructive trust arose in the earlier cases because the law of unjust enrichment was not sufficiently developed at that stage.[76]

Yet the historical development of the reasonable expectation constructive trust also does not answer the objection today. In the earlier cases between de facto partners without the addition of an express trust, there was no issue of the legal owner of the property being restrained in their ability to so deal with the property, nor was there any other party affected who could claim a prior equitable interest. For that reason, the stronger claim – the constructive trust – became the accepted claim. The constructive trust has the effect of preventing an unjust enrichment, and so its application in those simpler cases corrected the injustice. But the point is that the constructive trust does more than that; it also reallocates property rights. It is this feature of the constructive trust to which this second objection is directed, and which cannot be justified given the analysis in the preceding section.

The personal restitutionary claim is the better fit in these cases. This can be illustrated by the outcome in *Vervoort*. A constructive trust was rejected on the facts because Ms Vervoort had already received benefits from the trust property equivalent to the contributions she had made in the form of the funding of her lifestyle during the de facto relationship. In other words, any enrichment to the trust property (and therefore indirectly to the beneficiaries) brought about by her contributions had been neutralised by other benefits she received such that the enrichment had been restored to her already. This reasoning justifies the refusal of a personal remedy for unjust enrichment, but it should not justify the loss of a proprietary interest in favour of the claimant if there had been one. That could only have been denied for the reasons explained above, namely, that the claimant's equitable interest is defeated by the beneficiaries' prior interest.

75 *Lankow* [1995] 1 NZLR 277 at 282.
76 *Vervoort* [2016] NZCA 375 at [68].

It seems, then, that these are not, in fact, constructive trust cases. This is not to say that there can be no relief for the contributing party. Claims might potentially be mounted in unjust enrichment, estoppel or for an improver's lien. This requires, first, consideration of whether such claims could ordinarily apply as a matter of principle to the factual scenarios in issue here, and then, second, whether the existence of the express trust throws up any difficulties for those claims.

An unjust enrichment claim leading to a restitutionary award of the value of the contributions conferred by the claimant on the beneficiaries may be justified in these situations because the basis upon which the claimant made the contributions – an expectation of a property interest in return – failed. This describes the action more colloquially known among lawyers as quantum meruit and the reason for the action (or the 'unjust factor') as a failure of basis.[77] The focus of the remedy is not the expected benefit of which the claimant has been deprived, but the value of the services that the claimant provided.[78]

In order to give rise to a right to restitution, the basis upon which the contributions were made must be mutual.[79] In the absence of any shared understanding, the claimant is merely a risk-taker.[80] Some argue that the failure of basis requires, first, a condition to have been agreed between the parties, to which the benefit conferred was made subject. Where such a condition exists and fails, the appropriate action is in contract, to repay the benefit. If there is no contract, there ought to be no claim.[81] However, as Havelock has shown, although failure of basis *appears* to be contractual, the action in fact belongs to the law of unjust enrichment, the function of which is subsidiary where there is no other juridical explanation for the arrangement.[82]

There are at least two difficulties with the quantum meruit claim in the present context. First, if the claim is against the beneficiaries, the reasonable expectation shared between claimant and controlling settlor-trustee of an interest does not establish a mutual basis shared by the beneficiaries. Second, with regard to the claimant's position and as was problematic for the reasonable expectation requirement, if the claimant has notice of the existence of the trust and therefore that there are beneficiaries with a claim to the property who are unlikely to accept the basis upon which the claimant is enriching them, then the claimant cannot reasonably believe the basis for her contribution is that she will take a property interest. There is then no basis to fail, and no ground for restitution.

77 A. Burrows, *The Law of Restitution* (3rd ed, 2010, Oxford University Press), p. 319; *Fibrosa Spolka Akcyjna* v. *Fairburn Lawson Combe Barbour Ltd* [1943] AC 32; *Pavey & Matthews Pty Ltd* v. *Paul* (1987) 162 CLR 221.

78 *Cobbe* v. *Yeoman's Row* [2008] UKHL 55 at [4] (Lord Scott).

79 G. Virgo, *The Principles of the Law of Restitution* (3rd ed, 2015, Oxford University Press), p. 306; P. Birks, *An Introduction to the Law of Restitution* (1991, Clarendon, Oxford University Press), p. 115.

80 R. Havelock, 'A Taxonomic Approach to Quantum Meruit' (2016) 132 *Law Quarterly Review* 470.

81 See, for example, P. Jaffey, *The Nature and Scope of Restitution* (2000, Hart), pp. 44–45.

82 Havelock, 'A Taxonomic Approach to Quantum Meruit'; see also R. Grantham and C. Rickett, 'On the Subsidiarity of Unjust Enrichment' (2001) 117 *Law Quarterly Review* 273.

An alternative claim in promissory estoppel has similar difficulties. To establish an estoppel, the claimant must show that as a result of a belief or expectation that the claimant would share in the property created or encouraged by the trustee, it was reasonable for the claimant to rely to her detriment on such expectation and make contributions to the property.[83] The relevant belief or expectation is not reasonable in the presence of notice of the trust.

However, it may be possible that an estoppel-based claim could be made by the claimant against the controlling settlor-trustee on the basis of an expectation that the trustee would cause the trust property to be shared with the claimant on account of her contributions. This would be a personal claim against the trustee, with the possibility of an expectation-based measure of recovery against him,[84] assuming he has personal wealth from which to draw. The Court in *Vervoort* acknowledged as much when it rejected an alternative claim in estoppel against the beneficiaries on account of the particular representations relied upon having been made by the controlling settlor-trustee in his personal capacity.[85]

Having established that the remedy being given in these constructive trust upon express trust cases is really better analysed as a personal award, this clears away the objection from the preceding section with regard to the beneficiaries' competing claim. However, consideration of the principles relevant to alternative actions in unjust enrichment and promissory estoppel against the beneficiaries shows that such actions will be dependent on whether the claimant had notice of the existence of the express trust. If she did, she will be limited to an estoppel claim against the controlling settlor-trustee personally.

In the rare situation where the claimant had no notice of the trust, she is able to rely on the conduct of the controlling settlor-trustee, as any party external to a trust and dealing with the trustee can, in order to establish either a shared basis that failed justifying a restitutionary award, or an encouraged belief or expectation upon which she detrimentally relied justifying an estoppel. Both of these claims would result in a monetary order. Of course, it would then be open to the beneficiaries to claim breach of trust by the controlling settlor-trustee.

## 6 THE NUISANCE REMAINS: THE CONTROLLING SETTLOR-TRUSTEE

The analysis of this chapter has sought to show that it is not appropriate to recognise a constructive trust arising upon property subject to a prior express trust. First, as a matter of proprietary rights, the beneficiaries' equitable interest in the trust property

[83] *Central London Property Trust Ltd* v. *High Trees House Ltd* [1947] KB 130; *Wilson Parking NZ Ltd* v. *Fanshawe 136 Ltd* [2014] NZCA 407.

[84] *Wilson Parking NZ Ltd* [2014] NZCA 407.

[85] *Vervoort* [2016] NZCA 375 at [82], such representation being, as it related to the property, that he would provide her with a property settlement and proper maintenance that would be fair ([78]).

is not defeated by the creation of the claimant's equitable interest pursuant to the constructive trust. Rather the later equitable interest must necessarily be subordinate to the persisting beneficiaries' interest. Second, the relief given in those cases that have recognised a constructive trust is more accurately understood as responding to a claim in unjust enrichment or on the basis of an estoppel. Such claims are unlikely to succeed where the claimant knows of the prior express trust and cannot thus establish either a basis or an expectation reasonably relied upon.

As was referred to at the outset of this chapter, the alienating effect that trusts have had on the property expectations of spouses, partners, and creditors combined with an increasing propensity of settlors to remain in control either by way of formal powers in the deed, or simply by controlling conduct, has led in New Zealand to the development of some contentious judicial approaches.[86]

The real concern of the Court of Appeal in the constructive trust cases discussed in this chapter was clearly evident in their judgment in *Vervoort*. The Court made it plain that the modern context in which trusts are operating to defeat partnership claims demands a response[87]:

> It is acknowledging the reality of the New Zealand trust landscape as it has developed that has justified the recognition of the constructive trust beneficiary's claim. It is a further reality of that landscape that the trustees of family discretionary trusts are more often than not the beneficiaries of those trusts and in control of them. It is common in many trusts in New Zealand 'for the settlor to retain some extent of control or to vest that control in someone other than the trustee'. The effect is that the reality of a trustee's ability to give a third party expectations (in return for that third party's contributions) over trust property, which that trustee deals with as if their own, must be recognised.

While one may be sympathetic to the Court's object, the approach taken undermines the nature of the beneficial interest and will no doubt have significant implications for a coherent law of trusts and established principles of private property rights. Caution must be exercised before departing too readily from traditional trust principle on account of modern trust practice.

However, without the constructive trust, and if the alternative personal claim in unjust enrichment or estoppel against the beneficiaries is not available, an injustice remains that the claimant has contributed on account of the controlling settlor-trustee's behaviour. The true nuisance is the controlling settlor-trustee, and his propensity to act as if the property were his own and then fall back on the trust structure to deny the burdens that come with absolute ownership, whenever necessary.

What may very well be becoming clear is the need for a flexible doctrine of illusory trusts that honours equity's concern with substance over form. Notwithstanding

86 See further, J. Palmer 'Controlling the Trust' (2011) 12 *Otago Law Review* 473.
87 *Vervoort* [2016] NZCA 375 at [70], quoting Palmer, 'Controlling the Trust', 477–478.

the appearance of an apparently operative trust in correct or standard form, if the settlor-trustee's controlling conduct shows that she did not intend or understand the trust to require that all trustees must actively participate, then perhaps equity ought to be robust enough to recognise the trust as illusory. While such an approach may be open to the charge of also upsetting trust principles, it would at least be responding directly to the concern sought to be resolved, and its scope could more easily be kept in check. Maybe it is indeed time for recognition of a broader doctrine of abuse of trusts.[88]

[88] See Chapter 15 (Virgo).

# 15

# Abuse of Trust

*Graham Virgo*

## 1 INTRODUCTION

The trust can be a powerful instrument in managing and maintaining wealth and in creating significant rights and obligations. Settlors are given great freedom as to how they create a trust, with few restrictions on the provisions they can include in the trust instrument. But with this freedom comes responsibility to ensure that the trust is not abused. Equity will not tolerate such abuse, and if a trust is considered to have been abused, it may be void or unenforceable.

But when will a trust be considered to be abused? Surprisingly little attention has been paid by commentators or judges to the notion of abuse of trust, although there are particular doctrines, which can be analysed as constituting an abuse of trust that have received a significant amount of attention. This chapter will seek to draw these and other doctrines together, to identify common themes and so determine whether a distinct doctrine of abuse of trust can be identified.

For the purposes of this chapter a trust, or a trust power, will be considered to have been abused where the purpose of the settlor or trustee in creating the trust or in exercising the power is considered to be inconsistent with the purity of the trust, typically because the settlor or trustee is unacceptably motivated by self-interest. A breach of trust is not for these purposes considered to be an abuse of trust, regardless of the motive, because a breach involves a failure to do what the trust requires the trustee to do or a trustee doing what they should not do. Abuse of trust is more subtle because it concerns the motivation behind the creation of what purports to be a trust or the exercise of a power.

## 2 ABUSE OF RIGHTS

In setting the scene to determine whether a distinct doctrine of abuse of trust can be recognised in Equity, it is useful first to examine a possibly cognate doctrine, namely that of abuse of rights at Common Law. It has sometimes been suggested that where a defendant exercises a Common Law right, but does so for what might be considered an unacceptable motive, this constitutes an abuse of the right which is consequently unlawful. This is illustrated by *Hollywood Silver Fox Farm* v. *Emmett*[1] – where the claimant, a breeder of foxes, sued the defendant for the tort of nuisance, after the defendant, who was seeking to develop nearby land, arranged for guns to be fired on his land but in the vicinity of the claimant's land during the breeding season. It was found that the defendant's purpose was to frighten the claimant's vixens and prevent them from breeding, which is what happened. It was held that the defendant was liable to the claimant, even though he had exercised a right to fire guns on his own land. This suggests that the exercise of a right for an improper motive can result in liability being imposed.

But this should be contrasted with the earlier decision in *Bradford Corporation* v. *Pickles*,[2] which suggests that, where the defendant is exercising a lawful right, liability cannot be imposed simply because the motive is improper. In that case, the claimant owned land on which there were springs and streams which provided water for the inhabitants of Bradford. The defendant owned contiguous land which was uphill from that of the claimant. The defendant sank a shaft into his land to extract minerals, but the effect was to reduce the water available from the claimant's land. The claimant sought to stop the defendant from continuing to sink the shaft, because of the impact on its water supply. The claimant asserted that it was the defendant's intention to injure the claimant so that it would be induced to sell the land to the defendant. Despite this motive, the House of Lords held that the claimant was not entitled to a remedy. Lord Halsbury said:[3]

> This is not a case in which the state of mind of the person doing the act can affect the right to do it. If it was a lawful act, however ill the motive might be, he had the right to do it. If it was an unlawful act, however good his motive might be, he would have no right to do it. Motives and intentions in such a question as is now before your Lordships seem to be me to be absolutely irrelevant.

This suggests that the lawful exercise of a right cannot be rendered unlawful by the defendant's motive in exercising the right. Whilst *Hollywood Silver Fox Farm* appears to reach a different conclusion, this can be distinguished on the basis that the defendant's exercise of his right on his own land became unlawful because of the interference with the claimant's rights over its own land, particularly through the impact on the claimant's property and its right to the quiet enjoyment of its land; neither of these rights were infringed in the *Bradford Corporation* case.

It follows that the exercise of a right at Common Law cannot be rendered unlawful by virtue of the ulterior motive of the person exercising the right unless in so

1 *Hollywood Silver Fox Farm* v. *Emmett* [1936] 2 KB 468.
2 *Bradford Corporation* v. *Pickles* [1895] AC 587. Note also *Allen* v. *Flood* [1898] AC 1.
3 *Bradford Corporation* [1895] AC 587 at 594.

doing it directly interferes with the rights of another. This was expressed succinctly by Lord Watson in the *Bradford Corporation* case:[4]

> No use of property, which would be legal if due to a proper motive, can become illegal because it is prompted by a motive which is improper or even malicious.

If this was a fundamental proposition of law it would follow that a settlor who lawfully exercised a right to declare that their property is held on trust could not have the exercise of this right declared unlawful by virtue of an improper or malicious motive. As will be seen, however, this is not true of Equity, where the right to declare a trust or to exercise a trust power might be declared invalid for this very reason.

## 3 SHAM TRUSTS

A key example of a trust being declared invalid by virtue of the motive for its creation is where the trust is characterised as a sham. Although it might appear, on an objective interpretation of the facts, that the settlor lawfully intended to create a trust with a particular set of rights and obligations, this conclusion will be undermined where the real intention of the parties is to create a different set of rights and obligations. In such cases, the subjective intentions of the parties trump the objective appearance of a trust. This is a 'sham trust'. The essence of a sham was identified by Diplock LJ in *Snook* v. *London and West Riding Investments Ltd*:[5]

> it means acts done or documents executed by the parties to the 'sham' which are intended by them to give to third parties or to the court the appearance of creating between the parties legal rights and obligations different from the actual legal rights and obligations (if any) which the parties intend to create.

Whilst we typically describe the trust as a sham, it is actually the acts or documents relating to the creation of the trust which are the sham since they purport to be doing something different from what they are intended to do.[6] Nevertheless, the language of 'sham trust' provides a useful shorthand for this doctrine. The parties might have a variety of ulterior motives for creating the appearance of a trust, including misleading creditors or the tax authorities or seeking to shield assets from a divorced spouse.

### 3.1 *Identifying a Sham Trust*

Whether the trust is a sham will depend upon careful consideration of the evidence, but several principles can be identified to assist in this analysis.[7]

4 ibid at 598.

5 *Snook* v. *London and West Riding Investments Ltd* [1967] 2 QB 786 at 802. See also *Hitch* v. *Stone* [2001] EWCA Civ 63 at [63] (Arden LJ).

6 *Official Assignee* v. *Wilson* [2008] 3 NZLR 45 at [48]; *JSC Mezhdunarodniy* v. *Pugachev* [2017] EWHC 2426 (Ch) at [146] (Birss J).

7 See M. Conaglen, 'Sham Trusts' (2008) 67 *Cambridge Law Journal* 176.

(1) A finding of sham turns on intention. There must be an intention both to create a false or misleading appearance that a trust has been created and to deceive third parties or the court.[8] A party will satisfy the relevant fault requirement even though they did not intend the trust to be treated as a sham, if they knew or did not care that the act or documentation was misleading.[9] It follows that reckless indifference as to the sham is equated with intention, which is consistent with how intention is defined in other areas of the law.[10]

(2) It has been recognised that a 'finding of sham carries with it a finding of dishonesty'.[11] Despite this, there have been occasions when a sham trust has been recognised even though it was not declared with any obvious dishonest motive. For example, in *Midland Bank plc* v. *Wyatt*,[12] Wyatt had purported to declare a trust of his interest in the family home for the benefit of his wife and daughter. This was held not to be a valid declaration of trust because he lacked any real intent to hold the interest on trust for the benefit of his family. The trust document had been hidden in a safe, the wife and daughter were unaware of the declaration of trust, and Wyatt and his wife had continued to act as absolute owners, for example by mortgaging the property. Rather, the trust was purportedly declared to act as a safeguard if his company were to face financial difficulties, so it was a sham. It was recognised that this conclusion would have been reached even though there was no evidence that it had been created dishonestly, but as the result of, for example, mistaken legal advice.

In *JSC Mezhdunarodniy* v. *Pugachev*,[13] Birss J accepted that dishonesty is not a necessary component to establish a shamming intention. He illustrated this by the following example. The settlor may have prepared a sham document intending to mislead, but that document may have been put in the bottom drawer of a desk and never seen the light of day. Birss J considered that such a settlor might have intended to act dishonestly, but that such dishonesty is only latent; there can be no actual dishonesty until the document is produced to a third party. But this confuses dishonesty, a state of mind, with deception, an act of misrepresentation. Nobody needs to be deceived in order to establish a sham, since the focus is on the intention of the parties; fault here is inchoate. Birss J considered that dishonesty need not be proved because

[8] *Hitch* [2001] EWCA Civ 63 at [66] (Arden LJ); *Pankhania* v. *Chandegra* [2012] EWCA Civ 1438 at [20]–[21] (Patten LJ). See also *Scott* v. *Federal Commissioner of Taxation (No 2)* (1966) ALJR 265 at 279 (Windeyer J).

[9] *Midland Bank* v. *Wyatt* [1995] 1 FLR 696 at 699 (David Young QC); *JSC Mezhdunarodniy* [2017] EWHC 2426 (Ch) at [150] (iv).

[10] Such as the tort of inducing a breach of contract: *OBG Ltd* v. *Allan* [2008] 1 AC 1 at [40]–[41] (Lord Hoffmann); [192] (Lord Nicholls).

[11] *National Westminster Bank plc* v. *Jones* [2001] BCLC 98 at [59] (Neuberger J); *ND* v. *SD* [2017] EWHC 1507 (Fam) at [184] (Roberts J). See also Conaglen, 'Sham Trusts',187.

[12] *Midland Bank* [1995] 1 FLR 696.

[13] *JSC Mezhdunarodniy* [2017] EWHC 2426 (Ch) at [152].

of his confusion about the function of dishonesty and his recognition that to be a sham a document 'must be created with an intention to mislead, but the fact that the document is never deployed to mislead does not stop it being a sham'.[14] That is correct, but it does not follow that dishonesty is irrelevant. In determining whether there should be a separate requirement of dishonesty, it is necessary to consider how dishonesty is defined. This has been clarified by the UK Supreme Court in *Ivey* v. *Genting Casinos (UK) Ltd*,[15] which held that dishonesty is to be determined objectively by reference to what the reasonable person would consider to be dishonest, albeit in the light of the facts known by the defendant.[16] Whilst it might be appropriate to recognise that dishonesty defined in this way is indeed a separate requirement to establish a sham, this will invariably follow from the requirement that there be an intent both to create a false appearance and to deceive third parties. Indeed, even if Wyatt had misunderstood legal advice he would still be considered to have acted dishonestly if, in the light of what he knew, a reasonable person would describe his conduct as dishonest. Consequently, it should not be an independent requirement for a sham trust that the parties were dishonest.

(3) Where the settlor self-declares themself as trustee, it is only necessary to consider the intention of the settlor to mislead.[17] Where, however, the settlor purports to declare a trust with somebody else as trustee, the trust will be treated as a sham only if both the settlor and the trustee intend it to be so.[18] So, if the settlor lacks the intention to create a trust, but the trustee does not share this intention, the trust will still be valid.[19] The reason for requiring both parties to share the intention to mislead is unclear, and it has sometimes been suggested that it should be sufficient that one controlling mind should possess the shamming intention.[20]

Various reasons have, however, been suggested for the requirement of a common intention. Conaglen argued that it is because a high threshold must be met to ensure that apparent trusts are not upset too readily, so as to maintain the security of transactions.[21] To reach this threshold, what must be established is effectively a

14 ibid.

15 *Ivey* v. *Genting Casinos (UK) Ltd* [2017] UKSC 67, [2018] AC 391.

16 This has been recognised as the correct interpretation of dishonesty for the action for dishonestly assisting a breach of trust or fiduciary duty: *Group Seven Ltd* v. *Nasir* [2019] EWCA Civ 614, [2020] Ch 129.

17 *Painter* v. *Hutchison* [2007] EWHC 758 (Ch) at [109]–[115] (Lewison J).

18 *Hitch* [2001] EWCA Civ 63 at [68]; *Shalson* v. *Russo* [2003] EWHC 1637 (Ch), [2005] Ch 281 at [188] and [190] (Rimer J); A v. A [2007] EWHC 99 (Fam) at [52]; *JSC Mezhdunarodniy* [2017] EWHC 2426 (Ch) at [150](iii).

19 See also *Chase Manhattan Equities Ltd* v. *Goodman* [1991] BCLC 897; *Grupo Torras SA* v. *Al Sabah* [2004] WTLR 1 (Deputy Bailiff of the Royal Court of Jersey).

20 A. Hudson, *Equity and Trusts* (Routledge, 9th ed, 2017), p. 95. See also J. Palmer, 'Dealing with the Emerging Popularity of Sham Trusts' [2007] *New Zealand Law Review* 81, 93.

21 Conaglen, 'Sham Trusts', 188–190.

conspiracy between the settlor and trustee to mislead. A more convincing explanation of this requirement was provided by Rimer J in *Shalson* v. *Russo*:[22]

> When a settlor creates a settlement, he purports to divest himself of assets in favour of the trustee, and the trustee accepts them on the basis of the trusts of the settlement. The settlor may have an unspoken intention that the assets are in fact to be treated as his own and that the trustee will accede to his every request on demand. But unless that intention is from the outset shared by the trustee (or later becomes so shared), I fail to see how the settlement can be regarded as a sham. Once the assets are vested in the trustee, they will be held on the declared trusts, and he is entitled to regard them as so held and to ignore any demands from the settlor as to how to deal with them. I cannot understand on what basis a third party could claim, merely by reference to the unilateral intentions of the settlor, that the settlement was a sham and that assets in fact remained the settlor's property.

In other words, there is a need for a common intention to be established in order to rebut the objective appearance of a trust. If the settlor intends a sham, but the trustee is unaware of this and fulfils their trust obligations, the court should not interfere by declaring the trust a sham. The settlor's intentions will have been defeated, but since they were improper from the outset this should not be a cause for concern. If, on the other hand, the settlor intends a trust, there will be a real trust even if the trustee intends something else. In such circumstances, either the trustee will be liable for breach of trust, by not fulfilling their trust obligations, or the exercise of a trust power may be set aside as being fraudulent.[23] It is only where the settlor does not intend a trust and the trustee shares this intent that a sham, should be declared because there will be no trust and the trustee, as a party to the sham, cannot be considered to have legitimately assumed their trust powers and obligations.[24]

(4) A trust that was not a sham when created cannot be made a sham subsequently.[25] This is because, once a trust has been properly constituted and executed, there is a valid trust which determines what should happen to the trust property. As Munby J recognised in A v. A,[26] once a trustee has accepted office in good faith, they cannot divest themselves of their fiduciary obligations by improper acts. Consequently, if a trustee accepted their responsibilities without intending to be a party to a sham but then purported to treat the trust as a sham, there is a valid trust but they could be liable for breach of trust, and if the settlor subsequently agreed that the trust should be treated as a sham they might be liable for dishonestly assisting a breach of trust. Similarly, a trust will not become a sham if a trustee is appointed after the trust has been

[22] *Shalson* [2005] Ch 281 at [189].
[23] See Section 7.
[24] *Re Esteem Settlement* [2003] JRC 092, [2004] 1 WTLR 1 at [53].
[25] A [2007] EWHC 99 (Fam) at [43]); *JSC Mezhdunarodniy* [2017] EWHC 2426 (Ch) at [150] (v).
[26] A [2007] EWHC 99 (Fam) at [43].

properly constituted but with the intention of treating the trust as a sham. This is because the trust, being properly constituted, is not a sham and so the trustee will be subject to trust and fiduciary obligations.

A trust that was a sham when it was created can, however, be converted into a genuine trust if, for example, new trustees are appointed who are unaware of the sham intent, and who exercise their powers and duties in accordance with the terms of the trust.[27] Such a trust will have been properly constituted and the new trustee, lacking the intention that the trust be treated as a sham, cannot be treated as a party to the sham.

(5) In *Hitch* v. *Stone*[28] Arden LJ recognised that determining whether a trust is a sham requires careful analysis of the facts. In determining whether a document is a sham, the court is not confined to interpreting the document itself, but can have regard to external evidence, such as the parties' explanation, and circumstantial evidence, such as evidence of the subsequent conduct of the parties.

The courts tend to start with a presumption that a document, which purports to establish a trust means what is expressed on its face, and it will not lightly find a trust to be sham.[29] Various factors have been found to be relevant to the determination of whether there was an intention to mislead, such as the artificiality of the transaction,[30] and the extent to which the settlor can control the trustee's decision-making powers or treat the trust fund as their own to do with as they wish.[31] A good indicator that a trust is a sham is where it appears that the settlor has been divested of property but the trustee does not truly have the power to administer the property and the settlor continues to exercise real control over it. It is a question of degree whether or not the settlor retains such power over the property that the trust is treated as a sham.[32] The more powers the settlor retains the more likely it is that the trust is a sham,[33] although the fact that a settlor has reserved powers does not necessarily mean that the trust is a sham.[34] The fact that an arrangement is artificial also does not necessarily mean that it is a sham,[35] but artificiality will be relevant evidence. A particularly

27 ibid at [45].
28 *Hitch* [2001] EWCA Civ 63 at [64]–[65].
29 *Heinrich* v. *Pantrust International* SA [2018] JRC081A. See S. Alexander, 'Intention and Sham' (2018) 24 *Trusts and Trustees* 1031. See also *National Westminster Bank plc* [2001] 1 BCLC 98 at [59] (Neuberger J).
30 ibid at [39] (Neuberger J).
31 See *Shalson* [2005] Ch 281 at [195]. Although this was not established on the facts.
32 See Conaglen, 'Sham Trusts'.
33 D. Harris, 'No Such Thing as a Sham Trust?' (2004) *Private Client Business* 95.
34 L. Ho, 'Breaking Bad: Settlor's Reserved Powers' in R. C. Nolan, K. Low, and H. W. Tang (eds), *Trusts and Modern Wealth Management* (Cambridge University Press, 2018), pp. 39–42.
35 A [2007] EWHC 99 (Fam) at [33].

good example of the type of evidence, which may be relied on to establish a sham is the decision of the Ontario Superior Court of Justice in *Re McGoey*,[36] where the face of the relevant document was just as significant as its contents. McGoey, a bankrupt, and his wife alleged that the family home and another property were held on trust for their children. Trust documents were produced, but these were held to be sham because an expert in typography had testified that the fonts used[37] were not in existence when the documents were purported to be created.

In *JSC Mezhdunarodniy* v. *Pugachev*, Birss J recognised that evidence that the trustees may have done something after the trust was set up which was contrary to the terms of the trust may not support a finding of a sham, since it might simply constitute a breach of trust.[38] Equally, if the trustee does something subsequently which is consistent with the terms of the trust it does not necessarily follow that there is no sham, especially if the trustee is acting at a time when they know that they are under close scrutiny; actions when no one is looking carry more weight.

### 3.2 *Consequences of Finding a Sham*

If the trust is a sham it will be void.[39] Any property which has been transferred will be held on resulting trust for the settlor. However, holding the trust to be void might adversely affect innocent third parties who have relied upon the apparently valid express trust. In such cases, third parties should be protected and the doctrine of estoppel might be employed to prevent parties to the sham from denying the existence of a trust to the detriment of those who have innocently relied upon it.[40] In *Carman* v. *Yates*, Charles J noted that:[41]

> as against an innocent third party it cannot lie in the mouths of the pretenders to assert to the disadvantage of that innocent third party that the transaction is a sham, or pretence, and thus of no effect.

This seems entirely appropriate, but it is not clear how the court would deal with the situation where the interests of various innocent third parties conflict, such that some would insist on the trust being a sham and others the contrary.[42] Charles J in *Carman* v. *Yates* suggested that the courts would benefit from a degree of flexibility in such a situation.[43] Conaglen has cautioned against unconstrained judicial

36 *Re McGoey* 2019 ONSC 80.

37 Cambria and Calibri, both released in 2007, whereas the trust documents were executed in 1995 and 2004.

38 *JSC Mezhdunarodniy* [2017] EWHC 2426 (Ch) at [150](v).

39 *Hitch* [2001] EWCA Civ 63 at [87].

40 ibid at [87]; *National Westminster Bank* [2001] 1 BCLC 98 at [60].

41 *Carman* v. *Yates* [2004] EWHC 3448 (Ch) at [219].

42 Neuberger J recognised that the court would have to consider such a scenario if and when it arises: *National Westminster Bank* [2001] 1 BCLC 98 at [60].

43 *Carman* [2004] EWHC 3448 (Ch) at [220].

discretion in this area, preferring instead to focus upon established principles concerning estoppel and the priority of competing equities.[44] Even so there may be some merit in allowing the courts the flexibility to achieve the most satisfactory outcome on the facts of the case. This is now the position as regards the impact of illegality on trusts,[45] with which the doctrine of sham is closely related, at least where the parties are motivated by an illegal purpose.

It might be considered to be odd to conclude that a sham trust should be treated as void, for if both the settlor and trustee intended to deceive and this is dishonest, would not the more equitable response be to defeat their dishonesty by treating the trust in all cases as valid? But this confuses the objective evidence of the trust with the parties' subjective motives. The parties want there to be the appearance of a trust to enable them to pursue their dishonest purpose. Far better for the trust to be regarded as invalid, and so expose the reality of what they intended so as to make, for example, the putative settlor's assets available for their creditors, save where the rights of third parties need to be protected, and here estoppel is the most appropriate doctrine on which to rely.

### 3.3 *Sham as a Distinct Doctrine?*

Conaglen has argued[46] that the doctrine of sham trusts is a distinct doctrine from that concerning certainty of intent to declare a trust, since the focus is on establishing the true subjective intent of the person declaring the trust rather than objective evidence of the trust. This has been challenged by S. Douglas and B. McFarlane,[47] who argue that there is no distinct doctrine of sham trusts since the focus is simply on establishing the objective intent of the settlor to determine whether the trust was intended to take effect on the terms set out in the trust deed. Whilst establishing a sham can have regard to the oral communication between the parties, they consider that this still involves an objective interpretation to determine what these communications would have reasonably conveyed to the recipient of them. But this is inconsistent with the clear dichotomy identified in the cases between the usual objective rules of construction to establish a trust and the rules for establishing a different subjective intent which underpins the doctrine of sham.[48] This dichotomy is identified well in *Snell's Equity*:[49]

44 Conaglen, 'Sham Trusts', 205–206.
45 See Section 6.2.2.
46 Conaglen, 'Sham Trusts'.
47 S. Douglas and B. McFarlane, 'Sham Trusts' in H. Conway and R. Hickey (eds), *Modern Studies in Property Law*) (Hart Publishing, 2017), Ch. 13.
48 *Webb* v. *Webb* [2017] CKCA 4 at [56].
49 J. McGhee and S. Elliott, *Snell's Equity* (Sweet and Maxwell, 34th ed, 2019), 22-071. See also *Hitch* [2001] EWCA Civ 63 at [64]–[65].

(i) An intention to declare a trust requires a focus on the proper construction of the words used in the relevant documentation. Here the focus is on the unilateral intention of the settlor alone, objectively determined, with narrow rules of construction which have little regard to the background circumstances.
(ii) When considering whether a trust is a sham, the focus is on the reality of the declaration, so a wider range of evidence external to the document can be taken into account to determine that the purported declaration does not reflect the true agreement between the parties. This can include circumstantial evidence, such as the subsequent conduct of the parties.

It follows that it is appropriate to recognise the sham trust as a distinct doctrine and not simply as a matter of construction.

### 3.4 *Sham Trust as an Abuse of Trust*

By virtue of the usual conclusion that a sham trust is void, and so does not exist, it might be concluded that a sham trust does not involve any abuse of trust, because there is no trust to be abused. But this would miss the point. On the face of it there is a valid trust, but the parties have abused trust law principles to create the appearance of a trust by virtue of their deceptive motive as a result of which the trust should be treated as invalid: this is an abuse of trust.

## 4 ILLUSORY TRUSTS

It has sometimes been recognised that a trust might be illusory[50] and so ineffective to create rights and obligations. An illusory trust can be considered to be an abuse of the trust by creating the appearance of a trust which is never actually there. This is distinct from a sham trust which appears to be valid and effective with reference to the objective facts, but it is determined that the actual intention of the parties was to mislead. An illusory trust, on the other hand, purports to be a trust but the nature of the obligations identified are inconsistent with those which operate in a trust and so what has been created is not a trust. For example, in *Re AQ Revocable Trust*,[51] the settlor was the sole trustee of a trust which gave him the power to absolve himself of any breaches of trust, so he could not be held accountable as a trustee, and he also had the power to revoke the trust whenever he wished. It was held that these powers rendered the trust illusory, because he could never be called to account. Similarly, in *Webb* v. *Webb*[52] a trust was not recognised where the purported settlor had retained rights that were indistinguishable from ownership, such as the power

50 See Ho, 'Breaking Bad', pp. 42–47.
51 *Re AQ Revocable Trust* [2010] 13 ITELR 260 (Bermuda).
52 *Webb* v. *Webb* [2020] UKPC 22.

to nominate himself as settlor as the sole beneficiary in place of all existing beneficiaries and the power to pay the whole capital and income to himself as a beneficiary for his personal use. In such a case, the settlor had not effectively alienated the trust property so that there was no valid trust.

The notion that a trust cannot be recognised because it is illusory has been challenged. In the New Zealand case of *Clayton* v. *Clayton*,[53] Mr Clayton was the sole trustee of a discretionary trust, the objects of which were himself, his wife, and their daughter. According to the terms of the trust, Clayton could exercise the power of appointment in his own favour. In the Court of Appeal, it was held that the trust was not illusory, because, once a valid trust had been established, it should not be possible to treat it as not being in existence simply because the trustee has wide powers of control over the trust property. The Supreme Court rejected the finding that the trust was not illusory and then, somewhat unhelpfully, declined to rule on the point whether or not the trust was illusory since the issue did not arise on the facts. The Court recognised that there is no value in using the label 'illusory', it being sufficient simply to say that there was no valid trust.[54] The real issue was considered to be whether the powers identified in the trust instrument were so broad that what was intended to be a trust was not actually a trust, but it was not considered to be necessary to determine whether this was true of the discretionary trust on the facts of this case.[55]

Birss J reflected on this putative doctrine of illusory trust in *JSC Mezhdunarodniy* v. *Pugachev*.[56] He too rejected the language of an 'illusory' trust and said that the focus should be on the 'true effects of the trust'.[57] The doctrine of sham was distinguished, since that involves determining the true meaning of a document with reference to the subjective intention of the parties,[58] whereas determining the true effect of the trust requires the court to construe the powers and duties of the trustee as a whole and consider what is going on as a matter of substance.[59] Birss J suggested that, since in *Clayton* v. *Clayton* it appeared that the trustee had effectively retained the powers of ownership, it could have been determined that there was not a true trust.

In the light of the analysis in *Clayton* and *Pugachev*, there is clearly a distinct doctrine from that of sham trust and one which requires an objective determination of whether what purports to be a trust is actually a trust when judged by its true effect. But, despite the rejection of the phrase 'illusory trust', this is actually a useful descriptor of the doctrine. For, if what the settlor has purported to create

53 *Clayton* v. *Clayton* [2015] NZCA 30; [2016] NZSC 29.
54 *Clayton* [2016] NZSC 29 at [123]. This was also the language used by the Privy Council in *Webb* [2020] UKPC 22, where the phrase 'illusory trust' was not used.
55 *Clayton* [2016] NZSC 29 at [130].
56 *JSC Mezhdunarodniy* [2017] EWHC 2426 (Ch).
57 ibid at [169].
58 ibid at [168].
59 ibid at [167].

cannot be considered to satisfy the core requirements of a trust, then it is not a trust which has been created: the trust is an illusion and the attempt to create can be considered to be an abuse. How this abuse should be determined will require careful analysis of the facts, but it is clear that the doctrine of the irreducible core of trust obligations, as recognised by Millett LJ in *Armitage* v. *Nurse*,[60] will be relevant, since these are the obligations owed by the trustee to the beneficiaries which are 'fundamental to the concept of a trust. If the beneficiaries have no rights enforceable against the trustees there are no trusts'.[61] The fundamental duty of all trustees is to perform the trust honestly and in good faith for the benefit of the beneficiaries. If a trustee has reserved so much power to themself as trustee, this calls into question the irreducible core of the trustee obligations and means that there is no valid trust at all.

Whilst the doctrine of illusory trust should be considered to be an abuse of trust like a sham trust, the two doctrines are distinct. A sham trust requires consideration of the subjective intention of the parties to identify a motive to mislead. Whether a trust is illusory is a question of objective determination, without any need to prove dishonesty or purpose to deceive. It is simply a matter of determining that what purports to be a trust cannot be classified as such if it lacks the core components of a trust, even if the settlor has described it as a trust and subjectively intends it to be a trust.

## 5 DEFRAUDING CREDITORS

A declaration of trust can be set aside by statute in the United Kingdom[62] where it is made to defraud creditors, such as where the settlor's purpose is to put assets beyond the reach of creditors[63] or to prejudice creditors' interests in a claim against the settlor.[64] That this involves a response to an abuse of trust is illustrated by *IRC* v. *Hashmi*,[65] where a tenant had acquired the freehold of certain property and purported to declare a trust of this for his son. In concluding that the tenant's purpose had been to use the trust to defraud his creditors, Arden LJ said:[66]

> [Section 423 of the Insolvency Act 1986] does not require the inquiry to be made whether the purpose was a dominant purpose. It is sufficient if the statutory purpose can properly be described as a purpose and not merely as a consequence [...] it will often be the case that the motive to defeat creditors and the motive to secure

[60] *Armitage* v. *Nurse* [1998] Ch 241 at 253.
[61] ibid at 253.
[62] Insolvency Act 1986, s. 423.
[63] *IRC* v. *Hashmi* [2002] EWCA Civ 981.
[64] *Hill* v. *Spread Trustee Co Ltd* [2006] EWCA Civ 542.
[65] *Hashmi* [2002] EWCA Civ 981.
[66] *Hashmi* [2002] EWCA Civ 981 at [23]–[25].

> family protection will co-exist in such a way that even the transferor himself may be unable to say what was uppermost in his mind [...] for something to be a purpose it must be a real substantial purpose.

This focus on the purpose or motive of the settlor in creating the trust means that this can be considered to be a statutory example of abuse of trust.

It is also unlawful for a person to declare themself to be holding property on trust for one creditor, or group of creditors, to the detriment of other creditors: this is known as a 'voidable preference'.[67] In such circumstances, a sufficiently certain intention to create a trust may be established, but that intention is not given effect due to the policy underpinning the Insolvency Act 1986, which requires that unsecured creditors should be treated equally amongst themselves. Whether or not an unfair preference is at issue depends on the particular circumstances of the case. In *Re Kayford Ltd*,[68] Megarry J held that the trust was valid where a company, experiencing financial difficulties, set up a separate account, called the 'Customer's Trust Deposit Account', to ring-fence deposits received from its customers. The company only intended to take the money out of the account once goods were delivered to the customers. The judge held that this was not an unlawful preference in favour of the new depositors:[69]

> on the facts of the case [counsel] was unable to contend that any question of a fraudulent preference arose. If one leaves on one side any case in which an insolvent company seeks to declare a trust in favour of creditors, one is concerned here with the question not of preferring creditors but of preventing those who pay money from becoming creditors, by making them beneficiaries under a trust.

This decision can be justified since, without the protection offered by a trust, the company may have been less likely to receive orders from customers. Without such orders, the company may simply have entered liquidation even earlier, so its other creditors would not have been in any better position by opposing the creation of a trust. This, therefore, was not an abuse of trust.

## 6 ILLEGALITY

The trust might be considered to be abused where it is tainted by illegality, particularly where the operation of the trust infringes the criminal law. Two distinct but related scenarios can be identified. First, where the trust itself, despite being apparently validly declared, and so not a sham or illusory, is created solely to perpetrate illegal activity; these are extrinsically illegal trusts. Second, where the trust is again

67 Insolvency Act 1986, ss. 238, 239.

68 *Re Kayford Ltd* [1974] 1 WLR 279.

69 ibid at 281.

apparently valid but is operated in such a way as either to hide illegality or the trustee may be motivated by an illegal purpose; these are trusts which are tainted by illegality.

### 6.1 *Extrinsically Illegal Trusts*

A trust is extrinsically illegal where the trustee inevitably commits an illegal act in fulfilling their trust obligations, regardless of whether the illegality involves the commission of a crime or conduct which is considered to be contrary to public policy. Such a trust will be void as being an abuse of trust.

The Law Commission in its consultation paper on illegality,[70] usefully identified five instances when a trust should be treated as illegal:

(1) a trust which is legally wrongful to create or to impose;
(2) a trust which is created to facilitate fraud or some other legal wrong. So, for example, where a settlor transferred money to a company to hold on trust for him, the trust was void because he was motivated to ensure that the company appeared to have a credit balance;[71]
(3) a trust created in return for the commission of a wrong or a promise to commit a wrong;
(4) a trust which expressly or necessarily requires a trustee or a beneficiary to commit a legal wrong or which tends or is intended to do so; and
(5) a trust which is contrary to public policy at common law. So, for example, in *Thrupp* v. *Collett*[72] a trust which provided for the paying of fines of convicted poachers was held to be void as being contrary to public policy since it would encourage the commission of crime. Famously, in *Re Pinion*[73] Harman LJ stated that a school for pickpockets or prostitutes would not be a charitable trust, as being subversive of public morality.

### 6.2 *Trusts Tainted by Illegality*

There will be other circumstances where a trust is created lawfully and can operate lawfully, but where one or more of the parties is tainted by an illegal purpose in carrying out the trust. Such trusts, being tainted by illegal purposes, may be unenforceable as being an abuse of trust. Determining when the taint of illegality constitutes an abuse has long been a matter of controversy, with the English courts, at least, having adopted a particularly confused regime for responding to illegality.

70 The Law Commission, *Illegal Transactions: The Effect of Illegality on Contract and Trusts* (Law Com No 154, 1999).
71 *Re Great Berlin Steamboat Company* (1884) 26 Ch D 616.
72 *Thrupp* v. *Collett* (1858) 26 Beav 125.
73 *Re Pinion* [1965] Ch 85 at 105.

### 6.2.1 Traditional Approach

The traditional approach to illegality in private law has been founded on the maxim *ex turpi causa non oritur actio* ('no action can arise from a base cause'),[74] meaning that the courts will not assist a claimant to obtain a remedy where the action is founded on illegal conduct. As Lord Goff said in *Tinsley* v. *Milligan*, a case concerning resulting trusts:[75]

> it is a principle of policy, whose application is indiscriminate and so can lead to unfair consequences as between the parties to litigation. Moreover the principle allows no room for the exercise of any discretion by the court in favour of one party or the other.

This has been extended to defeat express trusts[76] and common intention constructive trusts.[77] But the *ex turpi causa* rule was never absolute; it was qualified by various doctrines. Two of these have been particularly significant to trusts.

6.2.1.1 NO RELIANCE ON ILLEGALITY A claim relating to a trust may succeed where it can be established without needing to rely on the illegality. In *Tinsley* v. *Milligan*,[78] the House of Lords recognised that Milligan could enforce her equitable proprietary right against Tinsley even though Milligan had participated in an illegal transaction. They had both contributed to the purchase of a house, but it was registered in the sole name of Tinsley on the understanding that they would have joint beneficial interests in it. This arrangement was to make it appear that Milligan was a lodger, so that she could make fraudulent claims for housing benefit. Both parties had participated in the fraud and benefited from it. Subsequently, their relationship ended, and Tinsley brought an action for possession of the house, asserting that she had sole ownership of it. Milligan counterclaimed that she had a beneficial interest in the property, because the nature of their relationship was such that a resulting trust could be presumed. Tinsley argued that Milligan could not ask the court to enforce the trust in her favour because of her illegal conduct in perpetrating benefit fraud. It was held that Milligan's counterclaim should succeed: to trigger the presumption of resulting trust, she simply needed to show that she had contributed to the purchase price and did not need to refer to the illegal purpose to establish this. The only way in which Tinsley could have sought to rebut this presumption was by showing that Milligan had intended Tinsley to have sole title to the property to enable her to perpetrate the fraud. But Tinsley could not do this

74 *Holman* v. *Johnson* (1775) 1 Cowp 341 at 343 (Lord Mansfield).
75 *Tinsley* v. *Milligan* [1994] 1 AC 340 at 355.
76 *Collier* v. *Collier* [2002] EWCA Civ 1095.
77 *Davies* v. *O'Kelly* [2014] EWCA Civ 1606.
78 *Tinsley* [1994] 1 AC 340 at 376 (Lord Browne-Wilkinson).

because it would have involved her pleading that the transaction was intended to effect an illegal purpose.

Whether the claimant can establish the claim without relying on illegality turns on chance. The result in *Tinsley* v. *Milligan* would have been different had the presumption of advancement applied, for then the claimant would have needed to plead the illegal agreement to rebut the presumption.

6.2.1.2 WITHDRAWAL FROM AN ILLEGAL TRANSACTION Where the claimant has effectively withdrawn from an illegal transaction before any part of it has been performed, they will no longer be tainted by the illegality and can enforce their claim. This withdrawal principle has long been recognised as a reason why a claim should succeed despite the taint of illegality.[79] Whilst originally the principle required proof of repentance by the claimant,[80] over time this requirement was dropped,[81] it being sufficient that the claimant sought to distance themself from the illegality, even if this occurred for reasons outside the claimant's control, such as where the transaction had been frustrated;[82] withdrawal does not require any voluntary change of mind on the part of the claimant. The operation of this principle is illustrated by *Tribe* v. *Tribe*.[83] The claimant feared that he would be forced to sell his shares in the family business to meet potential liabilities to creditors. Consequently, he transferred them to his son, who never paid for them and was never intended to do so. This transfer of shares was illegal because the claimant's purpose was to defraud his creditors. No creditors were deceived, however, because alternative arrangements were made which prevented the liabilities from arising. Once the risk that the shares would be taken had passed, the claimant requested his son to return them to him, but he refused to do so. Since the equitable presumption of advancement applies in respect of transfers of property from a father to his son, it was presumed that the claimant had given the shares to his son. To rebut this presumption the claimant needed to plead his purpose that the shares were not transferred to the son absolutely, but only until the threat from his creditors had passed; but this was an illegal purpose on which he could not rely. Despite this, it was held that the father had withdrawn from the illegal transaction because no part of the illegal purpose had been carried into effect, since no creditors had been deceived. Consequently, he ceased to be tainted by the illegality and could plead his true intention in transferring the shares to his son and so enforce the resulting trust. If, however, the illegal purpose had been carried into effect, even if only partly, the claim would fail.[84]

79 See *Taylor* v. *Bowers* (1876) 1 QBD 291.
80 *Bigos* v. *Bousted* [1951] 1 All ER 92.
81 *Tribe* v. *Tribe* [1996] Ch 107 at 135 (Millett LJ).
82 As had been recognised by the Court of Appeal in *Patel* v. *Mirza* [2014] EWCA Civ 1047.
83 *Tribe* [1996] Ch 107.
84 *Collier* [2002] EWCA Civ 1095.

### 6.2.2 Modern Approach

The decision of the Supreme Court in *Patel* v. *Mirza*[85] is now the leading authority on the operation of illegality in private law claims in England. Although the decision is of specific relevance to the law of unjust enrichment, it will also be of significance to claims relating to a trust. Whilst the nine Justices sitting in the Supreme Court sought to place the law of illegality on a secure and principled footing, the approach which has been adopted is likely to create more uncertainty.

The Respondent had transferred £620,000 to the Appellant, a City trader who had suggested the scheme, so that the Appellant could use the money to bet on share price movements based on inside information. Such insider dealing is a crime under Part V of the Criminal Justice Act 1993. The inside information was not forthcoming and so the agreement was not carried out. The Respondent sought restitution of the money paid on the ground that the Appellant had been unjustly enriched at his expense, the ground of restitution being that the basis for the transfer had failed totally. Because the parties had committed a conspiracy to commit insider dealing, and so were tainted by illegality, the Appellant refused to make restitution. The Supreme Court unanimously held that the Respondent should recover the money. The logic of restitution prevailed, despite the taint of illegality, such that all the Justices recognised that it was appropriate to restore the status quo rather than to allow the Appellant to profit from his participation in the illegal transaction. As Lord Sumption recognised, 'an order for restitution would not give effect to the illegal act or to any right derived from it'.[86]

The wider significance of *Patel* v. *Mirza* relates to the operation of illegality generally. There was consensus that the rationale behind illegality defeating a claim is that it would be contrary to the public interest to enforce a claim if to do so would be harmful to the integrity of the legal system. But there was disagreement amongst the Justices as to whether the effect of illegality should be flexible and context-dependent or certain and principled. The flexible approach was adopted by a majority. The new approach to illegality involves a trio of considerations:[87]

> one cannot judge whether allowing a claim which is in some way tainted by illegality would be contrary to the public interest, because it would be harmful to the integrity of the legal system without (a) considering the underlying purpose of the prohibition which has been transgressed, (b) considering conversely any other relevant public policies which may be rendered ineffective or less effective by denial of the claim, and (c) keeping in mind the possibility of overkill unless the law is applied with a due sense of proportionality.

Various factors were identified to assess the question of proportionality of denying relief, including the seriousness of the conduct, its centrality to the claim and

85 *Patel* v. *Mirza* [2016] UKSC 42, [2017] AC 467.

86 ibid at [268].

87 ibid at [101]; see also [120].

whether there was a marked disparity in the parties' respective culpability. But the question of proportionality requires a quantitative assessment against some objective guide, and no such guide was identified. Lord Sumption rejected the approach of the majority considering it to be:[88]

> far too vague and potentially far too wide to serve as the basis on which a person may be denied his legal rights. It converts a legal principle into an exercise of judicial discretion, in the process exhibiting all the vices of 'complexity, uncertainty, arbitrariness and lack of transparency' which Lord Toulson attributes to the present law.

Lord Toulson's response to this was to acknowledge that the trio of considerations might result in uncertainty, but the existing law was already riven with uncertainties and, anyway, certainty was not a relevant consideration when dealing with people who were contemplating unlawful activity. But surely Lord Sumption's analysis is correct. Whilst the trio of considerations purport to be principled, there is a significant danger that when applied by a judge they will not provide the guidance to judicial decision-making that is required of a legal principle. It is, for example, unclear how the considerations were applied on the facts of *Patel* v. *Mirza* itself, although it is clear that they did not operate to defeat the claim. But the majority did not identify reasons why insider dealing was made a crime or explain why this was relevant to the determination of the impact of illegality. Neither were any policies identified, which would have been affected had the claim been denied, nor was the question of proportionality considered explicitly.

Whilst much of the analysis of the law by the Supreme Court focused on illegality as it relates to the law of unjust enrichment, the decision is of profound importance to the law of trusts. Any allegation of illegality in an equitable claim will now have to be examined with reference to the trio of considerations to determine what the effect of the illegality on the claim should be. But of particular significance is whether the no-reliance and withdrawal principles remain relevant to claims involving trusts.

6.2.2.1 NO RELIANCE The majority in *Patel* recognised that the 'no-reliance' principle should be rejected.[89] This is primarily because of its perceived procedural nature and its arbitrary consequences. It follows that an equitable claim will not be defeated simply because the claimant needs to establish the illegality of the transaction to make the claim. Even so, the majority considered that *Tinsley* v. *Milligan* would have been decided the same way, but without the artifice of considering whether it was necessary to rely on the illegality to establish the claim.

[88] *Patel* [2017] AC 467 at [265].
[89] Confirmed by Sir Kim Lewison in *Cenoc* v. *Shafer (Saint Lucia)* [2016] UKPC 25 at [20].

Rather, the nature of the illegality would need to be considered explicitly, and the majority in *Patel* would have concluded that it would have been disproportionate to have prevented Milligan from enforcing her equitable proprietary interest which had arisen under a resulting trust, because this would have resulted in Tinsley being unjustly enriched.[90]

More significantly to an analysis of abuse of trust, the application of the trio of considerations would presumably confirm the result in *Collier* v. *Collier*[91] but using different reasoning.[92] In that case, a father had purported to grant a lease of premises to his daughter to be held on trust for him, in order to deceive his creditors.[93] It was held that the father was unable to establish his beneficial interest in the lease because he needed to rely on an unlawful agreement to establish the trust. Instead, the focus on the trio of considerations would now enable the court to determine whether enforcing the trust constitutes an abuse of trust in the circumstances.

6.2.2.2 WITHDRAWAL The continued operation of the withdrawal principle is doubtful following *Patel* v. *Mirza*. Lord Toulson did not consider that this doctrine was relevant on the facts of the case, so he did not examine it. But the doctrine appears to be inconsistent with the trio of considerations which he identified, or, if it remains relevant, it will be subsumed into one of the relevant factors to assess the disproportionality of denying relief. It follows that *Tribe* v. *Tribe* would presumably be decided in the same way, save if the application of the trio of considerations would defeat the claim.

6.2.2.3 ILLEGALITY AS ABUSE OF TRUST The approach of the majority in *Patel* v. *Mirza* has proved controversial. It has been rejected in Singapore,[94] where a more restricted form of the withdrawal principle has been recognised and the no-reliance principle has been replaced with a test based on stultification of the law. Whilst it is the case that the 'trio of considerations' creates significant uncertainty, in the context of the recognition and enforcement of trusts, it does enable the courts to develop principles that focus explicitly on whether there has been an abuse of

90 *Patel* [2017] AC 467 at [110] (Lord Toulson); [136] (Lord Clarke).

91 *Collier* [2002] EWCA Civ 1095.

92 Although Lord Mance recognised that restoration of the property should have been allowed: *Patel* [2017] AC 467 at [200].

93 If this was a shared intent to deceive by father and daughter, this could be treated as a sham trust. See section 3, above.

94 *Ochroid Trading Ltd* v. *Chua Siek Lui* [2018] SGCA 5. The Court did not depart from *Tinsley* [1994] 1 AC 340 in its application to the law of trusts, since the case concerned a claim to recover benefits conferred under an illegal contract, but it was acknowledged that if Singapore law was to depart from *Tinsley* a test based on stultification of the law would be applied: at [168]. See also *Baker Michael A* v. *BCS Business Consulting Services Pte Ltd* [2020] 4 SLR 85 at [273]–[275].

trust; an approach preferable to the extreme artificiality of depending on whether a party needs to rely on the illegality or is deemed to have withdrawn from the illegal transaction.

## 7 FRAUD ON THE POWER

Where a trustee exercises a trust power for an improper purpose, that exercise will be invalid by virtue of the doctrine of fraud on the power.[95] This is another example of a principle that falls within the doctrine of abuse of trust by a trustee, since the otherwise lawful exercise of a power may be rendered unlawful by virtue of the motive which relates to its exercise.

An improper purpose encompasses an exercise of the power for a collateral purpose,[96] or capriciously.[97] A 'capricious decision' has been described as one that is 'irrational, perverse or irrelevant to any sensible expectations of the settlor'.[98] The notion of fraud for these purposes does not necessarily require conduct that amounts to fraud at Common Law or conduct that could be termed dishonest or immoral, but simply involves the power being exercised for a purpose that is beyond that anticipated by the trust instrument.[99] This was expressed well by Lord Westbury LC in *Duke of Portland* v. *Topham*:[100]

> the donee [...] shall at the time of the exercise of that power and for any purpose for which it is used, act with good faith and sincerity, and with an entire and single view to the real purpose and object of the power, and not for the purpose of accomplishing or carrying into effect any bye or sinister object (I mean sinister in the sense of its being beyond the purpose and intent of the power) which he may desire to effect in the exercise of the power.

Significantly, in *Eclairs Group Ltd* v. *JKX Oil and Gas plc*,[101] Lord Sumption emphasised that fraud on the power is not concerned with an excess of power but is an 'abuse of power, by doing acts which are within its scope but done for an improper reason'.[102] There will be fraud on the power if the trustee's purpose in exercising the power is to secure a benefit for themself or a third party who is not an object of the power. For example, there was fraud in the exercise of a power in *Cloutte* v. *Storey*,[103] in which a power of appointment was exercised by

95 *Balls* v. *Strutt* (1841) 1 Hare 146 at 149 (Sir James Wigram V-C). See P. Sales, 'Fraud on a Power: The Interface between Contract and Equity' (lecture to the Chancery Bar Association, April 2019).

96 *Hillsdown Holdings plc* v. *Pensions Ombudsman* [1997] 1 All ER 862 at 883 (Knox J).

97 *Pilkington* v. *IRC* [1964] AC 612 at 641 (Viscount Radcliffe).

98 *Re Manisty* [1974] 1 Ch 17 at 23 (Templeman J).

99 *Vatcher* v. *Paull* [1915] AC 372 at 378 (Lord Parker of Waddington).

100 *Duke of Portland* v. *Topham* (1864) 11 HLC 32 at 54.

101 *Eclairs Group Ltd* v. *JKX Oil and Gas plc* [2015] UKSC 71.

102 ibid at [15].

103 *Cloutte* v. *Storey* [1911] 1 Ch 18.

the trustee in favour of his child, who was a legitimate object of the power, but pursuant to a covert private arrangement in which the benefit was passed back to the father. In *Klug* v. *Klug*,[104] one of two trustees refused to agree to the exercise of a power of advancement to provide funds to her beneficiary daughter to enable her to pay a legacy duty. It appeared that the mother's refusal to exercise the power was motivated by anger that her daughter had married without her consent. This was considered to be an inappropriate reason for the trustee's decision to refuse to exercise the power. Further, in *Hillsdown Holdings plc* v. *Pensions Ombudsman*,[105] a pension fund had a surplus, but its rules prevented the trustees from paying this to the employer. The trustees transferred the fund to another pension scheme, which was able to pay the surplus to the employer. Even though the employer had agreed to increase the members' benefits under the new pension scheme in return for receiving the surplus, it was held that the transfer of the funds to this other pension scheme constituted fraud on the power, because the transfer was motivated by the collateral purpose of benefiting the employer.

Where the doctrine of fraud on the power applies, the exercise of the power will be void since it is as though the power had not been exercised.[106] An unfortunate consequence of this is that third parties may suffer, because they, being unaware of the hidden purpose of the trustee, would conclude that everything that was done was entirely in order. Consequently, it would be preferable to treat the doctrine as rendering the transaction voidable, such that it would be valid until it had been rescinded. This would prevent the disposition from being set aside if the third party had acquired rights under it for value and was acting in good faith. This is not the law, although in *Pitt* v. *Holt*[107] Lord Walker said that the decision in *Cloutte* v. *Storey*, which had recognised that the effect of the doctrine is to render the transaction void, might have to be 'revisited one day'. It should be. This would ensure consistency with the more flexible approach which is adopted and should be adopted for other aspects of abuse of trust, notably illegality and sham.

## 8 CONCLUSIONS

At Common Law, a doctrine of abuse of rights does not exist. It is possible to exercise a right lawfully regardless of the motive for exercising it. But in Equity, matters are different. Purposes and motives can be relevant when exercising rights, including the right to create a trust in the first place.

[104] *Klug* v. *Klug* [1918] 2 Ch 67.
[105] *Hillsdown Holdings plc* [1997] 1 All ER 862.
[106] *Cloutte* [1911] 1 Ch 18.
[107] *Pitt* v. *Holt* [2013] 2 AC 108 at [62].

The time has come to recognise an equitable doctrine of abuse of trust. This is an umbrella doctrine under which a variety of different principles logically sit, including sham trusts, illusory trusts, illegality, and fraud on the power. The law relating to each of these principles has different components, with some focusing on subjective intentions and others concerned with objective interpretations of what constitutes a trust. But there is a common thread running through all of them, which relates to the pure nature of the trust and of trust powers. The trust, and the rights and powers created by it, is powerful but must not be abused. Purity of motive and purpose are expected; self-interest and self-aggrandisement are not. Ultimately, the trust is predicated on good faith and honesty; bad faith and dishonesty, however defined, are an abuse of trust.

# Index